NORTH SEA

Margate
Ramsgate
Canterbury
Ostend

FLANDERS
BELGIUM

Sandling
Hythe
Shorncliffe
Dover
Folkestone
Lydd

PASSCHENDAELE
1917

STRAIT OF DOVER

Calais

YPRES
1915

MOUNT
SORREL
1916

Courtrai

Boulogne
St Omer
Armentières
Tourcoing
Roubaix

A R T O I S

Lys
Lille
Tournai

Bethune
Escaut

HILL 70
1917
Lens
Scarpe
Valenciennes

VIMY
RIDGE
1917
Douai

Arras

FRONT LINE

Cambrai

P I C A R D Y

SOMME
1916

31 DEC 1917

Somme

Dieppe

Amiens

FRONT LINE

St Quentin

N

la Fère

Laon

Rouen

Beauvais

FRONT LINE
30 NOV 1914

A

Soissons
Aisne

Oise

Seine

Marne

Evreux

10 0 10 20 30 40 50
MILES

PARIS

TO SEIZE THE VICTORY

A great leader. Lieutenant-General Sir Arthur Currie,
Commander of the Canadian Corps.

TO SEIZE THE VICTORY

The Canadian Corps in World War I

JOHN SWETTENHAM

The Ryerson Press Toronto

PRINTED AND BOUND IN CANADA BY THE RYERSON PRESS, TORONTO

TO THOSE WHO ENDURED

FOREWORD

The history of the Canadian Corps in World War I is inseparably linked with the name of General Sir Arthur Currie who rose to its command following the capture of Vimy Ridge in the great battles of April, 1917.

General Currie's appointment was made in the field, by his British military superiors. This action was not well received by some Canadian authorities, civil and military, both in the United Kingdom and in Canada, who had concerned themselves with matters other than military experience and proved capacity for command and leadership. Despite this fact, the arrangement for the command of the Canadian Corps and the consequent change in the 1st Canadian Division were eventually recognized. Nevertheless, until the end of the war and even after, the clash with these Canadian political personalities and others of their persuasion continued, eventually culminating in the vicious statement published on 13 June, 1927, in a local Ontario newspaper, the *Port Hope Guide*.

At this time General Currie was on his way to a meeting of the Institute of International Affairs in Honolulu. On his return to Canada he gave the most anxious consideration to the newspaper article. He sought the advice of many of his friends, including former members of the Canadian Corps and the British First Army under which the Canadian Corps had served in much of the heavy fighting of 1917 and 1918.

It is evident from the record that General Currie was most deeply concerned for the good name of the Canadian Corps; he deplored the feelings of cruel distrust and anxiety that had been raised in Canada. No doubt the charges had originated with some malicious individuals and had been perpetuated by others, perhaps ill-informed and careless of the truth. Such smears had continued to spread for more than a decade and, in his view, it was necessary that these matters be fully investigated. Despite any trouble or risk to himself, he decided that the doubts that had been raised should be dispelled once and for all to relieve the minds of bereaved Canadian families.

Accordingly, in February, 1928, notice of a suit for libel was served against the proprietor of the newspaper and the author of the article concerned for the specific assertion that there had been "deliberate and useless waste of human life" at Mons *for the glorification of Canadian Headquarters*.

vii

To particularize the libel that had been circulated the author of this book starts with an account of the trial. He then turns back in time to give a general account of the Great War, which presents the reader with a concept of the momentous events in which the Canadian Corps had played its part. Then, in more detail, he goes on to recount the battle story of the several formations successively commanded by General Currie: the 2nd Infantry Brigade, the 1st Canadian Division and the Canadian Corps. The narrative includes references to the operations that the higher command had suggested the Canadian Corps might undertake and that, for good reasons advanced by General Currie, were not carried out. The operations proposed instead, and the significant results thereby achieved against the enemy, are described. An account is given of the outstanding generalship displayed by General Currie, of the novelty of his plans to gain surprise within the over-all task assigned to his command, of the apt tactical methods evolved; and, above all, of the great care he always exercised to ensure that the troops would go into battle with the maximum support of the artillery and engineers and, in fact, of all the arms and services. In planning, the care and early evacuation of casualties invariably received the closest attention.

The result was that, under General Currie's leadership, the Canadian Corps became, without any doubt, the most formidable battle formation of its size on the Western Front. It was inspired by confidence in leadership and its morale was unequalled. Its record of tasks performed on schedule with minimum casualties was unmatched, and all this is made evident by the author's glowing and concise account.

Some there are who will think that the full story of the part played by General Currie and the Canadian Corps is in itself enough to dispel the myths of criticism, so that the laurels won will shine through as a bright page of Canadian military history. Some there are who will think that those who sought to destroy General Currie's reputation should be left unnamed; but even with the favourable verdict of the court and all that has since been written and published in praise of the Canadian Corps and its commander, there still comes an occasional echo of past criticisms and insinuations. Unless these allegations are analysed in some detail and their source exposed there can be no assurance, even now, that Currie's name has been fully and finally cleared.

The major facts were well and, it now turns out, correctly known and assessed in the Canadian Corps itself. With the passage of time, much additional information in the form of letters and diaries and other accounts of the period has become available to serious students of history. The author has carried out the review of this material meticulously and has used it with moderation and restraint; yet the motives of those who made the principal attacks have been effectively disclosed.

All the sources have been cited for ready reference, and their perusal carries confidence that the author has marshalled all relevant facts, that his conclusions are soundly based, well taken and correctly expressed in a way that should end further debate.

It is my view that Canada has been well served by the author and that now, at last, the record of the Corps and of its commander stands clear and unchallengeable for the enduring satisfaction of those who took part in its memorable operations and of the people of Canada of whom they were an expression and a part.

Armistice Day
1965

PREFACE

This book tells the story of the Canadian Corps: how it was contributed from negligible beginnings by a country small in terms of population, and how it grew into a formidable fighting machine that achieved a reputation second to none in the First World War. The principal actors are Sir Sam Hughes, Canada's Minister of Militia and Defence for the first two years of the war, and General Sir Arthur Currie who commanded the Corps from the summer of 1917 onward. The drama lies in the influence these men had, for better or for worse, on thousands of sturdy troops thrown into the holocaust from every section of Canadian life. The supporting cast is large. It includes statesmen and politicians, both Canadian and British: Sir Douglas Haig and his army commanders; Joffre, Nivelle, Pétain and Foch; Moltke, Falkenhayn, Hindenburg and Ludendorff; and the colleagues and subordinates of the major figures.

Paradoxically, the achievements of the Corps and the stature of Currie grow greater with increasing distance. From Vimy on, the record of the Canadians was one of unbroken success; and this in a war where failure was common and the reputations of generals were shot to pieces, either while the conflict continued or in the white-hot glare of later analysis.

Today, unfortunately, the story is not so well known as it should be, and even at the time not enough credit was given to the Canadians. Canadians fought as part of the British armies and were often classed as British troops. In Sir Douglas Haig's despatches, for example, the fighting at Mount Sorrel, where the Corps suffered eight thousand casualties, is given one short paragraph and only one Canadian division is specified. The danger now lies in the flood of literature, television features and movies prepared in the United States for American readers and viewers, which are pouring across our borders. These give an inadequate and sometimes distorted picture of Canada's part in the First World War, and it is vital for Canadians of the present day, particularly young people, to be reminded of the facts.

In the interests of the truth the author has not avoided facts that disturb; no history can be complete if these are censored or glossed over. Such facts are included, not in any spirit of vindictiveness but because it would be a waste of time merely to list the events in chronological order and to eulogize the persons taking part. If history is written for the guidance of posterity it must contain something more than a bald recital of achievements and something less than inordinate praise.

The research for this book has been done in the main at the Dominion Public Archives, where the author was given the privilege of examining the papers of General Sir Arthur Currie and other pertinent documents. The papers of Sir Sam Hughes were destroyed many years ago by "a government agency in need of filing space," but sufficient documents were found in the available papers of Borden and others on which to base an account of Hughes as Canada's Defence Minister.

A great many persons gave valuable assistance in the writing of the book and to all of them the author is profoundly grateful.

He would specially acknowledge his indebtedness to General the Honourable A. G. L. McNaughton, P.C., C.H., C.B., C.M.G., D.S.O., C.D., for his valuable comments on the manuscript and for consenting to write the Foreword; this eminent soldier has done far more than can be stated here to ensure the accuracy of the accounts of operations.

A particular debt of gratitude is owed to Major Garner Currie who made his father's papers available and who gave many excellent suggestions.

Special thanks are also due to Dr. J. S. Moir of Carleton University for his encouragement and discussion of the theme, and to Dr. A. M. J. Hyatt of the University of Western Ontario who provided the author with the results of his detailed research into Currie as a soldier. The help given by members of the Army Historical Section—Lieutenant-Colonel H. F. Wood and Captain D. P. Morton—and by Lieutenant H. P. Noble has proved invaluable; all read the manuscript and offered useful criticism. The work of Captain F. R. McGuire, who was generous and untiring in the specialized assistance that he provided, is particularly acknowledged.

To the foregoing must be added the names of Mr. W. I. Smith of the Manuscript Division at the Archives; Mr. Henry Logan of the Public Archives Records Centre and Mr. L. F. Murray of the Canadian War Museum for their assistance with the photographs; Sergeant A. A. Azar for the compilation of the index; Mrs. D. Power and Miss H. Lefaivre for their accurate typing; and Mr. Harry Ellwand for the provision of six excellent maps.

Miss Doris Beer, Mr. Garry Lovatt and Mrs. Susan Damania of The Ryerson Press rate special mention for their patience and understanding and for their technical knowledge in the shaping of the book.

The author alone is responsible for the opinions expressed and for any errors or omissions that the book may contain.

                                                J. A. S.

CONTENTS

CONTENTS

ILLUSTRATIONS

ILLUSTRATIONS

MAPS

ONE.
AN AFTERMATH OF WAR: GENERAL CURRIE FIGHTS THE GHOST OF SIR SAM HUGHES

On 16 April, 1928, in the normally peaceful Ontario town of Cobourg, a large crowd pressed into the small courtroom within the imposing, stone-built Victoria Hall. It was the opening day of perhaps one of the most sensational trials ever conducted in Canada. The proceedings of the next few days were to echo and re-echo across the nation, and were even to be reported in considerable detail in Britain.

The origin of the trial lay in an article published almost a year before, on 13 June, 1927, in a small-town newspaper, *The Port Hope Guide*. Taking advantage of a press release describing the unveiling of a bronze plaque at Mons commemorating the capture of the city by the Canadians on 11 November, 1918, *The Guide* had carried a scathing attack on "this worse than drunken spree by Canadian Headquarters." The article alleged "deliberate and useless waste of human life . . . in the so-called capture of Mons" and placed the blame for it squarely on the Commander-in-Chief who had "conceived the mad idea" of taking the city to "glorify the Canadian Headquarters Staff." Sir Arthur Currie, who had commanded the Canadian Corps at Mons and who was now the Principal and Vice-Chancellor of McGill University, claimed that the words were defamatory to his character and standing, and brought a libel action against the writer and the newspaper's proprietor. The trial at Cobourg in the spring of 1928 was the result.

At the time of the trial, the war had been over almost ten years. The general public had largely forgotten the bitter controversies over Canadian leadership that had arisen immediately after the war. Furthermore, *The Port Hope Guide* was a small newspaper with but a limited circulation* that would hardly reach the mainstream of Canadian public opinion; thus an article contained in it, no matter how scurrilous, could do little injury to Currie's reputation. In these circumstances, the practical wisdom of causing the spotlight of publicity to be focused on a military action after such a lapse of time might be questioned. Would it not have been a better and more effective course

*Estimated at 1,000 (*Ottawa Journal*, 28 April, 1928).

1

to treat the whole matter with silent contempt? It would have been very understandable if Currie—formerly the commander of a national army, a hero of the First World War, and now the occupant of the dignified position of Principal of McGill—had ignored the pinprick of an article in a little-read local paper.

That the libel action would involve risk, both to Sir Arthur and to the country, was clear. A local paper, a local journalist, and no doubt a popular local publisher would be put on trial before a jury composed of their neighbours, who were, as it turned out, farmers and tradesmen from Northumberland and Durham counties. This, Currie could hardly have failed to recognize, would be perilous territory for him to invade. His acts as a war commander would be submitted to the adjudication of these men who would be subjected to highly technical descriptions of military operations, abstruse discourses on military administration with emphasis on the keeping of records, and who would have to try to follow the complicated chain of command. Documents, maps, war diaries, operation orders, casualty lists and the like would without doubt be read and scrutinized. And it would be a national calamity if justice should miscarry. A soldier of Currie's reputation could never again be a private individual. Any blot upon such a man's reputation must reflect upon his country and exercise a sinister influence on recruiting, wartime patriotism and sacrifice in the contingency of future wars. The trial would, in its way, be a far more important engagement than that at Mons.

The reason behind Currie's action, however, is not to be found in the newspaper article alone. Since the end of the war his leadership had been the subject of slander and calumny; he himself had been the victim of a deliberately fostered campaign of persecution. Although he had made speeches all across Canada giving the facts, so that he might reasonably have supposed the insidious rumours had at last been silenced, *The Port Hope Guide* convinced him the issue was still alive. But at least the secret whispering and sibilant slander had appeared where Currie could get at it. The matter, therefore, had to be brought into the open, to be settled, once and for all. It is in that context that the libel trial at Cobourg must be considered.

The decision to prosecute was not an easy one for Currie to make. From May to September, 1927, he had been on leave of absence from McGill to attend a meeting of the Institute of International Affairs at Honolulu. The article in *The Port Hope Guide* came to his attention on his return to Montreal. For five months he debated whether to take legal action. And then, even after notice of suit was served on the newspaper owner in February, 1928, Currie tried to reach an amicable settlement with him. Mr. F. W. Wilson, who besides owning the paper was the editor and publisher, saw the General at his invitation in Montreal. Sir Arthur stated at that interview quite bluntly that the article was untrue in every respect and produced orders and maps to show Wilson exactly what had taken place at Mons. After detailed explanations of the operations there, he pointed out, step by step, why the article was libellous and unfair and why it should be withdrawn. But Wilson would not retract. What had been written was, he contended, substantially a true statement.[1] Currie resolved, therefore, to face the trial and what would, he well knew, be the climax to the deliberate campaign to blacken his name, which had begun almost ten years before.

That campaign had started, ironically enough, with a tribute paid in the House of Commons to the men under Currie's command. On 25 February, shortly after the opening of the 1919 Session, Sir Thomas White (who, in the absence of Borden at the Peace Conference, was acting Prime Minister) lauded the "courage, sacrifices and achievements of the Canadian Expeditionary Force." From Ypres to Mons, he told the Commons, "an unbroken series of victories, often against the most desperate odds, attests the valour which has won the unstinted admiration of the world, and which will for all times be the most cherished tradition of the Canadian people." The people of Canada would be eternally proud that the "first troops to enter Cambrai, which was the great bastion of German defence on the west, wore the uniform of Canada." It would also be a source of "noble pride to the people of this country that on the last day of the war Canadian troops entered Mons from which the British forces at the beginning of the war had been driven by overwhelming enemy forces."[2]

This seemingly innocent and well-merited tribute gave an opening to one member of the House which was seized one week later. Lieutenant-General Sir Sam Hughes, who had been Minister of Militia and Defence in Borden's cabinet during the first two years of the war, rose ponderously. Gazing straight ahead with an unwavering blue-eyed stare, Hughes led into his attack obliquely but left little doubt as to its future direction. "Colonel John A. Currie, Member for North Simcoe," he began, "served at the front with distinction at the Battle of St. Julien. I want to point [out] again that the name of Colonel John A. Currie has been confounded with that of another, and deeds have been attributed to him that have not been creditable and that have absolutely no connection with Colonel John A. Currie."[3]

After this sighting-shot there was no doubt that Hughes had gained the attention of the House. In a silence that could almost be felt, he made reference to the acting Prime Minister's tribute, particularly as it related to Cambrai and Mons.

"Now, about Cambrai," Hughes continued weightily, "I know Cambrai well . . . It is a dirty, little, one-horse town, with narrow streets, an ideal position for machine-gun positions and booby traps.

Why any man of common sense would send soldiers in there, unless it were for his own glorification, I cannot comprehend." He then quoted a letter he had written to Sir Robert Borden on 1 October, 1917, in which he said: "I have on other occasions drawn your attention to the massacres of Lens, Passchendaele etc., where the only apparent object was to glorify the General in command, and make it impossible, through butchery, to have a Fifth and Sixth Division and two Army Corps . . ." Sir Sam shuffled the papers he was holding, shifted the weight of his stocky body to the other foot, then continued to read from the letter. "I think the time has arrived when you should assert yourself along positive lines, demand the removal of incompetents and have this needless slaughter—for I can call it nothing else—of our Canadian lads stopped."

Hughes' major broadside, however, was reserved for Mons. By now, he was in full sail. "I have just this to say about Mons," he asserted. "Were I in authority, the officer who, four hours before the Armistice was signed, although he had been notified beforehand that the Armistice was to begin at eleven o'clock, ordered the attack on Mons thus needlessly sacrificing the lives of Canadian soldiers, would be tried summarily by court martial and punished so far as the law would allow. There was no glory to be gained, and you cannot find one Canadian soldier returning from France who will not curse the name of the officer who ordered the attack on Mons."[4]

The strong words used by Sir Sam Hughes momentarily shocked the House into silence; to hear the leading soldier of Canada accused of incompetence, "butchery," "needless slaughter" and of "needlessly sacrificing the lives of Canadian soldiers" for his own glorification, left the members badly shaken; and coming from a former minister, there were many who believed.

On the same day Mr. Joseph Read, the Member for Prince, P.E.I., took up the cry. He referred to the "terrible sacrifice in Canadian life that has taken place in France and Flanders for the glory of certain individuals over there . . ." and he continued, "When we get it from the ex-Minister of Militia, who knows the circumstances, it is one of the most terrible indictments that was ever made in any parliament on the character of the men who were supposed to be looking after our military affairs."[5] The indictment was, as Mr. Richard Clive Cooper (South Vancouver) pointed out, one of "wholesale murder."[6]

General Currie was not without defenders. On the floor of the House members who had served under his command rose to support him. One member, after scorning Hughes' charges, suggested that it was up to the government to make Sir Arthur a "monetary grant of generous proportions" as a recognition of his service, "something worthy of the glory which he has brought to us."[7] The *Toronto Globe* stated flatly that Sir Sam Hughes had been more dangerous to the men in France than the Germans. "The enemy never dealt a fouler blow than that directed by Sir Sam Hughes against the leaders of the Canadian Army still in the field and unable to defend themselves."[8] Nevertheless, as Mr. Duncan Campbell Ross (West Middlesex) pointed out, no matter what evidence to the contrary might be produced, the damage had been done. "It is very easy to cast aspersions or to put blame on any person, and it is very hard to overtake these aspersions once they have gone amongst the public."[9]

The government did not come out immediately in absolute support of Sir Arthur Currie. Two months passed before Sir Edward Kemp (Minister of the Overseas Military Forces), when reporting in the Commons on the work of his department, praised Currie "who was ever considerate of the men under him." But that praise was tepid in comparison with the warm thanks tendered Lieutenant-General Sir Richard Turner, his own Chief of Staff, a man of the "very highest character and integrity" who was "beloved by the soldiers and a very gallant officer."[10]

In all fairness and justice, commented the Honourable Rodolphe Lemieux, a former member of Borden's cabinet, Kemp should have taken up Currie's quarrel and "defended him against the attacks of a gentleman who was his colleague for many years in the Government." But, he wryly concluded, the Minister was "more in a position to know about those charges than your humble servant."[11] Kemp protested that he had indeed paid tribute to Sir Arthur. "Which means," pursued Lemieux, "that my honourable friend has no confidence at all in the honourable member for Victoria [Sir Sam Hughes] and that—" "Not at all," said Kemp.[12]

Since Kemp's position was ambiguous in the extreme, where did the truth lie: in Hughes' accusations, or in the defence put up by Currie's late subordinates and the press? In the absence of a clear government statement there was growing general conviction that the bluff Hughes —no respecter of persons or reputations—was right. But then, on his return from Europe, Prime Minister Sir Robert Borden rose to silence even the most unreasoning criticism.

On 7 July, 1919, Borden accorded an official vote of thanks to the Canadian Military Forces and had this to say of Currie: "There has been a whisper of criticism that he was not sufficiently mindful of his duty to safeguard the lives of those under his command. In my judgment no criticism could be more unjust. Indeed, I know that on more than one occasion, and especially on one notable occasion, he took a stand in defiance of military precedent, a stand which would have been impossible except for his independent position as a Canadian General, a stand which involved risk to his own status and reputation. That stand he took for one reason and one reason alone; his duty to avoid any needless sacrifice of the troops under his command. No

General at the front more fully realized that solemn duty; and during the last eighteen months of the war there was no General whose judgement was more respected, none whose ability and thoroughness were more relied upon, than he who then commanded the Canadian Corps."[13]

If Hughes had deliberately set about to slander Currie, Borden's words were bound to undo the mischief. In this predicament it is hardly surprising to find that the redoubtable Sam did not let the Prime Minister's tribute go unchallenged. The seeds he had sown having been dug up by Borden and exposed to the withering wind of truth, it was now up to him to replant them in fertile soil and to recultivate them.

Sir Sam's second attack was made in September—carefully, and with great deliberation. He was not, he assured the House, making charges lightly. "The man is a coward, unworthy of association with his fellow-man and woman, who unjustly and deliberately deprecates another," was his tautly controlled opening; "and he who would wantonly by word or pen, or by silence dishonour the fair name of a comrade by permitting falsehood, misrepresentation or slander in deed or word, active or passive, should occupy the pit of infamy."[14] Hughes did not regard himself as an infamous man. He knew the facts, he said, and "knowing the honest convictions of my own heart and conscience" he had presented those facts for the consideration of Parliament, the country and his fellows.[15] His charges had been measured, therefore, and his words weighed.

He reviewed at length the Canadian battles from Ypres—where, by inference, he painted Currie a coward—to Mons, and concluded: "Mons was not a city of any great importance; I would not give the snap of my finger for it. It is a nice little place, but to sacrifice the lives of Canadians on the eve of the armistice was quite out of place and more a piece of bravado than an attempt to help the great cause of liberty at an acceptable time."[16] Thus, having revived the rumours that Borden thought he had scotched, Hughes lowered himself into his seat, no doubt with immense satisfaction.

There the matter remained. Though Hughes died a few months later, his malicious charges lived on. For nine years, unprobed by investigation and helped along by the government's failure to give Currie any honour or, on his return from overseas, to give him the welcome he deserved, those charges haunted Currie. Finally, with characteristic courage, the old leader of the Canadian Corps brought them to a head at Cobourg.

On Monday, 16 April, 1928, a cool and sunny day, the trial of Mr. W. T. R. Preston, a former Liberal organizer for Ontario who admitted writing the article, and Mr. F. W. Wilson, the owner of *The Port Hope Guide*, began. Currie asked for "exemplary damages" against them in the amount of $50,000. Mr. Frank Regan of Toronto appeared for Wilson (Preston had no counsel) and Mr. W. N. Tilley for the plaintiff. Presiding was a man of wide legal experience, Mr. Justice Rose.

The jurymen, a little uncomfortable in their best suits, were for the most part men well on in life, the exceptions being two returned soldiers. The courtroom, with its panelled walls, mahogany ceiling and great royal coat of arms behind the bench, was filled to capacity. Nineteen reporters were present, and to facilitate the transmission of their reports, both the major telegraph companies had installed equipment and operators in one of the offices of the County Court building. There was a sprinkling of military uniforms, notably those of three serving officers, Colonel R. J. Orde (Deputy Judge Advocate General) Colonel Logie Armstrong (Director of Records) and Colonel Fortescue Duguid, (Director of the Army Historical Section). Sheriff Nesbitt, his constables, assistant counsel, clerks and other officials completed the scene.

The first witness, Ralph Hodgson, Registrar of Deeds for the East Riding of the County of Durham (in which pastoral county Hughes had been born), testified to having read the newspaper article. The "Commander-in-Chief" whose actions had been condemned he took to be General Currie, although he knew that Currie as a corps commander did not rate so exalted a title; the association with "Canadian Headquarters" left no doubt in his mind as to whom it referred.[17] The defendants themselves did not dispute this point.

Mr. Regan moved for non-suit on the grounds that the article was not libellous and that no damage had been done, but the judge sharply turned him down. With that, the onus of proving that the article was true, in substance and in fact, now rested upon the defendants.

Under the heading "Mons," the article read:

Cable despatches this morning give details of the unveiling of a bronze plaque at the Hotel de Ville (the City Hall) at Mons, commemorative of the capture of the city by the Canadians on November 11th, 1918. This is an event which might very possibly be allowed to pass into oblivion, very much regretted rather than glorified.

There was much waste of human life during the war, enormous loss of lives which should not have taken place. But it is doubtful whether in any case there was a more deliberate and useless waste of human life than in the so-called capture of Mons.

It was the last day; and the last hour, and almost the last minute, when to glorify the Canadian Headquarters Staff the Commander-in-Chief conceived the mad idea that it would be a fine thing to say that the Canadians had fired the last shot in the Great War, and had captured the last German entrenchment before the bugles sounded eleven o'clock, when the armistice which had been signed by both sides would begin officially.

Canadian Headquarters sounded the advance upon the retreating Germans, unsuspecting that any mad proposal for further and unnecessary fighting was even contemplated. The men were sent on in front to charge the enemy. Headquarters, with conspicuous bravery, brought up the rear. The fighting may have been more severe than was expected. Certain it is the Germans did not take the attack lying down.

Of course the town was taken just at the last minute before the official moment of the armistice arrived. But the penalty that was paid in useless waste of human life was appalling. There are hearts in Port Hope stricken with sorrow and mourning through this worse than drunken spree by Canadian Headquarters. Veterans who had passed through the whole four years of war lie buried in Belgian cemeteries as the result of the "glories of Mons."

Headquarters Staff assembled in the centre of the town as the eleven o'clock signal sounded that the official armistice was effective from that hour. Along the route that they had carefully and with safety made their way to the centre of the town, passing the dead and the dying and the wounded, victims of their madness [sic].

It was common talk among the soldiers that while the Staff were congratulating themselves upon the great victory and enjoying the pride upon having "fired the last shot in the Great War," a sergeant advanced and whispered to one of the Staff that unless they withdrew immediately to a place of safety, they would not be allowed to leave the place alive, as the guns of the indignant Canadian soldiers were already trained on them. In less time than it takes to tell the story, Headquarters got into motors and were fleeing for their lives.

It does not seem to be remembered that even Ottawa, neither by Government nor Parliament, gave Sir Arthur Currie any official vote of thanks or any special grant as an evidence of the esteem or appreciation for his services. And this is the only case of the kind in connection with any of the high commanding officers of the war. He was allowed to return to Canada unnoticed by officials of the Government or of Parliament and permitted to sink into comparative obscurity in a civilian position as President [sic] of McGill University. The official desire to glorify Mons, therefore, deserves more than a passing or silent notice. Canadian valour won Mons, but it was by such a shocking useless waste of human life that it is an eternal disgrace to the Headquarters that directed operations.[18]

The crux of the defence rested on the question of whether Sir Arthur Currie knew, before Mons was entered, if the armistice was signed or was likely to be signed. Regan contended that the testimony of ex-soldiers who were present at the capture of Mons would disclose that the taking of the city (shortly before the armistice was declared, and while the plaintiff knew, or had reason to know, that a cessation of hostilities was imminent) was an unjustifiable sacrifice of human life. Before calling his military witnesses, however, Regan introduced a civilian subpoenaed to bring copies of *The Times* of London dated from 8 October to 11 November, 1918, which contained reports dealing with the progress of peace between the Allies and Germany, Austria-Hungary, Bulgaria and Turkey. Currie, admittedly an ardent reader of *The Times*, must—Regan maintained—have known of the imminence of the armistice.

This naive assumption was rudely shattered by Tilley. "Nothing," he stated flatly, "that would appear in the London *Times* on October 8th could at all affect what was General Currie's duty on November 10th or November 11th." Currie had to carry out orders, and "does a general in the field get his views of what should be done by reading the London press?" "I should say it would be a dangerous procedure," commented Mr. Justice Rose. Tilley agreed. "They would have to wait till they got *The Times* to see what they should do." Furthermore, he pressed, *The Port Hope Guide* had made a big point of the imminence of the armistice being *known* when Sir Arthur Currie "conceived the mad idea" that sacrificed Canadian lives; therefore, what some person might have expected about the armistice from reading *The Times* could only be irrelevant. The judge agreed; he ruled the London *Times* inadmissible as evidence.[19]

Much was made of a General Order requesting passage through the lines before the armistice for the German negotiators. This had been issued from the headquarters of Marshal Foch on 8 November, and the effort was made to prove that the Canadian Corps, having received that message, should have called off offensive operations. Against that, however, was produced the order of Marshal Foch himself which directed that there should be no relaxation of pressure on the enemy.

Nor—save one—were Regan's military witnesses any more helpful on this point. According to them it was "common gossip" on 10 November that the armistice was "pretty close." But this was no more than hearsay evidence. What Regan seemed to think he was entitled to do was this: to say that the "fact" in the newspaper was common gossip, and then produce the gossip as proof of the "fact."

Fred Lindgard of Port Hope, however, who had been a signaller stationed at Valenciennes (a town to the west of Mons) put the defence on firmer ground. He testified that he had received a message from 4th Division Headquarters to 4th Brigade Headquarters between ten and eleven o'clock on the night of 10 November; that message concerned the armistice, had been transmitted by wireless, and he had taken it down. It was short, and he remembered the gist of it—that the armistice was to be signed on 11 November at 11 o'clock. That being so, Currie would have had at least twelve hours' notice of the armistice and any casualties resulting from an attack that occurred thereafter might well be laid at his door; having received the message, would not the more humane course have been to give a respite to the soldiers?

The defence swung onto the question of casualties. Currie had stated positively at the Examination for Discovery, held before the trial, that not one Canadian soldier had been killed on 11 November. Regan called witness after witness to the stand to describe the events of 11

November. Those witnesses, who had come into the city after it was in Canadian hands, swore that they had entered Mons on Armistice Day and had seen the bodies of dead Canadian soldiers lying in the streets. ("But I never seen them all covered up with flowers before," said one). Another, W. D. Teddiman, formerly acting Company Sergeant Major of "B" Company of the 52nd Battalion, entered Mons as late as the afternoon of the 11th. He testified to having seen three or four dead Canadian soldiers lying in the roadway on the way in. Whether they were killed on 11 November or not, he could not say with certitude. He felt, however, that it was inconceivable that the Belgian people, who received the Canadians with such exuberance, would allow the bodies of Canadian soldiers to lie in the road from the day before. For that reason, he believed that they must have been killed on the 11th. Almost all the witnesses spoke of a military funeral in Mons, "with from eight to ten caskets," which had been carried out on the 13th.[20]

Colonel Duguid of the Army Historical Section produced War Diaries for 9, 10 and 11 November at Mr. Regan's request in an attempt to verify on what day the casualties had occurred. He read what was written under the 9th with respect to casualties: "9th November, casualties; killed, four officers, 18 other ranks—"

"And the 10th?"

But the Colonel had not finished with the 9th. "—the 9th," he continued, "wounded, four officers, 91 other ranks. This includes November 9th, 10th, and 11th."

"This includes November 9th, 10th, and 11th?" repeated Regan increduously.

"Yes"

"Now read on the 10th," pursued Regan. "What entry have you got on the 10th?"

"Casualties, see November 9th."

"And then under the 11th?"

"Casualties, see November 9th."

"Why didn't they group them under November 11th?"

"I do not know," was the placid response, "I did not write the diary."[21]

It was explained to Mr. Regan at some length that the accurate report of casualties was contained in a separate Casualty Report, not a War Diary. After commenting that the whole thing was a "farce," Regan suggested that Casualty Reports, giving names, be produced for 9, 10 and 11 November. But these were in Ottawa, and it would take time to search and send them on. Meanwhile the trial continued.

On 20 April Regan stated that the defence would undertake to show that there had been "deliberate falsification of documents in order to suppress the true state of affairs" with regard to casualties on the 11th. Rebuttal came from an unexpected quarter when Mr.

Preston, co-defendant with Wilson, surprisingly and dramatically rushed to Currie's defence. Regan had gone too far. "Neither in the article nor in the pleading," he said, "is there any thought of implicating Sir Arthur Currie by inference or otherwise. I did not think so—will never think so—that there is any suggestion of any falsification of records, knowingly, directly or otherwise."[22]

The defence shifted ground again, and tried to show there had been enormous loss of life at Ypres due to the plaintiff's action. But the libel suit concerned Mons, not Ypres. The witness called by the defence, Colonel John A. Currie (no relation to Sir Arthur), enlivened the proceedings by persisting in trying to give evidence concerning Ypres, despite the judge's ruling that such evidence was out of order, and came within an ace of being jailed for contempt of court. The next day, Regan again summoned the same witness to answer a question. Tilley rose in protest; Mr. Justice Rose raised a hand to keep Currie out of the box until the relevancy of the question had been determined. At this point Colonel Currie, who had reached the witness stand, spoke: "My Lord, can't I make a statement?" The judge shook his head, and was speaking to Mr. Regan when again the witness broke in with a request to make a statement. Mr. Justice Rose by now had had enough. Beckoning to Sheriff Nesbitt, he ordered Colonel Currie removed from the courtroom. The Sheriff passed the order to one of the constables on duty, and the frustrated witness was conducted to the exit, to be seen no more.[23]

Thus, when the sound and the fury raised by the defence died down at the half-way mark of the trial, two main points of evidence had emerged for the jury to ponder—that of the signalman, who had testified to receiving the armistice message on the 10th, and that of the soldiers who had given evidence that on the 11th the streets of Mons were littered with Canadian dead.

Witnesses called by the plaintiff were now flocking into Cobourg as if the Canadian Corps had been remobilized. A glance at the hotel registers would have disclosed the presence of many former soldiers whose names were well known in the war years. The trial brought reunions of old comrades, and in hotel lobbies and smoke-rooms the battles that earned for the Canadian Corps the name of being the most efficient and formidable fighting force on the Western Front were fought and re-fought. The previously tranquil town, for the most part an artillery community, welcomed the infantry with open arms. For the moment it had outdone Ottawa as the news centre of Canada.

On 23 April Colonel Duguid reappeared on the stand and made an astounding statement. According to him, the official army records contained no report of any fighting whatsoever in Mons! There was very definite evidence of fighting to the north and south of the city, Duguid said, but none in Mons itself.

A second item of outstanding importance was the production by Colonel Allan A. Magee of Montreal of the original message received at Canadian Corps Headquarters announcing the order for the cessation of hostilities. This was scribbled on a scrap of paper just as Colonel Magee had taken it down over the telephone from a staff officer at headquarters of the British First Army. The message had reached Corps at about 6:30 on the morning of the 11th. Magee said that he had immediately phoned it to the 2nd and 3rd Divisions, operating in the forward zone, and then to the other divisions. He confirmed it later by ordinary signal message, giving it a right of way over all other messages. His actions were entered in the Corps Message Log, which was on record.

This evidence, it would appear, had satisfactorily disposed of Signalman Lindgard's testimony. In fact, another witness later in the hearing characterized the message Lindgard said he had received on the 10th from the 4th Division to 4th Brigade as "ridiculous." The 4th Brigade was part of the 2nd Division, not the 4th, and received orders through that formation.[24]

Sir Arthur Currie, whose billet was "across the street" from headquarters, was notified by Magee of the armistice shortly afterwards, and the Colonel agreed that 6:45 A.M. would probably be the time at which the Corps Commander obtained the order. Regan interrupted sarcastically: "I understand Sir Arthur was taking a bath when he got the news and continued with his bathing before taking any action in the matter?"

The witness hesitated. "Well, I . . . It may sometimes be considered the mark of a very strong people to show ingratitude to their great men," he resumed heatedly, "but this attack upon General Sir Arthur Currie—"

"Yes," the judge interposed, "what is the relevancy?"

"Well," replied Regan smugly, "the men at the front don't get baths, do they? They do the fighting and the dying . . ."

Some time later written confirmation of the memorable armistice message sent out by First Army at 7 o'clock reached Corps, and that too was on record:

> Hostilities will cease at 11:00 hours November 11th. Troops will stand fast on the line reached at that hour which will be reported to Army Headquarters. Defensive precautions will be maintained . . . From First Army. Time 0700.[25]

The reference to "defensive precautions," commented another witness with perfect justification, indicated that it was certainly not necessarily the end of the war. And as for hostilities ceasing at eleven o'clock, it might just as well have been said that hostilities would continue until that time. Another witness recalled his own doubts about the sincerity of the enemy when word of the armistice had first reached him. The Germans, he had thought, were just stalling for time to reorganize and dig in for the winter on a shorter line.

The next few days of the trial were taken up with descriptions of operations. Operations are rarely undertaken without casualties but it was on the extent of such casualties that the outcome of the suit hinged. Linked up with that was the question as to whether Sir Arthur Currie, as Corps Commander, had exceeded his orders or had confined himself to carrying out just what he was told to do and no more.

Evidence placed before the court revealed that Sir Douglas Haig, the British Commander-in-Chief, acting on the order of Marshal Foch to maintain pressure on the enemy, had issued orders on 2 November to the British First, Third and Fourth Armies to advance to the Avesnes-Maubeuge-Mons line. On 9 November, General Sir Arthur Currie testified, the Canadian Corps received more precise instructions from General Horne of the First Army, under whose command it was. Horne directed Currie "to high ground east and northeast of Mons sending mounted troops and advanced guards forward to keep touch with enemy. . . ." On the 10th, Currie continued, the Corps' objectives of the previous day not having been reached, the Canadians were directed by First Army to continue their advance, objectives as before. About midway on the Canadian front lay the city of Mons, and in order to reach the high ground "east and northeast" of it the city had to be entered or bypassed.

Currie, according to his own testimony, working with two divisions in the line, directed the 2nd to capture a hill east of Mons. This feature, crowned by a wood (the Bois la Haut), was known as Mount Pallisel. He ordered the 3rd to the northeast where it would capture the high ground and the suburb of Nimy in that area. Advanced troops and cavalry, he continued, would then be sent forward of the objectives. By the 10th, troops of the 3rd Division were on the outskirts of Mons, and Currie sent out further orders to its commander that he was not to capture Mons if that would result in undue loss of life.

"Anyway," Regan goaded Currie, "you captured Mons, and made a formal entry and signed your name in the Gold Book of Mons, did you not, General?"

"Yes."

"Right below that of the King of Belgium?"

"Yes," replied Currie, and then with a dig he could not resist, "at the time I was in my car fleeing for my life, practically."[26]

The approach to Mons, according to witnesses who had taken part in the advance, was totally different from anything previously experienced by Canadian troops. Valenciennes was the last full-scale attack, and even the assault on that town had been largely an artillery action against a neighbouring defended hill. From then on it was open warfare,

with the advancing troops marching along the roads of Belgium in
columns, preceded only by their precautionary troops, receiving the
acclaim of the liberated people. When the battalions ran into German
resistance, they stood fast until the retreating Germans yielded the
position, and then the Canadians advanced as before.

Such was the experience of the Princess Patricia's Canadian Light
Infantry. Former members of that battalion said they had been following up the retiring Germans for days until, on 9 November, they were
close up against Mons to the south and southwest, separated from the
boundary of the city by only a few hundred yards of open ground and
the Canal du Haine. Evidence showed that one company had pushed
forward towards the canal but, as this movement drew enemy machine-
gun fire, the commander had withdrawn his men to positions of cover
between the village of Cuesmes and Mons and established outposts.
His action proved sound. During the night 9-10 November, the enemy
launched no less than five attacks against the company positions, each
of which was beaten off. The Patricia's stood their ground and were
relieved on the 10th. Machine-guns continued to hold up any advance
towards Mons throughout the daylight hours of 10 November, and
the Canadians made no attempt to force an entry in face of their
stubborn fire.

The operations around Mons were illustrated for the court by a
large-scale map made by Albert J. Kelly, formerly scout officer of the
Patricia's. Kelly explained to the jury the various features of the map,
pointing out the Mons-Conde Canal, the Canal du Centre, the Canal
du Haine, the town of Jemappes and the village of Cuesmes, all of
which featured in the evidence. With these explanations the jurors
followed the recital of operations given by other witnesses.

The 42nd Battalion, Royal Highlanders of Canada (Black Watch),
relieved the Patricia's outside Mons on the afternoon of 10 November.
They lay low, apart from reconnaissance parties, but nevertheless suffered casualties from machine-gun fire that day, the last of them at
about 4:30 P.M. How the 42nd Battalion entered Mons was told by
Captain W. A. Grafftey, a company commander of the Highlanders,
who had accompanied one of his platoons in its advance across a farm-
yard, through the railway yards, until at eleven o'clock it had established a post on one of the boulevards inside the city. Having met no
opposition, Grafftey sent for his remaining platoons and the night
advance was carried on towards the Place de Flandres. All this had
taken place without a shot being fired. While Captain Grafftey's company was pushing its way through the streets from west to northeast,
another commanded by Captain Eric Finley was moving up from the
southern limits. Both companies advanced to the further side of Mons
and established defensive posts. The city, said Grafftey, had been
"exceedingly quiet"; the deserted streets "quite eerie." No shots had

UNDAY

D TO HOSPITAL

**sed Accident, Summoned
Driving and Had
vo Months**

ated his father's evidence and
at Douglas did not make any
to miss his car. A. Brown,
s travelling in a car behind,
tified along the same lines,
eaves also testified.

evidence, Douglas remarked
did not see the car approach-
n the west until it was too
void a crash. He tried to
but was too late, he added,
been driving a car for four

trate Campbell pointed out
uglas showed a distinct error
nent in handling his car and
of driving was dangerous to
ic and was the cause of many
s. The minimum fine of $10
ts was imposed and license
r two months.

cars had their front wheels
and mudguards shattered and
nage in each case would
to approximately $75.00.

uglas' car at the time of the
were Mr. and Mrs. Norman
id two children. Mrs. High
own out and received injuries
necessitated her removal to
Hope hospital.

VMANVILLE 9-5
IGHWAY GROUP

**ts Were Scarce, Locals
regation Against
e Does Fine
nd**

d out to centre, Brockenshire,
ut at first.—0 runs.
anville—Tyler and F. Piper
James flied out to 3rd.—0

INNINGS—

Hope—Friar singled, High-
at 1st, Hills walked, Curt's
to centre, Russell grounded
short, Friar scored on Hol-
ingle, Chalk singled scoring

Russell ss, Holman lf, Sleeman cf,
Friar rf.

MONS

Cable despatches this morning give details of the unveiling
of a bronze plaque at the Hotel de Ville (the City Hall) at Mons,
commemorative of the capture of the city by the Canadians on
November 11th, 1918. This is an event which might very properly be allowed to pass into oblivion, very much regretted rather
than glorified.

There was much waste of human life during the war, enormous loss of lives which should not have taken place. But it is
doubtful whether in any case there was a more deliberate and
useless waste of human life than in the so-called capture of
Mons.

It was the last day; and the last hour, and almost the last
minute, when to glorify the Canadian Head Quarters staff the
Commander-in-Chief conceived the mad idea that it would be
fine thing to say that the Canadians had fired the last shot in the
Great War, and had captured the last German entrenchment before the bugles sounded eleven o'clock, when the armistice which
had been signed by both sides would begin officially.

Canadian Headquarters sounded the advance upon the retreating Germans, unsuspecting that any mad proposal for further and unnecessary fighting was even contemplated. The men
were sent on in front to charge the enemy. Headquarters, with
conspicuous bravery, brought up the rear. The fighting may
have been more severe than was expected. Certain it is the
Germans did not take the attack lying down.

Of course the town was taken just at the last minute before
the official moment of the armistice arrived. But the penalty that
was paid in useless waste of human life was appalling. There
are hearts in Port Hope stricken with sorrow and mourning
through this worse than drunken spree by Canadian Headquarters. Veterans who had passed through the whole four years
of war lie buried in Belgian cemeteries as the result of the "glories
of Mons."

Headquarters Staff assembled in the centre of the town as
the eleven o'clock signal sounded that the official armistice was
effective from that hour. Along the route that they had
carefully and with safety made their way to the centre of the
town, passing the dead and dying and the wounded, victims of
their madness. It was common talk among the soldiers that while the
staff were congratulating themselves upon the great victory and
enjoying the pride upon having "fired the last shot in the Great
War," a sergeant advanced and whispered to one of the Staff that
unless they withdrew immediately to a place of safety, they would
not be allowed to leave the place alive, as the guns of the indignant Canadian soldiers were already trained on them. In less
time than it takes to tell the story, Headquarters got into motors
and were fleeing for their lives.

It does not seem to be remembered that even Ottawa, neither
by government nor Parliament, gave Sir Arthur Currie any official
vote of thanks, or any special grant as an evidence of the esteem
or appreciation for his services. And this is the only case of the
kind in connection with any of the high commanding officers of
the war. He was allowed to return to Canada unnoticed by
officials of the government or of Parliament and permitted to sink
into comparative obscurity in a civilian position as President of
McGill University. The official desire to glorify Mons, therefore,
deserves more than a passing or silent notice. Canadian valour
won Mons, but it was by such a shocking useless waste of human
life that it is an eternal disgrace to the Headquarters that directed operations.

DROWNING

Article in the *Port Hope Guide*. This defamatory article on Mons, which
appeared on 13 June, 1927, prompted Sir Arthur Currie to sue the newspaper for libel. The result was one of the most sensational trials in
Canadian history.

The trenches from the air. This photograph, taken from a kite balloon, shows the heavily defended Vimy Ridge.

The Ypres Salient. Stunted willows, sandbagged breastworks, festoons of wire, shell-torn ground, and pathetic scattered crosses.

been fired, no civilians seen, and it was plain that the enemy had evacuated the place. The entry had been, he concluded, "easy going."[27]

Early on the 11th the armistice message had been received, and with it the Highlanders' part in the war ended. Cavalry of the British 5th Lancers passed through their forward posts and took possession of the high ground northeast of Mons.

All the witnesses were unswerving in their testimony that there had been no fighting whatever in Mons and that the Highlanders had not fired a shot in the city. Nor could their evidence be shaken by the most rigid and gruelling cross-examination levelled at them by counsel for the defence. No *attack*, witnesses insisted, had been directed against Mons within the ordinary and accepted meaning of the word. One officer of the 42nd told of having to "rap on the window-gratings" to rouse the sleeping citizens; a non-commissioned officer of the same battalion declared that the only fighting he saw in Mons was a "scrap between some Belgian civilians in a courtyard."[28]

The only losses suffered by the 42nd Battalion in the Mons area had taken place on the 10th. Four men were killed that afternoon, two at the canal and two while crossing a road on the western outskirts of Mons; men had been wounded at various locations outside the city—the last at about 4:30. From that time on, the battalion had not been under fire. Long-range shelling accounted for further Canadian losses on that day, notably when a shell burst in a farrier's shop at Jemappes, about three miles west of Mons, killing two men outright and wounding ten more. Of the wounded, four subsequently died.

The witnesses' consistency was challenged by Regan. He complained bitterly that they were "too well-versed," and persisted in referring to the "War College at the Dunham Hotel" where a large number of ex-service men were staying. He took distinct exception to witnesses having been put through a lecture at the "War College" and then coming into court to tell their stories. His tirade, it seemed, might have continued indefinitely, but the judge cut it off with a stern rebuke. Despite what had been said about Mons, Regan resumed, the proper course to follow would have been to avoid Mons altogether, to capture the high ground to the east so that enemy troops in the city, being outflanked, would surrender. He totally ignored the mass of evidence that had gone before, all pointing to the fact that Mons had been evacuated before the Canadians went in.

Tilley tested this military theory of Regan's by putting a witness on the stand to describe what had actually happened on that flank. The 2nd Division had had the task of capturing the high ground, Mount Pallisel with its Bois la Haut, to the east of Mons. The witness had commanded the 20th Battalion in that operation. The battalion, he said, was approaching the hill during the morning of 10 November when it was caught in sudden and unexpected machine-gun and artillery fire from "wonderfully concealed and camouflaged" positions. The objective was described as a strong position, "a huge hill rising like a cone" and a "regular Gibraltar." Because of the heavy resistance, and acting on Currie's instructions not to incur casualties if these could be avoided, the battalion had dug in until dark. After dark the battalion "had the Bois la Haut by midnight." The Germans had withdrawn, presumably "because Mons was lost." In this operation the battalion suffered casualties: one officer killed, one officer wounded; two non-commissioned officers killed; nine men killed and thirty-three wounded —almost all when the unexpected fire suddenly came upon them.[29]

On Friday, 27 April, the tall soldierly figure of Sir Arthur Currie— slimmer now than in the war years—occupied the witness box again. Completely self-assured, his testimony with regard to Mons was brief. "We have heard a great deal about operations being confined to the capture of Mons; not at all." The troops, he continued, were moving in a line that ran, by the evening of Sunday the 10th, generally west of Mons. "Now troops that are ordered to advance keep testing the line, always, and the place to pierce a line is at its weakest point—that is surely sound military tactics." And while the pressure was being maintained all along the line, the weakest point, through testing, was disclosed. That point was at the railway station in Mons, and there the troops entered. "In a few hours," he concluded, "they had gone through the city and out on the other side."[30]

Regan then rose, and for seven hours subjected Currie to a cross-examination that was still not concluded when the General stepped down at 6 o'clock that night. The Corps Commander was asked why he was "not man enough, when the Government asked him about casualties, to put them in his report?" The lawyer accused him of "denying to the men who were killed at Mons the honour of recalling that they had laid down their lives in the capture of the city." All this, and a great deal more, was hurled across the courtroom.

"You kept the men going until the end," snarled Regan. "Weren't you satisfied that they had done enough fighting and had had enough casualties?"

"Absolutely satisfied, and I know a great deal more about the casualties, Mr. Regan, than you do."

"Do you?"

"Yes," replied Currie firmly. "I lived through the months of the war there, I saw those magnificent battalions go into battle and come out badly decimated and I have feelings about it that you can never appreciate."

"I can appreciate this," blustered Regan, "that there were too many casualties during the war. That I can appreciate. Listen to this. 'Along the road of a hundred days to that day in Mons nine years ago, the men of Canada fought three great battles, at Amiens, at Arras, at

Cambrai. They led the attack; they never failed. They broke the Hindenburg Line, they took over thirty thousand prisoners, they freed over two hundred cities and towns and five hundred square miles of France and Belgium. They met and crushed forty-seven divisions of the enemy—one corps of Canadians, four against forty-seven.' Is that statement correct?"

"Yes."

"Don't you think, Sir Arthur," said Regan quietly, "that in the dying hours of the war you might have spared your men a trifle more than you did?"

"No," burst out Currie. "You are the man who is suggesting that they should lie down and quit within two days of the final victory . . . You would have had them mutiny, you would have had them be guilty of treason, disregard the instructions of the Commander-in-Chief, disregard the instructions of Marshal Foch, and act in an unsoldierly way, right at the very last. Those were not men who did that sort of thing."[31]

At this point—suddenly, spontaneously—the whole courtroom signified its approval by breaking into a wild stamping of feet, which was suppressed with some difficulty by the sheriff. Currie, aware that the spectators were behind him, grew calm again and outlined why pressure had to be maintained until the last.

He knew, on 9 November, that an armistice was imminent. He hoped it would take place. He also knew the German envoys were through the line and had been in conference with Marshal Foch, but they had asked for a seventy-two-hour armistice. That would have enabled them to get to the line of the Meuse River twenty-five miles back—a strong line which they could have defended. Foch refused and the envoys returned to Spa to get in touch with their political headquarters again and communicate the suggested terms of the armistice—an ultimatum, more or less. They returned through the British lines again about nine o'clock on the 9th, and again they asked for an armistice until eleven o'clock on Monday morning. Foch refused to give them this and intimated to Haig that he was to use energy and initiative to force decisive results. He had reason, resumed Currie. The Allies were driving the enemy before them, and pressure had to be kept up to let the Germans know they were defeated—the only condition under which they would accept the Allied terms. Currie knew his orders were based on this reasoning and he could not depart from them. The pressure had to be relentlessly maintained if the armistice were to be permanent and not a mere temporary truce as wanted by the Germans.[32]

For the rest of the day, and during the next, Currie had no difficulty in rebutting Regan's charges. As to "self-glorification," there had certainly been a parade in Mons—the men had earned it. "All the big time," sneered Regan, "the signing of the Gold Book with the King of the Belgians—the great parade." But to Currie it had been historic;

Mons was the place where the British had first encountered the
Germans in 1914 and, heavily outnumbered, had had to give way.
Four years later that defeat was avenged by the Canadian Corps. On
Armistice Day, 1918, the cheering population of Mons witnessed the
march past of all arms of the Canadian Corps, Currie taking the salute,
while the ancient carillon rang out the notes of "O Canada." He was
not ashamed of it; it had been a proud moment both for him and for his
men. As to the outcome of the trial, he was not interested in money,
only in vindication.

The trial was now nearly over. Records of casualties, compiled in
Ottawa with scrupulous accuracy, revealed only one Canadian fatality
for 11 November. That man was killed after his battalion had occupied
a defensive position four and a half miles northeast of Mons, "by enemy
sniper near the canal at three minutes to eleven." He had left a position
of cover just before the official cease-fire, perhaps to see what the
Germans were doing, and had been shot through the right breast and
died shortly afterwards. "So this is the appalling penalty paid in useless
waste of human life," said Tilley.[33]

Fatalities for the 10th were: 34 killed in action and 23 men admitted
to hospital who subsequently died of wounds—listed as having died on
the 10th. Of these, only ten had remained in the forward area, and it
was these men who were buried in Mons on the 13th. The Senior
Chaplain of the 3rd Canadian Division gave moving testimony regarding the funeral. The City Fathers of Mons, he said, asked for, and were
given, permission to take care of the Canadian dead. They collected
the bodies, which had been covered with flowers by the Belgian people,
from the outskirts of Mons. "The people brought them in their carts to
the mortuary where they had provided the most elaborate coffins left in
the city. They were then conveyed into a large room in the City Hall,
which was draped in black and silver, and lighted, as is the custom
there, with innumerable candles. There was then a period during which
the citizens of Mons paid tribute, which they did by thousands, bringing
with them bay-leaf wreaths of various kinds until the room was filled
with them. On November 13th at 3 o'clock the *cortège* left the hall, the
42nd Pipe Band leading, then the *cortège* of coffins, the R.C.R. Band,
and myself in the position of chaplain immediately behind the band,
then divisional officers, representatives of brigade and units, the City
Council, and last, at the end, a rather pathetic group of old men
dressed, I am told, in the uniform of 1870, the last surviving veterans."

"Of the 1870 war?" asked Tilley.

"Yes. Then came the citizens, not in column of route, but surrounding the *cortège* on either side, and there must have been four or five
thousand citizens accompanied us to the cemetery, where the graves
were already prepared, and after the religious service which is customary in the army the Representatives of the Province of Hainault

and the mayor of the city delivered very eloquent addresses. . . One sentence, if I might be permitted to give it, I have from memory: 'There are those in your land who sorrow this day. Tell them that their sons are in our keeping. They rest in a corner of Belgium which is forever Canada.' "[34]

On Tuesday, 1 May, the trial ended. The judge, in a lengthy and carefully worded summary, dealt with every aspect of the trial, point by point. Certain evidence appeared irreconcilable, notably that given by the defence witnesses of bodies seen in Mons, and that for the plaintiff where one witness after another testified that not a shot had been fired in Mons. But Mons, as other witnesses had explained, was the centre of a very thickly populated country. All around were suburbs, with spacious boulevards in some places, with narrow, crooked streets in others. The difficulty was in knowing when one was actually in Mons and when one was in the suburbs. It was possible that the dead men seen in "Mons" were actually lying in the outskirts, inasmuch as none of the witnesses who had testified to seeing them had given any clear indication of the exact locality in which they lay. At all events, all the casualties incurred at Mons had been reported in the official records, which gave the date of the casualty and the disposition of the soldier. The question remained, was the Port Hope newspaper article true, and if not, did it hold Currie up to ridicule or contempt, or expose him to hatred, scorn, or injury?[35]

The jurymen retired at 11:48 A.M. and for three hours and forty minutes stayed in their room debating the evidence. At 3:28 in the afternoon the foreman returned a verdict of guilty. Though the action claimed $50,000 Sir Arthur had said on oath that he did not "want money" and the jury gave him what he had asked for—a token $500 and vindication. For half a minute the verdict was received in silence and then, the tension broken, spectators clapped and applauded. Throngs of men and women surged around Currie to congratulate him in a scene of enthusiasm such as the court at Cobourg had never witnessed before and possibly will never see again. Currie would make no statement to the press—nor would Wilson and Preston. It was over; the strange lawsuit, followed with an intensity of interest across Canada, had ended. Over the courthouse wires almost a score of reporters had sent nearly a million words.

On the 2nd, Arthur Currie returned to Montreal. Traffic halted on Windsor, Peel and Sherbrooke streets, and his route through the city became a triumphal march. People crowded into Windsor Station, scuffled with police, struggled to get near the General, shouted and cheered, sang and paraded. Then, the horse was removed from the shafts of the "Montreal fiacre" in which Currie was riding and the carriage, escorted by the crowd, was drawn by enthusiastic McGill students to the United Service Club on Sherbrooke Street West. From the steps of the club, in a resonant voice that revealed strong emotion and gratitude for the welcome given him, General Sir Arthur Currie briefly expressed his thanks.[36]

He had done much. His action had struck a blow toward cleansing public life of one of its greatest dangers—the evil of unchallenged vilification. Throughout the nation editorials applauded him.

More important, Hughes' charges—which, in an embellished form, had been repeated by a local newspaper without checking the facts— had called into question Canada's entire military effort on the Western Front. It had been inferred that the great sacrifices made by Canadian troops had been unnecessary, and that with wise direction they could have been avoided. Had those charges been upheld, Canadians would forever have had to turn in shame from a military record which, however impressive, had been achieved only through callous leadership. The vindication of Currie, therefore, had done more than erase a personal stigma. It meant that Canadians could remember with pride the achievements and sacrifices of their men in the First World War.

TWO.
MOBILIZATION: HUGHES' ONE-MAN SHOW

In October, 1911, Robert Borden formed his cabinet. The new Prime Minister willingly admitted that his selection of Colonel Sam Hughes for Militia and Defence was his most controversial appointment. It had not been made without misgivings and Borden felt obliged to subject his Minister of Militia to a fatherly lecture about past indiscretions and future responsibilities.[1]

Born in the rural Ontario county of Durham in 1853, Hughes taught English at a school in eastern Ontario and later in Toronto where he became a well-known athlete. He then moved to Lindsay, Ontario, made money in canal and railway speculation and bought a local weekly newspaper, the Victoria *Warder*. With that his fortune and influence grew, and within a few years he was Conservative Member of Parliament for Victoria North, a colonel in the local Militia and a past Grand Master of the Orange Lodge of Ontario. Hughes owed his success to driving energy and boundless self-confidence. He owed the Defence portfolio to long service as Conservative military critic in the Commons, to claims of past support for Borden in internal party squabbles and—by no means least—to the powerful Orange electoral interest in Ontario.

Borden's misgivings about Hughes dated to the South African War, when Hughes was the centre of a national controversy. In April, 1899, the Member for Victoria North—an ebullient Imperialist—raised in the House the perennial suggestion that a brigade of Canadians should be raised and enrolled in the British Army for use in any part of the world.[2] His proposal foundered but opportunity came to revive the idea when Britain went to war against the Boers later in the year. The Liberal government was very slow in offering troops; newspapers across the country generally condemned Sir Wilfrid Laurier for hanging back. " 'Closer the bonds of Empire knit,' sang a poet of Imperial unity. But Sir Wilfrid murmurs, 'Closer the bonds of Empire—nit!' "[3]

Acting in the spirit of his previous proposal and in his capacity as a Militia colonel, Hughes, on his own responsibility offered a contingent to Frederick Borden, then Defence Minister, and at the same time made his offer direct to Joseph Chamberlain, British Secretary of State for the Colonies. Major-General Hutton, the British officer who commanded Canada's forces, had thus been circumvented and he reacted as might be expected. After consulting Frederick Borden, Hutton curtly advised Hughes that he was not authorized to call for volunteers for service in the Transvaal and must put a stop to it. But the "gallant colonel paid no attention to the gentle hint." He went on calling for volunteers, though he did try to mollify Hutton by saying that his actions had merely amounted to such phrases as, "Say, Jim, will you go to the Transvaal in case of trouble?" He had not, he claimed, "usurped the functions of government."[4]

A few days later Hughes felt his position strengthened by the receipt of a letter from England. Chamberlain, grateful for the offer, had stipulated only that "good marksmanship should be regarded as the highest qualification" for troops to be despatched. "I am sure," Hughes quoted him as saying, "it will be universally conceded that your patriotism, zeal, and pluck, mark you as the man to command the Canadian corps." Hughes then openly admitted having received offers from "fully 20,000 men" to serve in "the good old cause."[5]

The Canadian Government was not too embarrassed by Hughes' actions. It was already raising a force of its own, which on 30 October sailed from Quebec City aboard the S.S. *Sardinian* with Chamberlain's thanks for the "rapid organization and embarkation of the Canadian Contingent."[6] But the Canadians were commanded by Lieutenant-Colonel W. D. Otter, not by Lieutenant-Colonel Sam Hughes, though Hughes was aboard the ship, as a civilian.

General Hutton was responsible for this indignity to Hughes. He had been a target of abusive and insubordinate letters from Hughes and had, in the interest of discipline, stated quite bluntly that the Colonel's retirement would be recommended on the grounds of being "devoid of any proper spirit of subordination" and being "deficient in military judgment." Hughes apologized and was accordingly permitted to travel to South Africa, but not in a military capacity. Two months later Hutton relented and recommended him as a captain in Strathcona's Horse, which did not interest the would-be contingent commander! Just before leaving, Hughes, as a Member of Parliament, saw the Prime Minister and suggested that General Hutton be recalled.[7]

The press now took up the cudgels on Hughes' behalf. His offence did not merit the punishment of "military ostracism";[8] a "temporary tyrant" had tried to "rob him of his right to fight for the Empire."[9] Another newspaper bemoaned the fact that "Col. Hughes is to-day walking the streets of Cape Town, unable to get to the front in any capacity, thanks to General Hutton."[10] There was in fact a general demand for a parliamentary inquiry to redress the wrongs done to Colonel Hughes.

The battle between the two men began at a training camp at Niagara-on-the-Lake the previous summer. Hughes, "a Canadian through and through and from the heels up," one newspaper reported, knew the area and installed his battalion on the best bit of ground. "Later on a city corps arrived and the General ordered the Colonel to move his regiment of farmers and give place to the city chaps. 'Not much,' said Colonel Sam, 'my boys are as good as any on the ground. If I move, I move home!' . . . Now you know why Col. Sam is not Major of the Contingent, and when you see the General's scalp hanging from the tower of the Parliament Buildings next spring you will know how it came there."[11]

Hutton's scalp did not decorate the tower but at the beginning of February, 1900, he was recalled from Canada to command a mounted brigade in South Africa. The British Government, the press claimed, had shown sense in removing the man who "made a martyr of Col. Sam Hughes . . . and kept him eating his heart out at Cape Town."[12]

A month later, the Canadian Minister of Militia laid on the table of the House of Commons copies of the correspondence that had passed between Hughes and Hutton. It was an amazing collection. Hughes, besides being grossly insubordinate, had displayed all the talents of a blatant egotist. He lauded his own "hereditary training," his military qualities, his athletic prowess ("victory having almost always followed every team I led or played with") and finally he quoted a poem written in his honour:

> Hughes, Sam Hughes, the war-cry rattles,
> As rang old Fritz in Europe's battles.[13]

He had, the *Toronto Evening News* said, "made an ass of himself." Hutton, it was clear, had acted in a "most considerate and generous manner towards a bad tempered and insolent subordinate . . . as an English officer and gentleman, while Colonel Hughes acted towards General Hutton like a South African Boer."[14]

With the publication of those letters, commented the *Toronto Telegram*, Hutton had been avenged. "How General Hutton must have laughed at his esteemed contemporaries, not excluding this journal, which rose up in defence of outraged Canadian nationality as embodied in the cruel wrongs of Col. Sam Hughes, M.P." The newspaper continued: "It would have been manifestly impossible for Hutton to allow Hughes to go to South Africa . . . If the Conservative leaders knew all the facts they should have stood by Hutton and deserted Hughes." "The journals," the article concluded, "which imagined that Col. Sam Hughes was a victim to General Hutton's prejudice against Colonial officers must feel like asking the earth to open up and swallow them when they read those awful letters and especially that gem of poetry."[15]

Meanwhile, Colonel Hughes was not languishing in Cape Town. He had secured employment with the British and did well as a transport officer on the staff of General Sir Charles Warren, but his record was not sufficiently distinguished to justify decorations, which he considered he had earned. He served for the better part of a year on duties which he himself described as "seeing that all dangerous places [on the railway] are guarded; to see the troops at these places; to see the guards on bridges, water tanks, water supply, and important points wherever there might be danger, and to examine that the line is in proper condition and is patrolled."

To the reporter who interviewed him he had expressed complete satisfaction with his lot, the "turn down by Gen. Hutton [being] the greatest possible favour done me."[16]

On his return Hughes battled for decorations and "recognition" with the Liberal government without success. In 1904 he carried the fight directly to the Governor General whose inquiry elicited the War Office response that the Colonel's services did not merit the issue of even the war gratuity. Four years later Hughes appealed to Laurier, and by this time his own assessment of his prowess had become considerably enhanced; he now claimed at least one Victoria Cross, and perhaps two. Again he was disappointed.

Despite Robert Borden's admonitions, Hughes did not let the matter drop even after assuming office. Field Marshal H. R. H. The Duke of Connaught was now Governor General and the new Minister of Militia decided to tackle him. This he did—directly—but with no better result than before. The Duke, in fact, counselled him sternly to forget the whole affair, but the sturdy Hughes retorted just as sternly that he should get him "justice" (a somewhat impossible task). That the Duke of Connaught, one year later, angrily vetoed an attempt by Hughes to have himself promoted major-general need cause no surprise.[17]

The responsibilities of office did not chasten Colonel Hughes; instead they served as a challenge and an outlet for his remarkable energies. For the first time in Canada's history a Minister of Militia actively campaigned in Parliament and out for greater military expenditures. These took fruit in an expansion of the Militia and in the provision of local armouries and drill halls across the country; during Hughes' period in office, a total of 56 armouries and drill halls were erected throughout Canada at a cost of about two million dollars.[18] As for manpower, the actual strength of the active Militia in 1913 was only 43,000 against an establishment of 60,000; by July, 1914, Hughes had increased the establishment to 77,323 all ranks, and units had recruited until they were approaching full strength.[19]

Apart from drill halls, training camps were required for summer use by the expanding Militia. Existing camps were enlarged and improved, notably Sarcee Camp, Calgary; Camp Hughes at Brandon; Niagara-on-the-Lake, Ontario; Aldershot, Nova Scotia; Sussex, New Brunswick;

and Vernon, British Columbia. Other large camps, such as Camp
Borden, Ontario, were Hughes' own creations, as was the magnificent
Connaught Range, twelve miles from Ottawa, which was under
construction when war broke out. Hughes was especially interested in
rifle-shooting; as a past President of the Dominion of Canada Rifle
Association and an excellent shot he brought some of his own enthusiasm for the weapon to men in training. Remembering Chamberlain's
stipulation for South Africa, he told the troops, "I want, first of all, men
who can pink the enemy every time."[20]

The Minister did not regard himself, despite his office, solely as a
civilian. Like the fiery Trotsky, who as war commissar had a predilec-
tion for descending on any hard-pressed Red Army front at the time of
the Russian Civil War, Hughes would don his uniform and make an
unheralded arrival at any camp that took his fancy, to give practical
direction in the handling of men. His manner was curt and decisive, his
power absolute. Many of his policies, however, were good; and most
officers, well aware that their careers were at his mercy, forbore to
criticize his methods.

Despite the driving impetus imparted to the Militia by Hughes, Canada
was ill-prepared for war. The report of Sir John French (Inspector
General of the Imperial Forces), who in 1910 investigated the Canadian
Militia at the invitation of the Canadian Government, made that clear.
A woeful disproportion of arms and services was disclosed; training was
poor, many officers and non-commissioned officers were unqualified,
transport, equipment and supplies were sadly lacking.[21] Like most
British officers, however, Sir John found the raw, Canadian, human
material impressive.

Hughes tackled the glaring defects with enthusiasm. He abandoned
the old system of military districts, under which military units were
collected without cohesion, and established six divisional areas across
Canada in which units were organized on divisional lines (or in
cavalry brigades capable of being brought together to form a cavalry
division in time of need). With this arrangement a proper proportion
of arms and services could be aimed at, the first-line troops in each area
forming the field formations and the second-line the lines-of-communi-
cation and defence units.[22] There was also more emphasis on training;
in the summer of 1914 more than 10,000 troops carried out combined
manoeuvres at Camp Petawawa under active service conditions.
Hughes took a group of officers to the annual manoeuvres of 1912 and
1913 carried out by the British, French, German and Swiss armies. In
addition, officers were exchanged with Britain, Australia and India
and sent to attend staff colleges; qualification examinations for other
officers and non-commissioned officers, which had long been urged,
were now insisted upon.[23] In the field of equipment, however, little was

achieved because the increase in manpower had outstripped Canadian industrial ability to supply certain needs; some other requirements for items of British manufacture could not immediately be met. The Dominion Arsenal was capable of meeting limited demands for small-arms ammunition and artillery shells; for insurance Hughes established a second point of manufacture (in his home town of Lindsay, Ontario).[24] The country also had its own rifle—the Ross—but for heavier armament was dependent on British factories. By 1912 numbers of 18-pounder field guns—first-class modern weapons *—were being delivered to the Canadian Militia. Other orders placed by Hughes in Britain were deferred. War Office orders took first priority, and out of twenty-seven 4.5-inch howitzers ordered in 1911, only seven had been delivered when war broke out.[25] Despite this disappointment, the prodigious efforts of Sam Hughes to increase the size and efficiency of the Canadian forces before the war was undoubtedly his best service to the country.

By August, 1914, Canada had a regular force of 3,000 all ranks and a volunteer militia of about 64,000.[26] Only twelve officers of the Permanent Force had completed Staff College Courses. Though Militia Staff Courses had been instituted and military courses established at universities (out of which the Canadian Officers' Training Corps emerged later) training was still inadequate by European standards. Artillery was available for only two out of six planned divisions; motor vehicles, and even transport wagons, were almost entirely lacking. There were insufficient uniforms, and many of those available were obsolete. In truth, an expeditionary force ready to take its place in the European conflict did not exist. It may be safely concluded that if, in German eyes, the British Army was insignificant, the Canadian was not even worth the reckoning.

But to have to fight nature produces a hardy race; and Canadians, occupying the northern half of the North American continent, had a rigid climate to endure which undoubtedly produced a virile race of finest quality. This the Germans were to learn to their cost. In the Militia, small, ill-equipped and partially trained though it was, Canada possessed a nucleus on which the raw masses of her male population could coalesce. With proper equipment and experience the country eventually produced a corps of four divisions together with a comprehensive establishment of Corps Troops and Heavy Artillery. It was a balanced fighting unit that could not be matched by the Central Powers, nor—if performance was a criterion—by the Allied armies.

*General A. G. L. McNaughton describes this gun as "probably the best weapon in relation to environment that the British Army has ever had either before or since."

The tortuous chain of events leading to the First World War are well enough known that a brief outline will suffice. On 28 June, 1914, at Serajevo, the Bosnian capital, the heir to the Austrian throne was assassinated by Slav nationalists who were agents of "The Black Hand," a Serbian secret society. Seizing this pretext, on 28 July Austria declared war on Serbia, having first taken the precaution of obtaining Germany's firm promise of help should the conflict widen. On 30 July, having received an appeal for help from Serbia, Russia ordered a general mobilization. Germany immediately demanded that these warlike preparations cease. Russia ignored the ultimatum and on 1 August Germany declared war on Russia. Since 1894 Russia and France had been linked in a defensive pact; and on 3 August, Germany declared war on France. Italy, the other member of the Triple Alliance with Germany and Austria-Hungary, remained aloof, and so for the moment did Britain. The latter, associated with France in the Anglo-French Convention of 1904 and a similar agreement with Russia in 1907, was bound by no formal agreement to assist either country in case of war. The British cabinet, the majority of its members anxious for peace and uncertain of public opinion, wavered.

Until almost the end of July the European situation aroused no particular apprehension in Canada. Parliament was prorogued on 12 June and the Governor General and members of the government made the most of that lovely summer away from Ottawa. The Duke of Connaught was in the West, Sir Robert Borden at Muskoka and Colonel Hughes at his home in Lindsay. On the day that Austria declared war on Serbia, Borden's "holiday dream" was shattered by a "terrible awakening." He received advice on the 28th that Great Britain would almost certainly be involved if France should be attacked.[27] The following day an ominous cable from the Colonial Secretary to the Governor General pointed to the direct involvement of Canada in an increasingly critical situation. Canada was advised to adopt the "Precautionary Stage" of a defence scheme drawn up by the Dominion, which was only to be put into effect when relations with any foreign power had become so strained that measures against a possible surprise attack were necessary.[28] The Governor General, after transmitting the contents of the telegram to Borden, left Banff for Ottawa on 1 August and on the same day Borden returned to the capital. Hughes, "confronted with an opportunity for which his Napoleonic soul had longed,"[29] had reached Ottawa four days earlier and on 30 July had presided over an emergency meeting of the Militia Council. He informed an apprehensive press that preparations were being made for the early despatch to Britain of 20,000 or 25,000 men.[30]

News of Germany's declaration of war against Russia and France came on 1 and 3 August—but still there was no news from Britain. Hughes burned with impatience until finally, angry and excited, he ordered his Military Secretary to haul down the British flag flying over his headquarters. "By God, I don't want to be a Britisher under such conditions," he fumed; "to think that they would want to go back on France!" The "offending bunting" was laid in a neat roll on the Minister's desk but shortly afterwards, under the influence of calmer counsel, it was restored to the top of the mast, "for the present," to await a statement of British policy.[31]

That statement was not long delayed. On the evening of 2 August Germany had served an ultimatum on Belgium demanding a free passage for her troops to march against France. Belgium, determined to protect her neutrality—which incidentally had been guaranteed by Germany together with Britain and France in 1839—requested French and British aid. On the morning of 4 August German troops invaded Belgium. British uncertainties vanished in the face of this unprovoked aggression and a British ultimatum that day demanded the withdrawal of German troops from Belgian soil by midnight. The time limit passed without reply. Britain, too, was now at war with Germany—and with Britain, Canada.

In 1914 Canada's constitutional position within the Empire gave her no part in declaring war but she had the right of deciding what form her participation should take. It was wholehearted. There was enthusiasm throughout most of Canada for this war. Germany was clearly the aggressor, and there was a profound conviction that Britain's cause was just. Even after the war, when rivers of blood had flowed, the Leader of the Opposition, Mr. D. D. Mackenzie, voiced the same conviction: "Germany made unlawful war on Belgium. There is no doubt in the world about that. Belgium had a right to suppose that Germany would abide by her solemn treaty; so had France; so had Great Britain; so had every other nation in the world. They had a right to suppose that they had only to make certain defences against Germany at certain places and that Germany would not attempt in an unlawful way to make war on France. Consequently it was in issue, as we say in the law, an illegal war, started illegally and continued illegally throughout."[32]

The North German Confederation, which expanded to become the German Empire, and the Canadian Confederation had come into being on the same day, 1 July, 1867. Germany, relatively small in territory but large in population, was founded not as a democracy but as an autocracy backed by military might. Probably in no other country in the history of the world was such great progress made during a period of fifty years in material development or in the perfecting of a military machine. When her military machine had reached such a degree of perfection that she believed it invincible, Germany did not hesitate to furnish Austria with a "blank cheque" for use against Serbia. This act "stands out predominant among the immediate causes of the war."[33]

Canada, large in territory and small in population, travelled a different road. With a democratic constitution under which government was carried on by the consent of the governed, the people of Canada devoted themselves not to military affairs but to subduing nature and developing the country, a task so engrossing that when they entered the war to oppose Germany's aggressive designs Canadians were not fully conscious of their own strength, of the extent of their own resources, nor of the full possibilities of their own efforts.

In Germany every physically fit male was liable to military service and from this enormous pool the state drew off a desired number for periods of full-time training lasting from two to three years, depending on the branch of service. The soldier then returned to civilian life as a member of the regular reserve, in which he remained from four to five years, taking part-time refresher training. After service in the regular reserve, the German was no longer called out for training, although he remained liable for service to the age of forty-five. In addition to this highly trained reserve, an *ersatz* reserve was made up from those not selected for full-time service.[34]

In this huge reserve and in the thoroughness of the training lay, as the eminent military historian Liddell Hart describes it, "the secret of the first great surprise of the war, one which almost proved decisive."[35] Through it, the Germans were able during mobilization to back up regular army corps with reserve corps of excellent quality and to throw them into battle from the very first. In this way they achieved an incredible preponderance of strength against the French. They had, moreover, foreseen the worth of heavy artillery and machine-guns; they alone had adequate numbers of heavy howitzers, with which they speedily reduced the Belgian fortresses. While other armies possessed machine-guns, German preparations in this field had been more thorough. Skilful use of the machine-gun enabled them to dominate the battlefield before other armies became fully awake to all the possibilities.[36] Furthermore, the state had taken care to inspire the human components of this powerful and smoothly-working machine with the will to win. There was "flaming patriotism," and a comradeship and pride in the German army that were matched in no other army of 1914.[37]

German railway communications had been developed to a high standard of efficiency. The number of lines of double track running west had grown from nine to thirteen before 1914. Between 6 and 16 August more than three million men were carried to the fronts in eleven thousand trains and one and a quarter million of them then surged forward in the massive march through Belgium.[38]

Canada's response to the British declaration of war was generous and immediate. As early as 1 August, Borden offered a force to Great Britain and five days later the offer was accepted. On 7 August the cabinet decided to contribute an expeditionary force of one division. Patriotic fervour swept the country. Demonstrations of loyalty took place in every town. In the words of the official historian, "The enthusiasm of crowds in the Montreal streets singing 'La Marseillaise' and 'Rule Britannia' was matched by the stirring spectacle of the impromptu parades, waving of flags, processions of decorated automobiles and impassioned speeches with which every western city from Winnipeg to Victoria received the news of war."[39]

The problem for the military authorities was how to raise the promised division. Two schemes for mobilization did exist, the first for the six Canadian divisions and a second drawn up in 1911 for an expeditionary force of volunteers formed into an infantry division and a cavalry brigade. The latter plan (obviously the one to adopt in the present case) was sufficiently detailed to reduce chaos and confusion to a minimum by providing a decentralized system. The commanders of divisional areas (and three military districts which still remained following Hughes' reforms) would be responsible for recruiting and, as far as possible, equipping contingents. They would then despatch them to Petawawa, the central place of concentration in summer, or in winter direct to the port of embarkation. Horses and wagons would also be purchased in the divisional areas or districts.[40] The adoption of this scheme would, as the official historian points out, have ensured "the provision of troops on a fair ratio throughout the Dominion for a contingent of the same strength as that subsequently mobilized in 1914."[41]

Colonel Hughes, however, consigned both plans to the ministerial waste-paper basket. In place of a carefully drawn-up scheme Hughes substituted his own improvised measure, which he afterwards described as "really a call to arms, like the fiery cross passing through the Highlands of Scotland or the mountains of Ireland in former days."[42] On 6 August, the day the great German deployment began, Hughes sent 226 night telegrams directly to unit commanders of the Militia. With this, normal channels of communication had been ignored, divisional and district commands by-passed and the mobilization centred in Hughes' hands. Unit commanders were instructed to interview prospective volunteers and forward to Ottawa lists of those who could meet prescribed standards. Ottawa was then supposed to examine the lists and tell the unit commander how many to enlist, until a total of 25,000 individuals had been obtained. The inevitable result was chaos from Halifax to Vancouver. The impracticability of the whole centralized and unwieldy process at last dawned on Sam Hughes, and the members of the Expeditionary Force were eventually obtained in virtually the same way as had been prescribed in the second of the pre-war schemes.[43]

Existing Militia infantry units with their traditions were ignored. The new Canadian Expeditionary Force was formed into numbered battalions that bore no relation to the time-honoured regimental titles. "The most unpardonable sin in the whole of the Canadian mobilization," commented one unit commander, "was the complete smashing of the regimental spirit."[44] There is truth in this point, as any soldier knows. When a second battalion of a famous regiment is formed its members ask themselves, "Can we measure up to the standard set by the parent battalion?" They know the traditions and do their best to maintain them. Paradoxically enough, one battalion raised at this time did have a name, a new one that was to become famous. Princess Patricia's Canadian Light Infantry, privately raised and equipped at a cost of $100,000 by Mr. Hamilton Gault, began traditions which it still perpetuates.

Yet another change in the mobilization plan was made by Hughes. The concentration would no longer take place at Camp Petawawa but at Valcartier, where there was no camp at all! The site was the wide valley where the swift Jacques Cartier River enters the St. Lawrence, in the vicinity of the port of embarkation, Quebec.

On 8 August Hughes took over the site and transferred to it the contractors who had been working on the Connaught Range, near Ottawa, together with excavating machinery and 400 workmen. Their job was to put in three miles of targets, an artillery range, to install a water system and make roads. The ground was marshy in places and covered with bush. William Price of Quebec, the head of a timber firm and a friend of the Minister, was given the task of preparing the site. He engaged thousands of men to clear and drain the land. Though work still continued after the first troops arrived, by 18 August tents could be pitched and the men housed. Price was subsequently knighted for his services.[45] That Valcartier could be used at all after such a short time is yet another tribute to the energy and driving force of Colonel Sam Hughes; but although it was a magnificent achievement, it was "wasteful and unnecessary."[46]

In the spirit of those days the mechanics of mobilization made little difference to the response. It is hard for the mind of to-day, conditioned by the Second World War and present Cold War tensions, to understand the innocent fervour which greeted the outbreak of the First World War. Perhaps it was revolt against the monotonous routine of daily life—the chance of adventure after the peace of a century broken only by minor wars. Whatever it was, the hunting spirit of man was rekindled and volunteers flocked from towns and cities, from woods and farms, to join the colours.

"Recruits are simply pouring in from all quarters," reported one unit commander.[47] Many of them even walked surprising distances. The call was for infantrymen, and so cavalrymen who volunteered were told they must be prepared to serve in either foot or artillery. "Every mother's son says, 'That's good enough for me.'"[48] Commanding officers could afford to be selective: ". . . with lots of men offering, we knew that we would have no difficulty in getting all we required."[49] Unlike all other armies of the day, every married man had to get his wife's permission in writing before he could enlist, but in that age of enthusiasm wives seldom refused.[50]

From assembly areas locally recruited contingents marched to the station where they entrained for Valcartier. Thousands of people lined the route; bands played, flags waved, and the excitement was intense. "Young ladies carried the men's rifles, others decorated them with flowers, others clung to their arms and the sidewalks were a mass of excited cheering humanity."[51] Similar scenes were enacted at halts across the country. Some men even boarded trains without permission in their eagerness to go along and had to be put off. "Poor beggars, they sat down on the grass and howled with vexation."[52] Between 18 August and 8 September all the contingents (carried in a hundred special trains) had reached Valcartier, filling the new camp to capacity. Pitchforked into a strange military world, the new infantryman experienced the terrible, lonely vulnerability of all recruits. He soon discovered that it was a world of barked commands, aggressive masculinity and tented discomfort devoid of any feminine features. An impressive total of 32,665 officers and men were finally assembled, 7,000 more than had been prescribed.[53]

In one of the trains travelled, as Jan Smuts later described him, a "soldier of no professional training, a civilian of doubtful ability."[54] Yet this man, Arthur William Currie, was destined to command the Canadian Corps as "the ablest Corps Commander in the British Forces" and to become, in Borden's eyes, "at least as capable as any Army Commander among them."[55] Approaching forty, he was well over six feet tall and weighed more than two hundred pounds. Despite his size he did not cut an impressive military figure. Later in life a white-haired and leaner Currie had a more soldierly appearance, but throughout the war he looked uncomfortable in uniform; his tunic bunched over the girth of his Sam Browne belt and was parted at the back by a seat of generous proportions. His stiff forage cap sat squarely above a long and heavily jowled face. Despite his biographer's description of him as a "happy-go-lucky overgrown boy,"[56] pictures of a smiling Currie are rare indeed. His letters, too, are sober and reveal a thoughtful rather than a brilliant mind. In discussion Currie could be persuasive; in argument he was firm and convincing.

Arthur Currie was born at Napperton in Middlesex County, Ontario, in 1875 and grew up a frail child on his father's farm. Lacking the means to study law or medicine, as he wished, he trained as a school teacher. During those formative years he gained an intimate knowledge of life on the land and farming, at that time the mainstay of Canada.

It gave him resourcefulness, an understanding of countrymen and an uncondescending sympathy with the ordinary man.

At the age of nineteen Currie left his family to live with an aunt in British Columbia (then just beginning its amazing development). There he taught primary school in the village of Sidney, near Victoria. The rewards of teaching were meagre and that, combined with a prolonged illness in 1899-1900 and his marriage to the daughter of an English family in 1901, probably influenced his change of occupation. He gave up teaching to sell insurance and to dabble on an increasing scale in real estate, at a time when land "jumped ten and twenty times in price if not in value almost overnight."[57] In 1913 the bubble burst. A minor recession throughout most of the world was, for Canada, a major one. Money grew scarce, land was unloaded and Currie, like many others, was caught. The exact amount of his liability is unknown* but to settle part of it he accepted loans of five thousand dollars and a thousand pounds from two of his subordinate commanders during the war. In 1917, when repaying one obligation of more than $10,000, Currie described how his debts had troubled him: "It is impossible for me to tell you . . . the efforts I have constantly made to meet the claim but I can tell you that for nearly three years the last thing I thought of at night and the first thing in the morning was this."[59] These debts, in the hands of those who opposed his appointment as Corps Commander, assumed considerable importance later on and almost cost him his career.

Hand in hand with teaching and his later, free-wheeling, business transactions, Currie had always had an absorbing interest in the Militia. In 1897 he had joined the 5th Regiment of the B.C. Brigade, Canadian Garrison Artillery, in the lowest rank. Commissioned in 1900, he rose to command the unit in 1909. Disillusioned by the wreck of his personal finances he resigned the command in 1913, but was persuaded to take over an infantry unit (for which he had little training) in January 1914.** The outbreak of war found him commanding the same unit (50th Regiment, Gordon Highlanders), with Major Garnet Hughes, a graduate of the Royal Military College and the son of the Minister of Militia, as one of his officers.

Colonel Urquhart, Currie's biographer, may have exaggerated when he claimed that Currie's Militia training was "vital to his ultimate success";[61] it was, however, vital to his first wartime appointment. Even if he had attended every summer camp for the maximum sixteen days from his date of commissioning, he would have completed only two hundred and eight days' training by 1914. A keen soldier, however,

*A file, "Currie's admission of default," was personally destroyed by Sir Robert Borden.[58]
**Currie laughed at the suggestion, and only took the appointment when it was made clear that the fate of the unit was at stake. He pictured himself in lurid language as "the last man likely to look soldierly in Highland dress."[60]

he had obtained a first-class certificate in gunnery for which he had had to attend four months' instruction given by British regulars attached to the Esquimalt Garrison. Of more importance was his graduation from the Militia Staff Course held in Vancouver in 1914, conducted by Major Louis James Lipsett, a British officer loaned by the War Office, who was serving as General Staff Officer, Western Canada. There he had studied both the theory and practice of military subjects, and qualified for "employment on the staff at camps of instruction and on mobilization."[62] Lipsett described him as an "excellent officer who, if war broke out . . . could not be held back."[63] A friendship grew up between the two men which was to be strengthened throughout the days to come.

A second friendship which had important consequences for Currie was that between himself and Garnet Hughes. As members of the same regiment they knew each other well and each respected the other. There is little doubt that Hughes' good opinion of Currie must have influenced the former's father when he selected Currie later for higher rank. But Currie did not achieve recognition simply because of the people he knew. Also important was his success as a commanding officer. The 5th Regiment won the Governor General's Cup for General Efficiency (open to all Garrison Artillery units in Canada) four times under Currie's command; three times it won second place in the Landsdowne Cup for efficiency and it came first in gun practice on three occasions.[64]

A story told by one of Currie's officers bears testimony to the skill of the 5th Regiment. During General Sir Ian Hamilton's inspection of the Canadian Militia in 1913 target-practice for light field guns, not properly the arm of the Garrison Artillery, was staged at Victoria. One battery fired at a canvas target towed by a fast launch at some distance out to sea and quickly riddled it. The inspecting team was about to turn away when Sir Ian Hamilton said, "Your fellows almost cut the tow rope, Colonel." "We haven't tried yet, sir," replied Currie. Turning to the battery commander, Currie ordered four rounds of rapid fire that parted the tow rope midway between the target and the swiftly moving launch. Sam Hughes was elated and the inspecting staff impressed. Someone remarked on the steady nerves of those in charge of the launch. "Oh," said the major in charge of the battery, "that's not the first time they've seen that done."[65]

Currie's unit had a formidable record which Sam Hughes was bound to notice. He had first met Currie in 1912 and had complimented him upon his unit then. On a later visit, when Currie and Hughes had taken opposing stands on the provision of a band to play for a semipolitical body, Currie had won his respect by stating point-blank that he, and not the Minister of Militia, commanded the regiment.

The outcome was the offer, after war had broken out, of an "infantry brigade at Valcartier."[66] Though he had had little training by regular standards, Currie's Militia experience probably made him an outstanding choice.

Currie hesitated. The offer of a brigade was a tempting one. He did not doubt his own ability but could not forget his debts. In the end Garnet Hughes wired his father to advise him of Currie's financial nightmare and to request that the offer be kept open for twenty-four hours. The Minister did more than that. Not only did he agree to wait, he referred his son to Sam Matson, the publisher and proprietor of the Victoria *Daily Colonist*, who would help Currie to effect a financial settlement.[67]

With that assistance Currie's affairs were straightened out sufficiently and Garnet notified his father that Currie would accept the appointment. A few days later, on 26 August, 1914, the "provisional brigadier-general" left Victoria for Valcartier on the first stage of an arduous and perilous journey that was to bring fame for himself and an unsurpassed reputation to the troops he commanded.

Currie arrived at Valcartier siding on 1 September, 1914, and nobody could have been more relieved than he to be done with the past. Garnet Hughes, who had preceded him, met the troop train and shared his tent. Currie found out from Hughes that he was to command the 1st (Provisional) Western Brigade consisting of the 5th, 6th, 7th, and 8th Battalions. On the following day this brigade was renumbered the 2nd. "The amateur soldier who had never handled more than four hundred all ranks in peacetime was now in command of four thousand in time of war."[68]

Currie had no headquarters and no staff; not before 8 September was a brigade major assigned to him. The day after his arrival, still without a tent, he moved into the lines of one of his battalions (the 8th) which was under the command of Lipsett, his old instructor. On the 18th Sam Hughes looked him up and told him that he would definitely command the 2nd Brigade in the force going overseas.[69]

Four brigades were organized on a provisional footing. The 1st, comprising the 1st, 2nd, 3rd and 4th battalions from Ontario, was commanded by Lieutenant-Colonel M. S. Mercer. The battalions for Currie's 2nd Brigade all came from the West, while those of Colonel R. E. W. Turner's 3rd Brigade were Scottish battalions (the 13th, 15th and 16th) from all across Canada and the composite 14th Battalion from the Maritimes and Montreal. Lieutenant-Colonel J. E. Cohoe commanded the 4th Brigade, made up of the 9th, 10th and 11th Battalions from the Prairies and the 12th from the Maritimes. Another battalion (the 17th Provisional) was formed to include infantry who went to England surplus to brigade requirements.[70]

The selection of a commander for the embryo division posed a special problem to Hughes. There is little doubt that the Minister would have relished the command himself. To discourage him, Borden prompted Mr. George Perley, the acting Canadian High Commissioner in London, to obtain a statement from Lord Kitchener, the British War Minister. Kitchener complied by forwarding his view that it would be a mistake to "change the Minister of Militia at this juncture." He also passed along to Hughes the names of three Canadian-born officers serving in the British Army. Hughes did not consider them sufficiently senior for divisional command. He himself had three British candidates in mind, and of these he thought Major-General E. A. H. Alderson "best qualified by far." Kitchener, in view of this preference, designated Alderson.[71]

The more than thirty-two thousand men making up the Expeditionary Force represented more than two hundred Militia units across Canada. The infantry units had undergone frequent minor organizational changes and a major one—from twelve battalions on 22 August to sixteen on 8 September—so there was little cohesion. Though organized as far as possible on a provincial basis, the new units were largely conglomerates in which officers and men did not know one another.[72] Training problems were thus aggravated. At the first review of the force by the Minister on 12 September the only units to perform creditably were a few which had not completely lost their regimental identity.[73]

The mobilization of other arms and services required to complete the divisional establishment followed the pre-war plan fairly closely. Militia units were designated and advantage was taken of the nucleus they represented. Artillery units mobilized separately under the Director of Artillery, and with far less confusion than the infantry. Three field artillery brigades (18-pounders) and one heavy battery (60-pounders) were formed, each with its ammunition column, and there was also a divisional ammunition column. A 4.5-inch howitzer brigade was required, but there were not enough howitzers in Canada to equip it. Three field companies of engineers, a company of signals, Army Service Corps units and the medical services eventually assembled. In addition to the arms and services of the division new units were authorized by the Minister, some of which proved useful. The Motor Machine-Gun Brigade was one such unit. A bad example was the Canadian Aviation Corps, whose one plane disappeared in England.[74]

Three Permanent Force units had been moved to Valcartier early in August, not as part of the Expeditionary Force but to run the camps and instruct the volunteers. They were the Royal Canadian Horse Artillery, the Royal Canadian Dragoons and Lord Strathcona's Horse. As with infantry units, orders changed. Hughes offered the War Office "one regular cavalry regiment and two regular horse artillery batteries" and these were accepted on 7 August. On 26 August orders reached Valcartier to mobilize the two batteries and to form a composite regiment made up of Dragoons and Strathconas. By the middle of September, the units having been amalgamated, the composite idea was dropped and troopers switched back to their parent units. Hughes had now decided to send both cavalry regiments overseas.[75]

There was, in fact, confusion throughout the camp, and it has been generally condemned by the official historians, Macphail, Duguid and Nicholson. In the words of Sir Andrew Macphail, the medical historian:

The men were without adequate tentage and without greatcoats in the autumn frosts and rain; the horses were without coverings. Catarrhal conditions developed. The Jacques Cartier river which flowed through the camp became polluted; swift precautions were taken; there was no epidemic of typhoid; only one case developed before England was reached. This method of concentration bore heavily upon the medical services. The officers were suddenly faced by forty thousand men for whom sanitary arrangements were required if epidemic sickness was to be avoided. Each recruit must be examined in a confused camp rather than in the peaceful leisure of his native town, where the established standards should have been applied. . . Military training was negligible. The time was occupied in organizing and reorganizing, issuing clothing and equipment, examining and inoculating recruits, writing new attestation papers, and preparing for reviews.[76]

The Governor General reviewed the force three times during September; on each occasion a martial Minister of Militia, mounted and in uniform, led the marching troops past the saluting base.

Nicholson describes further confusion in the infantry:

Having arrived with no unit organization, the men had to be medically examined, inoculated and attested, and issued with clothing and equipment—the last a protracted affair dependent upon deliveries from the manufacturers. All these processes played havoc with training programmes, which were further disrupted by repeated changes in the composition, location and command of the units to which the troops were assigned.[77]

Duguid, who in 1914 saw the chaos at Valcartier, was even more emphatic:

The composition, location and command of C.E.F. [infantry] units were repeatedly changed; officers and N.C.O.'s being temporary and provisional were on probation; until a few days before departure, one provisional battalion had four lieut.-colonels, another none, and so with the lower ranks; new appointments, promotions, replacements, transfers and reductions were of bewildering frequency in the hectic, alternating process of shaking up and shaking down.[78]

The ubiquitous Sam Hughes met every major contingent arriving at Valcartier, and even conducted them to their lines. Spending more time at the camp than in Ottawa he held parades and supervised training. Appointments were made solely by him in a seigniorial way without reference to the Militia Council or to his colleagues.[79] Colonel V. A. S. Williams, the Adjutant General, had been installed at Valcartier as Camp Commandant. But he had "no power whatever regarding appointments or seniority," and could give no satisfaction to colonels deprived of commands or to other officers who felt they had justifiable complaints. "Go and see the Minister," was invariably his advice.[80] Ralph Allen tells the story of one inspection by Hughes when a particular unit took his fancy. "A fine unit you have here, Major," Hughes remarked. "Pardon me, sir," corrected the embarrassed officer, "I'm only a captain." "You're a major now," returned the infallible Hughes, as he moved grandly away.[81] The story may be exaggerated, but it has the ring of truth. "With Sam out of the way," wrote a 1st Division diarist after Hughes had been removed in 1916, "promotion is likely to be according to seniority and ability, which is all that anyone can ask for."[82]

The camp swarmed with contractors, work parties drawn from units, and gangs of labourers still clearing bush. Horses, purchased by buyers scouring the country for them, arrived in droves. Military police hunted through the camp for hidden liquor—Sam, a fanatical teetotaller, decreed that Valcartier should be dry—while troops lined up at orderly rooms for short leave to Quebec to escape the ban. Against this background, units tried to train and the ranges rang with rifle fire.

Arthur Currie did what he could to speed the equipping and training of his command but he could accomplish little. He led his brigade for the three reviews by the Duke of Connaught and was present on the ranges when his brigade was firing.[83]

Hughes boasted later that on leaving Valcartier the men of the first contingent were "trained to handle a rifle as no men had ever handled it before."[84] As the maximum training requirement for infantry was fifty rounds fired at various ranges—and not all infantrymen completed even that—and as there was a shortage of competent instructors, the truth of his statement might well be questioned. Already defects in the Ross rifle were beginning to show up. "I saw three of the rifles jam," remarked one observer, "and listened to a sergeant who attempted to explain the reason. A more plausible yet wholly inadequate explanation I have seldom listened to."[85] On another occasion the same person commented: "Several of the rifles seemed to misfire too frequently for rifles that are going to be asked to stop the German rushes,"[86] while "the bayonet has an unfortunate habit of jumping off the rifle when firing is being carried on with bayonets fixed."[87] "The utility of the Ross rifle as a weapon of war," he concluded, "is summed up in the words of a driver who, after several tries to keep the bayonet on and to load from the clip said in disgust 'To hell with the gun, I'll take a club.' "[88]

Nor was some of the equipment provided by contractors much better. "Contractors appeared upon the scene," reported Macphail. "Without patterns, without supervision or direction, they poured into Quebec supplies that had no relation to the hard conditions of war."[89] Boots were an example. These looked fine, but soaked up water like a sponge. "I have a pair of these boots myself," wrote a senior officer, "and can answer for the fact that they are quite useless in wet weather. Mine are coated with dubbing and still let in water."[90] They had a veneer of leather on the sole, underneath which was a "kind of gum or glue"; the uppers were made of very soft porous leather which became soaked with the slightest rain. "I remember saying to one of my staff in Valcartier that the boots for the men should be studded with nails. I now understand his remark that 'perhaps they will not stand being nailed.' "[91] "Men going upon active service," concluded Macphail, "were furnished with boots that might do very well for a farmer making an excursion to his barn on a Sunday afternoon, or for his daughter going to church. After twelve parades, these boots were reduced to a sodden mass, and the paper from which the heels were made returned to its primitive pulp."[92] It was the same with greatcoats. These, too, looked and fitted well, but the cloth readily absorbed water and was soaked through in half an hour.[93]

Wagons, including the generally issued Bain type, were not designed in such a way that the wheels turned under the box, and as such were useless for the narrow roads of France and Belgium. "Wagons were assembled that might do very well on the illimitable prairie," wrote Macphail with gentle irony. "They were of all possible types, so that each maker and every town might have a chance to profit by public funds; but there was not a road in Europe wide enough to allow them to turn."[94] The bandoliers issued to the troops contained loops of leather to take single rounds—rather like those of Cossacks—and were of no use whatever for a clip-loading rifle such as the Ross; nor could they be converted.[95]

Then there were the horses. Altogether 8,150 were bought at about $175 each, but numbers of them could not possibly have been inspected. "Many were shot before they had been in Valcartier a week, for the poor skates were too weak to stand a three-day railway trip. Sixty miserable specimens were sold . . . and fetched a dollar a head."[96] Altogether some 500 were auctioned at Quebec and brought an average of $54.00 apiece.[97]

When Canada decided to raise a second division Hughes' *ad hoc* procedures for procuring infantrymen were dropped in favour of the pre-war plan. Men were enrolled in military areas and districts, formed into units, and remained where they were until just before embarkation.[98] But with the first contingent "the impossible had been attempted." It had proved that "Canada was strong in men alone."[99]

Yet on 27 September, 1914, embarkation began. Measured against either of the two essential standards, training and equipment, the force was not ready. Hughes, convinced that "speed in passing troops overseas to England was the sole principle," had single-handedly disrupted orderly mobilization. "Canada and the world must not miss the spectacle and advertisement of a new 'armada.' "[100] To the Canadian public, who saw just that—a vast body of men assembled and on its way to the war in record time—Hughes was a "man who got things done," and that impression persisted among his partisans to the end.

To others with an ounce of military acumen, however, it was obvious that the force was not ready to go to France. Though the men left Canada in high heart, they were unprepared for battle. Even the most optimistic observer foresaw a long delay in England to complete training and equipping after the chaos of Valcartier.

THREE.
SALISBURY PLAIN: A FORETASTE OF FLANDERS

Chaotic mobilization at Valcartier was matched by chaotic embarkation at Quebec. The Director of Supplies and Transport, as soon as Canada's 25,000-man contingent had been accepted, set busily to work on a plan allocating troops, horses and equipment to vessels. On 17 September his plans were ready—twenty-five vessels would be required and these he had chartered. Four days later it was decided at a conference between Hughes, the Prime Minister and other members of the cabinet held at the Minister of Militia's house at Valcartier that all effective men at the concentration point (in all, 31,200) would be sent overseas. A hasty revision of the embarkation plan to allow for the extra six-thousand troops was rejected by Hughes. Hughes also rejected the services of the Director of Supplies and Transport and appointed his friend William Price (the performer of such prodigious feats of construction at Valcartier) to supervise the embarkation "without reference to Headquarters or to previous schedule."[1]

The new "Director General of Embarkation," dressed in the brief authority of an honorary lieutenant-colonelcy, tackled his job with enthusiasm in the face of insurmountable obstacles. He had no staff, nor were sufficiently experienced officers available at Valcartier to help him. Additional vessels had to be chartered at short notice, and some of these it was discovered already had holds filled with cargoes for Britain such as flour. Loading tables were non-existent, so that Price, in his extremity, resorted to a system of trial and error. When a vessel arrived which reputedly had the right space for a particular infantry unit, that unit was called forward from Valcartier by rail direct to the docks. The heavily burdened infantrymen marched aboard, tramped across the decks, floundered down companion-ways and corridors and finally, heartily sick of the whole process, disemburdened themselves in their assigned accommodation, which usually consisted of little more than recently improvised wooden bunks. Wagons and equipment were swung aboard, eased through hatchways deep into the holds until, hours later, the sounds of shouting and rattling winches died away.

Too often it then became clear to the harassed Price, from the pile of stores remaining on the dockside and from the mutter of discontent from the troop decks below, that the ship was too small. The whole unit would then have to be marched back down the gangways and stores offloaded to await a larger vessel. A drizzle of rain was all that was needed to complete the misery. Such was the experience of Lipsett's 8th Battalion whose complement of 1,161 troops, wagons and baggage, were first crammed into the *Bermudian*; the vessel finally sailed, filled to capacity, but still with less than half that number aboard.[2]

"Chaos," in the words of one of Price's *ad hoc* assistants, "reigned supreme"; and Hughes did nothing to smooth the path of his amateur deputy. After about half the badly loaded transports had cleared the docks and anchored in the river, an afterthought by the Minister sent tugs butting into midstream carrying ammunition to the vessels, each of which, his belated order specified, had to have some aboard. Nevertheless, Price completed loading after a fashion. Mounted units started to go aboard on 23 September, and the infantry on the 27th. By the evening of 1 October thirty loaded transports had moved out into the river. Few unit vessels were complete as such—tag ends of baggage, vehicles and even a few left-over horses found their way onto other ships. A War Office request that accommodation stores (which would be wanted immediately on disembarkation) other than tents should accompany each unit to avoid "serious inconvenience" in England, was completely ignored. Mounted troops, in some cases, were separated from their horses, and the congestion on horse transports meant that one man sometimes had to look after sixteen animals rather than four, as laid down in military regulations. Ninety motor vehicles, 863 horses and piles of miscellaneous baggage still lined the docks when the last vessel cleared the harbour. Another ship was finally obtained and sailed independently on the 5th. The whole hectic business had been an eye-opener for Price. "Apparently," he bitterly commented, "the embarkation of this force was considered a matter of little importance and much ease."[3]

Troops aboard the earlier ships to load had a long wait for embarkation to be completed, but the bustle of Quebec provided a spectacle to relieve the tedium. As soon as each transport was loaded it pulled away from shore and dropped anchor in the stream off Cape Diamond. The distant tramp of battalions, the rumble of the batteries as they passed through the narrow city streets, could be faintly heard. People waving to the men who lined the ships' rails crowded the heights of Quebec. Hotels and boarding houses were filled with relatives and friends of the soldiers. At night the brilliantly lit city was full of life and activity. Cape Diamond, sparkling with hundreds of lights, reflected in the water, lived up to its name. Quebec had seen nothing to match this military activity since Wolfe's ships had lain in the river a century and a half before.

On the last day of September, in clear weather, the loaded transports, one by one, began to slip away down river. Currie, aboard the *Lapland* with his headquarters and the 5th and 6th Battalions, left about midday. He had a daylight voyage past the battlements of Quebec and could see the pastoral St. Lawrence villages sliding by in all the glory of their autumn settings. Towards dusk the vessel neared the Gaspé Peninsula backed by distant snow-powdered hills, steered around its shoulder, and anchored in Gaspé Basin where centuries ago the discoverers of the New World had harboured. All around were the vague shapes of other ships, but it was too dark to count them.

Next morning the troops, in high spirits now that the voyage had at last begun, looked eagerly out of portholes or clambered up on deck. The sight in Gaspé Basin was one they would never forget. The day was bright, clear and warm, and the water as smooth as oil. On its surface, clearly reflected, twenty-eight of the finest North Atlantic liners rode sluggishly at anchor. They kept company with a squadron of four light cruisers, *Diana*, *Eclipse*, *Talbot* and *Charybdis*. At noon a signaller on the *Charybdis* amused himself by semaphoring to the transports: "Is your bar open? How is the Scotch?" provoking baffled fury aboard the dry transports. During the day other troopships glided into the bay, until there were thirty* in all. The land-locked harbour was alive with movement; boats filled with cheering sightseers circled the ships; a tug fussed from vessel to vessel bearing the grand figure of the Minister of Militia. Hughes spent the day at Gaspé going the rounds of the fleet.

Sam brought with him bundles of a four-page valedictory, "Where Duty Leads," which he had composed himself. These were hauled aboard each of the ships he visited and handed out to the troops on deck. His self-adulation, praising his own production of an army of free men from "peaceful Canadian citizens" and sending them on their way to preserve the British Empire and the liberties of humanity, did not sit well with officers and soldiers who had experienced his methods. Nor did the troops appreciate his words, shouted through a megaphone, which assured them that but for the arduous duties of his office the Minister would have been aboard the transport to lead the contingent in person to victory over the enemy. The men, feeling relatively secure on the upper decks, answered with laughter, jeers and catcalls, and a snowstorm of printed speeches.[4] An observer wrote to the Prime Minister congratulating him on having a Minister "who can give us cause for a real hearty laugh"; the humour of his message to the departing contingent had been quite delicious, especially the poetry. The only "fly in the honey," he went on, "is a lurking fear that a

*Two other transports (including that carrying the Newfoundland Contingent) joined the convoy at sea.

somewhat captious world might fail to appreciate the monumental jest, and thus write us all down in company with your Minister." "By the way," he concluded, "do you not think that rope is about long enough by now?" [5]

Hughes also imparted the startling information that von Kluck had surrendered with 25,000 men. The troops wondered if the feverish inefficiencies of the past few weeks had been endured in vain, if they would get to the front in time. They were reassured four days later when the ships' wireless picked up reports that exposed Hughes' inspired bulletin for the "yarn" it was; the Germans were in fact doing quite nicely and had reached the suburbs of Antwerp. [6] The visit of the Minister had not been an unqualified success. It seemed to many in the contingent that they could not shake free from him, and some darkly predicted that he would be "waiting for us when we landed in England." [7]

From Gaspé the Minister, unimpressed by the naval protection for his armada, wired Borden: "Escort altogether inadequate, should increase strength." His concern was passed on to England by the Governor General. The Admiralty, it appeared, had acted on an original Canadian estimate of fourteen ships but, as the Governor General was reminded, on being given revised figures a fortnight earlier they had assured the Minister of Militia that two battleships would reinforce the cruiser squadron *en route*. Furthermore, the whole of the Grand Fleet, as Hughes had also been informed, would cover the escort from attack and would seal off any intervention from enemy ports. Another arrangement made by the Admiralty—for *The Princess Royal*, one of its best warships, to join the convoy in mid-Atlantic—was kept strictly secret even from the Canadian Government, in view of details appearing in the Canadian press of the transports at Gaspé and of the strength of the cruiser squadron. [8]

The delay at Gaspé enabled the convoy to gather and naval dispositions to be made. On Saturday, 3 October, with everything in readiness, the flotilla sailed with the ebb-tide. Three hours later the last in the line of ships, now strung out over twenty-one miles, cleared the harbour into the Gulf of St. Lawrence. It was a clear, frosty evening when the convoy steamed slowly away from the Canadian shore, and many of the troops nostalgically watched the orange sun go down below the Gaspé hills; they were eastward bound from the New World for whatever fate held in store for them on the battlefields of Europe. With every ship in its place and every light masked except for the poop lantern, and with the coastline a mere dark thread behind them, the new soldiers turned away and one by one went below.

That night the moon came up, the full hunter's moon of October, its haloed disk slowly riding behind thin, fleecy clouds. The ships, now in the open, gradually moved into three lines almost two miles apart, each with a cruiser ahead, the fourth cruiser lying well back astern.

Signal lights pulsed between the warships. The water was bright with moonlight, untroubled by sea or wind. All that night the convoy throbbed steadily through the waters of the gulf.

Next day, a Sunday, the calm weather continued. Life-boat drill and church parades were held on every ship. The convoy forged calmly ahead until, by evening, it was off Cape Race, Newfoundland, with its lighthouse and wireless station. On the 5th the clear weather gave way to haze but a wind blowing fresh from the west finally dispersed it. The men did physical drill and exercised. During the morning a man fell overboard from the *Royal Edward*, which was carrying Princess Patricia's Canadian Light Infantry; the ship swung out of line and managed to pick him up, exhausted but still alive after fifteen minutes in the icy water. Later in the day a great, grey battleship, H.M.S. *Glory*, slid in from the bright horizon, flashed at the cruisers, and took up position on the southern flank; it was comforting to see her there. A liner, lying hull-down ahead, was overhauled by one of the vigilant cruisers. This ship, the *Florizel*, carrying the Newfoundland Contingent, was marshalled into the convoy. The following days passed with few incidents until the night of the 7th, when the weather worsened, producing a heavy swell; and then, at about noon on the 8th, a big three-funnelled cruiser, the *Lancaster*, which had been covering the convoy from below the horizon, passed through the fleet.

Dawn on the 10th brought into sight the great *Princess Royal* and the *Majestic*, which took up positions north and south of the eastward-moving convoy; both vessels remained distant but in view throughout Sunday, the 11th, a day of brilliant sunshine. On Monday afternoon the powerful *Princess Royal* dropped back and passed at high speed in full review of the cheering troopships, her band playing "O Canada" and "The Maple Leaf Forever," her bows knifing through the waves, churning the sea to foam. It was obvious that the convoy had reached home waters. Next day, on a rough and squally morning, Fastnet Light was sighted and later, with the weather clearing, the curious troops could see the Cornish coast quite clearly. Woods shimmered a ruddy bronze-brown, while between them stretched fields and pastures of a much more vivid green than those of Canada. Admiralty reports of the presence of German submarines in the English Channel caused the intended destination of the convoy to be hastily changed from Southampton to Plymouth, and on 14 October the transports were divided into fast, medium and slow ships under white, blue and red pennants. Groups of vessels then made their way as fast as they could to Plymouth and cast anchor just outside the breakwater that almost closes the entrance to the Sound. Batteries on the headlands at either side of the port were easily made out, as were the white tents of some of "Kitchener's Army" pitched on the high, clear ground.

Tugs rushed out to welcome the transports with sirens blowing and towed them in to safe moorings in the Hamoaze, the inner harbour, amid the wild greetings of the waiting townsfolk. "From rock and ship, from road and wharf, from fort and housetop came the battle cry of Britain in 1914: 'Are we down-hearted?' and the contingent roared back a stalwart 'No!' "[9] The ships, and those behind them, became cheering masses of khaki as they answered the welcome from the shore. Riveters swarming over half-completed hulls stopped their clangour to wave their greasy caps. Sailors and cadets on every naval vessel in harbour dressed ship and cheered the approaching troops. Finally the anchors of the impressive convoy rattled down one by one to find a hold off Drake's Island, and the soldiers took stock of their surroundings. No one was to go ashore that night.

They could see the solid stone-built town and the busily plying craft of the harbour. The colossal statue of Sir Francis Drake towered over the Hoe, a public park thronged with people. His outraised hand seemed to welcome them. The arrival of the Canadians had stirred the town, and wharves and quays were crowded until far into the night. With dusk, searchlights flashed on, their beams sweeping hesitantly across the bay, pausing here and there to examine distant shapes and then, reassured, moving from side to side to search out others. Pipers on the *Megantic* softly played those ancient melodies that have sounded wherever Scotsmen gather. The troops on other ships listened and found them soothing. Though many were in a strange land and all were thousands of miles from Canada, the ancient ties of blood and the warmth of the Plymouth welcome made them feel at home. A large percentage of men in the "First Thirty-Thousand" had been born in the British Isles. "The men sang themselves to sleep that night," and their songs drifted up from the troop decks long after "Lights Out" had sounded.[10]

Lord Kitchener and the Mayor of Plymouth extended an official welcome. Churchill, the First Lord of the Admiralty, cabled his thanks to Ottawa. The people of Plymouth greeted the first troops to disembark on the 15th with "cheers, handshakes and kisses," and pressed cigarettes and drink upon them.[11] But for others it was not so pleasant. Thanks to the amateur loading at Quebec, the tangle of stores on the dockside at Plymouth was indescribable. Disembarkation was inevitably slowed, and troops hung about to see that their unit stores were landed safely. The 15th Battalion, for example, found that the horses were on one ship, the harness and wagons on others, and the wheels on yet another.[12] After nine days of being cooped up aboard ship in Plymouth Harbour, the last unit of the contingent finally disembarked, and even then a mountain of baggage of all sorts remained. Trainloads were eventually dumped at stations near the Canadian camps on Salisbury Plain to be sorted out by parent units at leisure; it was weeks before the mess was cleared away.

Currie managed to get ashore briefly the day after arrival. His first act was to reassure his wife by cable: "Arrived yesterday safe and well. Love to all. Arthur Currie." His name, the impecunious acting Brigadier-General noted incredulously, had had to be signed in full, and all this had cost him ten shillings![13] Five days later Currie disembarked officially with the first half of the 5th Battalion. Like others before him, he found a seven-hour rail journey ahead of him through Exeter and Newton Abbot to Lavington and Patney to the north, or Amesbury to the east. Currie went the northern way. The train reached Lavington on the 21st at the uninspiring hour of two in the morning, and the troops then faced a ten-mile march into the wilds of Salisbury Plain, burdened with kit-bags, blankets and full equipment. Nevertheless, stepping short and easy with frequent rests, the men covered the distance in four hours. On the way they struck up a song they had heard British troops use in Plymouth, a "Celtic croon with minor tones . . . nothing like 'Tommy Atkins' or 'Soldiers of the Queen' "[14] but catchy; and somehow on this long march, following winding English lanes in a darkness you could almost feel, it seemed appropriate. Its name was "Tipperary."

Units found their tents already put up either by British Territorials or the New Zealand advance guard and hot tea ready, but headquarters was not so fortunate. Currie found nothing but the bare ground and a peg bearing the legend, "2nd Infantry Brigade HQ." Nevertheless, his tent soon went up and, like the men, he rolled into his blankets and slept. That day it rained, the gusty beat of it on the taut canvas emphasizing the loneliness of the high, wind-swept plains.[15]

The following day was clear, and as the first parades to be held after arrival were open-air church services on the 25th, the men had leisure to clean up, assemble their gear and look about them. Salisbury Plain, they found, was a high plateau, in appearance much like the foothills of Alberta. Its past is rich in legend and history. In plain view of Currie's brigade and the 3rd stood the prehistoric relic, Stonehenge, whose twenty-foot slabs and pillars were of granite, a stone which is not found within a hundred miles of the spot. All around, on high ground, were tumuli or barrows, the burial grounds of an ancient British race. Over to the east, a mile and a half from Stonehenge, lay huge earthworks cast up by the Romans at Vespasian's Camp, while four miles south were the ruins of Old Sarum, a Roman city. In this part of England Alfred the Great had found ready warriors to stem the tide of Danish conquest. The Canadians were by no means the first armed men to tread the springy turf of Salisbury Plain.

The War Office held ninety square miles of the plain for use as a military training ground. Some permanent barracks had been built with artillery and rifle ranges, but most of the accommodation con-

sisted of tented camps provided for the summer training of Territorials.
Canadian troops were in four main areas extending in a five-mile strip
to the west of the military area. Bustard Camp housed the 1st Brigade,
the Divisional Mounted Troops and the battalion of Patricia's; there
General Alderson had set up his headquarters, comfortably installed at
the Bustard Inn. In West Down South Camp were the 2nd and 3rd
Brigades, while a mile beyond, in West Down North, the artillery and
the Divisional Supply Column were encamped. The remaining area,
Pond Farm Camp, housed the 4th Brigade, the cavalry, the 17th
Battalion and the Newfoundlanders. In the valleys throughout the
plain, especially that of the River Avon, smoke curled above the cottages of tiny Wiltshire villages clustering round tree-shaded churches
and country pubs. The latter acted like a magnet on thirsty troops
whose camps, like Valcartier, were dry.

Discipline, from the outset, was bad. A large proportion of the contingent was made up of raw recruits and it was not easy for these men of
independent mind to realize that they had to obey the orders of
superiors—corporals who the day before had been their comrades.
Newly appointed officers and NCOs had not yet learned the blend of
command and subtle cajolery (glorying in the name of man-manage-
ment) that without bullying, browbeating or ordering about causes a
man to conform and feel no rancour. Then there was the matter of
passes. Few men seemed to realize they could not leave camp without a
pass or formal leave of absence, and even those who did came back
either late or drunk. The widespread ill-discipline was not vicious, and
the soldiers remained popular in the local villages. As a member of the
Wiltshire Constabulary put it: "You Canadians certainly do drink
hard, but we have little trouble with you beyond noise."[16] Nevertheless,
the question was troublesome. In one unit, 400 strong, an officer
admitted that "if the alarm sounded right now we could not get 200
on parade."[17]

A week's experience on Salisbury Plain convinced Alderson that an
answer must be found, and on 28 October he announced his solution
at a meeting of the officers of the division. There was a need in the
camps, he stated, for wet canteens, and these would be established. The
sale of beer under military supervision would reduce the temptation to
make unsanctioned visits to neighbouring villages. Despite protests from
temperance organizations in Canada, the new arrangements were put
into effect, and from that time onward morale and discipline improved.
"The wet canteen," reported one of Currie's officers, "is a Godsend and
drinking has been reduced to a minimum. A man who is free to buy a
mug of beer a couple of times a day does not try to keep a bottle of
whiskey in his tent."[18] Cases of drunkenness dwindled and offences of all
sorts steadily decreased. Away from the camps, however, there were

"It was want of sleep that struck them most." Canadians in the front-line trenches, 1917.

Hughes visits France. Sir Sam Hughes, Canada's Minister of Militia and Defence, steps ashore at Boulogne on his visit to France in August, 1916.

King George V visited Canadian Corps HQ at Reninghelst behind the Ypres Salient during the Summer of 1916. He is seen here in conversation with the new Corps Commander, Sir Julian Byng. General Plumer, Commander of the Second Army, stands on the left. Facing His Majesty are the divisional commanders, Turner (left) and Currie (centre).

The leaning Virgin of Albert.

Major-General L. J. Lipsett, commanding the 3rd Canadian Division.

Fixing bayonets. Canadian troops at the Somme, 1916.

Over the top! Canadian troops at the Somme, 1916.

The village of Courcelette. The capture of Courcelette by the Canadians on 15 September, 1916, was an outstanding achievement of that year.

disturbances, notably in London. On Salisbury Plain, Canadians were noted for, if not indiscipline, a rugged independence, as the following exchange indicates:

> *Sentry:* 'Alt, who goes there?
> *Answer:* Scots Guards.
> *Sentry:* Pass, Scots Guards.
>
> *Sentry:* 'Alt, who goes there?
> *Answer:* The Buffs.
> *Sentry:* Pass, the Buffs.
>
> *Sentry:* 'Alt, who goes there?
> *Answer:* Any of your damn business?
> *Sentry:* Pass, Canadians.[19]

But by the time the division was ready to leave England, its discipline was not in question.

General Alderson, the 55-year-old Divisional Commander, knew Canadians. He had commanded the Royal Canadian Dragoons and the 2nd Canadian Mounted Rifles as part of his Mounted Infantry Column in South Africa, and this factor had not been overlooked by either Hughes or Kitchener when selecting a commander for the division. Dark and heavily moustached, he has been described as "a kind, gentle little man."[20] Currie first met Alderson as he boarded the ships in Plymouth Harbour to meet the senior Canadian officers, but he did not record his impressions. There is no doubt, however, that Alderson had taken a sensible first step; his policies on training and equipment were to prove just as sound.

Sam Hughes fulfilled the dark prophecies of those who had face-tiously predicted his presence in England. He crossed the Atlantic by fast ship from New York while the Canadian Contingent was still at sea. On Saturday, 24 October, he descended on Alderson's head-quarters at the Bustard Inn to "give him information of value respecting officers and other important matters."[21] He assured the British general in his grandiose way that the men he had raised were already trained and equipped to take the field; in fact, after three months' intensive training and the exchange of Canadian equipment at Alderson's instigation, Hughes went so far as to say in an address before the Canadian Club at Port Arthur on 16 January, 1915, that in his opinion the troops were not then as ready for service as when they had left Valcartier.[22] The Divisional Commander, having talked with the brigade commanders, having had ample time to view the piles of bag-gage at the dockside at Plymouth and at nearby railway stations, and who had noted bodies of men straggling off to neighbouring public-houses—and watched their return—had certain reservations about

the initial preparedness of the Canadians. His subsequent actions give
ample proof of this.

Colonel Hughes, according to the Prime Minister who had
sanctioned the visit, was in England for a holiday. His presence there
was entirely unofficial, and he was "not to assume any military
command or interfere in military matters."[23] Borden might as well
have led a thirsty horse to water and told it not to drink. Resplendent in
uniform, the Minister of Militia called at the War Office and exchanged
views with Kitchener about the conduct and duration of the war. At
that interview, it has been stated, Hughes defied an order which would
break up the Canadian regiments and farm out the men to British
units.[24] This, at least, the immodest Minister never claimed, and he
was just the man to do so had it really happened. The story seems far-
fetched. Hughes was not averse, when the contingent was assembling
at Valcartier, to sending independent brigades to fight with the British
in France;[25] it was Kitchener's decision that the Canadians should form
a division and fight as such![26]

At dinners and banquets in London the irrepressible Hughes spoke
with fiery eloquence. He had ignored Kitchener's advice about the
safety of the convoy, he claimed ambiguously, and his intervention had
prevented the contingent from being sunk by submarine.[27] The statement came back to haunt him later when, in reply to a reporter's
question, he did not recall saying anything about submarines: "I cannot
say anything about it. Why go into the past? I do not care to discuss it.
Can't you ask some sensible question?"[28] As for the war, the affairs of
his department would soon be in such shape that "almost anybody can
look after them, and I may then go to the front and share with you that
battle for Empire and liberty."[29] "If the struggle is not over by spring,"
he promised, "I will take the field myself."[30]

> 'Twould be hard to comprehend
> How this bloody war would end
> Were it not for fearless, beerless
> Gen'ral Hughes.[31]

Comment in Canada was scathing. The above newspaper extract
is one sample. A correspondent to the *Toronto Evening News* wrote: "If
this country had to face the enemy with such a leader, the cry of 'O God
our help in ages past' would drown out the noise of the guns."[32]

"His latest utterances in London last night," a Canadian Member
of Parliament wrote to Borden, "compel me to take the charitable view
that I believe the man is insane."[33] But the Prime Minister was having
his own troubles at home because of Sam. Streams of complaints were
reaching him, from senior officers, the Bishop of Montreal, the secretary
of a humane society, private citizens and even Hughes' friend, William
Price, all complaining of the Minister's words and high-handed actions

at Valcartier. "There must be a limit to the extent to which insults may with impunity be hurled at Bishops, officers, and other representative men in the Community," wrote one irate gentleman; "the Government must surely lose caste along with its Minister for such gross improprieties."[34]

Borden was anxious to keep his Minister in England. Irresponsible speeches there, it seemed to him, would be less embarrassing than the presence of Sam at home. In a diplomatically worded telegram he broached the matter with Perley, the acting High Commissioner in London:

In case Hughes should be desirous of going to the front, it would be advisable from political consideration to give him the opportunity as he has unfortunately aroused great antagonism by his peculiar methods and manners although he did splendid work in organizing the camp at Valcartier. If, therefore, he is so inclined and the British Government would co-operate, the situation would be considerably relieved.[35]

Kitchener gently but firmly declined. As yet there were no Canadian troops in France. The Minister, he thought, should return home where, no doubt, he had work to attend to.[36]

At the end of October, having first conducted the aged Lord Roberts (who had commanded the British forces in the South African War) to Salisbury Plain to review his men, Hughes returned to Canada. He stepped triumphantly on Canadian soil no longer a colonel. Now he sported the rank badges of a major-general! He had raised the matter with Borden before dashing off to England and waited impatiently there for confirmation. A telegram, "No report rank from you," brought the nervous response: "Are you specially desirous that your promotion should be made in meantime?" The former English teacher quickly assured him that he was. "Re promotion my deputy or others announced long ago it seeming everyone wondering what wrong."[37] That was quite sufficient to bludgeon Borden into acquiescence, and Hughes' promotion quickly followed.

Hughes, during this short visit, foresaw the need for a person to act for him in England, a person through whom he could keep a tight grip on the affairs of the Canadian Contingent. Thus, when the Minister embarked for Canada on 31 October, he left behind a "special representative," Colonel John Wallace Carson, who installed himself at the White Hart Hotel, Salisbury.[38] Carson—tall, portly, florid—had been a businessman and mining speculator in Montreal. He had also been a colonel of the Royal Highlanders until a Liberal Minister of Militia had promoted another officer over his head, when he had indignantly resigned. Later, under the Conservatives, Carson renewed his association with the Militia and had reorganized the Prince of Wales' Fusiliers into the Canadian Grenadier Guards. Hughes knew and liked him

well, and had sent his crony to England late in September as the head
of a small advance party for the main contingent, but with no specific
statement of duties. Carson saw Perley in London and discovered that
neither of them knew exactly what he was supposed to do "except that
he had been asked to arrange so that things would be as comfortable as
possible on the arrival of the troops.[39] Carson thereupon took up
residence in Salisbury, reasonably near the camps, but found practically
nothing to do until Hughes, anxious to retain a grip on the new
division, selected him as his representative with vague powers defined
in Contingent Orders as "representing the Canadian Government as
regards certain financial and other questions in connection with the
Canadian Contingent."[40] The way in which Carson exercised those
duties will be examined in detail later.

Meanwhile, the troops trained on Salisbury Plain under appalling
conditions of rain and mud. It was the worst winter in living memory.
The average rainfall from the middle of October to the middle of
February for the past thirty-two years had been almost 12 inches; while
the Canadians were there rain fell on 89 days out of 123, until 24 inches
had fallen.[41] "Salisbury Cathedral itself was awash."[42] The waterlogged
soil overlying solid chalk was churned to mud by vehicles and marching
feet. Men contemplated their soaked greatcoats and soggy boots, knowing well that in damp tents these would have to dry on their backs and
feet. On 11 November a violent storm of rain and wind swept the
plain, billowing and flattening tents and drenching the area with
sheets of water. Canvas "ballooned like the mains'l of a schooner running before the wind,"[43] pegs gave way, and sodden tents slumped
down into the oozy mud. A second gale, a month later, was classed by
Currie as the "worst wind and storms I ever saw."[44] In Canada, where
timber is plentiful, trees would have been used to construct hard-
standings, especially for the horses which were up to their knees in
mud. This was impossible in England where restrictions imposed by the
British forbade even the cutting of small trees.* Small wonder that the
move into hastily erected huts during November and December was
welcomed. Conditions, in fact, were so notoriously bad that the
Australian and New Zealand contingents, profiting by the Canadian
experience, broke their journey to England in Egypt and went into
canvas near Cairo.[45]

Nevertheless, training continued. During the first week in November
Alderson had accurately gauged the state of training. From then on,

*A year later in Flanders, where "the trenches are rivers," Corporal M. W.
Campbell ("B" Battery, R.C.H.A.) was to record in his diary: "Last year we
were in the richest country in the world which couldn't afford any better
shelter for us than tents and not good ones at that. Here we can (at a little
personal risk) take what we want from the ruined villages . . . and so make
ourselves and our horses comfortable."

five weeks of company training, two of battalion training and a similar period for the training of brigades led to exercises of the division as a whole.[46] Company officers got to know their junior leaders and their men; units found cohesion; brigade and divisional staffs were practised in command. From a ragged and shaky start the progress made was startling as is instanced by the revealing comments of one senior officer —surplus to battalion requirements and thus with time on his hands to watch training in the various areas.

Early in the training syllabus, he saw units doing squad drill and "making a very poor attempt to master the manual"; there were "too many people giving orders at the same time." Entrenching was poor, "the parapets were certainly not thick enough, nor had the sod been used to hide the chalk thrown up," and on the ranges the gunners did not impress him. As for infantry patrols, "the men did not know what they were supposed to be doing" and it seemed to him that the Canadians were "a long way from either France or the front."[47] After two months, however, his comments grew steadily more favourable. Artillerymen were on "much better terms with their guns. There was an alertness, and desire to find the target, that bodes ill for many Germans." The infantry battalions were "in excellent shape and had improved almost out of knowledge."[48]

"Notes from the Front" came back from France to be incorporated in the training programme, so that, unlike those at Valcartier, exercises had at last stepped out of the Boer War era. Forty machine-guns arrived and a divisional course for the Machine-Gun Section of each battalion was held in December, followed by practice on the ranges. Twenty-seven hours of musketry, fifteen of drill, night work, outpost training, route marching and entrenching were packed into the first three weeks, no matter what the weather. Bayonet fighting, supervised by five instructors loaned by the British, also took place. Competition with British units for use of the rifle ranges was severe, but even then every infantryman fired 155 rounds, each man practising rapid fire.[49] Again, the Ross revealed its faults. "The men began to get dubiously acquainted with the weaknesses of the Ross Rifle . . . They were to suffer the bitter consequences of being armed with a defective weapon, impracticable for battle purposes, some few months later."[50] And not only was the Ross unpopular with the infantry; the gunners hated it because it did not fit the limber brackets, slipped sideways and fouled and chipped the wheel spokes.

For the artillery, engineers and signals, training was equally intensive. The gunners practised horsemanship and driving, gun-laying, battery tactics, ranging and methods of fire, as well as digging-in and concealing guns; a British instructor, fresh from the front, assisted. Each battery fired fifty live rounds on the artillery ranges. The engineers entrenched, bridged, wired and demolished, but their training was seriously curtailed through assisting in hut construction. Signals training was at least practical. They maintained day-to-day communications between the scattered camps by means of lamp, flag, heliograph (when the sun shone), telegraph and telephone. Motor-cycle despatch riders received an early indoctrination into conditions of mud and wet.[51]

Throughout this period Arthur Currie was intensely interested in producing a good brigade. To do that, he concentrated on discipline, training and equipment, and did not spare himself in getting results. "I want so to act here that you will be proud of me," he wrote to his mother. "It is a great responsibility, and although I try not to do so I cannot help worrying . . . I take little leave and am morning, noon and night on the job."[52] His diary testifies to his supervision of schemes both day and night, in the course of which, time after time, he got "soaking wet."[53] He wrote often to his mother and to his wife and family in Victoria; letters from them were an event and found mention in his diaries. "Two letters from home, replied same night." Family occasions were affectionately remembered as in this entry which concerned his daughter: "December 2nd, Marjorie's birthday, God bless her."[54]

Only the more serious disciplinary cases were referred to him and with these he adopted a humane and practical approach. Currie could hardly fail to be aware of the depressing conditions on Salisbury Plain, and of the burning desire of the men to get to the front. He was at first lenient: "Do that again and you will not be allowed to go to France." But incorrigibles he firmly weeded out and dealt with severely.[55] By the time the 2nd Brigade left England in February, 1915, Currie could be reasonably sure that the men in his battalions could be relied upon.

His supervision of unit training assured him that good progress was being made, and "except when a direct issue was raised he left his battalion commanders pretty much to themselves."[56] Indeed, he himself had little infantry training and he was wise to use this period of adjustment to feel his way, to improve his knowledge and gain experience. He was not afraid to ask questions of his battalion commanders (or to defer to them if he thought that they were right), and in Lipsett, his old instructor, he possessed a strong counsellor, guide and friend. With his staff it was the same: "he was tolerant of his staff, but not worrying overmuch as to who did the work so long as it was done."[57] Currie did, however, size up his officers carefully, and knew with whom he was dealing. He abruptly changed many a battalion commander's favourable assessment of his officers when he knew the man and thought it warranted.[58]

Currie's devotion to training (both his own and that of his men) brought good results and, by December, the 2nd Brigade could be regarded as a team. Even on free evenings, Currie moved within the confined circle of his brigade, dining at the various battalion messes for friendly discussions. His friend Garnet Hughes, now brigade major of the 3rd Brigade, often joined him, but there is no record of Currie going to that brigade. "He seems to have been particularly happy in the midst of his own military family at 2nd Brigade Headquarters. He liked all of his officers grouped around him there. . . When speaking of his staff collectively he wrote: 'I would not change them for all other staffs together.' "[59] Thus, at divisional exercises held at the middle of December, the brigade functioned smoothly and well; Alderson sought Currie out to compliment him.[60]

Relations with Divisional Headquarters were important. Orders came from there, and Currie could only make recommendations for General Alderson's decision on such matters as equipment and policy. "Faulty weapons and equipment, unsatisfactory communications, shoddy foot-wear, and changes in the establishment of tactical units," his biographer writes, were a daily concern to Currie.[61] The Brigade Commander's method of presenting these problems to Alderson was one of "conciliation and suggestion."[62] On Alderson's visits to 2nd Brigade Headquarters, Currie did not complain or criticize; instead he put the difficulties forward with comments and recommendations as to how they could be solved. Again, when orders reached Brigade which seemed to make no sense—as when in January Currie's 6th Battalion was taken from him and replaced by the 10th—Currie would ask the particular staff officer dealing with the matter if he would come over and discuss it. Currie would then put his views forward, and if Divisional Headquarters still insisted on the order, Currie would fall in with the plan and make it work. His alarm at losing a battalion which was disciplined, trained and part of his team just before going to France is understandable; but the unit included a large number of cavalrymen who were wanted in Base Reserve. As it turned out, the 10th Battalion was not a misfit but a well-trained unit, which dovetailed into Currie's team and proved itself at Ypres.[63]

The impressions of Arthur Currie, given by British staff officers who were professionals, are revealing. "He listened to the other side of the matter under discussion," wrote Major E. W. Gordon Hall, on the staff of 1st Canadian Division, "he did not blindly and violently push forward his own interests and without prejudice . . . accepted the position. If he could not attain what he considered the best he was quite ready to do the best he could with what was available."[64] Another, Colonel F. T. Burchell Wood, found him sincere, forceful, and intensely human, but "he never let his humanity stand in the way of his judgement"; this accurately sums up Currie's approach to disciplinary cases. "In negotiations he preferred the personal interview to the written word, and in approach he was good-natured, natural, and imperturbable."[65]

His leadership in battle as yet untried, Arthur Currie had nevertheless made a sound and practical start as a brigade commander. He had

used the time in England well, to gain experience and to improve his
men. Only once had he taken leave—to London for four days, in a party
of nine (including Garnet Hughes and Lipsett), before intensive training had started. There he saw the usual sights, went to theatres, ordered
uniforms and attended a dinner for Sam Hughes at the Automobile
Club. On 31 October, with Garnet, he saw the newly promoted
General Hughes off at Euston Station before returning to camp on the
following day.[66]

Not only was the time in England used to train, it was also used to
reorganize battalions and to change equipment. Canadian battalions
had eight companies, as opposed to the British four. The War Office
toyed with the idea of leaving all Dominion forces on an eight-company
establishment while keeping their own regular and territorial forces as
they were. In January, 1915, after the War Office had changed its mind
six times, the four-company organization was finally adopted, with the
consequent reshuffling of officers and men.[67] The equipment situation
was less open to doubt. After strict scrutiny by selected officers of the
1st Division and War Office inspectors, much of it was replaced from
British Ordnance Stores.

Hughes had appointed special "purchasing agents" in Canada, giving them honorary commissions so that, "If I found any sharp work
going on . . . I could put them through Court Martial."[68] These agents
bought 853 wagons of eight different makes, of which the parts were
not interchangeable. Sir Andrew Macphail, the official medical historian, described them as being of soft "green wood . . . and would not
stand any wear and tear. The result was that almost all of the wagons
were warped, split and splintered, and practically worn out."[69] These
had to be replaced; so had the harness, which, though of satisfactory
quality, was of inappropriate design. Ammunition Column wagons,
both divisional and brigade, were discarded in favour of the British
pattern, as it was doubted "if they would stand the strain of a load of
ammunition."[70] The cylindrical tanks of water carts, mounted on four
wheels, had been built in such a way that they could not be cleaned;
"there was no appliance for filtering or clarifying the water," and
furthermore, when full, they were too heavy to haul. Brakes were so
weak that they would give way "under pressure of the driver's foot."[71]
Water carts, too, were condemned. The record fails to show, however,
that any purchasing agents of officer status were ever court-martialed.

The Webb equipment, worn by only five battalions, could carry 150
rounds of ammunition. The others had "Oliver" equipment which
carried only 50 to 80 rounds, cut wearers under the arms, and had
neither pack nor a sling for carrying the indispensable entrenching tool.
It had other faults; its canvas valise tore away from leather braces; its
waist belt was too narrow; and its colour was too light. Even when

modified, Oliver equipment was "observed to interfere with the men's respiration."[72] Issues of new Webb equipment were made to seven Canadian battalions.

The contingent's trucks were excellent[73] and in tests out-performed the British lorries. But the vehicles were of North American pattern with spares some thousands of miles away. Spares for British transport, on the other hand, were readily available in France, so that the 1st Division took British vehicles with them, leaving their own in England (where breakdowns would not be of much consequence) for use by Canadian troops. Bicycles and telephones, too light for active service, were replaced with more rugged patterns of British origin. The uniform, though of inferior cloth, was not immediately withdrawn; all replacements in France, however, were made from British stocks.[74]

One item of personal equipment for the men in which Sam Hughes was greatly interested was a device known as the "MacAdam shovel." The patent for this, a combined shield and entrenching tool, was held by his secretary, Miss Ena MacAdam. The contraption consisted of a spade with holes in the middle, one to shoot through and a smaller one to sight through, and a four-inch handle. Twenty-five thousand, costing $1.35 each, were taken to England, where they proved absolutely useless even after a special folding handle had been improvised.[75] They were "heavy and difficult to carry, chafed the thighs and banged about"; and, more important, they were awkward to dig with and would not stop a bullet.[76] They were eventually sold for scrap.

An infuriated Hughes cabled from Canada to "hold a tight hand on all that improper work over there,"[77] but British tools were issued notwithstanding. With that, the name of Alderson was added to the growing list of Hughes' real or fancied enemies. The Minister took positive action to re-impose his personal control on the supply of future Canadian troops in England, which reflects his indignation at what he considered the wholesale rejection of Canadian equipment. This he did through Carson. An Order in Council of 15 January, 1915, defined Carson's role more definitely. He now would be ". . . appointed during pleasure, to represent the Militia Department of Canada in the United Kingdom, in connection with supplies and other requirements for the Canadian Overseas Expeditionary Force." He would act "as the agent of the Minister of Militia in maintaining the depots of articles of equipment and other supplies necessary for the upkeep and subsistence of the Canadian Expeditionary Force both in the United Kingdom and at the Seat of War."[78] The most important personal weapon in the whole division, however, was not exchanged.

The Ross rifle, as Ralph Allen so aptly points out, was no mere inanimate object for use by Canadian infantrymen in battle; it was a "symbol."[79] Canada, unable to purchase British Lee-Enfield rifles at the time of the South African War (when the War Office absorbed all

arms production), had turned to her own resources. In 1901 Sir Charles
Ross, a British inventor and businessman, was invited to Canada to
demonstrate a sporting rifle that he sponsored, a straight-pull bolt
action weapon of great range and accuracy, patterned on the Austrian
Mannlicher. Though abnormally long, the original model was light
and had good balance.[80]

The new rifle was tested against the Lee-Enfield before a five-man
committee appointed to report on the weapon by Sir Frederick Borden,
then Minister of Militia. The committee included Lieutenant-Colonel
Sam Hughes, at that time an opposition M.P., and a marksman of some
repute. The Ross compared very favourably with the Lee-Enfield in
the first ten tests, but in a test using cartridges deliberately over-
charged only the Lee-Enfield functioned normally. The bolt of the Ross
jammed after one round and had to be hammered open with the heel
of a boot. The final test was for prolonged fire. After a thousand rounds
the robust Lee-Enfield still worked smoothly, whereas, after fifty rounds,
the bolt of the Ross grew progressively stiffer and "misfed and jammed
repeatedly." After three hundred rounds the barrel was too hot to
touch, so hot in fact that it melted the solder holding the foresight in
place.[81]

Sir Charles Ross put forward a plausible reason for the failings of
his weapon. The design of the rifle had been based on American and
Austrian ammunition, more precisely manufactured than British-type
cartridges made in Canada. To modify the weapon, now that details
of Canadian ammunition were known, would be a simple matter.
Subject to these modifications, but without further tests, the committee
recommended that Canada should adopt the Ross as its own weapon,
and Sir Frederick Borden signed an agreement to purchase 12,000, to
be manufactured in Canada during 1903, and all other rifles required
thereafter. One committee member alone recorded a dissenting opinion; he noted that the action became "decidedly stiff when hot"; but
then he was only Major Gaudet, the Superintendent of the Government Cartridge Factory.[82]

The British authorities pointed out the dangers of failing to adhere to
"absolute uniformity of pattern . . . in the forces of the Empire" and of
discarding a proven weapon in favour of a doubtful one. They themselves had carried out tests between the Lee-Enfield and the Ross in
which the inferiority of the Ross had been "very marked."[83] This
warning was sufficient to inflame Canadian championship of the Ross
to a degree that went beyond all logic, and the future of the rifle as the
basic weapon of the Canadian infantryman was fully assured. Controversy at home, however, still persisted.

Such controversy forced no fewer than eighty modifications to the
weapon in its dozen years of active life. Each modification caused a
mark or star to be stamped into the rifle's metal until the proliferation

of these revealed too much of a spotty past; Hughes ordered a redesignation that would "blot out the stars and cover up the changes." He could not, however, change the fact that the original Ross had been altered almost beyond recognition. The once light, well-balanced weapon had become almost eight inches longer than the Lee-Enfield and more than a pound heavier. A proposed shorter model was not endorsed by Hughes, who had "no use for a short barrel"; thus "the advocates of a target rifle again triumphed, and the man in the ranks— already burdened with a heavy kit—was doomed to carry a heavier and less handy weapon."[84]

No provision for a bayonet had been made on the earlier models, and the later modifications allowing for this were never wholly satisfactory. But this did not worry Hughes. He had "little use for a bayonet, that is for practical purposes; but it serves a useful sentimental object."[85] In fact, the rifle to Sam—a prisoner of his own enthusiasm for it in 1902 —was almost holy, and when the King's Prize at Bisley was won with a "Canadian" Ross in 1911 and again in 1913, he would brook no further criticism. The Ross to him was far superior to the British rifle. It was apt to jam? So was the Enfield. He would "swallow any Lee-Enfield which did not jam when he fired it." The Ross was the "most perfect military rifle in every sense in the World today."[86]

And so, jamming and misfiring under rapid fire, and with the bayonet jumping off into the mud, the Ross was tried out by the Canadian Contingent at Valcartier, and later on at Salisbury Plain. General Alderson soon heard the many complaints and reported them, with the result that a worried Sir Charles Ross visited the division himself to "sponsor his weapon by lectures and personal examination of every Ross rifle on Salisbury Plain." Further modifications followed; the chambers were reamed; sights were enlarged; the magazine-retaining springs were chamfered; and a tiny hole was bored in the bottom of each magazine. Armed with his again-modified "best friend," the long-suffering Canadian infantryman crossed to France.[87]

The troops had had Christmas and New Year's in England, a good many of them taking leave and making the most of the free transportation offered by the railways to any point in the British Isles. Then on 4 February the division was inspected by H. M. King George V and Lord Kitchener, a sure sign of impending departure. The plain did not relent even for that occasion. A morning threat of rain, sleet or snow turned to a steady downpour by the time the battalions marched to the reviewing ground on a new line of railway built west of the camps by the Canadians. It was not the first visit by His Majesty— he had come before to welcome the troops—but the division knew instinctively that this was the last inspection.

The King arrived by train at a newly erected platform over which a flagstaff had been mounted. As his khaki-clad figure stepped out of the second coach, the great Royal Standard was broken out, magnificently gold and scarlet for a time before darkening in the rain and settling limply against the mast. The "Royal Salute" was given, and twenty-five thousand bayonets flashed into the "Present Arms," while the massed bands of the division played six bars of the anthem. The division was drawn up in two lines at two hundred paces distance: on the right the cavalry; then the artillery, engineers, signals and auxiliaries; and on the left the three brigades of infantry. The King and Kitchener, accompanied by Alderson, walked down the whole line, almost two miles long, wishing each commander good luck for himself and his "fine battalion." His Majesty looked healthy and in good spirits, while the fiercely moustached Kitchener "wore a smile like a summer morning."[88]

The King returned to the saluting base, and the great-coated division marched past—cavalry eight deep in fours, artillery by sections, two guns abreast, and the infantry in double lines of fours. It was a stirring sight. The troops then lined the railway and as the King rode by at the window of his coach, they cheered and cheered, hats aloft on bayonets. They had been smart and steady and they knew inside themselves that they were a credit to their country.

That same day Arthur Currie was promoted colonel, and five days later the division light-heartedly embarked for France. The men were sure that the worst of their troubles were over.

FOUR.
THE SEARCH FOR VICTORY

The contrast between the finely drawn plans of the belligerents of 1914 and their ultimate descent into colossal and bloody stalemate is the classic irony of the war. For years the rulers and statesmen of Europe had arranged their shrewd alliances; for years the generals had perfected their deadly schemes. Sublimely ignorant of the power of modern technological progress and the capabilities of a nation—as opposed to that of an army—in harness with the war machine, almost all predicted a quick success. * According to popular prophecy, the contest would be fought out by professional armies raised to peak strength by a system of conscription; the mass of the people would cheer the departure and welcome home the victorious troops. War, should it come, "would be a matter of six weeks' autumn manoeuvres with live ammunition."[2]

The German people reacted to the war with "indescribable enthusiasm from Memel to the tiniest hamlet in the southern German mountains, enthusiasm which in its volume and unity swept everything irresistibly before it."[3] In France, though the reception of the General Mobilization Order had been grave and restrained, people cheered and sang as troops left for the front. Trains pulled out of the Paris stations to the sound of the "Marseillaise."

Crowds were gathered at every station . . . Cries of *"Vive la France! Vive l'armée!"* could be heard everywhere, while people waved handkerchiefs and hats. The women were throwing kisses and heaped flowers upon our convoy. The young men were shouting: *"Au revoir! A bientôt!"* At one grade crossing, a young woman lifted her baby towards us, shouting: "He too, like you, will go some day, and do his duty!"[4]

*A singular exception was von Moltke, who told the Kaiser in 1905, "It will become a war between peoples which is not to be concluded with a single battle but which will be a long, weary struggle with a country that will not acknowledge defeat until the whole strength of its people is broken; a war that even if we should be the victors will push our own people, too, to the limits of exhaustion."[1]

And in St. Petersburg an enormous crowd congregated at the Winter Palace Square with flags, ikons and portraits of the Tsar.

The Emperor appeared on the balcony. The entire crowd at once knelt and sang the Russian national anthem. To those thousands of men on their knees at that moment the Tsar was really the autocrat appointed of God, the military, political, and religious leader of his people, the absolute master of their bodies and souls.[5]

The Kaiser, serene in the knowledge of the "Schlieffen Plan," assured troops departing for the war that they would be home "before the leaves have fallen."[6]

The Kaiser's confidence was almost justified. Graf Schlieffen, Chief of the German General Staff from 1891 to 1906, working on the assumption that war would be fought on two fronts against the French and Russian armies, conceived a plan for a speedy decision against the French while the Russians were being held in check. Only ten divisions were allowed for use against the Russians. The mass of the German forces were to be concentrated against the French. Nearly three-quarters of the German Army were to mass on a heavy right wing for a wheel through Holland and Belgium, through Northern France, across the Seine west of (and thus enclosing) Paris. This wing was then to drive southeast to press the French back against Switzerland and the German defences in Lorraine; there, squeezed in an iron grip, the hapless French would be annihilated. The German left wing, opposite the French frontier, was to be kept deliberately slender, for if it fell back under the main French attack, as was envisaged, the enemy would be drawn farther and farther from the decisive outflanking blow falling towards Paris from Belgium. This was the basic plan which von Moltke put into effect in August, 1914; had he not modified it he might have brought it off.

The Russian plan was to strike first at Austria, before Germany could give support; then, when the proverbially slow Russian mobilization had become fully effective, to turn on Germany. Had this been done, and no more, good results would undoubtedly have been obtained against an Austria preoccupied with the Serbs. But the French, reeling back and anxious to relieve German pressure against themselves, urged a simultaneous Russian offensive against East Prussia. The Russians, without much mobility and badly organized, loyally accepted a dual offensive using four armies. Two moved south against the Austrians in Galicia, while the others moved northerly into East Prussia.

The French scheme, Plan XVII, was in essence drastically simple. It called for an immediate and violent offensive into the two provinces, Alsace and Lorraine, which had been lost to Germany in 1871. The plan was based on a complete misconception of German intentions: it was considered that the greater part of the enemy forces would be concentrated on the common frontier. The French also underestimated the strength of the enemy in the west—it was thought that he must divide his forces between the eastern and the western fronts. Nevertheless, Plan XVII was to go into force *whatever the circumstances*.[7] French superiority in numbers, it was confidently assumed, must cause the Germans to abandon any offensive they might undertake to counter the French thrust, and the enemy would thus be forced to conform to the strategy of the French. In the event, it worked the other way.

France, far from having more troops than the Germans, was in fact outnumbered three to two on the crucial northern wing. Inferior arms made the disparity even worse. The Germans had eighteen 105 mm. light howitzers per division and sixteen 150 mm. heavy howitzers per corps. In divisions or corps, the French had no medium artillery whatsoever. Only in field artillery were the French better off. They had a hundred and twenty of their 75 mm. field pieces per corps against a hundred and eight 77 mm. guns in a German corps of roughly the same size. In total, moreover, German firepower, based on repeating rifles, machine-guns and light and medium artillery, was far superior to that of the French whose infantry relied on the old Lebel rifle (retained until 1915), the tubular magazine of which had to be recharged one bullet at a time.[8] "Usually it is the victor of the last war who, complacent with success, fails to progress in weapons and methods; the vanquished who is spurred by defeat into reform. However, it was the victor of 1870, not the vanquished, who had made the better preparations in doctrine, training and equipment for 1914."[9] And no matter how imbued with the spirit of attack was the French Army at the outbreak of war, offensive spirit and courage could hardly triumph against overwhelming firepower. That the French were woefully ignorant of this is revealed in their adoption of Plan XVII at all.

Britain, aloof from these continental schemes, had no real plan of her own. She had no military obligation to either France or Russia should they become embroiled with Germany. In the event, German violation of Belgian neutrality was needed to force Britain into a declaration of war. Once committed, though, she was virtually pledged to support and co-operate directly with the French. As a result, Britain despatched to France an Expeditionary Force numbering 160,000, highly trained especially in musketry. This force was armed with the Lee-Enfield rifle, a robust weapon that was capable of a high rate of accurate, medium and close-range fire and that was very satisfactory with the bayonet. The British force reached France on 16 August and concentrated on the extreme left of the French line.

Through the years 1906 to 1914 Moltke had altered Schlieffen's plan. Of nine new divisions that had become available in those eight years, eight were placed on the left and only one on the decisive, wheeling right. The left, thus strengthened, would, therefore, make penetration by the French, an essential part of the Schlieffen Plan, far less likely. Furthermore, the move through Holland, which Schlieffen had calculated would so alarm the French that they themselves would violate Belgium's neutrality to defend the line of the Meuse, was abandoned for a direct thrust on Belgium and the fortress town of Liège—a move which added Britain to Germany's adversaries.

Nevertheless, the German right, consisting of five superbly equipped armies, was massive enough. The forts at Liège, dominating the Meuse passage into the north Belgian plain, were pulverized into rubble under the hammer blows of heavy howitzers. The Belgian Army, completely unsupported because of French preoccupation with the idea of attacking the other flank, fell back to Antwerp from where, at least, they could threaten German communications; as a result, the enemy was forced to leave two corps to mask the city. The Germans, an irresistible mass of grey, steadily marching through the hot August days under the dust clouds that they raised, entered Brussels. That same day, the 20th, they came within sight of Namur, the last fortress on the road to France.

Meanwhile, Joffre, the French commander, blindly mounted the attack that Plan XVII demanded "whatever the circumstances," circumstances rendered critical indeed by the immensity of the German blow poised and ready to fall on Joffre's undefended left. A French thrust into Alsace actually reached the Rhine—the last glimpse the French would have of the Rhine for more than four years—until Joffre, at last alive to his danger, broke off the action and recalled his troops at the end of August. His main offensive, launched into Lorraine by two armies on 14 August, carried wildly charging French infantrymen with their bright red trousers, dark blue coats and flashing bayonets deep into a lost province of France. The Germans on that flank, unnecessarily stiffened by Moltke's eight divisions and his orders to detain the French if possible, decided they could do that best by attacking. Schlieffen's master plan of drawing the French farther and farther from the decisive scene of battle was discarded, and at Morhange-Sarrebourg the French were bowled over like ninepins by the concentrated firepower of long- and short-range weapons. But not all were casualties. Remnants of the First and Second Armies fell back into France, where they eventually took part in the "Miracle of the Marne." German pursuit, sanctioned by Moltke, unconsciously abetted French concentration.

Joffre, a phlegmatic engineer who was not easily daunted, picked up the pieces of his shattered Plan XVII and decided to throw two armies into the Ardennes, between Lorraine and Belgium. Events at Morhange-Sarrebourg made him believe that the Germans had been strong—actually it was their weakest flank—and reports indicated that they were strong in Belgium. Therefore, he reasoned, they must be weak in the centre. In fact, the farther west one went along the line, the stronger the Germans grew. The attack by the French Third and Fourth Armies delivered on 22 August into the broken country of the Ardennes ran smack into two German armies. "The untried warriors grappled, bled, and died."[10] The French 75, with its flat trajectory, was of little use in hilly ground, whereas the German howitzers were. Four savage engagements were fought on the first day—Virton, Ethe, Rossignol and Neufchâteau—snuffing out the French offensive like a red and spluttering candle.

Again the French armies were not outflanked. True, they fell back in confusion, but in what proved to be the right direction—towards the Meuse. Even so, the sardonic Lanrezac, commanding the Fifth French Army in the path of the colossal German thrust west of Namur, saw nothing but disaster. He viewed sourly the *débâcle* that had exposed his right and waited for the blow to fall.

The Germans were not slow to exploit the opportunity of enveloping at least one French army. Their 1st (commanded by Kluck) and 2nd (Bülow) Armies were closing on Lanrezac from the north and the 3rd (Hausen) from the east. The French Fifth, in the apex between the Sambre and the Meuse, with forces on both those rivers, was well disposed to counter a thrust direct from Namur but not a pincer movement. The Germans planned to attack on 23 August, using the 2nd Army against the Sambre line and the 3rd against the Meuse. The 1st was to sweep southwards through Mons to cut Lanrezac off from the rear. But the German plan miscarried. Bülow, without troubling to inform Hausen, stormed the Sambre a day early; Hausen, unaware of the change, crossed the Meuse on the following day. The German converging movement had thus failed to converge and Lanrezac extricated himself by moving southwards. Nor could Kluck cut him off. Moving down from the north, the German general unexpectedly encountered the British (then thought by German intelligence to be on the way up from the port of Le Havre) at Mons. Throughout the 23rd, Sir John French, the British commander, held Mons to cover Lanrezac's left, standing off six enemy divisions until nightfall by superb rifle-shooting. He retreated that night, abandoned by the French. He pulled back just in time. The collapse of the French left wing at last aroused Joffre to the realities of the tremendous German plan. The great battles of the frontier had gone in Germany's favour. There was nothing for him to do now other than to pull the French and British back and inspire them with some of his own imperturbable strength.

There was jubilation in Germany. They were driving the enemy before them. "The entirely favourable news that arrived every day from the right wing . . . created the belief that, together with the great victory in Lorraine of August 20-23, the great decisive battle of the

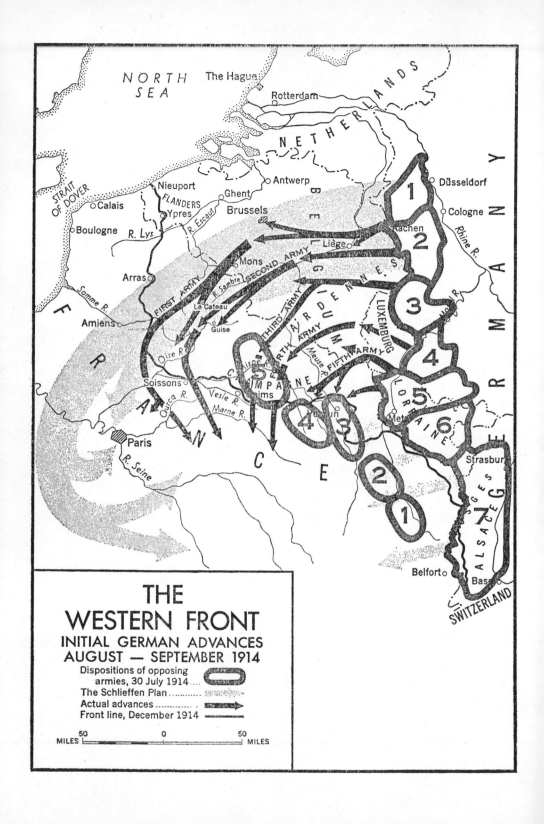

THE WESTERN FRONT
INITIAL GERMAN ADVANCES
AUGUST — SEPTEMBER 1914

Dispositions of opposing armies, 30 July 1914....
The Schlieffen Plan.............
Actual advances ....
Front line, December 1914

50   0   50
MILES   MILES

western front had taken place and had been favourable to us."[11] "The Kaiser", Admiral Müller reported, "is radiant."[12]

But a decisive victory on the frontiers had not been achieved. The great strategic surprise gained by Germany had not brought about the annihilation of any French army. From now on surprise had gone and, with lengthening communications, strength would wane. The enemy alone would, through concentration, grow in strength. The intelligent and sensitive Moltke realized this. "Don't let's deceive ourselves," he said, ". . . the victor has prisoners. Where are our prisoners?"[13]

Furthermore, the Germans, alarmed at Russian progress on the Eastern Front, detached two corps from the west before a real decision had been reached, corps which would have proved invaluable at the Marne later on. On 17 August the Russians, loyally pushing into East Prussia in answer to French pleas, defeated the Germans at Stallu-pönen. Three days later they brought off a similar feat at Gumbinnen, while the Austrians had been forced back across the river Drina by savage Serbian attacks. Prittwitz, the German commander in East Prussia, had been badly shaken by the early appearance of so powerful a Russian force and advised Moltke that he was ordering a general retreat behind the Vistula. Moltke's answer was to send reinforcements and to replace Prittwitz with the powerful combination of Hindenburg and Ludendorff who, on 29 August, smashed the Russians at Tannenberg.

Throughout the last week of August and the first few days of September, German troops marched ponderously across northern France, closely following tired French and British forces. But Moltke, still in Germany with no over-all commander in the field, was becoming more and more out of touch with his armies. He had "never stepped out of peacetime—never heard the thunderous weight of the light and heavy howitzers crushing French attacks, seen that splendid German infantry swinging down, eyes shut with fatigue, into the heart of France."[14] The movements of his northern armies were becoming more and more disjointed under a check delivered by the British at Le Cateau and a riposte delivered by Lanrezac at Guise, which caused Kluck to wheel inwards to the assistance of Bülow. Moltke's orders on 4 September for the 1st and 2nd Armies to remain *east* of Paris, and to transfer the offensive to the left wing on either side of Verdun, mark his ultimate departure from the Schlieffen Plan. Those orders threw away final victory

The German 1st Army was now ripe for a stroke in flank to be delivered by the Paris garrison. Galliéni, Military Governor of Paris where the Sixth French Army was now assembled, had instantly realized the significance of Kluck's left wheel and urged Joffre's sanc-tion for attack. On the 4th, the Sixth Army struck, and that evening Joffre, who had spent the afternoon solemnly reflecting on Galliéni's message in the shade of a schoolhouse tree, at last made up his mind. The attack would be general. Every unit, now glumly retreating from Paris, would stop in its tracks, turn, and march into the face of the enemy.

Thus, on 7 September, began the Battle of the Marne. The French and British, footsore and bone-weary, had one fight left in them yet. Between the 9th and 11th, the Germans, shaken by the Allied attack and unsure of their own strength and dispositions, though not defeated, nervously pulled back to the Aisne. It was, for the Allies, a strategic victory. Moltke's left and centre, pivoting on Verdun, achieved nothing to compensate for the failure of the German right. French defences there were too strong, and enemy efforts to envelop Verdun became bogged down in bloody deadlock. Falkenhayn replaced Moltke on 14 September.

The Germans consolidated their positions along the River Aisne and, still trying to turn the Allied flank, moved northwards, seizing the more defensible ground as they went, only to be countered time after time by the Allies who were trying to do the same thing. By this constant process of move, check, and move again, the coast between Dunkirk and Ostend was eventually reached. As the armies clashed and fought, pits were dug for shelter. Gradually there developed a defensive system stretching all the way from the North Sea to Switzerland, a line that was to vary little over the course of the next few years.

On 10 October, Antwerp fell, freeing German troops for the front line. The Belgian Army, covered by a British relieving force that had been landed at Ostend and Zeebrugge to help raise the siege, escaped down the Flanders coast to man part of the Allied line. Then, on 20 October, Falkenhayn struck at Ypres in a belated attempt to capture the Channel ports, which had been wide open to Moltke at the time of the great retreat. Sir John French chose that day to advance his line from Ypres to Menin. A savage encounter and a three-week battle (First Ypres) ensued, building up to peaks of fury on 31 October and 11 November when the Germans launched wave after wave of excellent young troops in stubborn attack. Shot to a standstill, they called the attack off to clear the dead and lick their wounds. Small wonder that they termed it *Der Kindermord von Ypern*. The crumbling line was still in Allied hands, but the small British professional army was finished. Ypres was its burial place.

Ypres and the virtual loss of her regular army taught Britain the true nature of the war. With the fighting closer at hand, France had already learned it; and the lesson was being brought home to Germany and Russia. The twentieth century had engulfed nineteenth-century notions that war was for professional armies. Now, it was to be total, truly a war of people—people in battalions, in factories, in laboratories, and people on the farms. Manpower and resources were to be poured out to the point of exhaustion in a desperate search for victory.

Ypres pointed up another lesson, which the military leaders had *not* learned yet: the defensive was stronger than the offensive, even when sketchy trenches were only thinly manned and wired, and firepower was a mere shadow of what it was to become. Ypres was in fact the beginning of a stalemate. Those who thought otherwise and fed on the illusion of a great break-through were dreamers who brought massacres in their wake. But what else could they do? They commanded great forces, backed by artillery; public opinion and political pressure forced them to use this power. A compromise peace might have been acceptable to a Germany in firm possession of Belgium and the richest part of France, but such a peace would be intolerable to the Allied powers. Thus, despite frightening and steadily mounting losses, repeated attempts were made over the next four years to push the invaders off the soil of France by means of a break-through.

Christmas of 1914 brought a brief respite from the digging of trenches and the erection of barbed wire entanglements (both of which were steadily multiplying on the Western Front between Switzerland and the sea). There was even fraternization in No-Man's-Land between the opposing troops. Far behind the raw and clammy trenches, however, in the châteaux of the mighty, plans were being considered for the coming year. Every one of the elaborate schemes, so carefully thought out for years, had miscarried; new strategy was urgently required.

In the west the continuous front offered no flank that could be turned. The Allies were in the unfortunate position of having relinquished ground under conditions of open warfare and having to wrest it back in the face of dominating ground and strong defences. The use of barbed wire, closely associated with machine-guns, called for prolonged artillery fire to destroy it; this meant for both sides the loss of all surprise, a master principle of war. Though guns and ammunition in the vast quantities required did not then exist, the Allies used what guns they had and tried to break through the German lines repeatedly in 1915.

Falkenhayn, like his predecessor, was a "Westerner"; he believed that the war could only be won on the Western Front. Hindenburg and Ludendorff, on the other hand, pressed strongly for a continuation of the eastern offensive to knock out Russia. In mid-January the Kaiser settled the matter—the Eastern Front would be reinforced. Hindenburg and Conrad von Hötzendorff, the Austrian commander, would then launch converging offensives from East Prussia and the Carpathians. German activities in the west would lapse into a strict defensive. In 1915, therefore, Germany turned to the east, leaving the French and British to "shatter their armies against her trench lines in France," while the Russian armies were largely destroyed.[15]

The opposing defensive lines in the east were certainly weaker than in the west. The ground, frozen iron-hard in winter, was proof against entrenching tools and stakes for barbed wire. The Germans and Austrians were holding a line nearly two thousand miles long with insufficient troops to man it effectively. A large percentage of the Austrian troops, moreover, came from Slav races who were closely related to the Russians and were thus prone to defection. On the other side, Russia's overwhelming strength in numbers was neutralized by deficiencies in arms and munitions. The output of Russian factories could not even make up for the daily consumption of ammunition, and to make good the loss of guns and rifles in the opening battles of the war would take months. Without them, as Hindenburg and Ludendorff shrewdly calculated, the Russian forces were extremely vulnerable.

It might have been expected that France and Britain would divert some of their own production to Russia and limit their own attacks. They need not have sent heavy-calibre weapons; the weak Austro-German line could have been broken with light weapons in the hands of the numerically superior Russians. The French, however, were naturally obsessed with the idea of driving the Germans out of northern France. The British leaders in France shared this desire. Thus Joffre and Sir John French saw France as the only vital theatre and devoted themselves to the task of rolling the Germans back to the Rhine—entailing what Churchill was to call the "brutal expedient" of the frontal attack.

There were two men of cabinet rank in England—Churchill (First Lord of the Admiralty) and Lloyd George—who recognized that for a maritime power the true strategy for 1915 lay, not in flinging armies against the impregnable positions in the west, but in turning a flank by sea to help Russia. Churchill had always acknowledged the practicability of amphibious operations to turn a flank. His recent experience on the Belgian coast with naval and marine brigades sent to assist beleaguered Antwerp had confirmed his views. He had also visited France and knew what the front was like. His lively imagination and broad vision surveyed the defensive line; he pictured it at the sea where the entanglement climbed over the yellow coastal dunes to the last rusty iron picket breasting the grey-green waters of the North Sea. There, he knew, the flank could be turned.

Two plans came under consideration: one by the First Sea Lord (Lord Fisher) that aimed at the domination of the Baltic after an invasion of Schleswig-Holstein and the seizure of the Kiel Canal, and Churchill's own scheme for the seizure of the Gallipoli Peninsula, enabling the British Fleet to pass through the Dardanelles and link up with the Russian Black Sea Fleet. In January, 1915, Grand Duke Nicholas of Russia, the commander of the Tsar's armies, appealed to Lord Kitchener for a demonstration, either naval or military, to relieve

Turkish pressure in the Caucasus. This appeal provided the incentive required to swing support behind Churchill's Dardanelles scheme.

At the end of October, 1914, Turkey had entered the war on the German side. With the Turkish entry, the Dardanelles had been closed, thus barring any flow of munitions to Russia by the easiest route. To force the Dardanelles would be a smaller and less dangerous enterprise than Fisher's Baltic plan. Germany could not offer the same massive resistance in the east, as Serbia lay across her communications with Turkey. Possession of the Gallipoli Peninsula, giving Allied access by sea to Constantinople, would knock Turkey out of the war. And there were wider goals. Four of the Balkan states, mustering armies of 1,100,000 men (Serbia 250,000, Greece 200,000, Bulgaria 300,000, Roumania 350,000), were the natural enemies of both Turkey and Austria and could only expand at the expense of those countries. Serbia was already fighting against Austria; Greece had made an offer at the outbreak of war to help Britain take Gallipoli although, as Turkey was not at that time in the war and as it was hoped to keep her neutral, the offer was declined. If all four states could be induced to stop their internal quarrelling—a preliminary conference to settle difficulties and arrange the spoils would be essential—the defeat of Turkey in 1915 was certain and that of Austria, confronted by a Balkan confederation, was likely. Nor would Italy, the hereditary enemy of Austria, remain indifferent to such decisive action; there was every chance that Italy, with an army of two million, would enter the war on the Allied side.[16]

Kitchener claimed that he had no troops to spare from the Western Front. The Admiralty, therefore, agreed to carry out the demonstration which the Grand Duke required by attempting to force the Dardanelles with ships alone. Most of those assigned to the operation were from an outdated class of battleship due for scrapping later in the year and thus were expendable.

The Gallipoli venture began on 19 February, 1915, when British ships, unassisted by troops, sailed in to bombard the outer forts of the Dardanelles. Twelve days later the forts had been destroyed. The effect on the Balkan states and Italy was as had been expected. Bulgaria moved on Adrianople, forcing the Turks to open a protective front. Roumania, sympathetic towards Russia but wary, again veered towards war. Italy spoke of receiving a share of Turkish territories. On 3 March Greece repeated the offer of a land force for Gallipoli. Russia, with an eye on Constantinople, would not tolerate such action, and the Greek offer was again declined. "Russia," as Liddell Hart put it, "would not help . . . to clear her own windpipe."[17]

For the first two weeks of March the British fleet, assisted by a French squadron, moved on the inner defences of the Dardanelles. Meanwhile, Kitchener at last awoke to the glittering prospects and began to as-

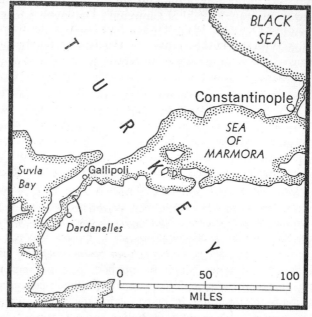

GALLIPOLI

semble an army in Egypt—not to work with the attacking ships, but to occupy Constantinople later on. On 18 March the fleet sailed in to tackle the strongest part of the strait—the Narrows.

Throughout the morning the attack went well. By midday the forts, crushed by heavy shells, were almost silent, and not a single ship had been sunk or badly damaged. Then, in the early afternoon, one single row of mines that had been missed by the sweepers sank three battle-ships and damaged a fourth. The officer in charge, Admiral de Robeck, ignoring the expendability of the ships, grew alarmed and called off the naval operation. On 22 March, knowing that an army was being assembled, de Robeck declared that it was his conviction that the fleet could not get through without the help of troops. The Admiralty, as always, abided by the decision of the man on the spot. The all-naval operation was never resumed.

It is now known that on the evening of 18 March the Turkish com-mand was willing to concede defeat. Their guns were largely destroyed and gun crews demoralized. Half the ammunition had been expended and there was no replacement; nor were there any more mines. The Sultan and his court were packed, ready to leave Constantinople. German officers on the spot had little hope of successful resistance should the fleet attack next day. They predicted that a revolution would follow the arrival of the fleet at the Golden Horn and that Turkey would sign a separate peace.

Why had de Robeck thrown away the victory so nearly gained? He was new in command, but he was certainly enough of a sailor to know that success had been within his grasp. The answer probably lies, as Churchill suggests, in a sentimental regard for the ships he was called upon to expend. He had been a midshipman aboard those ships, then the power and pride of the navy, and he could not see that they were now a "thing" to be profitably sacrificed. The artilleryman will give his life to save his guns; the infantryman will die to protect the colour; de Robeck would risk a little delay in forcing the Dardanelles to preserve the old ships he still adored. There was little to lose, he thought, by waiting; soldiers willing to complete the attack so well begun were in the offing.

The rub now was that the land forces, which de Robeck had thought to be ready for immediate descent, were held back. Only one regular division, the 29th, had been earmarked for Gallipoli, and Kitchener ruled that no operations were to be carried out until it arrived. In France, Sir John French, with Joffre's support, had opposed the detachment of the 29th Division from what he considered the vital theatre, and Kitchener, to placate him, had let it stay. For three weeks the unhappy division was batted about like a shuttlecock between "Easterners" and "Westerners" at a time when its early arrival at Gallipoli was absolutely vital. Not until 10 March did Kitchener finally make up his mind to send it to Gallipoli. Because of his long indecision the assaulting force numbering 75,000, supported by the fleet, could not be launched against the Gallipoli defences before 25 April—two months after the naval operations had first begun.

At the middle of March, Liman von Sanders, the German commander at the Dardanelles, had prayed for time to build up a defensive force. "If only the English will leave me alone for eight days!"[18] he said. They gave him over a month; and for every man to guard Gallipoli when the naval attack began, he had six when the attack was renewed. The British could no longer hope for surprise; that had disappeared when the ships began to pound the outer forts.

The land operations always trembled on the brink of success and finally failed. The critical decision, to order a temporary defensive in France while staging the main effort at Gallipoli, was never made. With hardly enough ammunition for one theatre, Sir John French was permitted to take the offensive in France while the Gallipoli force, starved for men and ammunition, was still expected to get results. In a three-day battle at Gallipoli (Krithia, 6-8 May, 1915), for example, 20,000 troops struck for the Narrows. They expended 18,500 shells and advanced 600 yards at a cost of 6,500 casualties. The following day (the 9th) Haig tackled Aubers Ridge in France with 30,000 men and an uncommitted reserve of 25,000. Guns fired 80,000 rounds that day. Not a yard was gained, yet Haig suffered 11,000 casualties and when night fell abandoned the attack as a useless waste of human life. The Gallipoli troops would have made no difference to Haig; his reserve was never thrown in. But had even two of the three divisions used by Haig been available at Krithia, to say nothing of the 80,000 shells, they might, the British official history concludes, "have carried Sir Ian Hamilton to the Narrows and the fleet to Constantinople."[19] But the French view of the Western Front as the decisive theatre was never seriously challenged, despite the fact that Britain's sea-power and growing military strength enabled her to strike the enemy at his weakest rather than his strongest point.

Only in July did the war policy of Britain, appalled at losses in France so out of proportion to the results gained, veer around in full support of the Dardanelles.[20] Thirteen British divisions eventually reached Gallipoli, but not in time to ensure success. The Newfoundland Regiment, which arrived to reinforce the 29th Division on 19 September, 1915, saw its first action of the war at Suvla Bay, where it was in the trenches from 16 November until the end of the campaign. There it held on grimly day and night under persistent Turkish bombardment.[21] At the turn of the year the complete force was evacuated. There was a last touch of irony. Admiral Wemyss, who relieved the passive de Robeck in the final phase, brought with him a positive attitude: he wanted to "force the straits and control them for an indefinite period."[22] By then military opinion had hardened against any continuance.

The Gallipoli venture failed—but by a hair's breadth. We can be reasonably certain that a combined operation using both naval and land forces would have succeeded. We can be equally certain that a purely naval attack (had there been no land force tantalizingly in sight) could have been pressed home to ultimate victory. As it was, the operation teetered first towards naval attack, then towards land, and finally collapsed between the two.

Unsuccessful as Gallipoli was, on 26 April, 1915 (the day after the initial landings), Italy pledged herself under a secret treaty, the Pact of London, to enter the war on the Allied side in return for Austrian and Turkish territories; a declaration of war with Austria followed on 23 May and with Germany fifteen months later. The failure at Gallipoli caused Roumania to hesitate; only in 1916, after Russia's successful summer offensive, and when the Salonika campaign that followed Gallipoli had opened, did Roumania enter the war on the Allied side.[23] Likewise, Bulgaria hesitated to join the Central Powers. She remained watchful until the Turks finally got the upper hand in the touch-and-go battle of Suvla Bay and then decided for the Germans. At the end of September, 1915, Bulgaria mobilized against Serbia and in concert with Germany and Austria routed the Serbian army in mid-October.

Greece, rebuffed twice and unwilling to lend support in Salonika after the Gallipoli failure, remained neutral.

Gallipoli was the one bright flash of British strategy during the war. In Admiral von Tirpitz's words, the capsizing of Turkey might have "affected fatally the whole course of the war."[24] The opening of the Dardanelles—and there is abundant proof that this was within the capabilities of British strength, properly applied—would have brought aid to Russia and could well have saved her from defeat. Whether Russia would have been saved from revolution and the world from Communism is no more than speculation. "The men of Gallipoli *might* have changed the fate of the world."[25]

FIVE.
CANADA'S ORDEAL AT YPRES

With the abandonment of the Gallipoli campaign, the major strategy of the war for Britain was finally settled. Thereafter, apart from "side-shows," the main effort in men and munitions was to be made in the trench lines of France and Flanders. It was in this theatre that the Canadians made their sacrifice.

They came in February, 1915, for a week's indoctrination with British units holding the line in front of Armentières. Every man, from company commander down to private, spent forty-eight hours with his opposite number for individual training—a thorough introduction to the mysteries of trench warfare. That was followed by twenty-four hours of platoon training, during which the Canadian platoons took over the responsibility for a definite length of trench. The men—eager, doubtful, anxious—marched up from their billets along the glistening *pavé* roads. They passed smashed and broken farmhouses and cottages, stunted willows, stagnant ditches, battery pits and torn-up mounds; then, through zig-zag cuttings in the marshy ground containing tangles of signal wire, they reached the trenches.

The "trenches" in this low-lying area were breastworks, ridges cast up on both sides of a shallow trench dug down to the water level. These earthen walls, capped with sandbags, were held in place by brushwood hurdles, corrugated iron and wired stakes and frames. Beneath the trench floor of boards and slats (duckboards) foul-smelling water sloshed about. Duties began with the "stand to arms" at first light, the likely hour for attack; then the protective wire was checked, to be thickened if need be the following night; the inspection of stores, rifles and localities followed; then housekeeping tasks such as the strengthening of breastworks were put in hand. At night patrols went out and, worst of all, listening-posts, pushed forward into the "devil's strip," were manned.

It was a quiet sector, but still the fresh troops felt the brooding presence of the front. New digging disclosed rusty metal, bones, rotted cloth and putrescent flesh. A good deal of lime was needed. The zone

76

between the opposing trenches, often only forty yards apart, was bullet-beaten. Bullets zipped overhead or wailed in ricochetting agony from strands of wire and jagged metal. As yet the full possibilities of artillery had not been realized; a few shells would occasionally go screaming by. Others fell close at hand, prompting a quick "Get Down!" from experienced Tommies who had learned to interpret the deadly sounds; the ground was gouged into a shower of spouting mud; the parapet jumped and danced in bright explosions, while blasts of heated air and fragmented metal soughed and whined above.

Yet the line was held with some degree of contentment. "Live and let live" was the policy adopted by both sides, if no liberties were taken.[1] Bursts of Lewis gunfire or rifle grenades, which the Canadians were encouraged to fire, brought the instant response of bullets that smacked and flayed the sandbags. Once a toy horse appeared above the German parapet; promptly knocked down by rifle fire, it appeared a few seconds afterwards bandaged around the neck and rump.

Nights were a strange experience. German flares soared up to curve back to the ground or, suspended by parachute, sank slowly, distorting the torn landscape with eerie light and shadows. The enemy's parapet sprang out frighteningly close. Men caught in No-Man's-Land froze prone upon the ground until the light had died. But it was the want of sleep that struck the men most. Huddled on the raw wet firestep, they snatched what rest they could, legs brushed aside by passers-by, a rifle going off at the nearest slit, artillery rumbling in the distance, or friendly guns crashing out behind. Only a groundsheet protected them from the February snow and chilling rain, and then, stiff and weary, the morning "stand to arms" aroused them.

There were casualties that week, but no more than the normal "wastage" in the trenches. Currie's brigade lost two men killed (properly buried behind the lines by their shocked friends) and twenty-two wounded.[2] Death was not yet commonplace.

The week of indoctrination finished, the 1st Canadian Division took over on 3 March four miles of line in the Armentières sector. Its role was purely defensive. The first seven days passed quietly enough, but early on the morning of the 10th the divisional artillery opened up with every gun at targets to the front, while three miles away on the right, a fury was loosed. The startled men watched the distant bombardment. In the grey light of morning, smoke, crimson-tinged and shot through with orange flashes, billowed in rolling folds over the hamlet of Neuve Chapelle. Signal lights arced up, sparkling like fire-flies. The din of gunfire, fading then thundering back in gigantic bursts, and the hysterical crackle of small-arms fire terrified the ears. It was, as Currie tersely recorded, "terrific cannonading and rifle fire."[3] That was the Battle of Neuve Chapelle, for which the Canadians were to keep up diversionary fire and to be ready when called upon to exploit success—a break-through that was confidently expected.

Sir John French entrusted the attack to Haig's First Army, and the first day was completely successful. The bombardment was short—thirty minutes—and the sudden attack that followed took the enemy by surprise. Within an hour the limited objective of Neuve Chapelle had fallen. But Haig's sights were set too high. He aimed at Aubers Ridge, three miles beyond. With communications cut, troops waited at Neuve Chapelle for orders to press on that did not come until mid-afternoon. Meanwhile, the Germans reinforced and the advance was halted. Sir John French naïvely hailed that day's success—and looked for more next day. He forgot that surprise had been forfeited. The 11th was a day of dismal failure. It cost the British 3,266 soldiers every hour.[4] On the 12th, after throwing back a German counter-attack, Haig dug in and established a new defensive line. The Canadians had not been called.

On 5 April the Canadian division marched north to take over part of the Ypres Salient from the French. They were soon to look back on the quiet Armentières trenches with nostalgia. But Ypres was an important task. The Belgian Army was fighting on the Allied side, and the salient was Belgian territory. Though open to bombardment from all sides, for political and sentimental reasons it could not be yielded. On the 14th, after a seven-day rest, London double-decker buses—incongruous on the country roads of Flanders—carried the Canadians towards the front.[5] By 17 April three French divisions had been relieved by the 1st Canadian and two British divisions. One French division (45th Algerian) remained in the salient to hold the northern flank. (Though the French Army was at last adopting a less conspicuous uniform (horizon blue), these colonial troops still wore *le pantalon rouge*.) Then came, in order, the Canadians, the 28th, the 27th; and the 5th British in the south. In the Canadian sector the 3rd Brigade adjoined the French, with Currie's brigade between Turner (3rd Brigade) and the 28th. The Canadian 1st Brigade, alerted for a possible attack on Hill 60, was not committed.

On the 15th, his first day in the line, Brigadier-General Currie*, as did others, received warning of attack. "Attack expected at night to be preceded by the sending of poisonous gases to our lines and sending up three red lights."[6] That day there was heavy shelling that continued up to midnight, but no attack. Some precautions were taken, amounting in the Canadian sector to strengthening the line and searching out the German front-line trenches with artillery in the hope of bursting gas containers should these have been assembled, as had been reported likely by the French corps on the left. The front trenches, taken over from the French, were weak. The policy of the French, with faith

*Promoted on 4 March, 1915.

pinned to the offensive, had been to hold the forward positions with a minimum of troops; they relied on field guns farther back to repulse enemy attacks. British tactics, reflecting traditional faith in the defensive ability of their men, were less sophisticated. The Canadians dug to the British pattern—once again breastworks in the low-lying ground—and connected isolated portions of trench situated, in the main, on the forward slope or at the foot of the Gravenstafel Ridge. Behind the front line, a thousand yards back on the crest of the ridge, the planned Subsidiary Line so far existed only on paper. From one to three miles behind the ridge were a series of redoubts, four to five hundred yards apart, known as the GHQ Line. These formed the inner defences of Ypres.

The Germans, as we have seen, decided to adopt the strategic defensive in the west during 1915, while striking a main blow against Russia in the east. Their eastern preparations would be covered by local attacks on the Western Front so far as modest numbers would permit.[7] The assault upon the Ypres Salient in April, 1915, was part of this general pattern, and it had the additional purpose of trying out tactically the effects of chlorine gas, which *might* give the opportunity of straightening out the salient. To this end they built up a small local superiority in numbers opposite Ypres—to six Allied divisions the Germans opposed seven and a half supported by a far greater weight of artillery—and those deadly cylinders of gas.

The German release of gas at Ypres was not their first use of it in the First World War. The first battlefield experiment occurred on 27 October, 1914, in front of Neuve Chapelle. There they fired three thousand shells, including gas as well as shrapnel, but the effect was so weak that it was not even noticed and only came to light when the Germans themselves proffered the information after the war.[8] Again, on 31 January, 1915, they used gas shells in Poland, where they proved useless in conditions of intense cold.[9] Because of these early disappointments the German High Command had little faith in the use of gas— the cylinders looked so innocuous when viewed side by side with huge, smoothly recoiling howitzers which were already pounding Ypres— and they neglected to provide reserves to exploit the four-mile gap the gas created.

The Battle of Ypres, 1915, began on 22nd April. Only the first two battles, Gravenstafel Ridge and St. Julien, concern us; their story is briefly told. At 5 o'clock the hush of a perfect spring evening was shattered. German artillery crashed out, hurling shells at Ypres, the neighbouring fenland villages within the salient and the French defences. At the same time, the valves of more than five thousand cylinders buried along the northern face of the salient hissed open, emitting clouds of chlorine gas on the light evening breeze that was blowing towards the French. A dense olive-green cloud formed and then moved forward, rolling slowly along the ground in the direction of the French defences. One survivor had the impression of "looking through green glasses."[10] Whole enemy ranks, hideous in respirators or mouth protectors and with bayonets fixed, leisurely followed the writhing vapour. The gas took the defenders by the throat. On the left of the 3rd Brigade, Algerian troops had to contend not only with the enemy but with panic:

. . . running blindly in the gas-cloud, and dropping with breasts heaving in agony and the slow poison of suffocation mantling their dark faces. Hundreds of them fell and died; others lay helpless, froth upon their agonized lips and their racked bodies powerfully sick, with tearing nausea at short intervals. They too would die later—a slow lingering death of agony unspeakable . . .

The whole air was tainted with the acrid smell of chlorine that caught at the back of men's throats and filled their mouths with its metallic taste. Behind the gas-cloud came the advancing hordes of Germans, under cover of a violent artillery fire.[11]

Small wonder that the French troops broke and fled, leaving open a four-mile gap on the Canadian left without a living soul to defend it. Two French divisions in all had melted as if by magic. Then, after a two-mile advance with the key to the deadlock on the Western Front in their grasp, the Germans halted as had been prearranged, to await the morning. They were without immediate reserves. Thus, for very small gains, they threw away the surprise achieved. The chance did not come again. The antidote was soon developed, and thereafter gas became more of a nuisance than a threat. In the end, when the Allies, too, had gas, the Germans were at a disadvantage: the prevailing winds were westerly.

A German push to Ypres—only four miles away—and a southward move along the Yser Canal would have put 50,000 Canadian and British troops in jeopardy. They would have had to retire from the forward defences or be trapped between the enemy's main positions and his advance in the rear. Such an advance could only have meant the fall of the Ypres Salient, with its large garrison and 150 guns.

Unaware that the Germans had halted, the Canadians made feverish attempts that night to close the extensive gap on their immediate left, now the left flank of the whole Second British Army. The main task of the 2nd and 3rd Brigades was to keep the enemy off the Gravenstafel Ridge; the 3rd Brigade, on whom the brunt would fall, had to defend the St. Julien area, behind the ridge, so that the feature would not be outflanked from the south and west. It seemed to Brigadier-General Turner (3rd Brigade) that he could best fulfil his task by driving the enemy out of a wood about a mile and a half west of St. Julien—the obvious jumping-off point for further attacks.

Sympathy for fellow sufferers. Canadians dress the wounds of German
prisoners during the Somme fighting, 1916.

The ordeal is over for the present. Weary Canadian troops march back
from the Somme fighting.

Hughes and Aitken. Sir Max Aitken (later Lord Beaverbrook) points out an interesting landmark for Sir Sam Hughes on their visit to France, August, 1916.

Hughes in London. In August, 1916, Sir Sam Hughes returned to London after his visit to France. He is shown here being helped into a cab by Major-General J. W. Carson.

Sir Robert Borden in France. Between meetings of the Imperial War Cabinet in London Sir Robert Borden made a four-day visit to Canadian troops on the Vimy front during March, 1917.

The bombardment of Vimy Ridge. This six-inch naval gun of the Canadian Heavy Artillery seen here firing at night, helped maintain the bombardment—termed by the Germans "the week of suffering."

Storming Vimy Ridge. Disarmed prisoners, overrun by the first wave of
Canadians, make for the rear. They are seen here passing through the
second wave, towards bursting shells fired by their own countrymen.

On Vimy. A respite after a job well done.

Turner attacked the wood at midnight using the 10th and 16th Battalions from divisional reserve, while the remainder of his force, with British units and French remnants, improvised ragged defences along the open flank; but at daybreak gaps still remained. His counter-stroke against the wood, meanwhile, had some success. Troops never before used in the attack hurled themselves into the unknown at night —a tricky operation even for battle-hardened men without reconnaissance—and took their objective. Extremely exposed in that position, however, they pulled back south before daybreak, helpless under German fire to recover the dead and the wounded. The 10th Battalion brought out only five officers and 188 men of the more than eight hundred who had taken part, and the 16th was similarly hit. At 5:45 A.M. Turner ordered a second counter-attack towards Pilckem, west of the wood, by the 1st and 4th Battalions. The attack failed, and losses were severe. Twelve hours later, having been reinforced by the British 13th Brigade and French units, Turner tried a third attack west of the Pilckem road using his new troops and the sorely tried 1st and 4th Battalions. The first enemy trench was carried, but the men could go no further. By evening the 4th Battalion had been reduced to company strength.

With daylight on the 23rd, the Germans failed to advance as had been expected. Canadian resistance around and north of St. Julien might well account for this. Though they did not drive the enemy back, save briefly, they bewildered him by attacks when at the most he had expected a patchy defence. By so doing, they kept him too preoccupied to attempt his own move forward.

Nightfall on the 23rd found the Canadians holding every one of their positions at the crucial apex of the salient where the enemy had made his deepest penetration. Under cover of darkness, the 3rd Brigade flattened out the apex by withdrawing to stronger ground on the western end of the Gravenstafel Ridge. The day's operations, so expensive in terms of blood, had bought time to close the flank. British, French and Canadian troops, thinly stretched but digging hard, had by evening barred the way to Ypres.

One battle was over; a grimmer one awaited. Saturday, the 24th, began with a violent bombardment, and another cloud of death, this time pointed directly at the Canadians holding the salient's blunted apex. Now the key, which two days before had unlocked four and a half miles of front, rasped and broke on the flinty courage of unyielding men. The gas at its heaviest rolled over the 8th Battalion (2nd Brigade) entrenched on the forward slope of the ridge and on the 15th holding the northern fringe of St. Julien village. Cotton bandoliers soaked in water were the only protection they had. Coughing, choking, even suffocating and with streaming eyes, the men endured and held their ground. The waves of assaulting German infantry following up the gas met volley after volley of rifle and machine-gun fire and were thrown back. The 8th, in fact, held onto their positions throughout the day, tearing at jammed rifle bolts with bleeding hands, sobbing with exasperation, still throwing the Germans back with machine-gun bursts and bayonet thrusts. The 15th, on their left, had worse positions from which they were literally blown out by field guns at short range; they suffered over six hundred casualties that day. With the 15th forced back, the whole of the 3rd Brigade front withdrew six hundred yards to a line south of St. Julien.

A counter-attack using battalions of the British York and Durham Brigade in conjunction with the 3rd Brigade was planned, but before it could be mounted General Alderson's headquarters received reports of Germans massing for what seemed an all-out effort to break the line. Turner was ordered not to counter-attack but to use the British units to "strengthen your line and hold on."[12] For some reason never satisfactorily explained, Turner interpreted that to mean the GHQ line, more than a mile back, and not his present frontage just short of St. Julien. Without reference to Currie, he pulled back leaving the left flank of the 2nd Brigade completely in the air.

The 2nd Brigade still stood firm but in constant danger of being outflanked. All day Currie worked unceasingly at getting reinforcements up to fill the ground vacated by the 3rd Brigade. One company of his 7th Battalion held on until hardly a man remained. In the words of the official history, "At the finish there was no ammunition and almost every rifle bolt had stuck."[13] At last, in the middle of the afternoon, his men almost finished yet still hanging on, the British battalions arrived. By that time, the Germans had seized the western tip of the Gravenstafel Ridge. During the night Currie himself mustered what men he could from the 7th and 10th Battalions and put them in on the left of Lipsett's rock-like 8th. A precarious flank was thus established but his men had little left to give after almost three days' continuous fighting. All but one company of the 8th were relieved by the Durhams during the night. At least the remaining company was spared from taking part in a counter-attack at dawn next morning. Mounted by the British 10th Brigade, the attacking troops swept into St. Julien, but with half their strength gone they were forced back almost to the starting point by murderous fire. The attack checked any further enemy advance but did no more.

The day of Sunday, 25 April, passed. The company of the much-enduring 8th Battalion still held on until mid-afternoon when a German attack in overwhelming force swamped the battalion of Durhams; the Canadian company perished with them, wiped out to a man. Currie had no reserve and could obtain no reinforcements and, therefore, pulled back his line; but the 28th Division on his right did not conform. The men of the 2nd Brigade, pitifully small in numbers,

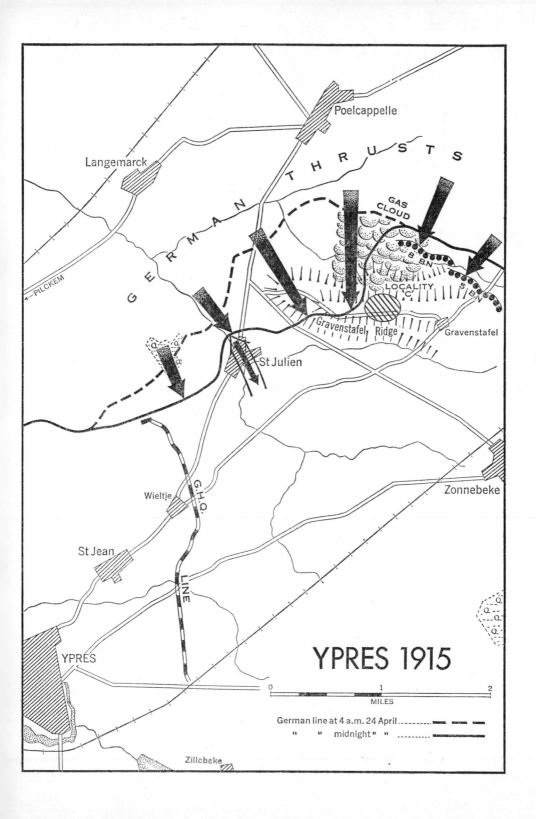

Poelcappelle

Langemarck

G E R M A N   T H R U S T S

GAS
CLOUD

PILCKEM

LOCALITY
'C'

8 BN

5 BN

Gravenstafel Ridge

Gravenstafel

St Julien

G.H.Q.

Wieltje

Zonnebeke

St Jean

LINE

YPRES

YPRES 1915

0   1   2
MILES

German line at 4 a.m. 24 April _____
"   "   midnight "   "   _____

Zillcbeke

again went forward to keep the line intact. They held their part of Gravenstafel Ridge until taken out early on the 26th and moved into bivouac on the night of the 27th. The 1st and 3rd Brigades had been relieved from the front line on Monday, 26 April. Though the Ypres battles continued until the fourth week in May, the Canadian infantry had played their part and were not called upon for further sacrifice. Reserves had now assembled and the salient, though reduced in size, remained.

The significance of the Canadian role lay in the fact that the troops had not broken during the crucial first three days of battle, even under the horrible surprise of gas, and had held the vital left flank against many times their numbers. Had they given way, the British 27th and 28th Divisions would have been cut off; certainly they would not have got away a gun and probably not more than half the infantry. That is what the War Office communiqué that followed the defence meant when it said, "The Canadians . . . undoubtedly saved the situation."[14] That, for Canada, is the glory of Ypres.

But the cost had been high. More than six thousand officers and men, killed, wounded or missing, paid for the ground the Allies retained. Out of five thousand surviving infantrymen, 1,452 had thrown away their Ross rifles and picked up the Lee-Enfields of fallen British comrades.[15] The time for grandiloquent words was done. The ordinary soldier had given his verdict where it was most valid, not on the peaceful Bisley ranges on a sunny summer's day, but at Ypres with death blundering up to him only yards away from his useless rifle barrel.

Ypres tested the men of Canada and found them a match for German professionals. It was also a testing-time for Arthur Currie. The British official historian classed the fighting as a "soldiers' battle, fought by brigadiers, regimental officers, and other ranks,"[16] and because of that it is possible to get a brief glimpse of Currie as a battle-leader. It is worthwhile to analyze his actions in this first Canadian battle.

The evening of the 22nd found Currie's 5th (Tuxford) and 8th (Lipsett) Battalions in the line on the forward slope of the Gravenstafel Ridge. The 7th Battalion was in brigade reserve, and the 10th in divisional reserve. Currie himself was at his headquarters in a farm midway between the GHQ Line and his forward battalions. At 6 P.M., one hour after the first gas attack against the French, but with no developments against his front, he ordered the 7th Battalion to stand-to. Half an hour later he sent his intelligence officer northwest into the French area to report on the situation. The report was phoned at 7 P.M.—the French front in general had gone. How about the 3rd Brigade? Were they holding? "According to appearances, yes, they are!"[17] Not more than ten minutes later Currie received a message from HQ 3rd Brigade (Turner and his Brigade Major, Garnet Hughes): "We are forced back on GHQ Line. No troops left."[18] Currie well knew, from his intelligence officer's report, that this was incorrect. Had it been so, his left flank would have been entirely unprotected. Nevertheless, he put his alerted 7th Battalion on the left of the 8th and sent the 10th Battalion from divisional reserve to 3rd Brigade for use by Turner. He informed General Alderson (who concurred) and the British on his right of these changed dispositions.

For more than two hours, HQ 3rd Brigade left Currie in the dark as to the exact position on his left, despite two strongly worded requests. Finally, at 11 P.M., he despatched an officer to bring back the information: "Imperative I know strength and disposition of your line. Please inform bearer."[19] The officer returned with the reply that the 3rd Brigade line was holding on the left of the 2nd Brigade trenches. Currie was momentarily reassured. Then, at 2 A.M., following heavy losses in the attack on the wood near St. Julien, Turner again required help. Currie pulled out three companies of the 7th Battalion from his line and sent them off. He now had no reserves.

The 23rd, for the 2nd Brigade, was relatively calm. Currie used it to visit every Canadian artillery observation post on the Gravenstafel Ridge. He studied the artillery fields of fire, the topographical features and the forward positions of his own troops and those of the 3rd Brigade. He became convinced from his observations that a place on the ridge marked on the map as "Locality C" (shown as a strong point on the Subsidiary Line) was the tactical feature which must be held. The area contained a group of shattered buildings, a shallow trench north of them commanding the fields and farms of the Stroombeek Valley, and other trenches on the southern slope of the ridge. It thus supported Lipsett's 8th Battalion, at the foot of the northern slope of the Gravenstafel Ridge, and also covered the reverse slope of the ridge. If the area were strongly garrisoned and firmly held, Lipsett could not be outflanked. The locality was, however, very weak, a few strands of wire left from the 1914 fighting and decaying trenches being the only defences. Currie decided that it must be held in strength; not only was it vital to the safety of his own position, it covered the junction of the 2nd and 3rd Brigade fronts and was the key to the defence of all the salient. But his front line had to be manned; his reserves had gone to Turner's 3rd Brigade. Other than part of the 7th Battalion already at Locality C, he had no troops to spare.

At midnight on the 23rd, Turner reported his positions right down to platoons. He expressed "great satisfaction with the situation."[20] But Currie remained uneasy. His official narrative, written that night, is almost a soliloquy: "Uneasy about left . . . reserves of the 2nd Brigade . . . used up . . . 7th Battalion . . . sent as support to 3rd Brigade right, and 2nd Brigade left become first line troops."[21] He could do nothing, however, and dozed until the attack next day aroused him.

On 24 April the second gas attack came. The Canadians were alert, for at dusk the night before masked Germans had been seen preparing something outside the parapets of their trenches. At Currie's Command Post the gas "made the nose and eyes run and our heads ache."[22] The 8th, as we have seen, stood firm, but on Lipsett's left the 15th Battalion fell back. Lipsett sent all his reserves to the left flank, opened by the 15th's retirement. Tuxford, on Lipsett's right, sent three platoons from his 5th Battalion to reinforce Lipsett. The 3rd Brigade sent back what was left of Currie's 10th Battalion. Now, at last, Currie had reserves. He personally conducted the 10th to Locality C and exercised command over it himself during the critical hours of the morning of the 24th.

For hours after the battle began the 2nd and 3rd Brigade Headquarters were at cross-purposes. At 4:55 A.M., 3rd Brigade advised Alderson that the "left of 2nd Brigade has been driven in."[23] It was, in fact, the right of the 3rd. A message from Currie at 6:30 told Alderson that it was the right of the 3rd that was crumbling. Twenty minutes later Garnet Hughes sent a reassuring message back to Division: "We are holding trenches—am in constant touch with 2nd Brigade . . . do not feel uneasy."[24] But it was not until 9:10 A.M. that the first message passed between the two brigades! At 7:05 Hughes was forced to admit that the front of 3rd Brigade had indeed withdrawn. The result of this confusion was that Alderson was completely in the dark as to the true situation; British reinforcements were in the offing, but for some time he was in doubt as to which brigade should have first call on the limited help available. Two battalions of the York and Durham Brigade were, therefore, detailed to act as reserves to those two brigades (2nd and 3rd) as required. This disposition led to more confusion later on.

At about 7:30 on 24 April the Germans had advanced to within three hundred yards of Locality C and were trying to work behind the defence line held by the 5th and 8th Battalions. The situation was critical, and Currie took personal charge of it. He requested reinforcements, and was told by Alderson of the two York and Durham units. At 8:20 he directed a platoon of the 5th Battalion to Locality C. Between 9:30 and 10 A.M., he obtained a party of sappers from the 2nd Canadian Field Company and sent them there; at the same time he arranged for the close support of two field guns for the locality. At 9:50 he sent a member of his staff to guide the York and Durhams into his area.

Locality C was now held in force; it had artillery support; reinforcements were on the way. With the locality defended, Lipsett and Tuxford could hold the front. Currie could be satisfied.

Pressure against Lipsett's flank, however, continued. The Germans, it was reported, were working round the left of Locality C from the direction of 3rd Brigade, and at 10:50 A.M. Currie got in touch with Turner: he must reinforce the 2nd Brigade line "or the whole front is lost."[25] At about 11 A.M. Turner replied: he would counter-attack towards Locality C using his battalion of the York and Durhams when it came forward. This message, and Lipsett's assurance that he would "stick to the last" in the trenches, for the moment set Currie's fears at rest.[26] Then, at 11:40, a message arrived from Garnet Hughes to the effect that, based on "information from an unknown source" the two reinforcing battalions of the York and Durhams had been withdrawn. The 3rd Brigade could not now provide assistance on Currie's left.[27] With that information, Currie urged Lipsett to retire to the Gravenstafel Ridge; but Lipsett felt he could hold on for a while longer. Then, at 11:53 a message came from Alderson: the 3rd Brigade *was* being reinforced and would counter-attack towards Locality C.

The events of the day thus far had proved the soundness of Currie's defensive plan. The direction of enemy pressure had revealed their object—to envelop the Gravenstafel Ridge from the northwest. This could best be frustrated by a strong defence on the line Locality C-St. Julien. Lipsett's flank, stretching from his forward trenches at the foot of the ridge to Locality C, was tactically the critical point. At midday, both Lipsett's line and Locality C were holding, and it appeared to Currie that the German pressure against them could be loosened by a counter-attack mounted from the 3rd Brigade area, as had just been confirmed by Alderson.

At noon Lipsett phoned—telephone communications between the 8th Battalion and Currie fortunately remained intact throughout the day—to advise that the German advance had halted. He was not now uneasy. The question arose as to how the British reinforcements, without question available, could be brought forward. Currie had already made two attempts, one at 9:50 A.M. But the bearer of that message, Lieutenant M. K. Greene, had returned with the report that the York and Durhams had not yet come forward. Currie sent him off again to await the battalions' arrival in the forward area. Between 11 and 12 o'clock, the 4th Yorkshires came up and Greene delivered Currie's message. But the commanding officer would not act on it. His orders read that he was to reinforce both Canadian brigades, as required, and until he found out what proportions should go to each he would do nothing.

Currie knew that the Subsidiary Line lay open for fifteen hundred yards, covered only by the troops at Locality C. The situation would be desperate should German pressure be resumed. He therefore determined on the extreme step of leaving his Command Post to secure the reinforcements himself, "it being thought," he wrote, "that they might move for me when unlikely to move for officers of lesser rank."[28]

Lipsett supported the plan and urged him to go, with the only proviso that should the situation become critical he would act on Currie's previous retirement instruction. Currie agreed, if "forced by circumstances. As he was the man on the spot I left it to his judgment and Lipsett and myself had a clear understanding about it."[29] There is no record, however, of his having consulted Alderson. At about one o'clock he left.

The fact that Currie left his post was later used by General Hughes against him. At first, confused by the similarity in names, Hughes' opprobrium was directed at Colonel J. A. Currie, who commanded the 16th Battalion and who went back to the town of Ypres that afternoon to "look up any stragglers in the city and send them forward."[30] That was why Colonel Currie, to clear his name, was so anxious to give evidence on Ypres at the libel action that Arthur Currie brought in 1928. "He had lived with the charge," he said, "for ten years." Hughes' later charges levelled at Arthur Currie of "butchery" and "self-glorification" included more than a strong inference of cowardice, stemming from this hunt by Currie for reinforcements to save the situation at the front. "General Currie," said Hughes in 1920, "was promoted before these facts were known. Had I remained in office six weeks longer, not only General Currie, but several other officers would have been asked to hand in their resignations."[31] Truly, war hath no fury like the non-combatant!

Currie's journey was, however, without direct success. He did not bring the British battalions back with him. He sought out the commanding officer of the York and Durham Brigade and urged a counter-attack from the 3rd Brigade area as the best means of restoring the situation on his front. He also sought out General T. d'O. Snow, commanding Corps reserves in the salient, to urge his plan, but without result. What Currie did not know was this: at the time he left the front, Canadian Divisional Headquarters, having received reports that the enemy was massing east of St. Julien for what appeared to be an all-out attack, had cancelled 3rd Brigade's counter-attack and instead had ordered them to strengthen the line with the British York and Durhams, and to hold on. Turner, as noted, interpreted that order to mean the GHQ Line, a mile back. A 3rd Brigade order, signed by Garnet Hughes, put the withdrawal into effect, thus leaving the flank of the 2nd Brigade completely exposed.

Currie, when he found out about this, hurried back. On the way he encountered Canadian stragglers, sorted out the 2nd Brigade men, formed them up and personally led them to the battlefront. He found that Lipsett had had an anxious time. Faced with 3rd Brigade's retirement, he had been on the point of exercising the authority vested in him to retire when British battalions had restored the situation. General Snow had sent forward his last reserves (the Royal Irish) to the

Locality C–St. Julien area early in the afternoon. At 2:15 P.M. Snow had also commandeered the reserves of the 28th Division (1st Suffolks and 12th Londons) and sent them to the same general area. At 3 o'clock the two British battalions of the York and Durhams at last advanced towards St. Julien. These battalions, together with the Royal Irish, met a German attack (the final one that day) and pushed the enemy back beyond St. Julien. Lipsett, therefore, now reinforced by British troops, was still in position, as were the troops in Locality C. In fact, the 2nd Brigade had held firm throughout the day. During the night 24-25 April, Lipsett and Tuxford stabilized the line, and even in that Currie took a hand.

Lieutenant-Colonel Gordon Hall, on Alderson's staff, arrived at Currie's headquarters at about 3 A.M. on the 25th to confer with the forward brigades and to dispose them into a defensive line. He found:

Currie and his Brigade Major worn out and in a dead sleep. None of the other GOCs [General Officers Commanding brigades] had arrived but I was determined to proceed with the consultation, so I woke up those two officers, asked for details of the situation on the 2nd and adjacent brigade fronts, and was given them so fully that by the time the other brigadiers had arrived a plan had been decided upon.
I could not help being struck by Currie's attitude. He knew that the 5th and 8th Battalions still held and that the remnants of the 7th and 10th were near by, but as to what had happened to the latter units he did not know further than that they had gone to the assistance of the other brigadiers. He might have asked many questions, he might have demurred, but he raised no difficulties. He collected his staff, walked out into the night to get in touch with Lipsett and fill in, as far as he could, the gap between Lipsett's left and the General Headquarters Line.[32]

Currie's part in the Ypres fighting can be quickly summarized. On the 22nd he determined what was happening in the 3rd Brigade area on the vital left. He knew more about the situation there than did Head-quarters 3rd Brigade itself. Thereafter, without waiting to be told to do so, he sent every reserve he had (and even that of Division) to help 3rd Brigade hold the flank. Next day he took advantage of a lull to assess the ground. He then knew what was vital to be held. In the fighting on the critical 24th he, at least, was not confused. Throughout the day he worked towards one constant purpose—to hold that vital ground. For that reason his brigade stood firm.

On the morning of 6 May, Currie visited the remnants of his units now safely out of the salient and at rest. That afternoon General Smith-Dorrien, commanding the Second British Army, addressed the officers. "No words could be kinder or more full of praise. The whole army realized that it was only the gallant actions of the Canadians that saved Ypres: otherwise one of the greatest disasters in the history of the

British Army might have occurred." Following that, Currie "had the first decent night's rest in 15 days."[33]

The mutual confidence between Currie and Lipsett grew stronger after Ypres; but relations between Currie and Garnet Hughes deteriorated. The lapses on the part of 3rd Brigade staff—of whom Hughes was the principal staff officer—had not been lost on the commander of the 2nd Brigade. The two men remained friendly; but later, as Divisional Commander, Currie did not want Hughes in charge of one of his brigades nor, as Corps Commander, would he accept Hughes as a divisional commander. Here may be found the real reason for Sam Hughes' later attacks on Arthur Currie.

SIX.
1915: BREAK YOUR TEETH ON MY BARBED WIRE

The enthusiastic response in Canada, unchilled by events abroad, continued. In October, 1914, Canada began recruiting a second contingent. It was known on 2 November that a complete 2nd Division would be formed but volunteers came forward so briskly that it soon became apparent that additional battalions were in the offing. It was intended, though not announced at the time, that battalions surplus to the requirements of the division would be broken up in England to provide reinforcements for the 1st Division.[1]

To meet the wastage of a division for three months, the War Office calculated, 500 gunners and 5,400 infantrymen would be required. By 26 April, only three thousand infantry reinforcements had reached England, and at Ypres Alderson's division absorbed twice that number in four days. The call was made, therefore, for a further six thousand immediately and for the same number every three months thereafter. Reinforcements for the 2nd Division would double the requirement, so that in the future two or three transports sailed from Canada every month with reinforcements alone, in addition to those ships bringing complete units.[2] Meanwhile the 4th Brigade, which had remained in England, was broken up for Alderson's needs.

The 2nd Division was formed from the Second Contingent in England on 25 May, 1915. It trained all summer at Shorncliffe and crossed to France during the first two weeks of September. In May, from the 4th to the 24th, the shattered units of the 1st Division had rested, been reinforced and re-equipped; and at the end of the month gas protectors consisting of pads of cotton waste, impregnated with neutralizing chemicals and wrapped in gauze, were issued through the medical services.

Events on the Western Front for the remainder of 1915 were determined by the German design to retain territory gained and the French desire to recover it. German defences, therefore, became more and more formidable and, without a key to unlock them, British and French attacks were torn to pieces.

Joffre had planned two major offensives for the year. The first was to be against Vimy Ridge in May. For this, the British (see page 73) would attack simultaneously toward Aubers Ridge to create a diversion in favour of the French offensive. In September would come the second great offensive, delivered by the French from the two widely separated sectors of Artois and Champagne. Once the breakthrough had been achieved, all the French and British armies on the Western Front were to roll forward in a general offensive, which, according to Joffre, would "compel the Germans to retreat beyond the Meuse and possibly end the war."[3]

Joffre's intention of breaking through a wall of tangled wire, steel and concrete in the face of flame and metal would have been laudable if he had the means. But to return to a war of movement in the green countryside of the lost provinces of France required more than courage backed by guns and small-arms fire. Technologically, artillery and small arms were almost as advanced as in the Second World War and in 1915 their use favoured the defensive. What the artillery required for the attack were improved maps and intelligence, precise location of targets, calibration of guns, the ability to shoot close over the attacking infantry, and an instantaneous fuse for wire cutting. None of this had as yet been developed, nor was it then recognized that the object of supporting fire is to paralyze the enemy at the time the attacking troops are in the greatest danger. In order to carry off the attack, waves of troops were forced to expose themselves, stumbling across open, shell-pocked ground against barbed wire deliberately meshed to hinder movement. Over that ground, fired from behind steel rails, concrete, or sandbag emplacements, machine-guns sprayed their hail of death.

The machine-gun, "cheap, light, requiring few soldiers to man it and firing [in bursts at up to] 450 rounds per minute of relatively lightweight ammunition which posed no very difficult supply problem . . . was able to stultify almost every offensive from the winter of 1914 to the spring of 1918."[4] The artillery caused more casualties throughout the war, but mainly because shells could be lobbed into the trenches twenty-four hours a day. The machine-gun, with its flat trajectory could not do that; but against attacking troops in the open and used in *direct* fire against targets of opportunity it was the master killer, which mowed men down like wheat. Though Ypres, with its gas, had been an exception, offensives on the Western Front were almost invariably more costly to the attackers than to the defenders.

An armoured vehicle, impervious to bullets and capable of crushing wire and surmounting trenches, had not yet been developed. Meanwhile, artillery, firing relatively ineffective shrapnel, was used to breach the wire; 150 shells for a gap ten yards wide in a twenty-yard-thick entanglement. The German answer was to stretch out more wire, so that artillery concentrations in turn increased, and supply problems grew and grew. In sensitive areas the trench systems were multiplied into mile-wide belts of trenches—forward trenches, support trenches, reserve trenches—and all were made stronger. Deep dug-outs large enough to accommodate whole companies were built, and these troops, safe even under bombardment, emerged to counter-attack any exhausted attackers who had reached their lines.

Though wave after wave of men (an assault wave and others to follow-up and maintain momentum) advanced, and sometimes captured lengths of the German fire-trench and even parts of the support trench, it was seldom possible to retain even a foothold in the face of counter-attack. If the attack were bold enough and committed enough men, some would get through. But in the long run the gains were nil or small and tremendously costly. Therein lies the horror and the fascination of the First World War.

The true horror of World War I was not in its maimed and killed, not in the length of the war, and not in its barbarism or atrocities—it was in the fact that *so many men died and achieved nothing by it.*[5]*

In 1915 they died striving for a break-through that was unattainable with the equipment and the tactics available. The over-optimistic Allied generals, who saw only the unspoiled fields beyond and not the impregnability of the defensive lines, are to blame: they blinded themselves to the true state of affairs and hurled men forward in one useless attack after another.

The French attack on 9 May was carried out by the Tenth Army under Pétain. His troops were fresh and keen but they failed. The German front was penetrated with great loss, and the French poured up the slopes of Vimy Ridge, almost to the crest, only to be driven off by German reserves. Nevertheless, French thrusts persisted; the battle now became one of attrition—nibbling, Joffre called it—lasting until 15 May. On 15 June the French began another assault; the battle lasted four days but achieved nothing. The slaughter was appalling. The French suffered 100,000 casualties to 75,000 on the German side.

Haig's diversionary attack on Aubers Ridge, put in after a forty-minute bombardment, was equally abortive. The depth of barbed wire in front of the enemy's forward breastwork had been doubled; machine-guns, firing through steel-rail loop-holes, had been installed; and in a second defensive line, two hundred yards to the rear, dug-outs in the higher ground sheltered men ready to throw back the attacking waves immediately the bombardment stopped. Concrete machine-gun emplacements, half a mile back, were ready to stop any break-through but they were not needed.   Haig, exhibiting some good sense, called

*Author's italics.

off the attack at nightfall. But Sir John French remained undaunted; for the future, he decided, there would be "deliberate and persistent" attacks, by which the enemy would be "gradually and relentlessly worn down by exhaustion and loss until his defence collapses."[6] This policy of attrition, however, was a two-edged sword.

The first of French's new attacks took place on 16 May, against Festubert. The assault went in at night. Darkness enabled the British to grip the front-line breastwork, but the enemy merely retired to the next line of resistance farther back. On the 17th, the British could not get forward. Next day the Canadians, freshly reinforced with raw troops, took part in the renewed attack.

Turner's brigade was the first in action, in a flanking attack against a defended orchard beyond the captured breastwork. "They encountered such an effective barrage . . ." runs the German account, "that the attack collapsed after a few minutes and was not again renewed . . ."[7] Nor did the main thrust against the orchard by a British battalion of Guards fare any better.

On the 20th, the attacks were again renewed; 3rd Brigade against the orchard, and 2nd Brigade against two redoubts marked K5 on the inaccurate maps. The latter was a vague objective. Shelling had so changed the ground that features shown on the map could not be recognized, and Currie, to his credit, had protested. The operation should be postponed, he had advised Divisional Headquarters, until a thorough reconnaissance of the approaches and the objective could be made; but he had been overruled.[8] Turner's brigade, succeeding where the Guards had failed, captured the orchard on the evening of the 20th. It was afterwards known as "Canadian Orchard" and remained in Allied hands until the German offensive in the spring of 1918 swept this and other gains away. Currie's attack, "under a storm of fire" from machine-guns, waned and died; but he took the objective three nights later.[9] Then, on 25 May, Sir John French halted the battle.

For one small orchard and two muddy ditches the 1st Canadian Division had incurred 2,468 casualties. Not one man would have paid $250 for the whole parcel in Canada. Writing of the battle afterwards, Currie said: "I received the message, 'Well done, 2nd Brigade,' but while such messages are deeply appreciated, they do not console. There I lost 53 officers and 1,200 men."[10]

At the Battle of Givenchy, which followed on 15-16 June, only the 1st Brigade was involved. There an innovation was tried. Three field guns, with plated shields and muffled wheels, were dragged into the front line to blast a path at zero hour for the attacking infantry. Furthermore, a mine had been driven under the enemy line to be exploded just before the assaulting troops went over. Unfortunately, insufficient backfill had been used in the tunnel. The mine flashed back and caused as much damage to the attackers as to the defenders. The three forward guns knocked out six machine-gun posts and blew great gaps in the parapet and wire before they were themselves knocked out. But those gaps, through which the assault was funnelled, became the obvious targets for the enemy to rake. The story, therefore, was the same as before: heavy losses in No-Man's-Land, a quick hold on the German front-line trenches, the inevitable counter-attack, hand-to-hand fighting and the retirement of a crushed and limping remnant to the shelter of its own defences. The 3rd Battalion, to whom the attack had been entrusted, lost 20 officers and 846 men out of a thousand in casualties.[11] As the costly French experiment in Artois had now ended, Haig called a halt to the needless slaughter. The Canadians moved back to a familiar line near Armentières, this time north of Ploegsteert, where, from June to mid-September, "a strange tranquillity persisted."[12]

The Canadians now carried with them the short Lee-Enfield rifle which, by decree of Sir John French on 13 June, had replaced the Ross. The number of infantrymen who had thrown the Ross away had climbed to some three thousand, and French had merely endorsed the verdict of the troops. But the issue was not yet dead; the 2nd Division arrived in September with the Ross!

In the summer of 1915 in the Canadians' sector "life was as good as ever obtains on active service."[13] Trenches were close to the enemy, so close in fact that chicken wire was strung up to catch hand grenades. An elderly bearded German frequently wandered into No-Man's-Land looking for firewood. "No one fired at him and he came to be almost affectionately known as Von Tirpitz."[14] His appearances helped relieve the monotony and prompted the singing of "Keep the Home Fires Burning" by hundreds of lusty voices along the line. There is also the story of a sentry who set an old pail on the parapet, hoping for a machine-gun burst; it came, and he had a brazier. Others, seeing this and longing for a spell out of the line, held their right hands up, but no more bullets came over. It was at this time also that the men came to know Canon Scott; fearless in every way, he was "equally at home in a trench issuing candy or smokes, in an officers' mess or conducting a burial." Canon Scott earned many tributes; though he had been "advised, begged, ordered and warned to stay out of dangerous places, he insisted on sharing the danger and hardship with his 'boys.' "[15]

To this sector came the 2nd Division in mid-September of 1915. The appointment of its commander had been the subject of some discussion. Kitchener's offer of the pick of "all unemployed generals on the active list" had been rejected by Sam Hughes, who wanted Turner.[16] Sir George Perley* advised the British War Minister of the wisdom of appointing a Canadian, whereupon Kitchener indicated Currie, whom

*Perley had been knighted on 1 January, 1915.

Sir John French had recommended as the "most suitable of the three [Canadian] brigadiers" in France.[17] Nevertheless, Hughes appointed Turner; Currie would take over the 1st Division later.

While the 2nd Division was training in England, Hughes' representative (Carson) cabled Sam: "Why do you not . . . have our two divisions in the field as an Army Corps with your good self in command?"[18] But Sam demurred, although not from any doubts about his own capabilities: "To remain Minister of Militia and to hold an important military appointment at the Front," the Prime Minister commented later, "would have been the ideal situation so far as his outlook was concerned."[19] "Many here demand that if Army Corps is formed I should command it," Sam informed Carson; but he had tasted the drug of power as Minister and was loath to put it down.[20] Nevertheless, he acted on the suggestion that a corps be formed and informed Sir John French through the Canadian liaison officer at British General Headquarters that it was "the earnest desire of all in Canada to increase the existing division . . . into an army corps, first of two, later of three divisions."[21] Sir John, on whom Canadian gallantry at Ypres had not been lost, urged Kitchener to form the Corps under Alderson's command: "I think the best return we can make for the splendid service rendered by the Canadian Division is to meet their wishes."[22] Kitchener agreed—and Major-General Hughes was knighted on 24 August, 1915.

Thus, on 13 September, 1915, with the arrival of the 2nd Division, Alderson opened Corps Headquarters at Bailleul. The same day, he sent for Currie, removed the blue armband from his subordinate's sleeve and replaced it with his own of red, signifying that Currie had taken over command of the 1st Division. The new Divisional Commander cabled the news to his wife and to his mother that night; on the following day he was promoted major-general.[23] Currie's own replacement in command of the 2nd Brigade was his old instructor and friend, Lieutenant-Colonel L. J. Lipsett of the 8th Battalion.[24]

In October Major-General Sir Sam Hughes directed that his son, Garnet, who was then filling a second-grade General Staff appointment in Turner's 2nd Division, be given a brigade. Alderson posted him to command the 1st Brigade in place of Mercer who had been promoted to command the newly formed Corps Troops. Currie had no objections to Garnet Hughes as a man but, son of the Minister or not, did not feel that Hughes was qualified to command a brigade, especially one of his own. For three weeks he struggled against the appointment but in the end he was forced to accept it, and on 25 November Hughes took over. "It was a question of needs must," said Currie; "the Corps Commander and the Minister were against me."[25] Though the protest might have prejudiced his career he had, for the second time, done what he thought was right in the interests of the men. Previously, after Ypres, he had opposed Hughes by coming out firmly against the Ross, which, he declared, was an unsatisfactory weapon. Sir Sam Hughes, no doubt, was beginning to have second thoughts about Arthur Currie.

The first effort of the Canadian Corps was made on 25 September. The task was to provide a diversion (much as had been done by the 1st Division near Neuve Chapelle) for a British thrust at Loos. This time the Canadians used artillery and smoke to simulate a gas attack. It was, in fact, the first smoke screen of the war but it did not affect the battle.

Joffre's grand attack took place that same day—the French Second and Fourth Armies striking northward from Champagne against the 3rd German Army; at the same time, in a converging thrust, the French Tenth Army and the British First struck eastward from Artois against the German 6th. It was hoped that "successful offensives would cut off the three German armies (the 2nd, 1st and 7th) holding the Noyon Salient, leaving them to be defeated in detail."[26] This objective was, as usual, over-optimistic.

In Champagne, twenty French divisions advanced against only six on the German side. The French had 47 heavy guns per mile and a total of some 2,000 field guns, a great concentration of artillery. On the first day the attack gained up to 3,000 yards in places, for the Germans, well aware of French intentions, had thinned out the forward lines leaving the attackers to be dealt with farther back. On the next day the French encountered the main resistance and paid heavily for every yard.

The offensive in Artois, carried out simultaneously on 25 September, achieved no more. Five German divisions held off fourteen French. One division of the French Tenth Army managed to reach the crest of a smaller feature of Vimy Ridge, but that was all. Haig's First Army, much weaker in artillery than the French, attacked behind a cloud of chlorine gas. At least, the six assaulting British divisions should have been behind the gas, but the wind was unfavourable in some cases. Nevertheless, the attack had been prepared and all was ready; despite the wind, the taps of 5,243 cylinders were opened to emit hissing streams of vapour that built up into an enormous sickly cloud. The divisions in the centre and on the left saw the cloud pause, hesitate, then float back into their own trenches causing, in the words of the British official history, "great inconvenience and some loss." Those infantrymen who were not poisoned by their own gas were "soon stopped, and slaughtered by the ungassed German machine-gunners."[27] On the right, where the gas had carried in the direction of the enemy, however, a deep penetration was made. Hill 70, on the outskirts of Lens, was taken. But Sir John French's general reserve, intended to exploit the break-through, was *sixteen miles* to the rear. Thus the effects of surprise, as with the Germans at Ypres five months before, had been thrown away. The German second line of defences held firm and, in the absence of reserves, the British attack bogged down. That night the Germans reinforced their one and a third divisions holding off six British and thickened the defensive wire.

On the following day the British resumed the attack:

They had had to cross the No-Man's-Land of the previous day, that was littered with the corpses of the Devon and Highland Regiments, lying in long straggling rows as the German machine-guns had traversed along their ranks. Among these were still many wounded who called out piteously to the newcomers for water and assistance.[28]

Then, under intense fire themselves and without artillery support save for a few desultory rounds before the assault, they reached the entangled wire, four feet high and nineteen feet across. It was of hard steel, "too thick to be cut with the hand-clippers that had been issued . . . braced and criss-crossed among pine stakes and pit props driven thirty-five centimetres into the earth."[29] The men tore at it in frenzy, hurled themselves upon it, or ran up and down looking for a gap until the callous machine-gun and rifle fire from the safety of protected positions cut them down. The slaughter appalled even the Germans:

Before them was the "Leichenfeld [field of corpses] von Loos," and, as among them dozens of khaki-clad forms rose up once again and began to limp and crawl back to their own lines, "no shot was fired at them from the German trenches for the rest of the day, so great was the feeling of compassion and mercy for the enemy after such a victory."[30]

Of the 10,000 men in "Kitchener's Army" who carried out the attack on 26 September, 8,246 were casualties. There is a British song which runs: "If you want the sergeant-major, I know where he is . . ." A ribald classic to begin with, the song was now cynically amended:

> If you want the old battalion,
> I know where it is,
> I know where it is,
> I know where it is,
> If you want the old battalion,
> I know where it is,
> It's hanging on the old barbed wire!

Kitchener's order to French, that he must do his utmost to help Joffre's optimistic programme even though "we may suffer very heavy losses"[31] had been obeyed. But the battle—and especially the reserves— had been mishandled. At the end of the year Sir John returned to England to fill the less demanding post of Commander-in-Chief, Home Forces, and was succeeded in the field by Sir Douglas Haig.

On 28 September, 1915, Joffre called off the Champagne and Artois offensives in favour of a new general offensive; his thirst for the offensive had not yet been slaked. German counter-attacks, however, upset what synchronization there might have been so that, in the event, only disjointed attacks went in. On 6 October the French captured a village in Champagne; on the 11th they pried a piece of ground from the enemy in Artois; two days later the British, having lost Hill 70, seized several trenches north of Loos, only to be forced to give them up again. The longed-for break-through was as far away as ever. On 4 November the front lapsed sullenly into stalemate once again, with the Germans as strong as before. Since 25 September they had inflicted losses of almost two to one on the Allied armies—200,000 French and 60,000 British, against 150,000 German casualties.[32]

The Canadian Corps, apart from the demonstration on 25 September and a similar one on 13 October, had been spared from these insanities. Autumn turned to winter and with it came the steady rain of Flanders.

Raindrops dripped from rusting wire; the churned-up earth in No-Man's-Land turned to mud; shell holes and craters brimmed with water. And the trenches, gouged into the low-lying ground, filled like the ditches they were. The troops, hunched under glistening ground-sheets in the slanting rain, stood thigh-deep in water behind the dissolving breastworks. The enemy, on higher ground, was better off; and, to discommode his opponents still further, he drained his trenches —including sewage—in the Canadian direction.

High rubber boots were issued, but there were not enough to go round; "trench feet," arising from the cold and wet and an added infection from the soil, set in. As with frostbite, feet swelled and tissues deteriorated and would become gangrenous if not checked. Colds, influenza and even pneumonia were common, and lice were ever present. There was no warmth, no comfort, even in the shattered leaky billets behind the lines. Only the daily issue of rum was briefly cheering.

That winter the old *laissez-faire* winter doctrine was no longer observed. British policy, Corps was advised, would be to "foster an offensive and aggressive spirit throughout all ranks and on no account must any idea of 'live and let live' policy be tolerated for one moment."[33] Currie, aware that stagnation could only be injurious to morale, welcomed it and when two battalions of his old brigade (the 5th and 7th) requested permission to raid the enemy's line, he was enthusiastic.

For ten days before the raid the raiding parties, five officers and 85 men from each battalion, all volunteers, rehearsed night and day on ground resembling the objective. Preparations, as with everything undertaken by Currie, were thorough. The men practised crossing wire by means of special mats; portable bridging ladders for water-filled ditches were tried; the men wore *crêpe* masks and carried flashlights with which to dazzle the occupants of dug-outs. The route across No-Man's-Land was marked by white stakes; orders for the operation were clear and explicit.

On the night of the raid, 16 November, artillery shelled the enemy's wire and a cutting group clipped out what the guns had missed. Both parties then moved forward. That from the 5th Battalion encountered unexpected wire in a moat below the enemy's parapet, threw grenades, and then withdrew without a single casualty. The 7th Battalion's party took the enemy by surprise, killed or wounded some thirty Germans and brought back twelve prisoners complete with newly issued respirators, which intelligence officers welcomed. Only one Canadian was killed and another slightly wounded; the withdrawal had been orderly. A German counter-attack, put in forty minutes later, was easily repulsed. It was, in the words of the British official history, in all respects "a model raid,"[34] while the French requested four thousand copies of the detailed operation order for distribution to selected units.[35]

Currie's division staged another equally successful raid, again by the 5th Battalion, on the night 14-15 December. Thereafter the winter wore on in bleak misery through Christmas and the New Year. Though the Corps had been involved in no major operations since its formation in mid-September, it had sustained 2,692 casualties during the remaining months of the year, 688 of them fatal.[36] Such was the toll of the trenches.

On Christmas Day, 1915, another Canadian division—the 3rd—was formed under Major-General M. S. Mercer, formerly of the 1st Brigade and later commanding the Corps Troops. His brigades were the 7th, 8th and 9th, commanded by Brigadier-Generals Macdonell, Williams and Hill. Princess Patricia's Canadian Light Infantry came to the 7th Brigade after a year's service with the British, as did the Royal Canadian Regiment, which had been on garrison duty in Bermuda for almost a year. The P.P.C.L.I. brought their Lee-Enfield rifles with them. The 8th Brigade's four battalions were formed by converting six regiments of Canadian Mounted Rifles to infantry. The other battalions to complete the brigades were newly raised and, like the C.M.R., all carried the Ross rifle. During the first three months of 1916, Alderson indoctrinated the 3rd Division by relieving the 1st and 2nd Divisions in the line with either brigades or battalions from the new formation. On the night of 3 April, the Canadian Corps changed places with its northerly neighbour, V British Corps, and moved into the Ypres Salient to hold the southeast part from St. Eloi to the Menin Road, a front it was to hold until August.

In the salient, as had been the case with the 1st Division, Turner's 2nd Division had its first fight. The outcome this time, however, was not so satisfactory. General Plumer, commanding the British Second Army, had decided to force the enemy out of a small salient 100 yards deep from a 600-yard base near St. Eloi. The whole salient, slightly elevated, became known as "the Mound" in that flat country. The task of its capture was entrusted by V Corps to the British 3rd Division, and when that had been accomplished, the Canadian Corps would relieve the British corps; in particular the 2nd Division would take over the newly won ground from the British 3rd Division.

Alderson protested; the attack and the fighting that would follow should all be the responsibility of his 2nd Division. But the operation, which was to be marked by the blowing of six mines under the enemy positions, was planned for 15 March. A change in front could not be made in time; and any delay might mean enemy discovery of the mines. Plumer, therefore, vetoed Alderson's proposal. A postponement until 27 March through engineer delay in placing the mines did, however, become necessary, and this would reduce the time for the consolidation of the ground that the British proposed to take. Thus the ground, "having been seized by surprise and as a result of the enemy garrison being annihilated by the explosion of the mines, the area and its defence were made the responsibility of others,"[37] a major factor in the chaos that resulted.

An artillery barrage and the explosion of the mines beneath the salient preceded the British attack. The Mound and its surroundings heaved in six places as though "a giant mole was pushing up the earth. . . The mound rose to a fair height, then broke with a roar, and earth was shot into the air, blotting out the sun." And then, in a German effort to isolate the mine craters, even as "the tons of earth descended, the air became alive with screeching shells."[38]

Four craters, numbered 2, 3, 4 and 5, were forward, while 1 and 6 had been blown in No-Man's-Land beside an old crater, Number 7. What had been the Mound was now Crater Number 3—an enormous hole. In fact the blowing of the mines had changed the landscape completely so that the attacking troops were never sure which craters they occupied and this uncertainty persisted after the Canadians had relieved them. On the right, the attack went well. The German third line was taken, including three craters. On the left the enemy refused to be dislodged and it was not until 3 April that the last crater (Number 5) fell. Only one objective still remained uncaptured: a machine-gun emplacement, which the Germans made good use of in mounting counter-attacks. The British division by this time was exhausted; relief could not wait for the stabilization of the front.

Early on the morning of 4 April, the 2nd Division—the first Canadian troops to wear steel helmets—manned the craters and the sodden forward line. The blowing of the craters and the constant shellfire had disrupted drainage patterns so that the whole area was waterlogged. The fresh troops attempted to strengthen the line. But work went slowly. "Every German gun around the Ypres Salient," it seemed, "was concentrated on blasting the Canadian battalions out of the craters"[39] and digging and wiring had not been completed when, at 3 A.M. on the morning of 6 April, 1916, the Germans attacked in force.

Shells fell like rain, splitting the front into resisting groups that were overrun a half-hour later. The defenders on the right held on to Crater 1 but were driven back beyond Craters 2 and 3, and on the left beyond 4 and 5. The Canadians counter-attacked, retaining Craters 6 and 7 on the extreme left but in the confusion they believed these to be Craters 4 and 5. This mistake, under which they laboured for ten days, had

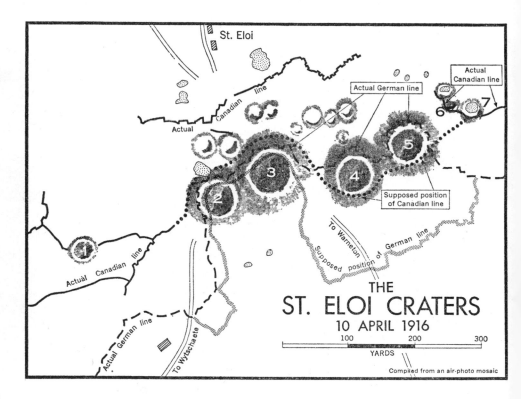

THE
ST. ELOI CRATERS
10 APRIL 1916

disastrous consequences. Craters 4 and 5 were well forward so that continued Canadian possession of them would mean that German attempts at penetration had failed. But the Canadians were not in the old German front lines as they reported but in No-Man's-Land. Army Headquarters, therefore, was completely misled as to the true state of affairs. Bad weather after 8 April lasted until the 16th; this precluded flying, which would have established the true position and ensured withdrawal from an impossible situation.

In consequence, successive battalions of the 2nd Division were thrown in, "doomed to destruction and knowing before they entered the crater zone that they were so doomed."[40] On the afternoon of 19

April, after a three-hour bombardment, the Germans cleared up the situation once and for all. The dazed defenders of 6 and 7 were finally swept away, and the only gain left after almost a month of fighting was Crater 1, one of the smaller craters on the extreme right. It had been a costly failure. The price for that hole in killed, wounded or missing, had been 1,953 Canadians.

Naturalists say that some species of warrior ants, moved by a blind instinct, keep going forward in the face of sure disaster. Some are said to march in columns, like soldiers, not deviating to the right or left. Should those in front be stamped on and destroyed, those behind continue to come on nevertheless, themselves to be crushed and annihilated in turn. That was the story of the 2nd Division at St. Eloi.[41]

Repercussions followed the battle. It had been a fiasco. According to Sir Douglas Haig, General Plumer wanted to remove General Turner of the 2nd Division and Brigadier-General Ketchen of the 6th Brigade, which had played the major part in the battle. It is indeed hard to understand why these officers remained ignorant of the true situation for so long. Air photographs taken on 8 April show Craters 6 and 7 full of water and the others almost dry. "Apparently," comments the Canadian official historian drily, "no use was made of this obvious means of identifying the positions held."[42] At any rate Plumer ordered Alderson to take "severe disciplinary measures," which the Divisional Commander did by initiating an adverse report on Ketchen. Turner refused to associate himself with this action against his subordinate, which led in turn to a request by Alderson for Turner's removal. Haig, however, knowing that the dismissal of two senior Canadian officers would be resented, and having weighed "the danger of a serious feud between the Canadians and the British" against "the retention of a couple of incompetent commanders," decided on 21 April that Turner must remain; under the extremely difficult conditions "all did their best." The two Canadian officers retained their commands.[43]

The matter, however, did not end there. Sir Max Aitken, another of Sir Sam Hughes' honorary colonels who had been appointed the general representative of Canada at the front (or "the Canadian Eye-witness" as he was sometimes known), left his office in London, crossed to France, and interviewed Haig's Chief of the General Staff on 23 April. At this time Aitken was thirty-six years old and had done no soldiering in either Canada or England; he knew very little about any of the Services in either country.* According to Aitken, in a message to Hughes, "the loss of Turner and Ketchen would affect disastrously [some copies read "nominally"] the Second Division and must be followed by many resignations." As we know, Haig had already

*Although raised in New Brunswick he resided in England, was a Member of Parliament there, and was elevated to the peerage as Lord Beaverbrook in January, 1917.

decided two days before that Turner would be kept on. Nevertheless, Aitken continued, he had "reluctantly" come to the conclusion that Alderson was the man to remove; he was "incapable of holding the Canadian Divisions together." Furthermore, he reported, Haig had "stipulated that Canada should give him the assistance he required in disposing of General Alderson."[44] This last statement raises an interesting question: Alderson belonged to the British Service; why then should Haig enter into any bargain over the disposal of General Alderson? The real reason for Aitken's message might well lie in the fact that Hughes' attitude towards Alderson was by this time extremely bitter, and Aitken was reporting what he knew would be acceptable to the Minister. And it would be certainly difficult for Alderson to work with Turner after what had occurred.

Hughes, incensed by Alderson's wholesale replacement of Canadian equipment on Salisbury Plain, had become even more so over the Corps Commander's uncompromising stand against the Ross rifle. In fact, it was generally believed for years that the cause of Alderson's removal had been the "differences of opinion between himself and the Minister of Militia regarding the use of the Ross Rifle,"[45] and this was undoubtedly a major factor. Alderson listed time and again the faults of the weapon: "I should not be fit for my position if I passed over anything which endangered men's lives or the success of our arms."[46] But Sir Sam, inflexible as ever, had turned the complaints aside with the contemptuous words: "It is not worth while, with men who know little or nothing about rifles, to take up these . . . points in detail, but some of them are so absolutely absurd and ridiculous that no one excepting a novice or for an excuse, would be found seriously advancing them."[47] That was in March. Hughes then undermined Alderson's position and authority completely by directing Carson, his special representative in London, to send copies of this letter to all commanders (down to officers commanding units) in both England and France. The Corps Commander made no reply; but on 2 May, following reports that the Ross had jammed during a German attack at St. Eloi, he forwarded a confidential questionnaire to all commanders down to the company level in the 2nd and 3rd Divisions calling for reports on the capabilities of the Ross when delivering or repelling an attack. Despite the confidential nature of the document, both Ketchen and Turner sent copies of Alderson's questionnaire to Carson, well knowing they would reach Sir Sam. Ketchen offered to furnish personal experiences regarding the good performance of the Ross "if capital is to be made for this," while Turner advised that whatever the men said about the Ross should be ignored; he feared that "action is being delayed too long as regards Alderson."[48] On 26 April the Prime Minister and his cabinet, after Aitken's message had been received, sanctioned Alderson's removal; a month later, to his surprise and intense regret, the Corps Commander was sent to be Inspector General of Canadian Forces in England, an appointment which lasted only until September.* His successor in the field was another British officer and a future Governor General of Canada, Lieutenant-General Sir Julian Byng.

Alderson's questionnaire on the Ross, however, though it undoubtedly contributed to his dismissal, still served a useful purpose. Answers to it were laid before Sir Douglas Haig after Alderson's departure. The British Commander-in-Chief at once advised the War Office that a large percentage of Ross rifles had jammed during an enemy attack at St. Eloi on 1 May; the men had lost confidence in the weapon. The War Office took it up with the Canadian Government. Now at last the matter lay in the hands of the Prime Minister and beyond the reach of Hughes. Borden reported that he was "content to abide by the Commander-in Chief's judgment after thorough investigations and adequate tests."[49]

The Canadian Corps spent the summer in the Ypres Salient, but it was no holiday idyll. The area, as always, was evil. A maze of trenches dissected the ground, many dating back to the old 1914 and 1915 fighting and in a state of disrepair, while all of them were laden with "a distillation of appalling stenches."[50] In the area north of Ypres-Comines Canal, one Canadian battalion took over a trench still "choked with the decomposed bodies of Scottish soldiers."[51]

There was no longer any optimism about an early victory. The first year had done no more than stem the German tide; 1915 had seen strong defensive lines develop that could be held by relatively weak enemy forces, and still could not be broken through; and 1916 might well see the speedy transfer of enemy troops that, having dulled the Russian steel, could be hurled once more against the west. The earlier enthusiasm had by now abated. Despite journalistic eulogies boosting near-disasters into far-reaching victories, returning wounded had reported otherwise. The men of the 3rd Division, though still untried, had talked to the veterans of the 1st and those of the 2nd so recently "blooded" at St. Eloi: they had no illusions.

Enemy shelling was violent. *Minenwerfer* (trench mortars) lobbed projectiles like small rum barrels onto the frail breastworks with devastating effect. Bullets whipped and cracked from all directions, some even entering the parapets from the wrong side, for this was the Ypres Salient and could be ranged on by German guns and small arms from around the semi-circle. And there was the ever-present danger of whole sections of trench leaping skywards through enemy mine-workings underneath. Even digging in dud-infested ground took its toll. There was no safety anywhere.

*Mount Alderson in Alberta, overlooking the Waterton Lakes, bears his name.

Above all there was the noise. It has been likened to an infernal orchestra made up of ear-splitting crashes from heavy artillery, the deeper roar of mined charges, the flailing crack of field pieces, the higher-pitched note of rifles, the ghastly staccato rattle of machine-guns, the shriek and wail of shells, and the insect zip and whine of bullets; but no words can ever describe it adequately.

Perhaps it can be comprehended by imagining the noise of a compressor operating outside one's window from early morning until late at night. The sound of its engine is bad enough, but one would accustom oneself to it were it not to be followed by the wild staccato clatter of the drill hammering into seasoned concrete for irregular intervals of time. Even that, through familiarity, might become tolerable—if it were sustained. But the noise changes from one to the other with no pattern or regularity, and while the hammering continues nerves are bunched in preparation for the engine noise that will surely follow. This persists during days of mounting tension until, when the daily inferno has at last ceased, the clangour is by then so firmly embedded in the brain that a return to the actual noise would be almost welcome to fill the screaming silence.

Multiply that noise a thousandfold, continually fluctuating with distance and the type and size of weapons, and you have the noise of war. The troops became connoisseurs of noise for they lived with it every day. Even back in billets behind the line they could distantly see the nightly show of pyrotechnics that had flickered over the front since the end of 1914 and hear the noise. In the front line, with tense nerves, they came to recognize the various types of shell—not only the devilish shriek of whizzbangs—from the ear-shattering noises made. They became resigned to noise and mocked it, for there was no respite, even if they were trying to snatch a little sleep on the eve of an attack. And so they found relief in singing "Hush, Here Comes a Whizzbang," composed by some unknown trench balladeer.

The bleak dreariness of trench warfare dragged on through May and into June, 1916. Farther south, part of Vimy Ridge, taken over from the French by British troops in March, was lost to the Germans on 21 May. The Canadians lived like beasts, more primitively than in Stone Age caves, in the blood-soaked, puzzling and filthy Ypres trenches. Even there, nature did not forget the habit of centuries. Crops, regardless of the lack of sowers, sowed themselves and grew in tiny patches on the tortured ground. A few leaves burst out of splintered willows. Blue and white cornflowers, blood-red poppies and yellow cabbage flowers sprang from the lips of decaying trenches in sickening profusion among the rusty wire. Birds soared in the sky and insects scurried in the dust—while on a plane between the two, man crouched behind sandbagged parapets, bent on his own destruction.

In mid-1916 the war had deteriorated into an endurance match in which the side to crack first would lose. The Canadians, nurtured in a hard climate, endured the horrors of trench life philosophically. In the south, the French, too, endured, but it was an ordeal that stretched them beyond the bearable limit and led, almost directly, to the mutinies of 1917.

SEVEN.
1916: THE ARTILLERY-DOMINATED
BATTLES OF ATTRITION

The initiative in 1916, as in 1914, once again rested with the Germans. The Chief of Staff, von Falkenhayn, at the beginning of the year determined to take the offensive on the Western Front. The Russians, though still in the field, had been badly weakened; Italy had been easily held. Only France and Britain were serious adversaries and, of these, France had suffered more through her 1915 offensives than she had gained. Germany, then, von Falkenhayn reasoned, must seek a decision in the west. Only thus could the war be ended.

He saw Britain as the more tenacious opponent, but the northern trench lines did not lend themselves to a major blow. In any case, Britain would survive a disaster in Flanders. The remaining alternative, then, was to strike at Britain through France for, with France prostrate, "England's best sword" would have been "knocked out of her hand."[1] A break-through in mass was not considered necessary; to "bleed France to death" would be sufficient and to do this a spot must be chosen that the French could not give up. Such a place was the fortress area of Verdun, the legendary key to the defence of France, which Falkenhayn with remorseless logic counted on being defended to the last. The French would, he confidently assumed, throw in every man they had to hold Verdun and in that area they would be drawn into a killing-ground of German artillery.

Verdun was to become an anvil upon which French military manhood was to be hammered to death by German cannon. The French were to be fastened to fixed positions by sentiment, and battered to pieces there by artillery.[2]

Joffre and Haig also had optimistic plans for 1916. In January Britain adopted conscription but it was recognized that time must be allowed for training the new troops. An offensive was timed for June astride the Somme. It would be a Franco-British operation on a front of fifty miles, and meanwhile the build-up of troops, heavy artillery and munitions would be started. In the event, however, German initiative dislocated the Allied scheme.

The Verdun battle opened on 21 February, 1916, and the German offensive continued for seven months. A French counter-offensive followed, which extended the fighting until 15 December, a duration record even by the "impossible" standards of the First World War. In the old days decisive battles were fought in hours. This one, in which early German gains were finally wiped out by the French, was inde-cisive; it merely demonstrated that a state of balance existed between the Central Powers and the Allies in terms of industrial resources.

Falkenhayn's concept was proved correct. Verdun was indeed a symbol that the French would not relinquish. But to the Germans the fortress became a symbol, too, which *had* to be captured; thus both became imprisoned in its horror.

The French front collapsed under the impact of more than three thousand guns. Falkenhayn had seen enough of the failure of Allied mass attacks not to imitate their methods. Only small probing parties would go forward after the annihilating barrage to report on the next line of resistance; this would then become the target for renewed artillery bombardment. Pétain was rushed to the scene and took command on 25 February. Reinforcements and two thousand French guns poured in. The battle dragged on for week after week of vast artillery duels. But inevitably the infantry on both sides were drawn into the mutually destroying process of attack and counter-attack. By June, two-thirds of the French Army (66 divisions out of a hundred) had passed through the "furnace" of Verdun, and yet by the end of the month the Germans had amalgamated enough miniscule amounts of ground to be almost in possession of the fortress.

Outside events then made their influence felt. On 4 June Russia, crippled but not defeated, loyally attacked to take the pressure off France as she had done briefly and unsuccessfully in March. This time the offensive continued throughout June and was resumed in August. It carried the Russians to the Carpathians, the last barrier to the Hungarian plain. There the Germans stemmed it. Russian success, however, compelled Falkenhayn to detach troops from the Western Front; it forced the Austrians to abandon an offensive against the Italians; it encouraged Roumania to enter the war on the Allied side and that led to the dismissal of Falkenhayn. But all this had been wrought at a heavy price. Russia never again played a significant part in the war; the sequel was revolution and collapse in 1917.

On 24 June the preparatory bombardment for Haig's relief offensive on the Somme began. A day later Falkenhayn stopped the flow of divisions and munitions to Verdun; and in the autumn the French wrested from the Germans the ground that they had won.

Verdun was the bloodiest battlefield in French history. Even today
. . . nothing useful will grow. The earth has been too badly infected
by the shellfire, and the ground is covered only by an ugly metallic-
green weed. The visitor to Verdun can see a concrete shed which
covers the "Trench of Bayonets" where the earth caved in on a unit of
the 137th Infantry Regiment, burying the men alive and leaving only
the bayonets on their rifles protruding above this mass grave. The
visitor can look out at the desolate battlefield from which, until 1932,
ten cartloads of bones were collected each day. And he can visit the
huge, ugly mortuary of Douaumont which is built over the skeletons
of thousands of unknown bodies collected from the surrounding fields.[3]

There were 460,000 French casualties at Verdun; but the Germans
themselves, whose spirit had "declined to a marked degree," lost
300,000 men.[4]

While these momentous events were taking place, the Canadian-held
sector of the Ypres Salient had been the target of a limited German
offensive during which, for the first time, the 3rd Division saw action.
The battle of Mount Sorrel began with a German attack on 2 June,
1916, in an attempt to delay preparations for the Somme offensive,
which the enemy well knew to be impending.

The Canadians held a roughly semi-circular line some two and a half
miles long from Hill 60 on the right, including Mount Sorrel, Hill 61,
Hill 62, through Sanctuary Wood, across an open valley known as
"the Gap," to the village of Hooge on the left. Behind them, between
the front line and Ypres, was the ruined village of Zillebeke and its
triangular reed-fringed lake. The summit of Hill 60, which completely
dominated the other features and the Flanders plain, was in enemy
hands giving him observation over Canadian movements throughout
the area. The 3rd Division, at the beginning of June, held the Canadian
line.

On 1 June an intermittent enemy bombardment, which lasted all
day, died at nightfall only to start up again early on the 2nd with
redoubled fury. A four-hour eruption of black shrapnel bursts and
sulphurous spouts of earth told of the agony of the 3rd Division. Its
commander, General Mercer (who had gone forward), died that morning; shellfire burst his eardrums, a bullet broke his leg and then, dazed
and crippled on the ground, a burst of shrapnel killed him. Brigadier-
General V. A. S. Williams, formerly Adjutant-General and later Camp
Commandant at Valcartier, was wounded and captured, the senior
Canadian prisoner of the war. The Mounted Rifles were literally
blown out of their trenches—a German eye-witness spoke of human
bodies and even trees hurled into the air—so that when the German
infantry went forward there was little opposition. By 2 P.M. the enemy
had captured Mount Sorrel, Hills 61 and 62, and had penetrated to a

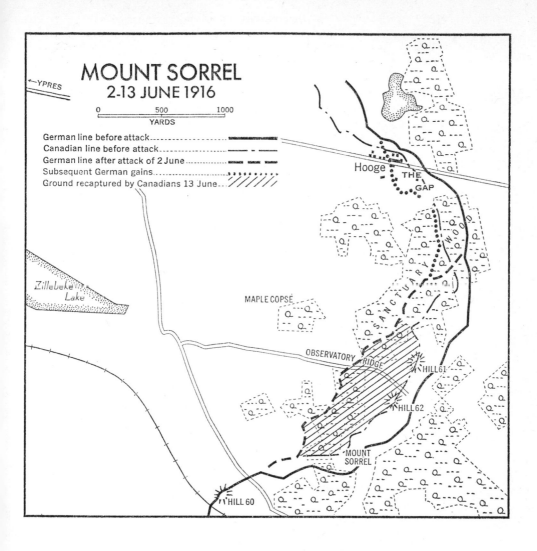

MOUNT SORREL
2-13 JUNE 1916

←YPRES

0   500   1000
YARDS

German line before attack
Canadian line before attack
German line after attack of 2 June
Subsequent German gains
Ground recaptured by Canadians 13 June

Zillebeke Lake

Hooge

THE GAP

SANCTUARY WOOD

MAPLE COPSE

OBSERVATORY RIDGE

HILL 61

HILL 62

MOUNT SORREL

HILL 60

depth of 1,200 yards. On the left, Hooge still held firm. Canadian reserves marched grimly toward the holocaust up forward and sealed off the German penetration after stubborn fighting.

Byng ordered a counter-attack for dawn on the 3rd, entrusting the task to the 1st Division. Currie suggested forming a defensive line from the support positions still in Canadian hands and attacking through it. His attack would thus be a prepared counter-attack from a firm base, but he was overruled. Time was pressing. As it was, the impromptu assault using Lipsett on Mount Sorrel and Tuxford on Hills 61 and 62 did not get off until full daylight. Both brigades failed.

The enemy made the next move on the 6th. He exploded four mines directly under the front line at Hooge, which he then occupied without much difficulty. But as the support trenches held firm further back he had merely gained a few yards; the forward trenches were left in his possession.

Byng was still determined on ousting the enemy from the high ground and once again he nominated Currie. On the 8th the 1st Division withdrew to rest and prepare; the 2nd Division replaced the badly shattered 3rd in the line. Behind the lines Currie drew up a thorough plan. The attacking battalions carefully rehearsed their co-ordinated roles; strong artillery support was arranged for; and every day reconnaissance parties reported on the enemy defences for comparison with aerial photographs of his trenches. Currie then reassured the battalions that were to attack in terms that foreshadow his later creed—to pay the price of victory in shells and not in the lives of men:

Tell the officers and men that we intend that the artillery will knock the fight out of the enemy. Our chief work is to consolidate quickly and hold on. We have plenty of artillery and ammunition. We will give them over 50,000 rounds from 18-pounder to 12-inch, and most of it is big stuff.[5]

Lipsett's brigade would again attack the Mount Sorrel position, and Tuxford's the two hills. The two commanders had been over the ground during the abortive attack on the 3rd; furthermore they were used to working together since their battalions had stood side by side at Ypres. Garnet Hughes' 1st Brigade was in reserve.

At 1.30 A.M. on the night 12-13 June, after a vicious bombardment three-quarters of an hour long, the attacking troops jumped off from prepared positions. It was pitch black with wind and rain, but even so smoke-shells were fired to conceal the discharge of weapons from enemy machine-gunners on Hill 60. The assault was almost too easy. After an hour all the objectives were in Canadian hands, and the troops consolidated on what was thought to be the old forward line. What had once been a system of trenches had been completely obliterated by Currie's promised artillery support—218 pieces in all, drawn from Canadian, British, Indian and South African sources.

The first "set-piece" attack to be delivered in force by the Canadian Corps had been successful. The Corps had by its own efforts, apart from artillery, restored the situation. And though enemy artillery lashed the Canadian positions savagely as a prelude to the inevitable counter-attack, the line remained firm and continued to do so throughout the summer. Corps' losses during the twelve-day battle, mostly suffered by the 3rd Division, numbered 9,600 as against 5,765 German casualties.

There were two important consequences: Lipsett was promoted major-general and appointed to the 3rd Division; and the Ross rifle was finally withdrawn. Despite the Minister's uncompromising defence of the weapon, and despite orders forbidding Canadian troops to arm themselves with Lee-Enfield rifles, complaints persisted and men often picked up the British weapon with the concurrence of their officers. The Prime Minister, as we have seen, determined to leave the matter to the judgment of Sir Douglas Haig who, a week after Mount Sorrel, firmly recommended that the Lee-Enfield should be issued to all the divisions of the Canadian Corps. On 16 August the 2nd and 3rd Divisions were re-armed with the Lee-Enfield; a few Ross rifles only were retained for snipers. A month later the newly arrived 4th Division exchanged its rifles for the British weapon in France. During March, 1917, the factory of the Ross Rifle Company was expropriated and the Canadian Government relied on British supplies thereafter. In October Sir Charles Ross relinquished his appointment as Consulting Officer, Small Arms, Ammunition and Ballistics, and with it the temporary rank of colonel. His factory was dismantled in March, 1918.*[6]

To the south, the great gamble of the Somme began on 1 July. The original conception, based on the French shouldering the major burden, had come to a bad end with Verdun. In the event, the British attacked with Rawlinson's Fourth Army (nineteen divisions plus two in Army reserve) on a front of eighteen miles while the French employed six divisions with two in reserve on a six-mile front. The main purposes of the offensive were to relieve pressure on the French at Verdun; to inflict as heavy losses as possible on the Germans; and to aid the Allies on other fronts by preventing the transfer of German divisions from the west. To these must be added Haig's hope for a break-through. To exploit the expected breach he concentrated five cavalry divisions

---

*After the war, General A. G. L. McNaughton, then DCGS, ordered all Ross rifles in Canada to be repaired and overhauled. This was done at the rate of about 5,000 a year for several years with the single exception of the Mark II, which was subject to blow-back if the bolt was incorrectly placed.

During the Second World War, after Dunkirk, McNaughton, who commanded the Canadian troops in England, cabled for these reconditioned weapons, which were sent by fast passenger ship. They were used to arm the Home Guard in the Canadian area for whom no weapons were available. Under *clean conditions* the rifles proved useful.

in GHQ reserve—and this twelve years after Sir Ian Hamilton, a British observer in the Russo-Japanese War, had reported that the "only thing that the cavalry could do in the face of entrenched machine-guns was to cook rice for the infantry."[7]

South of the Somme, the French sector was flat, but in the north where the British were to fight the countryside was open rolling chalkland, sprinkled with villages and woods. The main feature was a ridge stretching from Ginchy to Thiepval—the watershed between the Somme and its tributary, the Ancre—known as the Pozières Ridge, from the village of that name near the highest point. From that ridge the Germans looked down with a sense of domination at the blatant preparations that the British made. They felt confident; their enemy would be attacking uphill. The ground was not of Haig's choosing. It had been insisted upon by Joffre as the only sector where the French could mount a joint attack.

There could be no surprise. In any case, a seven-day preliminary bombardment gave the plan away. The enemy knew that this was leading up to an infantry assault. The Germans, secure in deep dug-outs, gripped their rifles and adjusted the belts of hand grenades strapped round them, waiting for the storm of shells to lift from the front defences onto those in the rear. At that moment, it would be vital to be out of the dug-outs and in position to repel the British.

Through trench periscopes installed at the dug-out entrances, a close watch was kept on the British parapets. At 7:30 on the morning of 1 July, a cloudless summer morning, the hurricane bombardment suddenly died and a line of steel helmets appeared like toadstools in the British trenches. The Germans knew that the moment had come. Gasping with exertion, they rapidly clambered up the shafts of the steep dug-outs and emerged into daylight, dragging machine-guns and heavy ammunition boxes behind them. The firing line was quickly formed.

Waves of British infantry with bayonets fixed had already started to cross No-Man's-Land in steady lines—on the Loos pattern, but this time as many as eight waves preceded by a few hardy grenade throwers. The pace was almost leisurely and it seemed to the waiting enemy that they believed that no resistance could have survived the long, crushing bombardment. In fact, they were weighted down with grenades, ammunition, rations, picks and shovels, even with rolls of barbed wire, so that the most they could manage was a steady walk. A light "battle-order" had not yet occurred to British generals.

In the German trenches machine-gunners adjusted their weapons for the best field of fire. Fingers tautened on the well-oiled triggers. Then, with the leading British infantry a hundred yards away, came the tensely awaited incisive command to fire, and the guns burst into life;

rifle flashes whipped out in ragged fury all across the front. Red rockets soared into the blue morning sky to signal the artillery to join the feast, and almost immediately afterwards a deluge of shells tore into the packed British ranks.

Men, it is said, laugh when they attack. A first trepidation when the warning is received gives way to listlessness and resignation. Then the moment comes. They screw up their courage. Once over the top, smelling "the mingled odour of blood, iodine, cordite, burnt flares, powder and recently upheaved earth, the spirit of the thing seized one and in the relief at being alive and doing something, most men laughed." [8]

On the first day of the Somme that laughter, if indeed they laughed, turned to cries and groans as bullets struck home and limbs were torn away. Arms reached out in agony; men collapsed in death; or badly wounded, rolled and twitched on the spouting ground. Others, less severely injured, dragged themselves into shell holes seeking shelter. The uninjured, remorseless as dripping water, closed ranks and stumbled on to close with the enemy. The Germans, now wildly excited at these close quarters, stood up regardless of safety and threw grenades at the smoke-blackened tattered remnants of the mass attack. Mills grenades came hurtling back followed by desperate bayonet rushes: a *mêlée* of hoarse shouts, bursting grenades, groans and the screams of death, while over all the din of the artillery continued. Wave after wave of infantry surged into the rock-like German defences and carried them; or were forced to recede time after time over ground littered with the piling dead.

Full success was gained only on the right where the village of Montauban, half a mile inside the German defences, was captured. In the centre, and on the left, it was a tale of partial success or of failure. The Newfoundland Regiment, in action for the first time since Gallipoli, attacked on the left against Beaumont Hamel where it suffered some seven hundred casualties; the objective was not taken.

Night at last brought relief from the horrors of that broiling summer's day. British casualties amounted to 57,470—the heaviest toll for a day's fighting in all that nation's history. These were the finest and bravest in the country, volunteers for the most part of the Territorial and Kitchener's new armies. Kitchener had increased the strength of the British Army from the six divisions comprising the old Expeditionary Force to seventy well-trained divisions in the spring of 1916. He himself, lost at sea on 5 June, 1916, while bound for Russia, was at least spared from knowing that the young men he had largely raised and trained had been thrown away in outmoded tactical formations on a single day in Picardy. Yet the British Army carried on the struggle at the Somme for another five months. Its courage remained unshaken, its morale unbroken.

The French, south of the Somme, captured all their objectives on 1 July through their use of more flexible tactics, which exposed fewer men to fire, and a heavier artillery concentration. It is also true that the German defences on this front were less strong, and that the French were opposed by fewer of the enemy. Six French divisions encountered only one German division plus a regiment. Nevertheless, the French alone could report a victory.

The Somme fighting continued in the form of exploiting success by attacks on the right, where the greatest penetration had been made. News of it reached the Canadians in the salient through Corps intelligence summaries and the daily press. The impression given was that of a titanic struggle, of the commitment of vast forces and artillery, of ammunition expended on an unprecedented and prodigal scale. Optimistic headings such as "The Big Drive" and "The Break-through" seemed justified as accounts naming certain villages gave way to reports mentioning others further forward; the whole line seemed to be steadily advancing. Then, in the middle of August, the Corps left the salient for training near St. Omer with no regret. It was warm and sunny and relatively peaceful "but the soft breezes wafted over Hill 60 carried a distillation of nauseating stenches from the decomposed bodies littering No-Man's-Land, and myriads of disease-laden blow-flies which had hatched in them."[9]

In the fresh Channel air, on rolling ground similar to that at the Somme, optimism mounted higher still through the type of training given. Manoeuvres taught the attack on *distant* objectives. There would be no more staring at the same parapets, ditches and blasted willows for days on end; an exhilarating war of movement, it seemed, might well be in sight.

In August, Sir Sam Hughes, on one of his periodic visits, addressed the Corps. The 4th Division had already arrived in France, and he was raising a fifth. When that division reached France, it was his hope that Canada would have two army corps, as did the Australians. The present Corps, he said, would be at the Somme in a matter of days.

At the end of the month the Corps reached the ruined city of Albert from the neighbourhood of which Haig's July offensive had been mounted. They saw the ruined church with its celebrated "Leaning Virgin" displaced by gunfire. When that precariously balanced statue toppled, it was said, the war would be lost by the side holding Albert at the time. As a precaution, for superstitions flourished under First World War conditions, the 3rd Canadian Field Company braced the leaning figure with heavy steel cable.

South Africans, Australians, New Zealanders, Newfoundlanders, Indians and British Tommies crowded the narrow, tortuous streets of Albert. There were ammunition dumps, engineering dumps, gasoline dumps, artillery parks, ordnance depots, horse lines and what seemed like miles of troughs. Up forward the ground climbed in barren shell-pocked ridges under a sky dotted with scores of observation balloons that roughly marked the winding battle line. The thunder of artillery could be plainly heard.

The Canadians marched along the Albert-Bapaume road into Sausage Valley with its lines of guns. Never had such support been dreamed of; piece after piece, the artillery seemed to stretch interminably, almost wheel to wheel. As the men climbed the ridge on the other side they could see rolling folds of ground east of the Ancre; there was a lift and a spaciousness to this battlefield very different from Flanders and its cramped trenches. Exhilarated by country that reminded them of home, the troops were almost cheerful as they followed Australian guides through the blurred outline of what had once been Pozières village, captured by the Australians on 4 August. And what had this entailed? "We have just come out of a place so terrible" wrote an Australian officer, "that . . . a raving lunatic could never imagine the horror of the last thirteen days."[10] The front line, just beyond the crest of Pozières Ridge, overlooked for miles the surrounding countryside with its hills, hamlets and church steeples. Even here, the roar of artillery reverberated among the hills, shells shrieked piercingly overhead, and there was an intermittent crackle of small-arms fire.

The Canadian Corps took over the line in this sector from the 1st ANZAC (Australian and New Zealand Army Corps) on 3 September, with Currie's division first into the line. The division went into action in the Somme area for the first time on 9 September, when the last section of the Pozières Ridge still held by the enemy was captured "with a precision that left nothing to be desired."[11] On the 11th and 12th the 1st Division was relieved in the line by the 2nd and 3rd Divisions and went back to rest west of Albert. With the whole of the ridge in Allied hands, preparations began for a further great offensive.

Sir Henry Rawlinson, commanding the Fourth British Army of which the Canadian Corps formed a part, recorded in his diary that Haig was anxious to "have a gamble with all available troops about September 15, with the object of breaking down German resistance and getting through to Bapaume."[12] His original break-through plan had failed; after that he professed faith in attrition. He had now recovered from the shock of 1 July sufficiently to gamble once again. And after that, inevitably, it would be more attrition.

In his hands Haig held the key to the western deadlock, had he used it properly. An armoured machine, impervious to bullets and able to cross barbed wire, had by now been developed. Forty-nine of these tanks out of the 150 built were already in France. Here were machines capable of being used in mass formation to restore the battle-winning talisman—surprise—to a moribund sector of the Western Front. Such a sector was not the Somme, which had been filled with roaring violence for more than two months, tearing up and ravaging the ground; there the Germans had concentrated artillery and reinforced since the offensive had begun, and their defences had grown steadily stronger. Nor did Haig wait until more tanks had been delivered. Instead he decided to commit tanks for the first time in penny packets on 15 September; to redeem, if he could, his dwindling prospects in the Somme offensive.

The battle that began at 6:20 on 15 September, a fine autumn day, has been styled the Battle of Flers-Courcelette. The advance was to be pushed on the easterly slopes of the ridge on a ten-mile front from Combles to Thiepval. Rawlinson's Fourth Army would deliver the main attack, its objectives the villages of Flers, Morval, Lesboeufs, and Gueudecourt. Sir Hubert Gough's Reserve Army (soon to be the Fifth Army) had the task of protecting the left flank, and planned to use the Canadian Corps to secure points of observation near Courcelette. The heavy artillery had been concentrated to provide a gun to every twenty-nine yards and an innovation was the method of fire. About half the guns would fire a "creeping" barrage (whereby the barrage crept forward in front of the infantry a certain number of yards every minute), and the rest standing barrages on fixed targets. Another novelty in the Fourth Army's assault was the introduction for the first time of an advance by limited bounds about a thousand yards apart to a series of successive objectives.

Then there were the tanks. Of 49 available, 42 went to the Fourth Army to be parcelled out to attacking divisions. The seven placed at the disposal of the Reserve Army were given to the Canadian Corps for use by the 2nd Division against a point of observation and an outer bastion of the Courcelette and Martinpuich defences known as the Sugar Factory.

That day, according to German sources, the defence was "as good as completely broken,"[13] but reinforcements bolstered up the front and held the British back. Nevertheless, the attackers seized a belt of ground a mile and a half deep along six miles of the front with a penetration of almost two miles at the centre. Four tanks had reached Flers and one had passed through the village accompanied by cheering men. Flers had been taken, as was Courcelette later in the day. It was an exhilarating victory in marked contrast to the days that followed.

The Canadians, an hour after the attack went in, had seized the Sugar Factory. In this they were undoubtedly assisted by the artillery, which had crushed the opposition in the front-line trenches, and by the tanks. Though tanks fared badly in the heavily cratered ground, one lumbered onto the objective, and its presence induced many Germans to surrender. One hundred and fifty Germans gave themselves up at the Factory.

The 2nd Division, having fulfilled its task with such early and surprising completeness, mounted an impromptu attack against Courcelette itself; meanwhile, on the left, the 3rd Division would push on to take the German trench system known as Fabeck Trench.

The 2nd, with no time for reconnaissance and with no jumping-off place in the nature of trenches, plunged on to the objective over open shell-swept ground. Two battalions cleared the village with the bayonet: the 22nd Battalion of French Canadians on the right and the 25th of Nova Scotians on the left. The Germans counter-attacked fanatically; the 22nd beat off no less than seven attacks that night, and the 25th four. Even the Germans in the village, ensconced in cellars and dug-outs, resisted desperately; mopping-up took all next day, and in the end a thousand prisoners were taken. "If hell is as bad as what I have seen at Courcelette," the commander of the 22nd Battalion wrote in his diary, "I would not wish my worst enemy to go there."[14]

The 3rd Division's attack took them into Fabeck Trench, portions of which they retained. The Patricia's on the right linked up with Canadian troops in Courcelette, while on the left the 4th C.M.R. established two blocks in the trenches to secure the flank. They, too, were subjected to counter-attacks delivered from north and east of Courcelette but beat them off. On the following day the central part of the trench, and thus the whole trench line, was cleared and another sixty Germans surrendered.

Thereafter the Battle of Flers-Courcelette bogged down. Gains were small against stiffening resistance until the battle ended on 22 September. The week's fighting had cost the Canadians 7,230 casualties, but casualties are more easily accepted where there has been some success. The troops, having met the Germans in hand-to-hand fighting and taken the objective and having thrown them back from it time after time, knew themselves to be superior. That knowledge was to sustain them in the battles still to come.

Very few tanks reached the objective at Flers-Courcelette and the enemy was misled as to their potentialities. But the part they played had impressed Haig. They had redeemed "in a limited degree the ill-success of the Somme offensive."[15] He ordered a thousand from the Ministry of Munitions, which were to vindicate themselves at Cambrai in 1917 and eventually led to Allied triumph in the last year of the war. The Germans did not copy the tank until 1918, when they produced a clumsy model with a clumsy name—*Panzerwagenmitraupengetriebe*.

Fighting at the Somme continued for two more months. The Canadian objective for the whole of that period was the German defensive line beyond Courcelette: Regina Trench. It was a solid slogging match

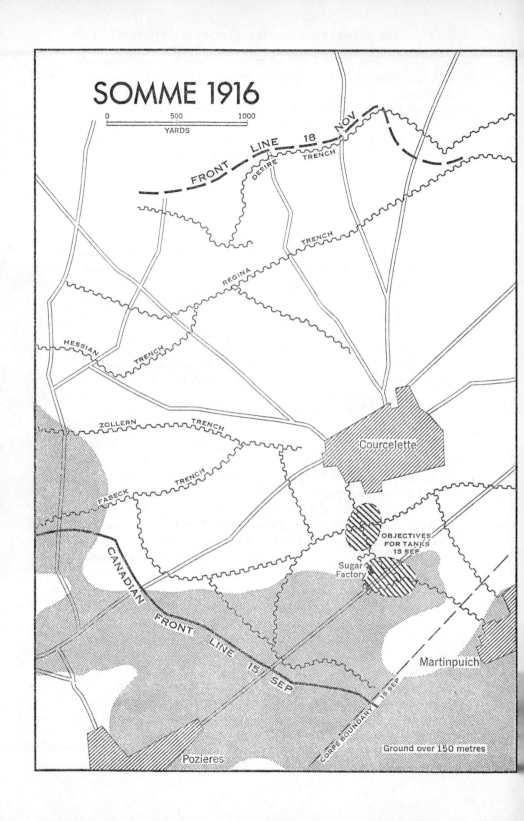

SOMME 1916

0 ____ 500 ____ 1000
YARDS

FRONT LINE 18 NOV

DESIRE TRENCH

TRENCH

REGINA TRENCH

HESSIAN TRENCH

ZOLLERN TRENCH

TRENCH

FABECK

Courcelette

OBJECTIVES
FOR TANKS
15 SEP

Sugar
Factory

CANADIAN FRONT LINE 15 SEP

Martinpuich

CORPS BOUNDARY 15 SEP

Ground over 150 metres

Pozieres

without any of the interest of 15 September, a tale of trifling gains and mounting losses without tactical significance; but in the end the new 4th Division, fighting for the first time, took Regina Trench.

The first attack on Regina Trench, by the 1st and 2nd Divisions, took place on 26 September, which advanced the line to within striking distance of the trench. Renewed on 1 October by the 2nd and 3rd Divisions, the line crept a little closer. A further attack on the 8th by the 1st and 3rd Divisions brought the Canadians closer still. The Army Commander, Gough, was not satisfied with the results of that attack. The trench had not been taken and the two divisions had incurred 1,364 casualties. Currie conducted an investigation and the results are on file.[16] The wire had not been cut by artillery fire though there is evidence that Currie had done his best to ensure that this was done. Major Brooke,* a British artillery staff officer at Corps Headquarters, had visited Divisional Headquarters before the attack at Currie's request. He recorded that after a conference Currie took him aside and said: "Brooke, I want you to realize how much depends on the guns; my boys haven't got the kick in them which they had; I look to the guns to put them into Regina Trench."[17]

After the assault Currie personally interviewed officers and at least three men in every company of the attacking battalions. He found that one battalion had not rehearsed as ordered. Objectives had been vague and ill-defined. It was not common sense to point to a map and order men to take point D 26 b 7.7; they should have been told how to locate that point—physically—on the ground. Yet the attack had been pressed home despite heavy enemy fire and intact barbed wire. The soldiers did not give up as long as ammunition and grenades held out, and even then they used their rifles as clubs.

Here, said Currie, was the heart of the problem. Though it was always possible for some men to get into the enemy trenches, these men could not hold out unless grenades and ammunition reached them; and for that communication trenches, which could only be dug at night, were necessary. The timing of most attacks, therefore, was wrong. Instead of jumping off at first light, attacks should begin much later in the day so that night would conceal the bringing up of reinforcements and supplies. Currie found no excuse for a battalion not having rehearsed its task; objectives, too, should have been properly defined. But if all that had been done, the wire would still have been uncut and ammunition and grenades would have run out just as soon. It is perhaps significant that no later Corps attack when planned by Currie was ever unsuccessful.

Following the attack of 8 October, the Canadian Corps was withdrawn from the Somme area to take over part of the Vimy front.

*Later Field-Marshal The Viscount Alanbrooke, a Chief of the Imperial General Staff in the Second World War.

Finally, the 4th Division, which reached the Somme on 10 October under its commander Major-General David Watson, took Regina Trench on 11 November and the support trenches behind it seven days later. The Canadians suffered almost twenty-five thousand casualties at the Somme, and about two-thirds of these were incurred in the desperate struggle for Regina Trench. That defensive line, commented the Canadian official historian, which "had cost so much blood, was no longer a position of strength. Repeated bombardments had reduced it to a mere depression in the chalk, in many places blown twenty feet wide, and for long stretches almost filled with debris and dead bodies."[18]

The attack of 18 November marked the limit of the 1916 advance. The Somme offensive ended, and on 28 November the 4th Division rejoined the Corps on the Lens-Arras front to take part in preparations for the attack on Vimy Ridge.

The seven weeks spent on the Somme by the 4th Division had been a nightmare of the foulest sort. The inexperienced troops were suddenly pitchforked into the obscenities of modern war in a battle of attrition against the strongest defences. They were pitted against German troops whose orders were explicit: any officer who gave up an inch of trench would be court-martialed; and any sector of lost trench must be counter-attacked immediately. Added to that, from October on, the weather had broken, turning the battleground into a morass.

Sad river mists filled the valleys, spangling khaki with cold raw dew. On the exposed ridges drizzling rain turned the grey-white chalk to treacherous slime. The low sun hardly shone through the gloomy skies. The rain persisted and the mud deepened to a mortar-like consistency that filled the trenches and oozed down dug-out entrances. Shell holes and craters became small lakes of grey "cement" or were turned brown by rust and blood. Bodies in strange attitudes and useless gear lay in pathetic bundles on the stripped and wasted ground.

Over that ground the men attacked "loaded with more cold iron than a gaol would give a murderer."[19] Shells snouted up the greyish mud in showers or skidded sickeningly on the limb-strewn ground. Soldiers sobbed with frustration as they tore themselves out of the muck and floundered forward. Some blundered shoulder deep into shell holes and were left screaming to their fate. And never before, except at Verdun, had so many shells saturated any battlefield.

Only the best of men in such conditions could go in and win. The 4th Division did that at the Somme.

In all, 125 square miles of "lunar" landscape had been wrested from the enemy. Verdun had certainly been relieved; the Germans had been held for the most part on the Western Front; and the enemy's strength had been worn down. German casualties had amounted to between 660,000 and 680,000 against 419,654 British Empire and 204,253

French—an Allied total of 623,907.[20] Nevertheless, the words of Lloyd George trouble the mind in any reflection of Haig's conduct of the Somme offensive:

No amount of circumspection can prevent war leading to the death of multitudes of brave men, but now that Generals are not partaking in the personal hazards of a fight, they ought to take greater personal risks in satisfying themselves as to the feasibility of their plans and as to whether the objectives they wish to attain are worth the sacrifice entailed, and whether there is no better way of achieving the same result at less cost of gallant lives.[21]

And the Australian official history asks pointed questions: "Was this great effort of our countrymen—so pregnant with trouble for our nation—directed by prudent and capable generalship? Was it guided along lines likely to render a return for which it was worth incurring these crushing casualties?"[22]

Falkenhayn's lack of success at Verdun and at the Somme—Roumania's entry into the war was given as the official reason—had led to his dismissal on 29 August, 1916. His successors, Hindenburg and his co-commander Ludendorff, shared Falkenhayn's opinion that a decision must be reached in the west, but they were not prepared to undergo another *Blutbad* at the Somme even though that had been a blood bath for the Allies, too. One of their first acts was to start the construction of a strong position further back, the Hindenburg Line, a shorter and straighter line that would be more defensible with fewer troops. Rather than await a second battering in the spring of 1917, they relinquished ground and withdrew to the Hindenburg Line.

Joffre, whose "strategy" had brought 1,300,000 casualties to France by December, 1916, and who had foreseen no danger at Verdun, had lost the confidence of the nation. In mid-December he was promoted Marshal and "retired" as Commander-in-Chief. His successor was Robert Nivelle, who had replaced Pétain at Verdun and conducted the successful French counter-offensive in the fall, and who now promised certain victory.

Haig alone remained, secure in his position as Commander-in-Chief of the British armies. Early in 1917 the King promoted him to Field Marshal "as a New Year's gift from myself and the country."[23]

EIGHT.
IN ENGLAND AND IN CANADA: AN INTERLUDE BEHIND THE SCENES

For the first two years of the war, while Canadian soldiers trained, fought, suffered and endured, events were taking place in England that resembled a perpetual game of musical chairs. The players scrambled for position and authority, constantly reacting to distant music in the form of peremptory and almost unintelligible cables from Canada or to louder passages intermittently pounded out on frequent visits to England by General Hughes.

The participants in this frivolity were the mature officers and aging veterans of senior rank who had been sent from Canada to administer the overseas troops in one capacity or another. One was Colonel J. W. Carson, the Minister's special representative; another was Brigadier-General J. C. MacDougall, Officer Commanding Canadian Troops in Great Britain; and the third was Major-General S. B. Steele, who commanded the Second Contingent before it crossed to France as the 2nd Division. Other performers, circling around the fringe and occasionally joining in, were Sir Max Aitken, "the Canadian Eyewitness" and future Lord Beaverbrook, and Brigadier-General Lord Brooke who commanded the Canadian Training Camp at Bramshott.

Of all the contestants for the major prize—the favour of Hughes and the power it brought—Carson had a head start over all the others. He arrived in England first. From his post at the White Hart Hotel in Salisbury, he kept a close eye on the conditions of wet and mud and on the exchange of Canadian equipment in the camps on Salisbury Plain. In the middle of December he returned to Canada and submitted reports concerning both these matters to the Prime Minister who was deeply struck by Carson's firm opinions. He directed that Hughes should give the Colonel definite status, something more than the vague terms of reference under which he had originally been despatched. Carson himself proposed that he be appointed Assistant High Commissioner under Perley[1] but Borden preferred the formula, which was finally incorporated in the Order in Council, appointing him to "represent the Militia Department" and to act "as the agent of the

Minister of Militia in maintaining the depots of articles of equipment and other supplies for the upkeep and subsistence of the Canadian Expeditionary Force . . ." This generous mandate did not satisfy Carson: he begged the Prime Minister to inform Alderson, Perley and the War Office that he, the Minister's representative, would be available for consultation on any subject about which they might seek advice.[2] In Borden's opinion the Order in Council went far enough.[3]

Back in England at the beginning of February, Carson found the 1st Division moving to France. Thereafter the Canadian military authorities in the United Kingdom would have three main tasks: to train and dispatch reinforcements; to organize and train new formations; and to rehabilitate casualties. The command of the Canadians left in England, other than cavalry, was vested in Colonel J. C. MacDougall, a permanent force officer who had crossed with the First Contingent, and who was now promoted brigadier-general. Carson, however, continued to regard himself as representing the Minister without any limitation imposed by the Order in Council; he assumed just as much military authority in England as Hughes (who had ignored the Militia Council in Ottawa for years) did in Canada. Thus, when a British inquiry whether any officer had been empowered to return incompetent officers to Canada reached Carson, he at once claimed that he alone could do so. "I am the only officer now serving in the country who would have that power," he replied, "and I would not hesitate to act if the necessity were unfortunately to arise."[4] He then set about actually obtaining from Sam the powers he had just claimed: ". . . cases of undesirable officers are bound to arise and there is no authority now in England capable of dealing with them,"[5] and he went still further. "Would it not be wise," he suggested, "for you to consider the appointment of a Senior Canadian Officer who would carry a rank not below that of Major-General, and put him in supreme central command of *all* the Canadian Troops who might be at any time in England . . . ?"[6] He left no doubt as to who that senior officer should be. "I find myself in the embarrassing position of having unending requests made on me for information and advice and even instructions, and as your Representative here, I am supposed to be able to fill all three functions but naturally I have no authority to give on these matters, and can only advise, which I am always willing to do."[7] In these schemes, Carson encountered little opposition from MacDougall; that officer was quite willing to use Carson as a channel to the Minister.

Hughes did not, however, follow Carson's suggestion. He replied a month later to the effect that MacDougall was in military command of all Canadian units in Britain except the cavalry, and that Carson would continue, as authorized by the Order in Council, to represent the Minister.[8] Even then, with his office now in the luxurious Savoy Hotel in London, Carson continued to regard himself as the Minister's representative in every military province, notwithstanding the restrictions imposed by the Order in Council, by Borden and now by Hughes. It would appear that neither Hughes nor MacDougall tried to curb him; both conducted correspondence through his office.

The arrival of Major-General Sam Steele, commanding the Second Contingent, complicated matters for both Carson and MacDougall. Steele had served in the Militia since 1868, had taken part in the Red River Expedition, had commanded Strathcona's Horse in South Africa, and was a founding member of the North West Mounted Police. Though an eminent and experienced officer, Steele at sixty-six was deemed by the War Office too old to command a division in France; thus, when the 2nd Division was formed from the Second Contingent, Steele would remain in England and, though Carson managed to get himself promoted brigadier-general in May, Steele was still senior to both Carson and MacDougall.

Carson took good care to cultivate friendly relations with such a high-ranking and well-known officer. A tactful welcoming letter greeted Steele, announcing that Carson, as "the representative in England of the Honourable the Minister of Militia and Defence and the Department of Militia and Defence," was very much at his service and disposal, as he also was to the division "which you so ably and effectively command."[9] Carson arranged an interview for Steele with Kitchener, and conducted the arrangements whereby MacDougall and Steele would have separate commands within the Shorncliffe area, part of the British Eastern Command where the Canadians were now encamped; one would command the Training Division and the other the 2nd Division before it crossed to France.

On 3 July, the Minister arrived in England. He promptly ruled that Steele would command the Southeastern District "including all Canadians in England."[10] MacDougall, however, would retain the Training Division and his rank of brigadier-general. A month later Steele took over the Shorncliffe District, and a fortnight after that Turner arrived from France to take over the 2nd Division. It would seem plain, therefore, that Steele had replaced MacDougall as General Officer Commanding Canadians in England. But it was never made clear. A myth circulated that MacDougall's original appointment had been confirmed by an Order in Council and that it could not be changed until the order was revoked; even Steele believed this fable, as did Carson—or he pretended to do so, well knowing that his claim to power could be sustained as long as ambiguity existed. From then on there were two who considered themselves "GOC Canadians" with all this meant in divided command. Five months later, Carson advised Steele quite bluntly that "General MacDougall remains in the position to which he was appointed by the Canadian Government, and approved of by the British Authorities, namely, General Officer

Commanding Canadians in England."[11] The War Office, perhaps, might have been tempted to ask, "Will the real GOC Canadians please step forward?" On 27 August Hughes returned to Canada, leaving a wake of confusion behind him.

No sooner was he out of the way than Carson put in his bid for absolute power. In a letter to Steele he claimed vice-ministerial status with "very extended powers . . . as my position is that of control as the Minister's direct representative of all our troops in England, whoever they are and wherever they may be."[12] In fact, he now openly claimed the same dictatorial powers in England that Sam enjoyed in Canada. Steele would command the Shorncliffe District but was to exercise his command only through MacDougall, who would not only command the Training Division but any other Canadian units arriving in the British Isles. Steele did not demur, and with that the War Office discovered that they had another officer, superior in his own estimation to both MacDougall and to Steele, with whom they must deal.

Were Carson's views those of the Minister? It seems unlikely. His earlier conduct indicates that he was not above falsifying his own authority, if that would enhance his prestige. He could be sure that the widespread terror of Hughes would prevent even senior officers from questioning what they were led to believe had come from the Minister. On the other hand, had Hughes granted such authority on impulse and without written confirmation, it would have been quite in keeping with his erratic methods; and less than a month later he promoted Carson to the rank of major-general. In either case it is evident that he failed to make his intentions clear to all the officers concerned, and he left the War Office and the Canadian High Commissioner completely in the dark.

On his return to Canada, the Minister decided to send another twelve thousand men to England before the winter. Though reinforcements, they were to be sent over in the battalions in which they had been recruited. The War Office, short of winter accommodation, began by protesting and then decided that room for five thousand could be made at Shorncliffe and for the balance in the Aldershot Command. Meanwhile, the movement of these troops remained shrouded in mystery—neither the War Office nor Carson received any details—until 11 October, 1915. That morning Carson was awakened with the news that a thousand Canadians had been deposited at Bramshott, a village near Aldershot. Nothing had been prepared for them; nor had they been met. Such were the beginnings of the huge Canadian camp at Bramshott.[13]

Command of the new camp was given to Brigadier-General Lord Brooke, the son and heir of the Earl of Warwick. After some years in the army, Lord Brooke had tried his hand at ranching in Western

Canada. He became a close friend of Sam Hughes, so much so that though Brooke had rejoined the British Army at the beginning of the war, Sam had personally intervened to give him a brigade in the 2nd Division. A month had convinced Turner that Brooke would have to go; but how could he remove him without upsetting Hughes? The opening-up of the new training camp in England gave the answer and on 19 November, 1915, Brooke took over as GOC Canadian Division, Bramshott.

The Canadian command system, confused before, now became absurd. Two training divisions were now in being, MacDougall's in the Shorncliffe District of Eastern Command, and Brooke's under the Aldershot Command at Bramshott, a hundred miles away. Steele, in charge of Shorncliffe District, had full authority to supervise Mac-Dougall's division (despite understandable friction between the two) but he had no jurisdiction over Brooke. MacDougall, on the other hand—still believed to be GOC Canadians—now became responsible for Canadian troops at Bramshott, too, and *had* authority over Brooke. Thus MacDougall could give orders at Bramshott, which his superior could not; and when doing so he need make no reference to Steele whatsoever.

Carson applied himself to the problem. He made a first attempt to resolve it through the War Office. Boundaries would have to be redrawn; Bramshott, he suggested, should be detached from Aldershot Command and added to the Shorncliffe District of Eastern Command. Tradition, however, is not so easily upset and the War Office did not reply. Carson then reviewed the personalities concerned and concluded that all would be well if he could only get rid of Steele, "a fifth wheel to a coach in any case."[14] "You are," he wrote to Steele, "and I say it without trying to throw any bouquets, a master hand on matters of inspection and the handling of men," and went on to propose that he should be Inspector General of Canadian Troops in England, with frequent trips to France. That would eliminate the elderly officer quite effectively, and he was gratified when Steele succumbed. The next step was to obtain the support of Hughes:

There is no question of friction between these two distinguished officers, and yet I do know that the only thing that prevents friction is the common sense displayed by both of them, and perhaps I should also say the presence of myself here always ready to throw oil on the troubled water at a moment's notice, and the thought has struck me, and struck me only to-day, could we not make much better use of General Steele's services by giving him an appointment similar to that which he held in Canada and make him Inspector General of all our forces in England? He could then . . . spend his time in inspecting from camp to camp, hospital to hospital, convalescent home to convalescent home, etc.[15]

Even this masterly effusion, as with the War Office, provoked no response and Carson knew better than to pester Hughes. He turned again to the War Office and revived his former proposal concerning boundaries. This elicited a reply that seemed to Carson quite perverse; but to the War Office it was very simple. Steele was the senior officer; he was authorized to supervise Bramshott as well as Shorncliffe, which, of course, greatly pleased Steele but not MacDougall. MacDougall protested to Carson, who once more took up the cudgels with a completely baffled War Office, explaining to them that MacDougall was "in command of all Canadian troops in England, under the supervision, however, of Major-General Steele." "At the moment," he emphasized, "Lord Brooke, the Commanding Officer in Bramshott, is serving under the orders and instructions of Brigadier-General MacDougall."[16] Carson then visited the War Office to define the situation more precisely, as a result of which he informed Steele that "everything was straightened out, and we all know just where we are and in consequence all attend to our own work without treading on anybody's corns."[17] Unfortunately Major-General Steele's equanimity was completely shattered when Carson went on to describe MacDougall as "responsible for the training and discipline of all Canadians in England."[18] If that were so, countered Steele, he himself would be prevented from exercising any authority or supervision over such matters; yet three months later Carson was still at his "wits' end to know how to unravel the tangle which has arisen,"[19] and as a result the personal relationships between Carson, MacDougall and Steele grew steadily more strained.

Inevitably, the administration and training of the Canadian troops in England suffered. The ineffective manner in which the divisions in France were reinforced was undoubtedly the most serious failing. Although there were more than 25,000 Canadians in England by February, 1916, only 2,000, Alderson was told, were available as reinforcements. The Corps Commander pressed the matter through the British; even if only semi-trained, they should be sent to fill his vacancies and complete their training in the field.[20] Carson, on this occasion, was forced to give in.[21] Other officers, frustrated by abortive correspondence, visited Shorncliffe in person to obtain the officers and men with which to rebuild their battalions. They returned to France empty-handed.[22] Currie was quite despondent about the whole situation: "I almost feel as if it is no further use making complaints," he wrote to Carson, "because the position is almost hopeless."[23] Major-General Mercer of the 3rd Division more forthrightly described Shorncliffe as "a joke," which made MacDougall extremely indignant. Statements such as Mercer's were "just the limit" and, he confided to Carson, "reflect upon us all." In this, at least, the two were in agreement.[24]

Another problem, which had begun with the landing of the First Contingent with more than four hundred surplus officers, was the number of unemployed officers in England. The problem was aggravated by Hughes' method of raising reinforcements by battalions instead of drafts. Almost all the senior officers for these new battalions were selected by Hughes on their presumed ability to attract recruits, and were either personal friends or men of political influence. Once in England the battalions were broken up to reinforce those in France, and brand-new colonels and majors saw their subalterns and privates sent away while they themselves remained. To return to Canada would have been shameful; to go to France would have meant a major sacrifice in rank and self-esteem. The majority of these frustrated officers, therefore, remained in England, completely idle, apart from two-week visits to the front line instituted as a face-saving device to salvage their honour, and which might induce some of them to return to Canada. The visits persisted until September, 1916, when the War Office requested that they cease.[25]

Opportunities to post some officers were frustrated by the replacing of officer casualties by promotion within units—a policy that commanders in France understandably preferred—instead of calling for reinforcement officers in the same rank. And then Hughes continued to grant commissions to all and sundry overseas; on one day, Carson's incoming mail included more than twenty letters and cables all on that subject alone. "Do you not think it would be a good plan to write the Minister," his staff captain suggested, "and remind him of the number of surplus officers we have on this side, and that if every Tom, Dick and Harry is granted a commission we will soon have a Brigade of officers run by a handful of privates?"[26]

The Corps Commander, starved of reinforcements, pointed to the source of all the chaos and inefficiency when, in a letter to Hughes, he complained of "quadruple control."[27] Carson, Steele, MacDougall and Brooke, said Alderson, all dealt directly with his headquarters. And both at Shorncliffe and Bramshott, the commanders failed to realize that their primary purpose was to train and feed the best possible material to the Corps in the field. Instead, they held on to officers and men in the hope that some day they could get rid of them altogether as units.[28] Perley and Aitken addressed correspondence to the Corps whenever they felt like it; and from the other side of the Atlantic the Militia Department in Ottawa sent messages to the War Office, to Carson, to Steele and to MacDougall without system and as the whim seemed to strike them. The War Office gave up trying to understand the Canadian "system" and seems to have corresponded with whomever might get results.

This pragmatism by the War Office led to one major instance of utter confusion. Both Brigadier-General MacDougall and Major-General Steele were ordered by the War Office to organize a new cavalry regiment for the Canadian Corps. They were not now on speaking terms and both, flattered by War Office attention, set to work with a will. MacDougall began to make one up from the Cavalry Training School at Shorncliffe. Steele, at the same time, crossed into what was generally regarded as MacDougall's territory and ordered Brooke at Bramshott to form an identical unit from the Canadian Mounted Rifles. The flurry had gone on for some time, and the units were almost ready to embark, when the error was detected with recriminations that may be left to the imagination.

"This absurd condition of affairs," wrote Carson to the British Under-Secretary of State for War, "and every other absurd condition of a like nature could be overcome . . . in one way only, and that is by these official instructions of the War Office coming to me as the representative in England of the Department of Militia and Defence, Canada, and to me alone, and I would see that prompt action is taken at all times and no mistakes made."[29] But the War Office had no instructions from Canada to deal through Carson; they, therefore, inquired of the Canadian Government if the powers assigned to Carson in the Order in Council of 21 January, 1915, had been extended and whether it was their wish that communications should be conducted through him.[30]

This cable passed through the Governor General and the Prime Minister at a time when Hughes was away. Major-General W. G. Gwatkin, Chief of the General Staff, took advantage of the Minister's absence to propose to the Prime Minister a centralized control in England by a local committee, answerable to the Militia Department, under a president who would distinctly not be Carson.

Carson had already come to a similar conclusion, but his suggestion as to a controlling figure was understandably different from Gwatkin's. Were he to be given absolute control, he urged Hughes, all would be well. He had discussed the matter fully with Sir Max Aitken and the two had concluded that they should "consolidate, and moreover, have a distinctive title." Carson would be the "Commissioner of War for Canada" and Aitken the "Assistant Commissioner of War for Canada." That solution would be "perfectly satisfactory to Sir Max Aitken and it would be perfectly satisfactory to me."[31]

Once again Hughes did not reply though, before 1915 was out, the need for a complete reorganization had occurred to him. In mid-November he had cabled his overseas representative for information, most of which he should have already known.

Kindly forward report on various organizations in England, system of training, chain of command and responsibility, schools organized, number of officers trained, system of ordnance, army service, remounts, everything. I wish a most concise yet clear framework of all under you.[32]

Carson gave him a general picture and in his reply recommended "almost a duplicate of your complete organization in Ottawa." "Either a Sub-Militia Council or a Financial Committee" should be established with, in addition to himself "as practically Acting Minister of Militia over here, as your representative, an Adjutant-General and Quartermaster General and an Inspector General's Branch." He concluded by hoping that the Minister would take "a short trip to England to personally oversee all these matters and personally authorize all these changes on the spot."[33]

Hughes finally got away in March, 1916. In the meantime the Canadian Government advised the War Office that Carson's original functions had not been extended, and that the Minister would investigate the whole situation while in Great Britain. Borden, as the time for Sir Sam's departure approached, became extremely reluctant to let him go. Apart from his "disinclination to remain steadily and constantly at his post performing the appropriate duties incident to the administration of so important a department,"[34] it was clear to Sir Robert that Hughes was about to be attacked in the House. Hughes told the Prime Minister that he had secretly approached the Opposition and obtained their promise not to attack the Militia Department when he was away and Borden, with misgivings, consented to his absence. Even before Sam was on the sea, the Liberals delivered an onslaught against shell contracts and profiteers. But the Minister was not available and Borden had to answer the charges in his stead.

Throughout the first year of the war Hughes had been a large and vulnerable target for the Opposition. His methods at Valcartier, the shoddy boots and uniforms, the purchase of unfit horses, the profiteering in wagons, equipment and even in jam, had been thoroughly aired; but these were lesser affairs. This present scandal was something else and amounted, briefly, to this: members of the Canadian Shell Committee had used munitions contracts for their own profit; contracts had not been put out to tender, with the result that there had been no competitive bidding; large orders, which could have been filled more cheaply and quickly in Canada, had been placed in the United States; and finally, J. Wesley Allison, a friend, honorary colonel and appointee of Sam Hughes, had turned all these practices to his own considerable gain.

The business began in Ottawa early in the war when Hughes, infuriated by the inference of two representatives of the giant United States' Steel Corporation (who were soliciting shell contracts) that Canada could not manufacture shells, had determined that Canada could and would make shells.[35] He set to work with characteristic energy and it is to his credit that, in a short time, Canada had a thriving and profitable industry which, before the war ended, had brought millions of dollars and greatly increased opportunities for employment to the country. To control the manufacture of some types of munitions and the purchase of others, Hughes set up a Shell Committee under the direction of a group of honorary colonels. Allison, a former contractor from Ohio, was associated with the committee as a free-lance purchasing agent.

Revelations in Parliament were startling. One concerned Allison and three American speculators who had set up a dubious concern known as the American Ammunition Company at a cost of $3,000. Allison placed orders for artillery fuses amounting to $10,000,000 with the new company on behalf of the Canadian Shell Committee, and since it had neither factory nor capital, got the Shell Committee to advance $1,500,000. The orders could then be filled. By the end of their game, at least one of the American fly-by-night speculators made $1,000,000, out of which he paid $220,000 to Colonel Allison. The Committee, in fact, paid "more than four dollars a fuse for twenty million dollars' worth of fuses when even the most perfunctory investigation would have shown the going price to be three dollars a fuse."[36]

In the face of this storm, Borden appointed a Royal Commission to investigate the scandal; and he asked Hughes to return from London. He had already decided that Hughes could not remain in the government,[37] but other members of the cabinet were doubtful if Borden's resolve would survive a reunion with Hughes. As Sir George Foster put it, "The danger ahead is the Premier's lack of will when Sam sits opposite."[38] Sir Sam arrived in Ottawa on 16 April to face a restive public, an aroused House and an angry cabinet. While in England, Hughes had discussed with Sir George Perley in very general terms a new system of command and control in England.[39] With Carson, however, he made more definite plans, which he confided neither to Perley nor the Prime Minister. The outcome was an "informal" council to be organized by Sir Max Aitken and authorized on 31 March. Its members would be Carson, Aitken, Brigadier-General David Watson* (to be brought back from France as Inspector General), Brigadier-General MacDougall (Adjutant-General), a quartermaster-general,

*Watson, a strong Tory and the owner of the Quebec Chronicle, was chosen by Hughes; he was a competent soldier.

the Director of Medical Services and, as an afterthought, Lord Brooke.
This was virtually the same old crew with one notable omission:
Major-General Steele.

Completely unaware of Sir Sam's activities, Borden had meanwhile
drafted his own ideas for an overseas council to act under the acting
High Commissioner, Sir George Perley. In this he was ably assisted by
Major-General Gwatkin. The Prime Minister had been astounded to
learn that out of the 240,000 Canadian troops raised, only 60,000 were
in France.[40]

The "informal" council met only twice and then it was sabotaged
by Aitken, as he himself cheerfully admitted. His reasons lay in
Watson's insistence on both Steele and MacDougall being removed
before he would take over in England; and to that end the council had
decided that "immediate steps should be taken through the friendly
influence of Colonel Sir Max Aitken to have Brigadier-General J. C.
MacDougall, C.M.G., attached to the Canadian Army Corps Headquarters in France for instructional purposes for an indefinite time."[41]
But MacDougall, though he would have been glad to accept a suitable
appointment in France, refused to be ousted on a pretext to get him
out of the way. Aitken then concluded that, since Watson's prereq-
uisite had not been met, he could not now count on the Brigadier-
General's support, and he was not prepared to head the council
without the full co-operation of all its members. He therefore informed
Sir Sam that he had "decided on my own account to place every
obstacle in the way of the formation of that Committee, and this I
have done." Watson, much relieved, took over the command of the
Fourth Division.[42]

Hughes passed a copy of Aitken's message to Borden, who might
have been expected to seize this unexpected opportunity to put into
effect his own plans for an overseas council under Perley. But he did
not do so. The Royal Commission was still inquiring into the shell
contracts scandal, and until it was concluded Borden administered
the Militia and Defence Department. Had the Prime Minister imple-
mented his own drastic reorganization, the publicity would almost
certainly have dealt another blow to Sam's prestige. Besides, Sir George
Perley was coming over to Canada later in the year and Sir Robert
probably thought it better to defer a change until he had discussed the
implications with him.

In England, the chaos continued. Out of twenty thousand men at
the Training Division, Shorncliffe, a quarter had been put to work on
odd jobs around the camps, to the detriment of their training. Six
hundred soldiers were held back from France to play in bands. It
seemed that the primary purpose of training reinforcements had been
forgotten.[43] And the jockeying for position went on as merrily as before,

aggravated in June by the arrival of Alderson, the former Corps Commander, to be Inspector General of Canadian Forces. Though Haig had imagined that the post would have some significance, Aitken made it quite clear to the War Office that it was purely nominal.[44] Of course this was not explained to Alderson, and he took his job seriously, roving around and writing embarrassing reports about the numbers of surplus officers.[45] Since Ottawa had no record of Alderson's appointment and treated any communication from him as unofficial, his letters were ignored.[46] Steele, in his turn unaware of how Alderson was regarded, considered the appointment a personal affront and accorded the new Inspector a chilly reception on his every visit to the Shorncliffe area.[47] In September Alderson thankfully quitted the scene to rejoin the British as Inspector of Infantry; that month Perley advised Borden that the military arrangements in England were "neither dignified nor effective."[48]

Perley sailed for Canada during the first week in July, 1916. The Royal Commission had not yet reported and Borden, still administering the Militia Department, was by now aware of its deficiencies. He and Perley, therefore, were of one mind when, on the day after Perley's arrival, the two met with Hughes and reiterated their views on the need for reorganization.[49]

By the middle of the month the Royal Commission on shell contracts handed its report to the Prime Minister. "Everyone was guilty, so in fairness to all, everyone was acquitted."[50] Though Hughes had made sure that the Shell Committee awarded some of its contracts to his own constituents, including his son-in-law, he was cleared of using undue influence and exonerated of complicity with Allison. Allison, who had deceived the Minister and the committee, was strongly censured, and in his case stern action was taken; he was deprived of his honorary colonelcy. Hughes, thus relieved of his anxieties, now decided to go to England to apply his administrative talents. He arrived there at the end of July.

Next day a cable arrived from Borden:

When you have reached conclusion respecting your proposals for the reorganization please cable them fully as they should be definitely embodied in Order-in-Council and it would be desirable to consider them before they are actually put in operation.[51]

Hughes' reply veered off at a tangent to talk about surplus officers; there were not fifteen in the whole of England, and in fact Carson had told him "we are short several hundred."[52] Strange, replied Borden, the Chief Paymaster was paying more than two hundred. He then asked for names, the number of non-effective troops in England, and other pointed questions that Sam ignored. Instead, he asked Borden to raise four divisions, and to send fifty to eighty thousand troops over immediately. "Big drive expected," he said, "and great desire that Canadians should be first in Berlin." Next day he was going to France to discuss it all with Haig.[53]

It was high time, thought Borden, to remind him of the purpose of his visit, which he did on 16 August. That day Hughes sent off a pleasant cable setting down a few passing thoughts on the shortage of timber in Britain, the supply of fish to Canadian soldiers and his opinion of Lloyd George. Yes, replied Borden on the 24th, but what about the reorganization?

Sir Sam had in fact been busy on that very problem; his cables were merely a smoke screen to cover his activities. His solution was to revive his "informal" council under another name, the Sub-Militia Council. It consisted of nine members including Carson (chairman), Steele and MacDougall, while Brooke was roped in later. Remembering Borden's warning that no final arrangements were to be made without reference to him, he added the prefix "acting" to the name of the council and on 5 September, 1916 it met. On the 6th he cabled Borden: "Hope to have full report based on most mature considerations from every viewpoint ready to mail by end of week. Meantime everything going splendidly."[54]

Banner headlines in the Ottawa *Journal* that very day were a disagreeable surprise to Sir Robert Borden: MILITARY COUNCIL FORMED IN LONDON TO SOLVE TROUBLES IN HIGH COMMAND. FIRST MEETING HELD TODAY.[55]

He indignantly telegraphed Hughes, referring to the "extraordinary press reports" and drawing attention to his cable of 31 July;[56] next day he requested Hughes' return. The Minister's reply was somewhat disconcerting: "Know nothing whatever about our . . . composition of proposed Council and cannot understand your peculiar message." He concluded with the information that he was off to Scotland "for a week inspection timber camps at various points. Absent about week."[57] Hughes left Aitken to mollify the outraged Prime Minister, and Sir Max did his best: "Minister has not made any statement to Press," he explained diplomatically, "but members of proposed Council are talking freely."[58]

At the end of September Hughes returned to Canada, leaving Carson to suggest at one council meeting, seconded by MacDougall, that a proposal be forwarded to the Minister for the founding of a Canadian decoration to be known as The Order of the Beaver and Maple Leaf.[59] Sir Sam's ship must have passed that of Sir George Perley, who had spent his stay in Canada thrashing out with Borden their own ideas for an overseas council. At least Hughes could be confident that the system he had established would effectively maintain his own authority over military affairs in England. To make doubly sure, he had insisted that his son-in-law, Major Byron Greene, be appointed secretary,[60] that he should be present at all discussions to record the individual votes and to submit the minutes for his scrutiny.

Borden did not immediately take Sir Sam to task when he returned to Ottawa despite the news from Perley that Hughes' new organization was "in the saddle."[61] Nor did he react to the acting High Commissioner's adverse report on the conduct of Colonel Bruce in the soon-to-be-notorious Bruce-Jones controversy.[62] The Prime Minister was busy putting the finishing touches to an Order in Council that would set up an overseas council as he wanted it, and destroy the creation of Sir Sam Hughes.

The Bruce-Jones battle had its beginning when, at the end of July, the Minister despatched Colonel Herbert A. Bruce, a doctor who had been commissioned and who had had just two weeks' military service, to England as "Special Inspector General" to report on the Canadian Medical Services under Major-General Guy Carleton Jones. "It would be interesting," commented the official medical historian, "to enquire into the mental process by which the Minister arrived at the conclusion that he had selected the proper person for so exacting a task; but that would be a problem in psychology."[63] Bruce, after a six-week investigation, issued his report on 20 September, and on 6 October the new Sub-Militia Council, a body "wise in giving decisions upon subjects of which they knew nothing,"[64] studied it, decided to adopt its recommendations completely, and furthermore voted that Bruce should replace Jones as head of the Medical Services so that he could give effect to the reorganization he had advocated. The Minister approved. Under Bruce's command, as a subsequent inquiry found, the morale of the Medical Services declined rapidly and the care and treatment of patients decreased in efficiency.[65] It was hardly surprising; Bruce, after all, had no knowledge or experience of military medical administration. He was relieved of his appointment on 30 December, 1916, after a board, convened in England, considered his report and General Jones' reply. Jones was reinstated in his stead.[66]

Borden, after sounding out the cabinet, was ready to see Hughes by the middle of October, and on the 17th he told him that an overseas ministry would be set up in England. Next day—on which Sir Sam became an honorary lieutenant-general in the British Army—he passed his draft Order in Council to Hughes. Why, it may be asked, had Borden decided that his version of an overseas council should be headed by a minister? There was no precedent; nor has there been a successor, even during the Second World War. The answer is, of course, that a minister alone would have the power and authority to remove the influence of the incompetent Minister of Militia from the conduct of military affairs abroad. No administrator of lesser rank, however strong and competent, could have brought order out of chaos and yet have remained under Sir Sam Hughes.

Hughes fought back. The idea was absurd. "There is no more necessity for a resident Minister in Britain than there is for a resident Minister at our camps in British Columbia, Calgary, Camp Hughes, Camp Borden, Valcartier . . ."[67] Then he detected a loop-hole: as yet the new minister had not been named, though he must have known it would be Perley. He wrote to the Prime Minister in conciliatory terms; his concern, he said, had been for "our mutual friend" Sir Max Aitken. "Please fill in his name," he begged, "let the office be attached to him instead of him to the office, and you have my exact wish."[68] Borden, unmoved by these blandishments, replied that the minister would be appointed after the department had been set up. Undaunted, Hughes cabled Aitken asking him if he would accept the post, but Sir Max for once proved unco-operative: he could not; he was, he admitted, not qualified.[69] In fact, Aitken was preoccupied with other matters. Two months later, through his part in the political arrangements that brought Lloyd George to power, he became Lord Beaverbrook, and he could no longer find time to be "the Canadian Eyewitness" at the front. He remained in London as Canadian Records Officer.

The Overseas Ministry became an accomplished fact by an Order in Council of 27 October, 1916. Hughes submitted one fevered letter after another to the Prime Minister. He even drafted his own Order in Council. His Sub-Militia Council should continue with Perley, as High Commissioner, as its head; Aitken should replace Carson as Hughes' representative; Aitken should be given Privy Council rank; and Perley should submit draft Orders for the mere formality of signature by Hughes.[70]

Borden coolly drew the Minister's attention to the efforts he had made from July until September to determine what plans Hughes had for reorganization. His recent proposals amounted to little more than what he had "actually put in operation before you left Great Britain although authority in Council had not been obtained therefor."[71] The Overseas Ministry would stand, and Sir George Perley was named to head it.[72]

With that, Hughes' frustration and fury could no longer be contained. Borden had already taken advantage of the Minister's absence to parcel out his "empire." Already J. W. Flavelle was controlling shells and munitions; A. E. Kemp, chairman of the War Purchasing Board, looked after the other aspects of procurement; R. B. Bennett, chairman of the National Service Board, was responsible for recruiting; and F. B. McCurdy, appointed Parliamentary Secretary of the Militia Department, kept the day-to-day administration going. Now Sir Sam was to be divorced from the overseas theatre in which he had paraded with considerable pleasure.

In a vitriolic outburst, Hughes poured scorn on commissions and Orders in Council. They looked "beautiful on paper" but few, if any, had been "anything like perfect in practice." As to Orders in Council, the "British Constitution does not exist on paper; no Order in Council is behind it," and had he conducted military affairs on such a formal basis, "the First Division would not have left Valcartier yet."

One other point and I am through. It might well be implied from your memorandum that my failing to secure authority by Order-in-Council for this Sub-Militia Council impelled you to the course you are now pursuing with Sir George Perley. May I be permitted to say that both you and I know to the contrary. I knew early in August that Sir George Perley had planned something on these very lines. You have, also, admitted that as early as the first week of September you had this matter under consideration by you and Perley earlier. You incidentally remarked yesterday that you had not consulted any of your colleagues. Of course, when I drew attention to the statement, you corrected yourself.[73]

Hughes never doubted that the Prime Minister would cave in as he always had before. Carried away by the Bruce Report, he began to deliver stormy denunciations of the Medical Services overseas, incorporating grave allegations. Addressing the Empire Club in Toronto on 9 November, 1916, he announced that "thousands of Canadians had lost months, and sometimes a year, in hospitals not under Canadian control, when they should have been back in the trenches," and that "Canadian soldiers were allowed to go under the knife of first-year medical men while the services of experienced surgeons from Canada were not being utilized."[74] That very day Borden demanded his resignation.

His demand was no angry reaction to an utterly irresponsible speech; it was the result of Borden's matured thought. The Prime Minister, nettled by the substantial truth of Hughes' accusations concerning his collusion with Perley, seized on the manner in which they had been presented to oust him. There could be no co-operation between his brainchild, the Overseas Ministry, and the Militia Department so long as Hughes held office. He consulted his colleagues and obtained their backing for what he was about to do. On 9 November, 1916, he accordingly informed Hughes what an embarrassment he had been to the government and called for his resignation:

Under conditions which at times were very trying and which gave me great concern, I have done my utmost to support you in the administration of your Department. This has been very difficult by reason of your strong tendency to assume powers which you do not possess and which can only be exercised by the Governor in Council. My time and energies, although urgently needed for more important duties, have been very frequently employed in removing difficulties thus unnecessarily created. You seemed activated by a desire and even an intention to administer your Department as if it were a separate Government in itself. On many occasions, but without much result, I have cautioned you against this course which has frequently led to well founded protests from your Colleagues as well as [being] detrimental to the public interest . . .

But more than that, your letter is couched in such terms that I cannot overlook it or excuse it. I take strong exception not only to statements which it contains but to its general character and tone. You must surely realize that I cannot retain in the Government a colleague who has addressed to me such a communication. I regret that you have imposed upon me the disagreeable duty of requesting your resignation as Minister of Militia and Defence.[75]

Hughes, stunned and incredulous, took two days to recover himself sufficiently to write a long and insulting letter in which he tendered his resignation with "much satisfaction."[76] On the 15th he removed the last of his belongings from his office and apprised Borden of the fact with a warning:

I leave with regret not on account of the office or anything special, outside of friendships which will last . . . but for the welfare of the soldiers. However a kindly watchful eye will be kept over [them] by your humble servant.[77]

The Honourable A. E. Kemp was appointed Minister in his place.

Well might the Prime Minister complain that Hughes had arrogated complete authority and had been a handicap to the government. The mystery is why he put up with him so long. The Minister of Militia, as the Toronto *Globe* predicted four months before the war, set himself up as "War Lord of Canada" on a very ample scale.[78] He completely disregarded the Militia Council and "insisted on being Minister and Commander-in-Chief too, an anomaly for which Sir Robert Borden will some day reap sore harvest."[79] His autocracy was such that, as Hughes himself pointed out to the Anglican Bishop of Montreal, he "was not going to be run by bishops, nor by Borden."[80]

Borden was well aware of the antagonism Hughes aroused; his own files, as well as the daily press, bristled with complaints. Soldiers had protested about his actions at Valcartier: "Everybody in camp really thinks he is crazy. . . He said to one officer [drilling his men], a captain, 'Pipe up, you little b-----, or get out of the service.' How long are officers to submit to such insults from a maniac?"[81] A doctor said, "The consensus of opinion among medical men who have taken sufficient interest to give thought to this question is that the Minister of War is *insane* and not responsible for that extreme vanity which he desires to gratify."[82] And politicians passed a similar judgement: "His latest utterances in London last night compel me to take the charitable view that I believe the man is insane."[83]

Newspapers had demanded Hughes' removal. The Toronto *Telegram* commented two months after the war began: "The letters which have appeared in these columns must prove conclusively that the country is practically a unit in desiring the removal of the Minister of Militia,"[84] and an open letter in the same paper had chided Sir Robert's indecision: "Your silence and inaction can only confirm the growing belief that the Minister . . . is your master and that you and your Cabinet are unequal to the task of right government."[85] Members of Borden's party, and his colleagues, had echoed these views. The president of the Conservative Association in Toronto said, "I do not know how long the Conservative Party can stand the egotism of the Minister of Militia. It is needless to say that I am more than ever convinced that it would be a wise thing, both for the country and the party, to have General Hughes step out of the Cabinet,"[86] while Perley, in England, remarked: "I cannot understand why you put up with his ways so long."[87]

Borden, according to his memoirs, had on many occasions doubted the usefulness of Hughes as a minister. "In my experience," he said, "his moods might be divided into three categories; during about half the time he was an able, reasonable and useful colleague, working with excellent judgment and indefatigable energy; for a certain other portion of the time he was extremely excitable, impatient of control and almost impossible to work with; and during the remainder his conduct and speech were so eccentric as to justify the conclusion that his mind was unbalanced."[88]

Yet, for some five years, he kept him. If he was afraid of incurring the wrath of the Orange Lodge through dismissing Hughes, the editor of the Toronto *Evening News* set his mind at rest as early as November, 1914:

I do not want to be regarded as a personal enemy of the Minister of Militia but so much criticism comes to me from every side that I begin to be appalled. I am writing this letter to convey to you this message from Mr. Hocken, now Mayor of the City and Editor of the Orange Sentinel. He says that if you find it necessary to make a change in the Department of Militia, he will undertake that no appeal to the Orangemen against the present Minister will be effective.[89]

It would seem that Hughes' own assessment of Borden—"a most lovely fellow; very capable, but not a good judge of men or of tactics; and is as gentle-hearted as a girl"[90]—was shrewd; he banked on the Prime Minister's peaceful nature while ignoring his frequent warnings and carrying on very much as a law unto himself. And he remained in office. Borden was the soul of patience; he waited until Hughes had overstepped even his own elastic limits before deciding that he could no longer be retained. And it may be that Borden believed Hughes' claims to popularity with the troops. Having made up his mind that Hughes must go, the Prime Minister called for an independent opinion

on how the troops would take his dismissal. In September he sent
Colonel George H. Bradbury (Tory M.P. for Selkirk and a later
senator) to tour the camps in England and the units in France.
Bradbury's report, received at the end of October, 1916, reads in part:

If you were to ask me whether Sir Sam was a strength or a weakness
to your Government, I would certainly have to state most emphatically
that . . . he is the biggest load you have to carry at the present moment.
Public opinion among the men in uniform is certainly against Sir Sam.
[They] look on him as a kind of joke. Men on this side of the water who
have had experience at the Front are very sore, and make some very
nasty statements regarding what would happen to Sir Sam if he
happened to lead a Division at the Front.
. . . There is a great deal of talk regarding the Ross rifle. There are
some awful stories told as to the result of the troops being forced to use
this rifle. This is not all from the ranks. I have heard personally from
Brigadier-Generals, and many other officers, who have [made] no bones
in stating that large casualties were occasioned from the fact that this
rifle was impracticable.[91]

Reassured by this and by the attitude of his colleagues, Borden at
last rid himself of Sir Sam Hughes.

In London, Perley faced a stupendous task. It was much worse than
even he had thought. Had he known "how difficult the situation is
here," he advised the Prime Minister, "I doubt if I should have
complied with your request to take it in hand."[92] He tackled it by
bringing back senior officers from France and supporting them to the
full. These men knew what the Corps required and so ordered matters
in England that the men at the front would benefit.

Training in the camps in England was put on a sound basis with a
fourteen-week syllabus for all. Seventy battalions in various states of
strength were grouped into twenty-six reserve battalions (excluding
units of the Fifth Division), and these in turn were grouped into six
reserve brigades. Perhaps more important for morale and *esprit de
corps*, the reserve battalions were affiliated on a territorial basis with
other battalions in France most of which had retained associations with
some part of Canada. Thus pledges made in Canada that friends and
neighbours would be kept together could be fulfilled.

Arrangements were completed with the War Office for the staff-
training of Canadian officers; henceforth trained officers would be
available to fill staff positions in their own Corps. Perley appointed
Colonel R. F. Manley Sims as representative in France with clearly
defined powers—unlike Aitken—and subordinate to the Minister; this
was the first step of many designed to secure more effective control of
the Corps so that, almost imperceptibly, it became less a Canadian
part of the British Army and more an autonomous contingent fighting
alongside the British forces. By June, 1917, the Canadian Corps at last
had its own commander in Arthur Currie.

Within four months of his appointment, Perley had eliminated all controversy in the Medical Services occasioned by the Bruce Report. He brought over an experienced officer, Major-General G. L. Foster, who had been Director of Medical Services in France, to take over the same position in England from Jones. Foster, an extremely capable officer, proved big enough for the job. Perley took similar action with the Veterinary and the Chaplains Services, both of which were experiencing difficulties.

All promotions and retirements of officers of the Canadian Expeditionary Force outside Canada were placed in Perley's hands, subject only to the formality of approval by the Army Council. Thus interference by Ottawa in overseas appointments, so prevalent in the Hughes era, was removed. Communications to and from Canada passed at the ministerial level so that Perley was kept fully informed. The relations of the new Minister remained good with the Minister of Militia, the cabinet and Parliament despite the obvious difficulties that there was no one in the House to speak for the Overseas Ministry, except the Minister of Militia or the Prime Minister who had to depend upon cabled information from London.

There is no doubt that the firm but diplomatic Minister, assisted by a competent staff, set the much-mismanaged overseas administration on a right footing and removed it from the expansive era of political favour and patronage. Two months after Perley's appointment the improvements could be sensed in France, where a senior officer reported: "Sir George Perley is rendering every possible assistance and doing very efficient work all around. I hear nothing but praise of him in every quarter. Think his appointment one of the most popular moves the Prime Minister ever made." [93]

At the end of June, 1917, Perley's deputy, Walter Gow, found relations between the Corps and London excellent:

Everywhere the statement was, "Things are so much better now than they were. The drafts . . . from England are much better trained and the relations between the field and the forces in England seem to be much closer and better in every way." [94]

In December, 1917, worn out by twelve months' work and responsibility, Perley relinquished the Overseas Ministry to his opposite number in Ottawa, now Sir Edward Kemp, who was succeeded as Minister of Militia by Major-General S. C. Mewburn. Sir George remained in London as High Commissioner. A tribute by Currie sums up the work he had performed:

. . . a most wonderful improvement has taken place since your appointment as Overseas Minister of Militia and on turning over that office to your successor you must be conscious of having done more than well. [95]

While these much-needed reforms were taking place, what of MacDougall, Steele, Brooke and Carson?

MacDougall, through his training and reinforcement role too intimately connected in the minds of officers at the front with the mismanagement of the past, returned a month after Perley's appointment for employment in Canada. Steele still strove for recognition; he recommended Carson to the new Overseas Minister as Deputy Minister and himself as Inspector General,[96] which Perley refused to consider. Perley suggested to Borden that he "might be most useful in Canada, particularly in connection with recruiting in the West, where he has great influence. . ."[97] but it was six months before Steele vacated the Shorncliffe command. Lord Brooke commanded the 12th Brigade in France; after being wounded at the front he dropped out of the Canadian Service.[98]

As for Major-General Sir John Wallace Carson, C.B.,* Perley obtained authority to establish a small commission under him to draw up plans for demobilization; but the Major-General did not relish such a humble task and preferred to go on leave. He remained on leave in Britain and in Canada until 31 January, 1918, when he was finally struck off strength. One of his last acts was to write to Currie begging him to recommend him for a Russian decoration "to round out my set" of British, French and Belgian honours. Currie turned down the request for his support with indignation. And yet, on 14 January, whilst still on leave, the persistent Carson (who had approached the matter through other channels) was rewarded; on that day he received the Russian Order of St. Stanislas (1st Class).[99]

*Knighted for his past services in May, 1917 (Court Circular, 25 May, 1917).

Vimy in Canadian hands. The loss of Vimy Ridge, considered an impregnable position by the Germans, placed the Canadians, as will be seen here, in a dominant position above the Douai plain.

Following the capture of Vimy Ridge in April, 1917, senior French officers visited the battlefield to study the Canadian operation. One of them is seen with Lieutenant-General Sir Julian Byng, inspecting captured German guns.

Following Vimy, Currie was knighted in the Birthday Honours List of 1917. Here he receives the accolade from King George V in a marquee erected in the ruined square of Albert, behind the Somme.

Hill 70. Canadian troops make their way through shattered enemy defensive lines to the summit of Hill 70 after its capture by the Corps on 15 August, 1917.

Hill 70. The shattered suburbs of Lens, infested with trenches and machine-gun posts, as seen from the slopes of Hill 70.

Canadian heavy artillery in action.

Currie and Haig. Arthur Currie and the Commander-in-Chief of the British armies, Field Marshal Sir Douglas Haig.

Passchendaele, 1917. The conditions under which this battle was fought are beyond description. After being immersed in its horrors, a wounded Canadian and German soldiers help each other through the mud.

NINE.
VIMY: CANADA'S EASTER GIFT TO FRANCE

The Canadian Corps spent the winter of 1916-17 in a relatively quiet sector of the First Army's front between Arras and a point opposite Lens. Before them loomed Vimy Ridge.

There were many new faces in the battalion ranks and many more arrived, as reinforcements poured in from England to strengthen units depleted at the Somme. Below the shoulder straps officers and men now wore an identification device; "Somme Patches" they were called. The 1st Division wore a two-inch square of red cloth, the 2nd blue, the 3rd black (later grey), and the 4th green. These were surmounted by a circle, semi-circle, triangle or square, which represented the four battalions, in order of seniority, in each brigade; and the colour of these told the brigade: green for the first, red for the second, and blue for the third in each division. Thus, for example, the 1st Battalion (the senior battalion of the 1st Brigade in the 1st Division) wore red patches surmounted by a circle in green, while the 2nd Canadian Mounted Rifles (the second battalion in the 2nd Brigade of the 3rd Division) wore a grey patch surmounted by a semi-circle in red. These patches were worn with a pride that passed into tradition, and even in the Canadian Army of today, though regimental titles have been revived, divisional patches have remained. A 1st Division man can still be recognized by the "Old Red Patch" he wears.

Artillery fire was rare, the odd desultory shot fired at first more from habit than anything else, until the Germans crawled out into No-Man's-Land to put up a notice: CUT OUT YOUR DAMNED ARTILLERY, WE TOO ARE FROM THE SOMME.[1] Later, the gunners said wryly, they fired only to clear their barrels of accumulating rust.[2] The infantry kept up intermittent hostilities by exchanging small-arms and mortar fire and by raids.

Some men welcomed raids or night patrols. To a few it meant action. To others it was the best way to be wounded, and a wound would be a means of getting out of the trenches for a spell or perhaps to Blighty; and that might last out the war. The best time for a wound was at night when the fire was unaimed and less likely to hit a vital spot.

Furthermore, the dressing stations were quiet then, and the back areas unshelled. Volunteers came forward, therefore, for night work in this quiet sector; but some of the raids were eerie.

Four men volunteered to obtain the identity of the unit opposite and went out into No-Man's-Land under a fitful moon. When almost half-way there and skirting a strange hump, the moon broke from behind ragged clouds to reveal that the hillock they were avoiding was a German, lying on his back, his arms stretched wide. He had been shot in the throat so that his chin and neck were black with blood, giving the impression of a full dark beard. His face was ashen grey and his wide-open eyes bright with reflected moonlight. The men recoiled in horror almost into the bodies of two Canadians who had died with their heads and shoulders thrust into shallow scrapings. It appeared that these men were from another battalion out on a similar errand and had exchanged shots with the German earlier that night. They had killed him, but not before being hit themselves; severely wounded, they had tried to crawl into a hollow and had died there. Their heads were turned from their assailant, almost as if they were trying to hide from "Bluebeard's" macabre face. The moon went back behind the clouds, and the men, recovering themselves, cut the identification from the German's tunic, and got safely back to their own trenches. Next day, the winter's sun revealed a No-Man's-Land as derelict and ordinary as before.

The winter was cold, the hardest for twenty-two years,[3] and the little Souchez River froze two feet thick; food, served hot, congealed to ice at the edge of mess-tins before it could be eaten. Nevertheless, despite its miseries, conditions were better than the year before. The trenches, which drained into the Zouave Valley, were reasonably dry, and the men had time to dig shelters in the chalk or frozen clay. There were the usual lice—*itchie-coos*, the men called them—and rats which, gorged on human remains, grew to enormous size.

Behind the lines, concert parties occasionally entertained the men in converted barns. Some of these parties were later grouped into the "Dumbells," organized from serving soldiers of the 3rd Division; they entertained in France and became well known throughout Canada after the war. The parties sang music-hall songs, danced, and gave skits based on army life; they even included female impersonators. A song that sent cheers and laughter echoing from the smoky beams was sung by a man wearing full equipment: tin hat, rifle, bayonet, grenades, entrenching tool, haversack, pack, water bottle, rubber boots slung over his shoulder, and gas mask. He shuffled on stage wearing an expression of mingled gloom, misery and disgust, pushed his tin hat forward onto his nose and sang in the most dismal possible way:

> I've got a mott-er,
> Always merry and bright.[4]

The favourite songs of this period were no longer jingoistic or patriotic; they were "Oh, What a Lovely War" and "Pack up Your Troubles in Your Old Kit-Bag."

The monotony of the winter was broken for Arthur Currie by two main events. The first arose from Perley's appointment as Overseas Minister and his desire to bring back a senior officer from France to be GOC Canadians in England. During November Sir George, in company with Sir Thomas White, Minister of Finance in Borden's cabinet, visited France for three days and interviewed senior officers of the Corps. On 22 November he wired Borden:

For G.O.C. Canadians, England, Currie is generally preferred by officers at front but objections might very likely be raised in some quarters. He says he used to work on Liberal side but got disgusted with politics and now takes no interest. Turner much beloved by everyone but perhaps not so firm or forceful as others . . . We like Lipsett who is splendid soldier very good at training but is regular English officer and might not be considered Canadian. Watson fine chap but is junior . . . White and I think Currie most capable for position but Turner would be more popular with our following . . .[5]

The upshot was that a reluctant Turner was finally selected, but before accepting he made one condition: "In the event of a Canadian General Officer being appointed to the command of the Canadian Corps," his claim as "the senior Major-General" should be respected.[6]

The vacancy in the 2nd Division caused by Turner's new appointment was seized on by the Prime Minister to propose promotion for Garnet Hughes, presumably to pacify his father, whose potential for trouble in Parliament was causing Borden alarm. But General Byng, the Corps Commander, had already selected Major-General Burstall, the commander of the Corps Artillery, for the 2nd Division; and Perley bravely backed the Corps Commander. Borden's annoyance is quite evident in the telegram he addressed to Perley:

I have no knowledge of military matters but with respect to personal ability, I have no doubt that man selected by Byng [Burstall] is much inferior to other mentioned [Hughes]. I would strongly advise you to have capable representative at Front who can keep you informed.[7]

Perley saw the need to find an appropriate place for Garnet Hughes. He found an opportunity within a month. Hughes was brought over to command the 5th Division in England, which was on the verge of being broken up to provide reinforcements for France. A compromise was arrived at. The division would be brought up to full strength but would not be sent overseas, nor would drafts be taken from it. And Garnet Hughes would be a major-general.

Currie, still in France as he desired, was one of a party of officers sent in January, 1917, by Sir Douglas Haig to visit the Verdun battlefield.[8] At Byng's request, he had prepared a report on the lessons learned at the Somme,[9] and now he was to prepare a similar report on the Verdun fighting. The British group met General Nivelle and other French officers at Verdun, and examined the battlefield in detail.

Currie accepted no statements at face value. He checked comments made by senior officers by questioning the junior commanders who had done the fighting. A senior officer would say that such and such had happened; Currie noted that he could find "no instance where this took place."[10] Another general would say that a particular lesson had been learned from a phase of the action. Currie commented: "I found no divisional commander agrees with such a contention."[11]

On his return, he wrote a sound tactical analysis of the Verdun battles, emphasizing the final French attacks. Of great importance, he found, was the preliminary infantry training before the assault. This training consisted of two parts: first, the troops went into the front line to become familiar with the ground over which they were to attack; secondly, they were withdrawn to the rear to practise over similar ground. During the second phase, the emphasis was on company and platoon tactics, each group determining the most effective way to accomplish its task; and as much rest as possible was deemed essential. Troops, "re-equipped, re-clothed, fed particularly well," went to concerts and "consequently returned to the line absolutely fresh and highly trained."[12] On return to the line their freshness was kept untarnished; in their absence other troops had carried out the fatiguing tasks necessary to the assault: the digging of assembly and communications trenches, dumping stores and making roads.

Currie's advocacy of platoon tactics is noteworthy. The British had in pre-war days stressed the importance of the platoon, but in the mass attacks of 1915/16 such a small tactical unit had been disregarded in favour of successive waves of men. The platoon being a smaller, less vulnerable target, said Currie, should spearhead the attack.

Get back to the pre-war, self-sufficient, self-reliant platoon; remember that now this self-sufficiency requires a number of weapons instead of the two (the rifle and bayonet) of pre-war days and the need for the efficient co-ordination of all of them.[13]

Currie deprecated the costly British method of attacking by waves. It was unnecessary with highly trained troops. At Verdun entire divisions had jumped-off to attack at one time, not in successive waves, and had been across No-Man's-Land before the enemy's artillery started firing. Every man, through training, knew what to expect and the troops had been absolutely fresh.

Currie was adamant about one thing: natural features, and not trench lines, should be the objectives of attacks. Features had been the objectives at Verdun: clearly defined hills and valleys, which had been taken. He undoubtedly had his own experience in mind. His own protest against the vaguely defined redoubt—K5—at Festubert had been overruled, and his first attack had failed. At the Somme, after failing at Regina Trench, he had again protested against orders that described objectives, not in relation to physical features, but by map reference only. On the way to the objective, the present British tactics, if they could be so described, neglected to use such ground cover as did exist. Troops must be taught the power of manoeuvre, he reasoned, to move around strongpoints and take them from flank and rear instead of waiting for them to be neutralized by artillery; a tedious business, and often unnecessary. Platoon tactics, once again, should be employed.[14]

Maps and air photographs, he conceded, were useful and had proved so at Verdun. But these should be up forward, once the assault began, for use by the front-line officers and not in the hands of those at the rear.[15]

The remainder of Currie's major comments were devoted to the use of artillery. French senior officers had been carried away with the results of the creeping barrage, so effective, they claimed, that little hostile machine-gun fire had been encountered by the advancing infantry. After questioning field commanders, Currie could not entirely agree. Nevertheless it had impressed him, as had the French use of artillery in general. He recommended that the British should adopt three procedures: first, heavy artillery, held at corps level, should be placed directly under the commander of the assaulting division, who alone was responsible for the destruction of hostile trenches, obstacles and guns on his own front;[16] secondly, more emphasis should be placed on "counter-battery" fire—just before the attack the enemy's batteries should be located and destroyed—the concept of which had been developed by the British V Corps at the Somme and eagerly taken up by the Canadians who placed all the counter-battery guns under the control of a single officer as early as December, 1916. Finally, there should be no noticeable change in the artillery fire, even on the day of the attack, so that surprise could still be achieved after an artillery preparation lasting several days.[17]

This report by Currie is significant on three counts, the first and most obvious being that he, the only Canadian observer, should have been selected to go to Verdun at all. Furthermore, it reveals a commander striving under the stultifying conditions of trench warfare to achieve the objective at less cost. Finally, most of his recommendations were adopted.

The Allied plans for 1917 had been drawn up by Joffre and Haig in November, 1916. These amounted to a Franco-British continuation of the Somme offensive, on a wider front, to be ready from the first week in February, 1917. But Nivelle, succeeding Joffre in December, produced a new plan which, instead of attrition, aimed at the complete destruction of the enemy's forces. North of the Somme River the

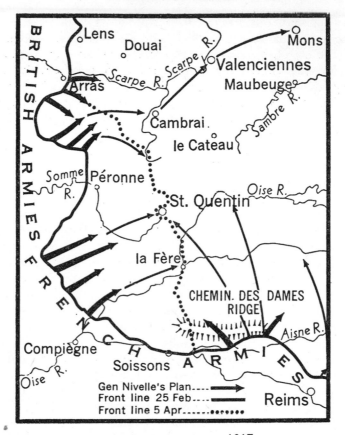

THE NIVELLE OFFENSIVE, 1917

British would attack on a wide front opposite Cambrai; south of it, the French would attack towards St. Quentin. But these would be only preliminary operations to pin the Germans down. Nivelle's main thrust, designed to break through the German line, would then be made along the Aisne in the Soissons-Reims sector. Nivelle counted on the shock tactics used at Verdun to gain his purpose and, once achieved, an Allied "mass of manoeuvre" consisting of three armies would pour through the gap to defeat decisively the enemy reserves "without chance of failure."[18] Thus the knockout blow appeared to be in the making. Haig, however, took the precaution of stipulating that should Nivelle's offensive fail to defeat the enemy as decisively as he hoped, then he would ask for the return of British divisions (which he had provided on the French left) to carry out his own offensive to free the Belgian coast.[19]

Haig's plan for a northern offensive seemed justified. The Admiralty were desperately anxious for the capture of Ostend and Zeebrugge from which German U-boats and destroyers emerged to sink shipping in the Channel. And the situation grew more critical as the months progressed. In February 470,000 tons of Allied ships were sunk; in April the tonnage had risen to 837,000. Sir John Jellicoe, the First Sea Lord, predicted a British collapse if the sinkings continued at their current rate.[20]

Before any offensives could be mounted, other events of far-reaching significance to the course of the war were taking place. On December 12, 1916, Bethmann-Hollweg, the German Chancellor, put out peace overtures, which were communicated to the Allies and to the United States. His action was prompted by the indecisive nature of the war, which might make a compromise peace possible, by the British blockade, which was bringing starvation to Germany, and by the fact that the only answer to the blockade lay in unrestricted submarine warfare. The effect that the last would have on the neutrals, especially the United States, appalled him. The moment seemed propitious for peace proposals. On 6 December the fall of Bucharest and the collapse of the Roumanian army prevented any danger of their being taken as a proof of weakness, but in fact they were unfortunately timed. Lloyd George had replaced Asquith as Prime Minister only five days before, and his policy was that of continuing the war until final victory. The German terms, which included the ceding of the Congo and the fortress of Liège by Belgium, the Briey-Longwy coal and steel area by France, and certain other territories by Italy and Roumania, were rejected. The Allies in turn made known to President Wilson their conditions, which were not unlike those finally imposed by the Treaty of Versailles. In January, 1917, an undefeated Germany rejected them.

Though a compromise peace was the logical outcome of stagnation on the Western Front, there was to be none in 1917. This is hardly surprising. Public opinion had not been taught to accept a peace without a victory. The troops in France knew the meaning of war with all its horrors, but they could not tell the people at home. How does one tell friends and loved ones, chattering bright nonsense culled from optimistic newspapers, the brutal truth of one's own experience? Remarque could not, as he makes clear in *All Quiet on the Western Front*,[21] nor could Robert Graves.[22] The civilians saw things in terms of black and white: on one side "our brave boys" and on the other "the beastly Hun." They could never have understood the sympathy a soldier could feel for his fellow-sufferer in the opposite trenches. A letter which appeared in the *Morning Post* after the Somme is typical of the prevailing war-madness of the time:

. . . we women, who demand to be heard, will tolerate no such cry as Peace! Peace! where there is no peace . . . We only need that force of character behind all motives to see this monstrous world tragedy brought to a victorious ending.[23]

And so it was to be war to the end. Bethmann-Hollweg's resignation followed the rejection of the peace proposals and the enemy turned to unrestricted submarine warfare by which they believed they could starve Britain into surrender in six months. On 1 February, 1917, submarines began to sink on sight: two months later the United States declared war on Germany.

Between those dates, the first of perhaps the two most significant events of the twentieth century took place in Russia. The March Revolution overthrew the Tsar. Though the government that replaced him con-tinued the war after a fashion, the Germans began to replace their tired divisions from the West with fresh ones from the Eastern Front. In November the Bolshevik Revolution, and the truce that followed, finally removed Russia from the war and enabled the Germans to put in hand the wholesale transfer of troops for an all-out offensive in the West. More than that, it allowed Germany to beat the Allied blockade. Russian grain, oil and minerals were then available to replenish the empty German storehouses.

It is ironical, and was for Germany an irreparable tragedy that she should have started unrestricted submarine warfare when she did. Shortly afterwards the stalemate it was designed to end broke without it.[24] With Russia out of the war, German military and industrial might could well have been too much for Britain and France. Through her submarine attacks, Germany had redressed the balance against her when the United States declared war on 6 April. Nevertheless, it would be at least a year before American manpower and industry could be sufficiently harnessed to the war machine to make its presence felt.

Before Nivelle's great plan for early 1917 could be put into operation, the Germans dislocated it by withdrawing to the Hindenburg Line. Anticipating a resumption of the Somme offensive—in fact, British pressure along the Ancre had gained five miles—the enemy, on the night of 12 March, began a methodical retirement from his awkward salient at the Somme. The whole area between the old line and the new had been utterly devastated before withdrawal. In the new, immensely strong line that had been completed twenty-five miles in the rear across the chord of the Arras-Compiègne-Reims bulge, they planned to take up the defensive until the outcome of unrestricted submarine warfare became clear.

By 15 March the withdrawal was complete. Since much of the ground that Nivelle planned to attack had been evacuated, a change in plan was imperatively necessary, but the French Commander-in-Chief clung to his original intention as if the Germans were still there. The British, however, limited their contribution to the Arras sector where the front had not changed; it was now to be an all-British operation.

The British attacks, known collectively as the Battle of Arras, would be mounted by Allenby's Third Army on an eight-mile front astride the River Scarpe (the First Battle of the Scarpe) and by the Canadian Corps, assisted by some formations of Horne's First Army, on the adjoining four miles of front (the Battle of Vimy Ridge). Planning for the Canadian assault had already become the "Scheme of Operations" on 5 March.

The capture of the ridge would be a most formidable undertaking. The Canadian line ran from where the River Souchez cut both the opposing lines in the north to a point opposite the southeast tip of Vimy Ridge, behind which was the village of Farbus, and Farbus Wood. The Souchez flowed through a narrow valley with high ground on either bank, the Lorette Spur in the Bois en Hache to the north and an elevation in Givenchy-en-Gohelle wood to the south known to Canadians as "the Pimple." South of the Pimple a depression housed the village of Givenchy-en-Gohelle, and immediately south of that the ridge itself ran southeast for four miles before descending gradually to the Scarpe valley in front of Arras. Midway along the ridge, and behind it, lay the village of Vimy. Though the ridge was not high, only 450 feet above sea level, it dominated all the surrounding country. Its two highest points, Hill 145 and Hill 135 (which lay on either side of the Arras-Lens road cutting the ridge roughly in half) gave observation over all the Canadian line. And even the slopes of the ridge were of advantage to the enemy. On the west the slope up which the Canadians would attack, though gentle, was very open. The reverse slope, on the contrary, was steep and well-wooded, providing excellent cover for enemy reserves and guns.

Most formidable of all, however, were the successive lines of enemy defences, the maze of trenches, deep dug-outs and interconnecting tunnels, and the concrete strongpoints. The Germans had no intention of yielding Vimy Ridge. It protected a vital mining and industrial district of France, centred on Lille, then in full production for the enemy. And it also covered the junction of the enemy defences stretching south from the Channel with the Hindenburg Line; thus it guarded the pivot of these two defensive systems. The British could not advance in the Arras sector if the ridge was firmly held.

Sir Julian Byng set to work with great thoroughness to justify the confidence which the British, by setting it this key task, had placed in the Canadian Corps. Byng was a popular commander. "This," reported one officer, "is a soldier—large, strong, lithe, with worn boots and frayed puttees. He carries his hand in his pocket, and returns a salute by lifting his hand as far as the pocket will allow"; his informality was to the Canadian taste, and the men responded.[25]

All four divisions would attack simultaneously and impetuously in line—4th, 3rd, 2nd and 1st from north to south—with all objectives set as the far side of the ridge from the Pimple to Farbus Wood. Each

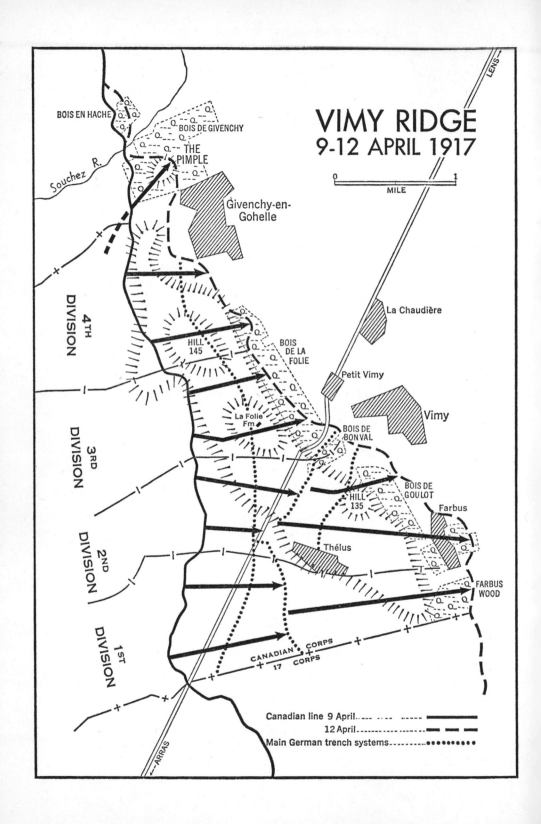

VIMY RIDGE
9-12 APRIL 1917

BOIS EN HACHE

BOIS DE GIVENCHY

THE PIMPLE

Souchez R.

Givenchy-en-Gohelle

LENS

La Chaudière

0   MILE   1

4TH DIVISION

HILL 145

BOIS DE LA FOLIE

Petit Vimy

Vimy

La Folie Fm

BOIS DE BONVAL

3RD DIVISION

BOIS DE GOULOT

HILL 135

Farbus

2ND DIVISION

Thélus

FARBUS WOOD

1ST DIVISION

CANADIAN   CORPS

17   CORPS

ARRAS

Canadian line 9 April
12 April
Main German trench systems

division came into the line on its assigned front to study the ground that lay before it. Commanders briefed their subordinates who in turn passed the method of attack on to the men; the troops knew where they were to go and what they were to do. On ground behind the lines a full-scale replica of the battleground was laid out under Byng's personal direction. It was kept up to date from air photographs and the reports of observers. German trenches and strongpoints were taped and clearly marked. Formations and units in reserve practised repeatedly on the model.

Byng took part in the training schemes, patiently accompanying battalions over the ground and pointing out the salient features. He exhorted officers to

make sure that every man knows his task. Explain it to him again and again; encourage him to ask you questions. Remember also, that no matter what sort of a fix you get into, you mustn't just sit down and hope that things will work themselves out. You must *do* something. In a crisis the man who does something may occasionally be wrong; but the man who does nothing is *always* wrong.[26]

Platoons rehearsed the tackling of strongpoints over deliberately broken ground; companies co-ordinated the actions of platoons; and battalions, brigades and divisions were exercised at each level. The rehearsals were realistic. The "attacking" troops carried exactly what they would carry on the day of the assault; thus equipped they practised getting out of jumping-off trenches as quickly as possible and keeping up with the barrage. And mounted officers, carrying flags, rode ahead of the men at the same pace as a rolling barrage.[27] Rest and intensive training inspired confidence and had the desired effect of raising the troops' morale.

Large dumps for the enormous quantities of ammunition to be expended in the preliminary bombardment and attack, and for other stores necessary for the assault, were prepared in good time by British and Canadian sappers assisted by labour units. Work was done at night. Roads and light railways for transportation were built in the Canadian forward areas. Twenty-five miles of road in all were repaired and maintained; three miles of new plank road were constructed, at which the Canadian engineers were particularly adept. Twenty miles of railroad in the Corps' area, over which gasoline-driven locomotives or even mules drew light trains, were reconditioned and extended until eight hundred tons of ammunition, engineer stores and rations came forward every day. Push-trucks were assembled forward for the evacuation of wounded. Stokes mortar positions, and projectors that could toss gas drums almost a mile forward, were installed. Signallers added to existing telephone circuits twenty-one miles of cable, buried seven feet deep to give immunity from enemy shelling, and more than sixty miles of unburied cable along the trenches.[28]

In these preparations the engineers excelled. Tunnelling companies dug four miles of subways through which troops could move to and from the front line with safety; these would prove invaluable for the evacuation of wounded later. Engineers carved chambers to accommodate brigade and battalion headquarters, dressing stations and stores into the walls of the tunnels. All were provided with piped water and lit by electricity.

Artillery preparations were no less thorough. There was, above all, a great weight of guns. In addition to the 1st and 2nd Canadian Heavy Artillery Brigades, First Army placed nine more groups at Byng's disposal, so that the Canadians would have the benefit of a total of 245 heavy guns and howitzers. The field pieces were similarly augmented to give the fire of seven divisional artilleries plus eight field artillery brigades, a total of 480 eighteen-pounders and 135 4.5-inch howitzers. The fire of heavy guns under First Army's command could be switched to Canadian targets at Byng's request and, more than that, I British Corps had 132 heavies and 102 field pieces available to the Canadians in case of need. The firepower thus provided was more than twice the density that had been achieved at the Somme.[29]

Plans included a modern touch. Eight tanks would precede the storming infantry and the Royal Flying Corps would bomb resisting strongpoints. But bad weather on the appointed day cancelled the air attack, and the tanks, misemployed on shell-saturated ground as they had been at the Somme, bogged down soon after leaving the start line. The success of the assault, therefore, depended on the infantry and artillery, unaided by air or armour.

A two-week preliminary bombardment for the Third Army and the Canadian Corps was decided upon—over the protests of Allenby, who wanted only forty-eight hours in the interests of surprise.[30] Fire on the forward slope of the ridge could easily be observed so that by day trenches, dug-outs, machine-gun emplacements, strongpoints and roads could be accurately engaged. At night harassing fire by artillery and machine-guns would hinder reconstruction. A new artillery fuse, designed to burst high explosive shells in the entanglements above the ground, was used with good effect to cut the German wire; this was totally unlike the disheartening experience at the Somme in endeavouring to cut wire with field gun shrapnel. And on the day of the assault the infantry would jump off behind a rolling barrage moving forward by hundred-yard lifts, while standing barrages poured fire on the enemy defensive systems. Some indication of the torrent of shells to be used can be gained from ammunition figures; for the two corps involved—the Canadian Corps assaulting with the I British Corps in support—each had a bulk ammunition allocation in excess of 42,500 tons and an extra 2,500 tons a day.[31]

The control of guns by the assaulting divisons and the concept of counter-battery work was carefully planned. The Canadian system of counter-battery fire was meticulously organized by Lieutenant-Colonel A. G. L. McNaughton,* Counter-Battery Staff Officer for the Corps, in association with survey companies, sound rangers, air squadrons (notably No. 16, then commanded by Major C. F. A. Portal who was to become Chief of the British Air Staff in the Second World War) and balloons. Field artillery, above the usual complement, was assigned to divisions under divisional control. The heavies formed three groups assigned to counter-battery tasks and four double-groups for trench destruction. Each division had one of the double-groups in direct support and could thus control the destruction of trenches and the cutting of wire with which they were intimately concerned.[32]

On the right Currie's 1st Division had the longest line of advance. Here, approaching Farbus Wood, his infantry would be out of field gun range. "Silent" batteries were, therefore, moved as far forward as possible behind the front line where they would take no part in the preliminary barrage or the early advance. Then, when the troops moved towards the wood in the final stage of the attack, they would spring into life to lend support.[33] On the left, from the Pimple, the enemy could enfilade the whole front of the 4th Division in the advance so that Watson wished to include it as a preliminary objective; Byng, however, wanted a sudden assault on the ridge itself, without preliminary objectives, in the interests of surprise. The Pimple, therefore, would be neutralized by gas and smoke at zero hour and left until later. The dominating features of the ridge—Hills 135 and 145—would be dealt with in the same way.

Easter Monday, 9 April, 1917, was set as the day for the attack. The preparatory bombardment began on 20 March, but for the first two weeks only half the guns, disposed in selected covered or semi-covered positions over a great arc, were used. It was considered desirable to conceal from the Germans the full extent of the massive artillery support that had been assembled. On 2 April the guns that had been silent added to the thunderous chorus. Thousands upon thousands of shells rushed overhead to batter the German defences during a period of intensive bombardment termed by the enemy "the week of suffering." In the interests of tactical surprise, the bombardment continued steadily up to zero hour; the customary final bombardment of targets farther back was dispensed with. By this means the enemy, immune

*McNaughton later became CGS at Ottawa. He relinquished this appointment in 1935 at the request of Prime Minister Bennett to become President of the National Research Council. On the outbreak of World War II he was recalled to military service and became GOC, First Canadian Army. In 1944 he joined Prime Minister Mackenzie King's government as Minister of National Defence.

from even the heaviest shellfire in deep dug-outs, might be induced to remain below ground until his assailants were upon him.[34]

On the night of the 8th the troops, guided by luminous stakes, moved quietly forward to assembly areas where a hot meal and rum issue were waiting. An early moon, just past the full, clouded over as the night wore on; in darkness the men filed through gaps in the Canadian wire to occupy jumping-off positions in No-Man's-Land. All around gun flashes lit up the sky, and an uninterrupted roar covered the slight sounds of movement. Ahead shells burst against the dark flank of the ridge—the red puff of shrapnel and the whiter flash of high explosives clearly distinguished—while in the air above flares soared inter-mittently, some red, some white, some green. It had turned very cold; frost hardened the muddy ground.[35]

Zero hour was timed for first light at 5:30. All units were in position by 4 A.M. Shortly afterwards the weather turned even colder and a bitter northwest wind blew up covering the backs of the waiting men with sleet and snow. The storm lengthened the hours of darkness beyond 5:30, but night befriends the well-trained soldier; to the fully rehearsed assaulting troops it helped more than otherwise. And the slanting sleet from behind blew into the faces of the Germans.[36]

The attack began dead on time. The intensive fixed bombardment yielded first place to the pulsing flame of almost a thousand guns and mortars and the continuous fire of 150 machine-guns flashing out together in the planned barrage and covering fire; seconds afterwards, it seemed, a crashing roar struck the ears. But the men were up and over. Fifteen thousand Canadians surged across No-Man's-Land in one wave to keep close up to the bursting shells. The first wave was fol-lowed by two more, equally strong, at intervals.

The ground was pocked and scarred by continuous shellfire; broken entanglements lay in the path of the eager infantry. But at least the wire was cut. Running, jumping, walking, the men kept moving steadily behind a barrage "lifting forward from objective to objective with clocklike precision and practically obliterating the German trenches as it passed."[37] This was not fire *preceding* movement, as in the early days of the Somme, but fire *combined* with movement.

The enemy had been taken by surprise. In the ruins of his foremost trenches only a few sentries were above ground and they were quickly dealt with; the rest of the defenders remained sheltered in deep dug-outs. Parties were left to guard the exits until the mopping-up wave took over, and the leading troops pressed on. Even in the second line of trenches, though some of the enemy had by now emerged, considerable numbers were similarly trapped. Here there was some hand-to-hand fighting before the attackers moved forward as before.

By now German distress rockets had curved upwards and their artillery answered the call. But the response was feeble and fell well behind the attacking troops. Gradually, however, the fire grew in intensity and fell on supporting units following up the early waves, thinning out their ranks.[38]

Beyond the second-line trenches opposition stiffened and well-concealed snipers and machine-guns, firing from concrete strong-points, took their toll. Platoon tactics came into their own. Men dropped to engage them from the front with rapid fire while others, taking advantage of the broken ground, skirted round to seize them, using bayonets and grenades from flank and rear. The advance kept moving.

What is to-day a peaceful hill, surmounted by twin commemorative pylons communing with the placid sky, was on that day a turmoil of moving men, spouting earth, drifting smoke and driving sleet:

The picture of this famous eminence in the throes of a great attack was strange and inspiring. The ebb and flow of the assault contributed to what looked like utter confusion, but what was in reality a high state of orderliness and discipline. Preceding the lines of attacking troops, the three waves which advanced steadily as if on parade, were the smoke and dirt of shells. The shrapnel burst in white puff-balls, mingling their metallic crash with the high explosive that erupted miniature vol-canoes of earth in black, gaseous clouds. Among the lines and in the rear laboured devoted stretcher parties, themselves subjected to the same dangers as the wounded men to whom they brought succour. Groups of prisoners, mud-stained and dejected, marched back across the battlefield that had lately been their own terrain; curious small columns followed the advance stolidly, carrying Stokes mortars, heavy Vickers machine-guns, stretchers, picks, shovels, ammunition, water and bombs.[39]

The two centre divisions (3rd and 2nd) and Currie's 1st on the right, after planned pauses on intermediate objectives to consolidate, reached the crest shortly before 8 A.M. Only the 4th, on the left, experienced major difficulty. The crest, for the 3rd, was almost on the objective, and it moved down to clear the woods and orchards of its final line, succeeding after heavy fighting. The men of the 2nd and 1st Divisions, with further to go, moved steadily over the ridge at either side of the ruined village of Thélus, the only village on the ridge, situated to the right of the Lens-Arras road. The sun shone through a sudden rift in the overcast sky, momentarily flooding the scene with light. The enemy saw the high ground about Thélus covered with Canadian infantry, some advancing and some consolidating positions. "Thus for a fleeting moment was revealed the final issue of the day: the Germans saw that the Ridge was lost, the Canadians knew that it was won."[40]

The 2nd Division, assisted by the 13th Brigade of the British 5th Division, continued to advance to the final line. The British brigade moved to the north of Hill 135 and seized the Bois de Bonval and the Bois de Goulot both final objectives—while the division itself wrested

Farbus from the enemy in the teeth of machine-guns and field guns firing at point-blank range.

Currie's division, with its long advance, still had three thousand yards to go to Farbus Wood, and as it was beyond the range of the barrage the enemy wire had not been cut. The previously "silent" batteries now came into play and behind this new barrage infantrymen cut the wire, and swept downhill to overrun German batteries and seize the wood.

As they pressed on behind the barrage . . . the sky suddenly became overcast, and a blizzard raged for a few minutes. That picture is one I shall never forget—the dark scarred wood in the distance, the line of bursting shells creeping slowly toward it, the long line of khaki figures following the barrage and minding the shells and bullets which thinned their ranks no more than the driven snowflakes which overcast the whole scene.[41]

Early in the afternoon, as soon as the outcome seemed certain, Byng had telephoned First Army to request cavalry to exploit the success in the centre and right. He foresaw the possibility of seizing important rail and canal crossings on the plain beyond the ridge. But the cavalry was under GHQ control, and not that of General Horne, and by the time Haig's permission had been given, the moment had passed.[42]

The 4th Division, on the left, suffered a serious check in front of the highest point of the ridge, Hill 145. Forward enemy trench lines, as with the other divisions, were taken with ease, but thereafter strong positions on the hill itself held up the advance. From the Pimple, which the artillery had had no orders to mask other than with gas and smoke, the enemy enfiladed the assaulting waves of infantry causing heavy casualties. By the middle of the afternoon, the enemy still holding out, it became necessary to repeat the whole attack with fresh troops to clear up the situation. Artillery preparation was impossible; isolated pockets of Canadian troops had dug in close to the stubbornly resisting enemy. It was not before the morning of the 10th that infantrymen, without benefit of artillery, had cleared the summit. By that time the forward brigade was too exhausted to do more.[43]

At 3:15 on the afternoon of 10 April the 10th Brigade relieved the 11th, and renewed the assault. Its battalions stormed forward across the hill and down the escarpment to make good the divisional objectives. With that, the four-mile length of Vimy Ridge to a depth of four thousand yards at its widest part was in Canadian hands. It remained only to bring up artillery to check counter-offensives that might develop and to capture the Pimple, from Prussian Guards, on the 12th.

On 11 April the Germans pulled back two miles to a defensive line outside the western suburbs of Lens, far enough back from the ridge to deprive the Canadians of effective close observation.* The commanding positions won had forced this on them:

From the crest the whole plain of Douai lay at the Canadians' feet. The vista was one of peaceful-looking villages, nestling in green woods, of prosperous towns on the far horizon, from whose high chimney stacks poured clouds of smoke, of railways over which trains were still travelling. The whole fertile plain was seared with roads, and the roads were alive with movement.[44]

By the 14th the Canadians had followed up the retiring Germans and established a line opposite them, firmly consolidating the additional ground gained. No immediate attack could be contemplated; the roads had been almost completely obliterated and it would take days to repair them sufficiently to bring up artillery and stores for a renewed offensive.

With that, the Battle of Vimy Ridge had ended. It had been a great and striking victory. On a four-mile frontage the Corps had overrun one of the enemy's most formidable positions from foremost defences to gun-line in a single day; it had gone on to achieve a maximum penetration of nearly five miles. And despite the almost impregnable defences, the Germans had suffered the greater losses. More than 4,000 prisoners alone were captured, excluding killed and wounded, at a cost of 3,598 fatal casualties. In addition, the Germans lost 54 guns of all calibres, 104 trench mortars, and 124 machine-guns.[45] The first day of the Somme offensive, with 57,470 casualties, had not brought this yield in ground, prisoners, or guns.

General Horne ascribed the victory to "soundness of plan, thoroughness of preparation, dash and determination in execution, and devotion to duty on the part of all concerned."[46] We have seen the part Arthur Currie played in the planning and preparations. The soundness of the plan was undoubtedly the major factor in the operation's success; but it could not have been realized without the courage, will and stamina of the Canadian soldier with an excellent artillery acting in harmony.

Vimy brought many tributes to Canadian arms. The Corps had now demonstrated its power and efficiency. "Canada will be proud . . ." wrote King George V to Haig, and the French termed the feat "an Easter gift from Canada to France."[47] And just as Currie had gone to Verdun, so senior French officers came to the ridge to study the Canadian operation in detail. Hindenburg consoled Ludendorff. He pressed his hand and said: "We have lived through more critical times than to-day together!"[48] But Ludendorff, who "had looked forward to the expected offensive with confidence" was "deeply depressed."[49] He relieved his feelings by removing the 6th Army's Chief of Staff, the

*The Germans themselves were still able to observe, and shell, Canadian traffic down the face of the ridge.

man responsible for "this heavy defeat."[50] Within a fortnight the Army Commander followed him from the field to take up the appointment of Governor General of Belgium.

Vimy, its significance for Canada notwithstanding, was not the only success of the Arras offensive. The Third Army, fighting at the Scarpe, achieved a like success over lower and softer ground. The enemy was again surprised. On the 9th Allenby advanced from between two to six thousand yards, capturing almost 6,000 prisoners and 36 guns. By the end of the offensive on 14 April, the total had swelled to 13,000 prisoners and 200 guns.[51] But the Hindenburg Line was still intact; and though the pressure was maintained to assist the forthcoming French offensive, gains petered out in the face of stiffening German resistance.

Attention was now focused on Nivelle's much-vaunted break-through thrust to the south, for which the Arras battle had been a preliminary. It was ill-starred from the very beginning. The German withdrawal to the Hindenburg Line not only showed that the enemy had the will to relinquish ground if circumstances warranted it, but it enabled the Germans to hold the line with thirteen fewer divisions. It also restricted the area of the Allied attack. No assault could be launched across the wasted ground, the devastation had been too thorough for that. It would take weeks to restore the facilities necessary for a First World War offensive; it took until 5 April to drive in even the outposts and to reach the main position. The areas of British and French attacks, therefore, had been restricted to the flanks of the evacuated area— around Arras in the north and, for the French, along the Aisne, north of Reims.

The Germans could be reasonably confident of the area that would be attacked, and that confidence became certainty with the capture early in April of a French divisional operation order and their observation of all the signs of impending attack. Not only did they know the place —they knew the date and time of the French assault. And though aware of this, with an obstinacy that seems incredible, Nivelle persisted in his plan apart from short postponements because of weather.

The weather was still atrocious when, on 16 April, the Second Battle of the Aisne opened. By that time the Germans had increased their forces from 18 to 42 divisions, 13 of them coming from the shortened line; but the French still had superiority in men and guns. Nevertheless, the attack failed disastrously as was obvious to Haig on the opening day. His diary entry for 16 April reads: "It is a pity that Nivelle was so very optimistic as regards breaking the enemy's line."[52]

The enemy, fully conversant with French plans, evacuated the forward areas and let them pound the ground to pieces. Then, when the French moved confidently forward, they brought down their own bombardment or subjected them to counter-attack by the troops they had preserved.

Nivelle still persisted. To achieve a break-through he would have to push forward ten miles over the *Chemin des Dames* Ridge where the defences were the thinnest. Yet when the battle ended on 9 May he had gained no more than four miles at enormous cost while his line north and east of Reims had hardly changed. And though the French Government at first suppressed figures of their losses (and later distorted them in the interests of morale) a total of 134,000 was later admitted to for the first ten days of the battle. For the entire offensive, they must have approached 200,000 against 163,000 on the German side.[53]

A disgusted government replaced Nivelle by Pétain on 17 May, 1917, and at the end of the month came the disastrous sequel to the Aisne fiasco. For this last offensive the French armies, undermined by the horrors of Verdun, had drawn on the dregs of their endurance; they had believed Nivelle's confident prediction that it would end the war. Completely disillusioned now, French discipline melted through despair.

Just as the Russians had revolted against similar futile massacres, the simmering discontent in the French armies—with Russia as an inspiration and example—bubbled over into open mutiny. The French Army had passed the limits of endurance.

TEN.
1917: CURRIE RETRIEVES HAIG'S REPUTATION FROM THE PASSCHENDAELE MUD

General Henri Philippe Pétain brought to the command of the French armies a realistic conception of strategy. He was fully convinced of the need for this even before the mutinies took place. With both his predecessors, and with Haig, he agreed that the enemy must be worn down; but the type of offensive they had waged for two barren years found no favour with him. Unlike them, Pétain had experienced modern war as a lowly brigade commander and thus had been in close touch with the realities of siege warfare on the Western Front. As one promised break-through after another wore out with terrible losses, his pessimism hardened; and what he saw later as the commander of a division, a corps, an army and a group of armies did nothing to change it.

Great offensives with distant objectives, Pétain pointed out, called for elaborate preparations with a complete loss of all surprise; thus warned, the enemy could reinforce his line. The attacking troops would eventually find themselves on a prepared killing-ground that made the offensive far more costly than the defensive. The right formula, Pétain considered, would be to unleash sudden, limited attacks well supported by artillery at several successive places, reasoning that each one would catch the enemy by surprise. Early gains would be quickly consolidated before the enemy could reinforce, and the battle then broken off. He did not expect more than shallow penetrations; but those were preferable to deep salients inviting bombardment and concentric counter-attack. To carry out the new policy, a network of good communications and stores dumps along the front would have to be built so that men and equipment could be switched rapidly from place to place. By these small surprise attacks Pétain hoped to inflict greater losses on the enemy than would be sustained by his own troops; only when German resources had finally been exhausted would he turn to the full offensive.

This was attrition without massacres; attrition based on cold realism and not on a desperate wish. It was certainly a departure from Joffre,

164

Haig and Nivelle's "too literal acceptance of Napoleon's and Clausewitz's ideas on the supreme power of will and the necessity of striking the enemy's centre of gravity. 'Will' came to mean obstinacy, or 'pluck'; the enemy's centre of gravity to mean his most powerful defences."[1]

Besides, America was now in the war. Surely the only sane policy was to wrest the initiative from the Germans without a major offensive, to keep them off balance and to force them to react to short yet powerful blows—pinned down, never able to disengage and slowly weakening—until the new, unwearied troops arrived to give the death blow? So, at any rate, thought Pétain.

Only an exceptional man could have stepped outside the military training and tradition of a lifetime, could have remained free from the influence of the desperate hope pressing upon him from politicians, public opinion and his own subordinates. Pétain was such a man.[2]

Other events, however, intervened. As early as 29 April the insubordinate mutterings and growlings amongst Nivelle's troops crystallized to the point of mutiny, but only in one shell-shocked battalion. Cut to a third of its strength on the first day, this unit had been pulled out of the line, only to be ordered back again on the 29th. The men refused to march. Next day a shaky discipline reasserted itself and the men obeyed; four alleged ringleaders were shot.[3]

On 3 May a division became infected. It, too, refused to march to the front. Orders had no effect; blandishments failed. This time too many armed men were involved for punishment. Finally, the men compromised to some extent; they would go to the trenches but they would not attack. Freed by universal action from any reprisals, the troops marched forward in suppressed triumph to confide their secret to the army.[4]

By the end of May, mutinies—formless, without leadership or goal save to put an end to attacks and appalling slaughter—had erupted throughout the front-line units and some behind the line. Not all were affected, but such was the trend that no unit could be relied upon; one that had been immune to date might flare into revolt tomorrow in the face of unpopular orders. Nervous officers, stripped of disciplinary powers by the magnitude of the movement, shrugged and spread their hands. They left the troops alone to sing The Internationale, to wave red flags, and to form their Soldiers' Councils. Some sympathized. The commander of a badly mauled light infantry regiment is reported to have said:

This is a regression. We haven't learned a thing. We are still sticking to the methods of 1915. Of course, we'll get citations and decorations, but we don't care. We'd rather throw them at the heads of our leaders; it's not the honours that we are interested in, but a wise policy, more sparing of human lives.

As for the men, "all their hopes have been deceived, and their faith destroyed: this is criminal."[5]

The soldiers, it seemed, regarded their own unit officers with no ill will. They, too, had stormed the *Chemin des Dames* against a hail of steel, and uncut barbed wire. Some men even fell in behind them and marched to the trenches but they still made a show of independence by baa-ing like lambs on the way to slaughter. But the staff officers were hated. These were the "drinkers of blood," who found it prudent to stay well away from mutinous units.[6] Yet up forward the trenches held. Guns still fired, and troops threw back the German rushes. The men were prepared to defend ground but not to take it, and the enemy had no inkling of the nearness of his triumph.

In June, 1917, the mutinies, with purloined regimental wine as fuel, became even more widespread. Between Paris and the front, a mere hundred kilometres away, there were, according to the War Minister, only two divisions that could be trusted.[7] The widening disorders, it seemed, had a serious aim; that "an honourable peace be concluded without delay."[8] For Pétain, newly promoted to command an army that was melting in his hands, the situation could not have been more terrifying.

Catastrophe was not a stranger. He had faced it at Verdun and still pulled the army through. But this was infinitely worse. Discipline had gone and attempts to revive it had proved powerless. Though a cloak of secrecy had been thrown over the suppurating mess, the Germans might get wind of it; and attack would bring the collapse of the front and the fall of Paris.

On 2 June Pétain sent General Debeney, his Chief of the General Staff, to see Haig and put the whole situation before him. He was to "conceal nothing."[9] Help promised by Nivelle to Haig for 10 June to attack alongside the British in Flanders could not now be given; but an assault by six divisions near the coast, promised for the middle of July, would be launched as planned.[10] There is little doubt that Haig, long desirous of a thrust in Flanders to destroy the submarine bases on the Belgian coast, was now more than ever convinced of its necessity. It seemed imperative to draw German attention away from the French front as soon as possible. Plans had already been made to open his northern offensive at Messines for 7 June and he decided to let the operation proceed.[11]

Pétain then turned to the suppression of the mutinies, and in this his own reputation was his sharpest weapon. He was a fighting commander who regarded soldiers as persons, not as numbers to be thrown away. No disasters were associated with his name, and at

Verdun he had turned what seemed certain defeat into victory. Even there the sacrifices had deeply touched him:

My heart lurched as I saw our young men of twenty going into the furnace of Verdun . . . how saddening it was when they came back . . . Their stares seemed to be fixed in a vision of unbelievable terror . . . they drooped beneath the weight of their horrifying memories. When I spoke to them, they could scarcely answer.[12]

During the first two weeks in June Pétain put in hand measures designed to alleviate the grievances of the troops: regular leave, better food and bunks in accommodation behind the line. Hand in hand with this, ringleaders were dealt with sharply and severely to deter the wavering units. Courts martial brought in 23,385 verdicts of guilty; 432 were sentenced to death, but of these only 55 were shot; the rest of the convicted men were shipped to penal settlements in the colonies.

While these measures were taking effect, Pétain toured the front talking to the men and leaving behind the impression that he really cared. Conditions would be improved; under him there would be no more grand offensives, and he kept his word. From then on the mutinies began to abate. By the middle of July they had ceased entirely, and with that the danger of revolution and a separate peace had gone.

Meanwhile, with Russia already discounted, France convalescent and American help in sight, Haig gladly undertook to engage the Germans alone.

On 7 June Plumer's Second Army (IX, X Corps and II ANZAC) stormed and took the Messines Ridge. It was a necessary preliminary to future operations from the Ypres Salient for, from this high ground, the enemy commanded the communications up to Ypres; furthermore, the ridge commanded trench positions within the salient. In British hands it would be a bastion from which the right flank could be held secure. As at Vimy, it was a limited attack for the ridge alone, but the method differed. This was a siege attack perfectly attuned to siege warfare. The key to success lay in the simultaneous explosion of nineteen enormous mines containing six hundred tons of explosives, which had been laid after six months' tunnelling. A vast array of artillery was assembled for a seven-day preliminary bombardment and a great barrage on the day of the attack, much as had been done at Vimy. Behind the barrage, nine divisions would storm forward.

The mines exploded successfully, wrecking the German front-line trenches, and at the same time the barrage crashed down. Within three hours the crest of the ridge had been won. That afternoon, when the artillery had been brought forward, a second leap cleared the entire ridge. A German counter-attack next day broke down in the face of a strong defence. The Second Army now held a position overlooking the southern part of the Passchendaele Ridge; this in turn dominated the low-lying ground over which Haig's main offensive to clear the Belgian coast would have to be launched.

Plumer pressed Haig strongly for permission to exploit his success in the direction of Passchendaele before German reserves arrived. But General Gough, whose Fifth Army would carry out the later blow planned for July, preferred to include the operation in his own tasks, and Haig, following Gough's advice, restrained Plumer from exploitation at that propitious time. Had he not done so, the later horrors at Passchendaele might never have taken place.

Further south, Haig had kept up a relentless pressure with four armies against the enemy north and south of Arras to assist Nivelle's April offensive which, as we have seen, dragged on into May. The Canadian Corps took part in these operations, still as part of the First Army.

Between the Souchez, which flows through Lens, and the Scarpe are the following villages from north to south: Avion, Méricourt, Arleux, Oppy, Gavrelle and Roeux. The Canadian sector, in the north, faced the first three. The enemy had adopted a strong defensive line, Avion-Méricourt-Oppy, with a loop of trenches to take in Arleux.

Haig resumed his attacks on the Scarpe—the Second Battle of the Scarpe—on 23 April. The main attack was carried out by the Third Army immediately south of the First. It gained one and a half miles. A division of the First Army, on the Canadian right, captured Gavrelle; as yet the Canadian Corps was not involved. These operations cost the British 10,000 casualties while taking 2,500 prisoners.[13]

On the 28th the pressure continued. The Third Army attacked astride the Scarpe, the British 2nd Division (First Army) against Oppy, and Currie's 1st Division to clear the Arleux Loop. The British attacks failed, mainly through poor tactics, the objectives being indicated by lines drawn across the map regardless of natural, and heavily defended, features. Currie's division, by clearing not only the loop but the village beyond, achieved what the British official historian described as "the only tangible success of the whole operation."[14]

Haig on 1 May advised the Chief of the Imperial General Staff of his intention to slacken the Scarpe operations prior to shifting his main effort to Flanders. But the French agony along the Aisne continued until the second week in May. Two days later Haig opened the Third Battle of the Scarpe out of loyalty to the French and to win a more defensible line. Oppy remained uncaptured, and beyond Arleux the Canadians now faced the village of Fresnoy at the tip of a long spur that commanded German-held ground behind it. The Canadian task —again the 1st Division—would be Fresnoy.

The First Army (XIII Corps) seized and held a narrow strip along the front, but not Oppy. South of the Scarpe one formation of the

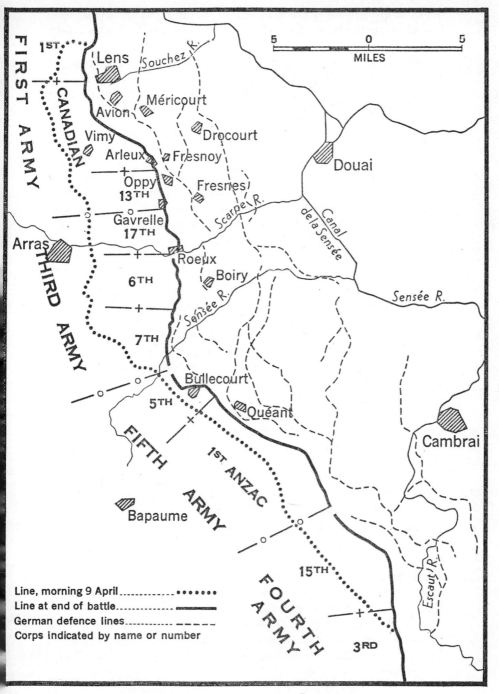

FIRST ARMY

1ST

CANADIAN

THIRD ARMY

FIFTH ARMY

FOURTH ARMY

1ST ANZAC

Lens

Souchez R.

Méricourt

Avion

Drocourt

Vimy

Arleux

Fresnoy

Oppy

13TH

Fresnes

Scarpe R.

Douai

Canal de la Sensée

Gavrelle

17TH

Arras

Roeux

Boiry

Sensée R.

6TH

Sensée R.

7TH

Bullecourt

5TH

Quéant

Cambrai

Bapaume

15TH

Escaut R.

3RD

Line, morning 9 April .... ● ● ● ● ● ●
Line at end of battle .... ──────
German defence lines .... ─ ─ ─ ─
Corps indicated by name or number

THE BATTLES OF THE SCARPE, APRIL-MAY, 1917.

Third Army advanced five hundred yards on a thousand-yard front but that was all. "The relieving feature," comments the British official historian, "of a day which many who witnessed it considered the blackest of the War"[15] was Currie's capture of Fresnoy. The 5th British Division relieved the 1st Division at Fresnoy on 5 May, and Currie's men pulled back to Corps reserve. Three days later the enemy, anxious to replace a vital stone knocked out of his defensive wall, counter-attacked after a two-day bombardment of exceptional weight and recovered the village.

With that, the Third Battle of the Scarpe ended. Further south, the Battle of Bullecourt, fought by the Fifth Army, lasted nine days longer. During that battle the Hindenburg Line, fortified with the keenest ingenuity, was breached after a pitifully small assault by a group of eleven tanks. Two got through, leading Australian troops into the open country a mile beyond. In insufficient strength, the tanks and some of the infantry were captured, but this tiny effort was proof of what might have been done by tanks deployed in mass and properly supported. The battle closed with Bullecourt in British hands.

In aggregate, these attacks, butting into the Arras sector for a continued period against defences that grew steadily stronger, proved costly and of no strategic value. The villages had been turned into slaughter yards. Ground had been gained on a twenty-mile front to a maximum depth of five miles; 158,660 casualties had been incurred against German losses of about 150,000, including 20,000 prisoners.[16] At the end of May Haig began the transfer of troops northwards in preparation for the Flanders offensive. The First Army, with the Canadian Corps under command, would resume operations towards Lens to distract enemy attention from this build-up.

For Currie, June was a momentous month. The Birthday Honours List of 1 June named him Sir Arthur Currie, K.C.M.G. Next day a bomb struck his headquarters, killing two and wounding fifteen. His own head was grazed by a flying fragment. Congratulatory messages on his knighthood—from Garnet Hughes, officers in France, and friends in England and in Canada—were still streaming in when, on the 6th, Currie was summoned to Corps Headquarters. There, Byng told him without preamble that the Third Army Commander, Allenby, had been named Commander-in-Chief in the Middle East, and that he himself had been selected to replace him. That left the Corps without a commander and, to fill Byng's shoes, Haig had decided on Currie. Two days later Currie moved to Corps Headquarters as acting Corps Commander.

Currie was the first non-regular officer to reach such high command. He found himself in the heady atmosphere that surrounds the commander of a national force. Suddenly he was faced not only with the military responsibility for the powerful Corps that had taken Vimy Ridge but, more disquieting, with political responsibility to the Canadian Government. This was a greater responsibility than ever confronted any corps commander in the British forces throughout the war, with one later exception: Monash, to the Australian Government.

It was logical that Currie should have been selected. His actions at St. Julien, the first time he had been in battle, demonstrated, as Lloyd George put it, his "natural aptitude for soldiering."[17] His cool head, sincerity and great ability had marked him for advancement throughout the later operations. Even after Vimy, in the preparations for which he had played such a notable part, it was his division alone that had never failed to take the assigned objective. Haig had personally congratulated him. So had Horne: "The 1st Canadian Division," he wrote, "is the pride and wonder of the British Army."[18] And even the Germans had paid unconscious tribute. "Wounded German officers say we must be a special assaulting division—they wouldn't believe that we are the same division which put them off Vimy Ridge and are still at it."[19] There was little doubt in British minds, therefore, that Currie was the right man for the job.

For Perley, the Overseas Minister, the promotion presented difficulties. First, he had not been consulted, and he protested to the British authorities. Furthermore, Turner, the GOC Canadians, was senior to Currie in the Overseas Forces, and had explicitly maintained his right to be considered for the Corps command when taking over his duties in London. Nevertheless, Perley was well aware that Currie had a distinguished fighting record and was in the strong position of being in France and already in command. Turner, on the other hand, had been away from the front for six months, and his record, in Haig's estimation, bore no comparison to that of Currie. Then again, Turner had done a first-class job in England and Perley had no wish to lose him.

Canadian sensitivities were soothed when a British explanation reached Perley that Haig's instructions for Currie "to take over command of the Canadian Corps" should have included the word "temporarily."[20] Perley, with that, could have put his own candidate forward, especially as the Prime Minister had left the matter to his judgment, though with a word of caution that the Overseas Minister should "take advice of higher command unless you see strong reason to contrary."[21] Borden also reminded Perley that Garnet Hughes should get the vacant division.[22]

Perley sent for Currie who arrived in London on the 14th. Next day the Overseas Minister "reached a most pleasant understanding" with Currie and Turner. Both would be promoted lieutenant-general, thereby preserving Turner's seniority, and would retain their present appointments.[23] The promotions took effect from 9 June. Currie, however, was quite firm in recommending Brigadier-General A. C. Macdonell for the command of the 1st Division; he refused to have Garnet Hughes, whom he considered an indifferent front-line soldier, and Perley accepted his arguments.[24] A powerful Hughes' interest, aware of Currie's lack of political friends and the dubious state of his finances, subjected him to pressure in Garnet's favour. But Currie would not change his stand.

On the evening of 15 June Garnet Hughes called on Currie at his hotel and asked point-blank for the 1st Division. Currie refused to recommend him. Though a personal friend of Hughes and aware that he owed his original appointment in some measure to his influence, his professional opinion of him had not changed. Hughes lost his temper and a bitter three-hour scene ensued. Currie remained firm and in the end Hughes stormed out, shouting: "God help the man who goes against my father!"

I am importuned, coaxed, threatened and they sought to bribe me. I was told that General Hughes would have to get the 1st Division: that there was a combination in England and in Canada for him that neither I nor any other man could beat: that his father wanted him to get the position and that God help the man who fell out with his father.[25]

Currie returned to France on the 16th. In England the intrigue against him, led by Lord Beaverbrook whose aid Garnet Hughes had enlisted, continued. Perley could not help but know it; he also suspected that Sir Robert Borden would welcome any means of mollifying the ex-Minister of Militia.[26]

Towards the end of June Perley sent his Deptuy Minister, Walter Gow, over to France to press Hughes' claims. Gow was unsuccessful, and his report convinced the Overseas Minister that both Currie and Macdonell's promotions were so popular in the Corps[27] that the issue was dead; for the remainder of Perley's term as Minister, relations between Currie and himself were governed by mutual confidence and respect.

The attempt through Perley to install Hughes as commander of the 1st Division having failed, Currie's enemies then resorted to more brutal methods to oust him from the Corps. They based their attack on Currie's debts. Creditors in Victoria were advised to demand instant settlement and to threaten legal action if their claims were not met. Currie had done his best to meet his obligations; he had already paid off one debt amounting to more than ten thousand dollars.[28] Hard-pressed and with insufficient funds to settle all his debts, Currie's plight was serious.

Throughout July, August and September his creditors continued to hound him. The matter reached Perley's ears in July, and the Minister feared disastrous consequences should the matter become public. So great was his concern, in fact, that he offered to shoulder half the debts if the Minister of Militia would do the same.[29] Kemp refused. Perley then referred Currie's dossier to Ottawa to be dealt with there.

On August 17 Currie's indebtedness was pondered over by the members of the Privy Council who eventually considered advancing money from the Department of Militia and Defence, subject to recovery after the war. A decision to that effect was reached but the Council directed the Paymaster General (for reasons which cannot now be ascertained) not to act on it for three months. Should legal proceedings be started before then, Currie's career would end.[30]

In September two senior officers in France came to the rescue of the harassed Corps Commander, putting up six thousand dollars between them to stave off Currie's creditors. (He paid his subordinates in instalments, clearing the last of these in June, 1919.)[31] With that, he could shake off the immediate worry that had haunted him, and return to the business of soldiering with an easier mind. But the breach between himself and the Hughes family, with its powerful following, had become irreparably wide. Currie could be sure that attacks against him would continue in another form.

Despite his inner turmoil Currie remained outwardly calm during his first months as commander and his capability was unimpaired. The task of the Corps at the end of May and the early part of June had been an attempt to break into the German position along the Souchez between Avion and the western fringe of Lens. The hamlet of La Coulotte, between the Canadian line and Avion, was seized on the night of 2-3 June but could not be held against strong German counter-attacks. Currie's first job as Corps Commander was to resume these operations.

On the day following the costly and abortive attempts on 3 June, he protested at a corps commanders' conference against holding newly won trenches. To remain on captured ground in this locality, on which the enemy concentrated overwhelming fire, brought heavy casualties. The purpose of keeping the enemy in the Lens area could be served equally well by large-scale raids whereby the troops would inflict as much damage as possible on the enemy and then withdraw. General Horne agreed.[32]

Such a raid, under Currie's direction, was carried out by the 3rd and 4th Divisions on a two-mile front in the Souchez-Avion sector. It was carefully rehearsed and went as planned. The attackers struck and withdrew, bringing back 136 prisoners, and leaving behind about 700 enemy casualties. The Canadians lost 100 men killed, and 609 wounded,[33] a result more favourable to the attackers than to the defenders.

Haig's preparations in the north were still proceeding. He directed Horne "to hold the enemy to his ground and prevent his moving troops elsewhere."[34] Accordingly, General Horne ordered an advance through the Oppy-Méricourt line and the capture of Lens. By the evening of 25 July the whole line had advanced about half a mile after fierce attacks; a heavy thunderstorm had given some surprise. The British were in the western outskirts of Oppy and held most of Avion while the Canadians had secured a continuous line of Avion Trench. A full-scale attack against Lens, however, could not be carried out immediately. Bad weather and flooding caused a postponement and the shortage of heavy artillery—most of it now in Flanders—meant considerable regrouping, which again would cause delay.

The capture of Lens remained as "the main objective of the First Army"—it was an obsession—for the first part of July.[35] Horne handed this task to the Canadian Corps and thus it became Currie's first major tactical operation as Corps Commander. He was ordered to plan for breaking through the Méricourt trench south of Lens and was then to advance and secure the line of the railway beyond, running northwest into Lens. On 10 July the Corps relieved I British Corps opposite Lens and Hill 70, in preparation for the assault.

It might have been expected that a newly appointed corps commander would have attacked as ordered. But Currie wanted to be sure that the assigned objectives were feasible and that to hold them would be useful. Much as he had done at Ypres, he climbed the *Bois de l'Hirondelle* spur behind the Canadian lines and, lying prone all morning, studied the ground. The Corps would be pushing forward into open ground, he saw, lower and more exposed than the ground which they then held. And the new ground was dominated from the north by Hill 70 and from the southeast by Sallaumines Hill. He did not doubt the ability of his corps to take the objectives, but what was the point?

. . . it would be an unwise thing to do so because it would leave us in a worse position than before. It would pull our guns farther out into the plain, would alter our general defensive system, and would not be a sufficient threat to the enemy to deceive him in any particular.[36]

This, then, would be a holding attack in its worst sense; attack for the sake of attack with no tactical objectives at the end of it, and one unlikely to deceive the enemy "in any particular." A holding attack, in any case, is perhaps the most difficult military operation for troops to understand. This one would have the purpose of keeping German men and guns away from Flanders; but troops see only the immediate attack, and when they are lacerated—seemingly for nothing—a sour

taste remains. If, however, a tangible objective with tactical significance could be substituted, then the attack would be worthwhile.

Therefore I went to see the Army Commander and told him what
my objections were. He asked me what I had to suggest and I said that
if we were to fight at all, let us fight for something worth having. I
named Hill 70 to the north of Lens or Sallaumines to the east of it. He
asked me which one I thought should be done first and I said Hill 70.[37]

The outcome was that Haig, advised of these objections by Horne,
visited the Corps and was finally convinced by Currie; he warned the
Canadian however that "the Boche would not let us have Hill 70."
The Flanders offensive would start on 31 July; Haig asked for the Hill
70 operation around 4 August. Again Currie demurred. "My boy,"
said Haig, "this is your own attack. I leave it to you to carry it out when
you are ready. You know what I want and I trust you to help me in
every way you can."[38]

Haig's trepidations concerning the enemy's reaction to a threat
against Hill 70 were natural. The loss of this feature—a bald dome of
chalky downland dominating Lens and providing observation over the
Douai plain beyond—would not be tolerated by the enemy. Even if this
strong position could be taken, as it had been by the British after Loos,
he would again counter-attack repeatedly to take it back. German
counter-attacks could be easily mounted against the hill. Between the
colliery town of Lens and Hill 70 were brick-built suburbs of miners'
houses reduced by shellfire to a blur of ruins; through this area a maze
of trenches wandered, protected by broken walls and piles of bricks.
Good cover was thus provided for the assembly of German troops.

Currie, however, planned to turn this German sensitivity towards
the loss of Hill 70 to his own advantage. He would position artillery to
cover the suburbs of Lens and deliberately provoke German counter-
attacks so that the enemy, drawn onto a killing-ground dominated by
the Canadian guns, would be destroyed. His scheme, therefore, must
include quick consolidation of the objective, rock-like defence, observation and warning of the enemy concentrations, and the domination of
the killing-ground between the Lens suburbs and Hill 70 with nearly
every gun he had.

While Currie put plans in hand, a preliminary operation went on to
keep the Germans occupied. Lipsett's 3rd Division was given the task
of simulating the original thrust on Lens itself that Horne had ordered.
This took the form of an assault through the Méricourt trench on the
night 22-23 July to destroy German positions on the railway beyond.
It was a raid, but even this concept had not been arrived at without
difficulty.

Horne, on studying the plan, drew Currie's attention to a new
injunction by Douglas Haig that, in order to increase the pressure on

Lens, all ground must be held.[39] GHQ's obsession, to capture Lens, still persisted. Again the new Corps Commander stood firm. It would be tactically unsound, he said, to try to hold a railway embankment commanded by high ground in front and subjected to fire in enfilade from either flank; and again his views prevailed. The raiders blew up enemy dug-outs and a tunnel along the railway, then withdrew with fifty prisoners.

The attack on Hill 70, delayed by bad weather and extensive planning, was set for 15 August. The preparations were very thorough, especially for the use of artillery to break up the inevitable counter-attacks storming forward to wrest the feature back. Two Canadian divisions would carry out the assault supported by nine artillery field brigades—five with the 1st Division and four with the 2nd—and their fire would be augmented by that of 160 machine-guns, which would go forward to lend close support as soon as the infantry were firmly on the hill. Each forward machine-gun position would form a strongpoint, the nucleus of infantry platoon groups well dug in. And as for Vimy, on ground similar to the battle area, the assault was rehearsed time and time again.[40] Well might Currie write on the flyleaf of his personal diary for 1917/18: "Thorough preparations must lead to success. Neglect nothing."[41]

Currie obtained from the British the services of special companies of Royal Engineers whose preliminary task consisted of a gas bombardment of the area to be attacked or from where enemy reserves would come. By 15 August, some 3,500 drums and a thousand shells containing gas had thudded into the city and its suburbs, a grim rejoinder to *Flammenwerfer* techniques and mustard gas, which the enemy had first introduced on this front in July. Nor was that all. At zero the artillery barrage was stiffened with 500 drums of blazing oil at selected targets, to build up a smoke screen and demoralize the defenders.

As dawn broke on the 15th the attack went in. In fact, there were two attacks: the main thrust against the hill and, to confuse the enemy, a diversionary blow directly on Lens by the 4th Division, which drew more retaliatory fire than did the main attack. The attack against Hill 70, ten battalions forward, went like clockwork. The infantry hugged a rolling barrage provided by more than two hundred field pieces, while four hundred yards ahead of that 4.5- and 6-inch howitzers concentrated on defensive lines and known strongpoints. Thick oil smoke screened the advancing khaki lines. And though the enemy artillery retaliated almost at once, counter-battery guns under Lieutenant-Colonel A. G. L. McNaughton, whose special task this was, neutralized their fire.

Within twenty minutes the troops had gained the crest; and by 6 A.M. some were on the final objective, which, as at Vimy, was the base of the hill on the enemy side. The 2nd Brigade, faced by a well-defended

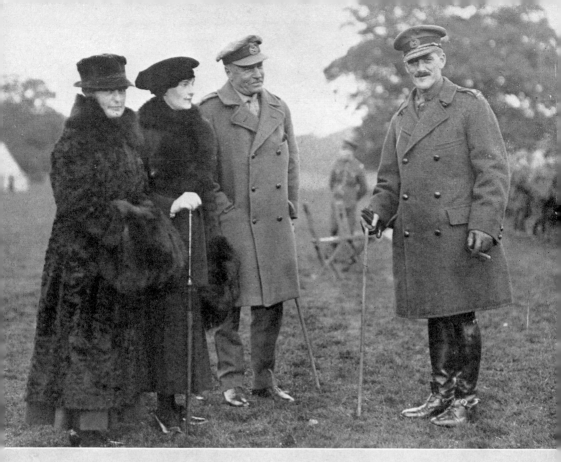

Major-General G. B. Hughes, commanding the 5th Canadian Division. The son of the Minister of Militia and Defence (right) attending a divisional sports meet held at Witley, in England, October, 1917.

Dominion Day, 1918. The 3rd Division concert party—the "Dumbells"—arriving at the Corps gathering at Tincques. The two leading female impersonators are, left to right, Privates Alan Murray and Ross Hamilton.

The Drocourt-Quéant Line. This striking photograph illustrates the heavy belts of wire of this formidable extension of the Hindenburg Line, pierced by the Canadians in September, 1918.

After Amiens. A tank halts on the Amiens-Roye Road after the great victory of 8 August. German prisoners carry back wounded Canadians.

Major Georges Vanier. Major Vanier (a future Governor General of Canada) lost his right leg on 28 August, 1918, while serving with the 22nd Battalion in the heavy fighting for the Fresnes-Rouvroy Line.

The Arras-Cambrai Road. Canadian supplies moving up from Arras during September, 1918, over a corduroy road built by the Canadian Engineers who were particularly adept at constructing this type of road.

Entering Cambrai. After forcing the formidable obstacle of the Canal du Nord, triumphant Canadian troops enter the deserted city of Cambrai on the morning of 8 October, 1918.

chalk quarry which imposed delay, had a tougher task. By this time the oil smoke had cleared, and machine-gun fire forced individual rushes from shellhole to shellhole, which did not achieve their purpose. It was not before midnight on the 16th, after repeated attacks, that the 2nd Brigade finally cleared up its front. It had gone into battle with 3,370 men; only 1,719 marched out when the 1st Brigade relieved it.[42]

As had been expected, German counter-attacks came thick and fast, the first before 9 A.M. on the morning of the 15th. By the 18th, when the enemy at last desisted, no fewer than twenty-one, delivered in strength and with great determination, had been beaten off. This period, for the majority of the Corps, marked the real fighting at Hill 70.[43]

Currie and his gunner team had planned for this. No sooner had the crest been captured than strongpoints, centred on Vickers machine-guns, were constructed. Artillery observers, dug deep into solid chalk, overlooked the German preparations. Aerial observers watched the German reserves start forward; ground observers saw them crowd into assembly areas along the front. And for the first time the guns could be registered instantly by the use of wireless communication with the forward ground observers. Wireless, it must be remembered, was in its infancy; but, as the British Signals historian observed, the Canadian Corps was "often more hospitable to fresh departures in signalling than the Imperial troops;"[44] it began to rely more and more on wireless after its successful use at Hill 70.

The pattern, then, was briefly this. Reports of the massing of German troops reached the Heavy Artillery by wireless from observation planes and by wireless and telephone from ground observers positioned on Hill 70. Concentration after concentration—a cascade of shells—poured down on the hapless enemy. But the planning was more subtle than that. The movement of German reserves, resulting from the earlier demonstrations and raids, had been reported by agents and carefully studied. The General Staff at Corps had estimated when the German formations in rear would be alarmed and start to move forward. They produced a march table showing their time of arrival at certain selected depths. Armed with this—and made more accurate by the reports of aerial observers—the artillerymen shelled them even before they reached the battle zone. Well might the infantry pay tribute to the gunners who did everything that was expected of them, and considerably more besides.

One heard of the enemy formation which, marching down the Lens-Carvin road in column of route, and hastening to the forward area, was completely destroyed by the Canadian gunners. The assembling of any sized groups of Germans brought instantaneous fire upon them.[45]

Currie exulted: "Our gunners, machine-gunners, and infantry never had such targets"[46] but, inevitably, some of the enemy got through. Many heavy artillery batteries had been withdrawn to Flanders. Only 164 heavy pieces remained, and some of these were so badly worn that they could only be used when limited accuracy—against German units advancing in depth—was acceptable.

The resolute enemy stormed the Canadian parapets repeatedly, hurling grenades into the trenches and sweeping them with scorching flame. So impetuous were these assaults that many trenches were entered—a *mêlée* of shouting, lunging, wrestling men until one side or the other was ejected. But the Germans were not allowed to keep their gains. Where sections, heavily pressed, recoiled, our men would not be bested. They leapt back, cursing, to savage the enemy until he, in his turn, recoiled. So it continued for four days and three nights of infernal noise, with quiet passages made horrible by the screams and groans of wounded men. On the 18th it ended with Hill 70 firmly in Canadian hands.

"It was," said Currie, "altogether the hardest battle in which the Corps has participated."[47] The battle was in fact Canadian in conception, execution and result—and it was a victory. The hill did not change hands again during the war. Strategically, as a holding attack, it was completely successful. The Germans admitted that the Canadians had attained their ends. Five enemy divisions had been met by Currie and had been badly smashed; the enemy had to replace those troops and, moreover, to reckon with a continued offensive. He thus could not transfer troops to the north or even relieve formations, battered in Flanders, from Lens as he had planned.[48]

The British were still obsessed with seizing Lens and the fighting continued until 25 August in the form of clearing trenches in the suburbs around the town. It was a mistake to forsake the advantages conferred by the high ground to meet the enemy on more equal terms. The Germans would not relinquish Lens itself without a struggle. To wrest it from them, ruined brick pile by crumbling mound, as the fighting in the suburbs proved, would be a formidable task with the slender artillery resources available. Horne kept the job in mind but did not press it. After the 25th the fighting lapsed into a surly stalemate until, six weeks later, the Canadians moved to Flanders. The period 15-25 August had brought them 9,198 casualties against an estimated 20,000 on the German side.[49]

Haig's northern thrust, as we have seen, opened brilliantly with the capture of Messines Ridge on 7 June. The offensive was not resumed until 31 July. In the interim, Lloyd George, who had sanctioned Haig's plans in May on the basis of French co-operation, was having second thoughts. Five days before Messines, Haig knew from Pétain's emissary

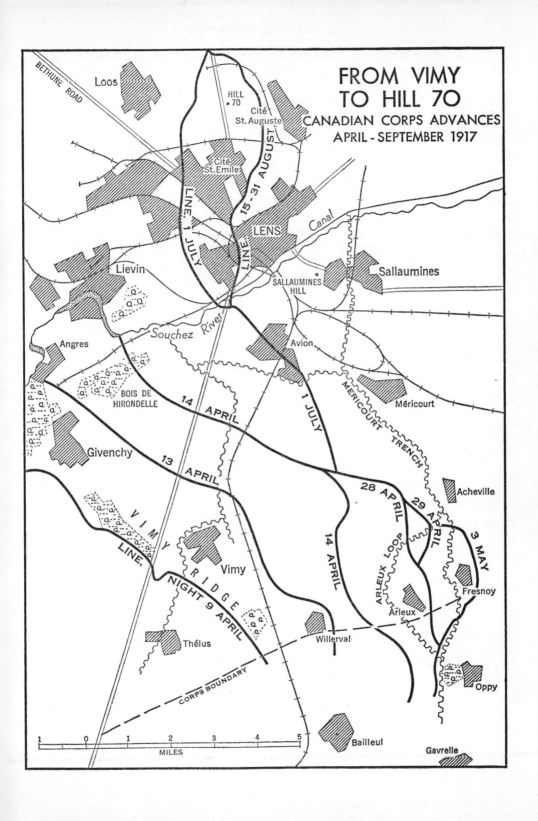

FROM VIMY
TO HILL 70
CANADIAN CORPS ADVANCES
APRIL - SEPTEMBER 1917

BETHUNE ROAD

Loos

HILL 70

Cité St. Auguste

Cité St. Emile

LINE 15-31 AUGUST

LINE 1 JULY

LENS

Canal

Lievin

Sallaumines

SALLAUMINES HILL

Angres

Souchez River

Avion

Méricourt

BOIS DE HIRONDELLE

14 APRIL

1 JULY

MÉRICOURT TRENCH

Givenchy

13 APRIL

28 APRIL

29 APRIL

Acheville

3 MAY

VIMY LINE

VIMY RIDGE

14 APRIL

ARLEUX LOOP

Fresnoy

Vimy

NIGHT 9 APRIL

Arleux

Thélus

Willerval

Oppy

CORPS BOUNDARY

1 0 1 2 3 4 5

MILES

Bailleul

Gavrelle

of the French mutinies but, fearing curtailment of his plans, he kept the information to himself and let the attack proceed. Heartened by the result, Haig continued with his preparations for a further blow which, he thought, would clear the Belgian coast that summer and might lead to a German collapse.[50] The Director of Military Intelligence at the War Office, on the other hand, saw no chance of success; he advised the War Cabinet that the best plan would be to remain on the defensive and await the build-up of American troops.[51] The British Prime Minister, by the middle of June, had become convinced that the right policy would be to conserve strength until 1918 (which he saw as the decisive year of the war), apart from sending artillery units to the support of Italy. Three hundred batteries was the figure mentioned.[52] Lloyd George feared that Haig's plan would exhaust the British Army by the winter, without bringing much result.[53]

Haig travelled to London on 19 June to present his case. He demonstrated that an advance of only twenty-five miles would be necessary to free Ostend and Zeebrugge; but Lloyd George was not convinced of the ease of the task. He predicted no more than small gains; and these would be in the initial stages. More difficult to deal with than Haig's optimism, however, was a grave pronouncement by Admiral Jellicoe that because of losses to shipping Britain must have Zeebrugge by the end of the year or accept defeat. Haig noted the scepticism with which this statement was received by the others present, but nevertheless he had received support from a powerful quarter—the navy. The Prime Minister still pushed his scheme for the support of Italy, which Haig, considering it "the act of a lunatic,"[54] refuted point by point on his return to France. On 21 July, the War Cabinet, hesitating to rule out the northern plan over Haig and Jellicoe's objections, grudgingly allowed the offensive to go forward.[55]

The policy which Haig advocated and fought for so tenaciously was probably right for May and even for June. The parlous state of the French Army and the submarine crisis were both sound reasons to justify it at that time. But the situation had altered by the end of July when the main offensive was launched. The French Army was well on the way to recovery. On 20 August, only three weeks later, it attacked brilliantly at Verdun in one of Pétain's "limited" attacks and captured ten thousand prisoners, more than twice the yield of Vimy; Haig, in recording this result, himself admitted that the French Army had had the quiet time which Pétain had hoped for to recover from the Nivelle offensive.[56] Nevertheless, he refused to call off his own offensive then, although it had already bogged down, and stubbornly continued it for almost three more months under shocking conditions and in the face of appalling casualties. The qualities of the First French Army, fighting on his left, must in any case have convinced him that the French were not done yet. Haig's claims that he *had* to go on attacking because of the *"awful"* state of the French troops were post-war attempts to vindicate his forlorn offensive and are contradicted by his diary entries at the time. How, for example, can his claim that he was under French pressure to continue the offensive in Flanders possibly stand up when President Poincaré, on 11 October, asked him when the operation would *stop* as he wanted the British to take over more of the line? [57]

And the peak of the submarine crisis had been reached and passed. The convoy system, introduced that month on a general scale, brought immediate results. Shipping losses steadily declined, more sharply than could possibly have been achieved by the capture of the Flanders ports.

While the strategic results envisaged in May no longer applied by August, the plans of the Commander-in-Chief remained unaltered. His reason lay in the fact that Lloyd George was pressing for the transfer of troops elsewhere. So long as the policy of the offensive prevailed, the War Cabinet could hardly reduce his strength. Were it to be abandoned, it was obvious to Haig that Lloyd George would insist in directing some of his forces to Italy. He was, therefore, determined to undertake, as Foch put it, his "duck's march" through Flanders. The direction of the offensive and the site were all wrong, as Foch implied. Without valid strategic aims the purpose of the offensive could only be attrition; and a better place might have been found for that. The axis of advance swung towards the coast, away from the enemy's main communications, so that there was no profitable basis even for wearing down the German strength; the security of Germany's position in France would not be endangered by Haig's advance. As for the site, Haig knew the Ypres area well. If he had used his eyes when going from place to place he must have seen that the surface water was so high that parapets had to take the place of trenches. And in any case, before the battle, his own Tank Corps pointed out that bombardment of the Ypres area would destroy the drainage system and turn the battleground into a swamp. [58] Haig disregarded the warning and that is exactly what happened. A preparatory bombardment of four million shells hurtled down on reclaimed bogland, and disrupted drainage patterns. It created in front of the British Army a self-made obstacle that doomed the offensive before it was even launched.

There was no surprise. The Germans had expected an attack since the Battle of Messines, seven weeks before. They had prepared a method of defence that entirely suited the water-logged conditions. Instead of trenches they constructed strongpoints, sited in depth, from which ground could be held by machine-gun fire with as few men as possible. Houses, haystacks and barns screened a cylindrical core of reinforced concrete. Gunfire exposed the embrasured concrete structures, whose squat shape reminded the British of pillboxes. "Pillboxes" they became. The forward positions were lightly held, and this economy enabled the enemy to mass reserves in the rear for prompt counter-attack should this be needed.[59]

Haig's offensive, officially known as the Battles of Ypres, 1917, but better known as Passchendaele, divides itself into three phases: first, the opening assault from 31 July to 2 August by Gough's Fifth Army; second, the limited advances made on 20 September, 26 September and 4 October by Plumer's Second Army; and third, the closing phase culminating in the capture of Passchendaele village on 6 November.

During the first phase some gains were made, by the left of Gough's Fifth Army aided by the First French Army between it and the coast. The villages of Bixschoote and St. Julien and the Pilckem Ridge were all taken. Hard counter-attacks robbed the right wing of any results. Already, when this phase ended on 2 August, the ground was a morass with slush two feet deep. Half the tanks, as might be expected, had been lost in this first battle, and the casualty list showed the grim total of 31,850.[60]

A further abortive attempt by Gough on 16 August brought an aftermath of discontent. The men felt they were being uselessly thrown away. Complaints against the Fifth Army's staff work grew bitter and widespread. The main task of advancing to the Passchendaele Ridge then fell on Plumer's shoulders. A reasonably good phase in late September and early October followed deliberate planning for limited objectives, mighty barrages, and heavily pressed infantry attacks on narrow frontages to give sufficient force to overcome German counter-attacks.

"The enemy" [said Ludendorff] "charged like a wild bull against the iron wall which kept him from our submarine bases . . . We knew that the enemy suffered heavily. But we also knew he was amazingly strong and, what was equally important, had an extraordinarily stubborn will."[61]

Three battles—Menin Road Ridge, Polygon Wood and Broodseinde— were successful. The Second Army obtained a footing on Passchendaele Ridge, though at terrible cost. And then the rains set in.

By the first week in September, according to Haig's Chief of Intelligence, letters from London revealed a "very marked weakening of trust" in Douglas Haig.[62] By the middle of October, when the weather had broken, Haig was "still trying to find some grounds for hope that we might still win through here this year, but there is none."[63] Nevertheless, with a stubborn obstinacy that had been foreshadowed at the Somme, and against the advice of both Gough and Plumer, Haig determined to have the ridge at Passchendaele for his winter line.

On 5 October, the day following the capture of Broodseinde, Haig

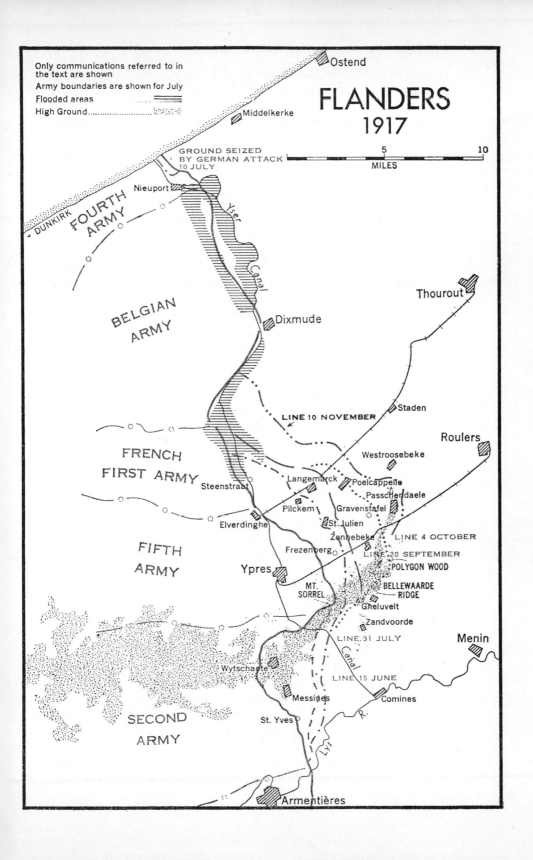

Only communications referred to in
the text are shown
Army boundaries are shown for July
Flooded areas
High Ground.........................

GROUND SEIZED
BY GERMAN ATTACK
10 JULY

FLANDERS
1917

5   10
MILES

Ostend

Middelkerke

Thourout

DUNKIRK

FOURTH
ARMY

Nieuport

Yser

BELGIAN
ARMY

Canal

Dixmude

Staden

LINE 10 NOVEMBER

Roulers

Westroosebeke

FRENCH
FIRST ARMY

Steenstraat

Langemarck

Poelcappelle

Passchendaele

Pilckem

Gravenstafel

Elverdinghe

St. Julien

Zonnebeke

LINE 4 OCTOBER

FIFTH
ARMY

Frezenberg

LINE 20 SEPTEMBER

POLYGON WOOD

Ypres

MT.
SORREL

BELLEWAARDE
RIDGE

Gheluvelt

Zandvoorde

Menin

LINE 31 JULY

Canal

LINE 15 JUNE

Wytschaete

Comines

R.

Messines

SECOND
ARMY

St. Yves

Lys

Armentières

decided to employ the Canadian Corps. It was to go to Gough's Fifth Army, but Currie objected strongly. He had worked under Gough at the Somme and still remembered Regina Trench. Haig then arranged for the Corps to go to Plumer, not to Gough, "because the Canadians do not work kindly with the latter. The idea seems to be prevalent," Haig continued, "that he drove them too much in the Somme fighting last year." [64]

And so by the middle of October the Corps returned to Ypres. The veterans, fewer now, remembered it as an accursed place, not only for battles—Gravenstafel Ridge, St. Julien, Mount Sorrel—but for the daily fighting in the exposed breastworks, a slow bleeding to death. They passed through the city that has given its name to so many battles —First, Second and now Third Ypres—but they hardly knew the place. Even ruins have their degrees. Ypres, in the summer of 1915, when not a house was whole, seemed to represent the limit of destruction. Two years later, when shells had obliterated even shellholes, little remained but rubble and broken ruins. Even then, strange corners, with broken staircases climbing to the open autumn sky, still survived. Outside the town, little crosses marked the places where British and Canadian troops lay side by side, often disinterred by bursting shells. The Corps marched forward into an unrecognizable wasteland of deepening mud until, on 18 October, they took over ground from the 2nd ANZAC which stirred, for some, a faint chord of memory. It was a little forward—a few hundred yards at most—of the same front they had taken over from the French at Gravenstafel Ridge before the gas attack in 1915. Despite all they had endured here they were at the point of beginning; well might they reflect on war's futility.

The commander of the Second Army ordered Currie to submit plans for the capture of Passchendaele as soon as possible. Sir Douglas Haig, knowing Currie and his methods, cautioned Plumer not to rush him; no attack should be made until Currie was satisfied that his preparations were complete. [65]

Currie first went forward to look at the battlefield. The greatest difficulty was, of course, the mud. In all, nearly half the area in front of Passchendaele was covered with water or deep mud—so deep that men often had to wade through boglands holding their rifles above their heads while all the time the enemy were firing at them. In some places, half a mile wide, the bogs could not be crossed even by infantry. Guns had sunk down and remained, badly bunched, because it was almost impossible to move them. They were extremely vulnerable to enemy artillery. More than that, their rate of fire was extremely slow; without firm platforms, after every round they would move or sink and had to be constantly re-aimed. Ahead was the German position, on drier ground and extremely strong, consisting of concrete emplacements sited on the forbidding hogs-backs and spurs of Passchendaele Ridge.

The whole area was littered with the debris of the recent fighting, which neither side could clear because of the continuous shelling. The swollen flanks of dead horses and mules shone in the rain; rusty tanks, locomotives buried to their boilers, and broken wagons tilted up grotesquely. Human remains, some like frozen swimmers, lay on every side. Not every dead face was caked with mud. Some of the recently killed were white; others grey, green, black or decomposed. A disgusting smell like marsh gas pressed heavily on the senses. Currie turned away. "Battlefield looks bad," he confided to his diary, "no salvaging has been done, and very few of the dead buried."[66]

What he had seen convinced Currie that his corps should not be committed to this attack. The operation was impossible, except at great cost, and futile. He protested to both Plumer and to Haig:

I carried my protest to the extreme limit . . . which I believe would have resulted in my being sent home had I been other than the Canadian Corps Commander. I pointed out what the casualties were bound to be, and asked if a success would justify the sacrifice. I was ordered to go and make the attack.[67]

Currie put the cost of making the attempt at sixteen thousand casualties. He overestimated by only 346.* Haig gave no reason for his rigid order, apart from saying, "Some day I will tell you why, but Passchendaele must be taken."[69] He said this with some emotion. Haig was not an emotional man, and this from him led Currie to believe that Haig had a deep and significant reason for the order. Actually, as Haig confided to Currie when he met him at the Peace Conference during February, 1919, in order to "help the morale of the French Army and of the French people and the British people, he was determined to finish the fighting of 1917 with a victory."[70] This is hardly the same as having to continue the offensive at the direct request of the French. The Canadian had protested and been overruled. He could do no more than go in and make the assault a success.

He saw the guns as the key to victory. There must be enough of them; and they had to be able to move forward as the infantry advanced to lend close support and to neutralize the enemy's artillery. Of 360 field guns taken over from the Australians only 220 were in working order, while more than a hundred could not be found. Currie asked for them. He was told they must be there. In the unlikely contingency that some were not, then at least he must have been handed copies of the indents! Currie angrily retorted that he could not "fight the Boche with indents," and he got the guns.[71]

They would have to have firm platforms to fire from in the mud, and these were prepared ahead of time and staged at various positions forward. Roads had to be built for the guns to move from one position

*15,054.[68]

to another. While some guns fired, others would be moving forward. Continuous fire, it was hoped, though this was never fully realized, could thus be provided from firm bases, avoiding the necessity of re-laying after every round.

A barrage laid in front of the assaulting foot soldiers he deemed essential. But the rate of advance over that terrain could not be predicted with any accuracy. Just how fast could the infantry tear themselves free from the cloying mud? To keep the barrage just ahead of them would require careful planning, great flexibility and close liaison by observers working with the attacking troops.

Passchendaele village was still a mile away from Plumer's exhausted troops. And between Ypres and them lay six miles of shell-ploughed ground. Currie ordered roads—new plank roads or road repairs—over that distance to bring up reinforcements, munitions and supplies and to evacuate the wounded. Hand in hand with this went the construction of tramways and light railways. The engineers—Canadian and Second Army—worked and suffered around the clock to get things ready. There were three thousand casualties before they were through.

On the 23rd Haig lunched at Corps Headquarters and approved Currie's plans. During the afternoon he inspected a clay model of the battlefield, which is now at the Imperial War Museum in London. He was cheerful when he left the Corps. If contemporary reports are to be believed, that is as close as Haig or any of his senior staff officers ever got to the battleground itself.[72] In November, however, after the fighting had ended, General Kiggell (Haig's Chief of Staff) left headquarters in the fortress of Montreuil to visit the battle zone for the first time. The story has been told in almost every account of Passchendaele. As his staff car ploughed through the mud near Ypres, still well back from the front where the conditions were ten times worse, he became more and more uneasy. Finally he broke down, burst into tears, and muttered, "Good God, did we really send men to fight in that?"

Next day Haig's equanimity was shattered. The Germans smashed completely through the Italian defences at Caparetto, penetrated eighty miles, and captured an estimated quarter of a million prisoners and three thousand guns. By the end of the month Lloyd George, understandably enough, was hunting for the scalp of Haig who had assured him that Italy could hold out unaided. "The Cabinet," recorded Haig's Chief of Intelligence, "are in full cry against D.H. and against our strategy."[73] Haig now awaited with some anxiety the outcome of Currie's battle.

The conditions under which it would be fought were at their very worst. The defensive wire, as well as the pillboxes which showed only a few feet above the ground, impervious to anything but a direct hit, and difficult targets, would have to be attacked frontally. The original front had narrowed to a salient vulnerable from three sides. And only two plank roads, accurately marked down and shelled, crossed at either side of the main swamp to the front line. Currie stretched Haig's patience to the utmost by insisting on three phases, and before the first of these he and his staff officers were almost continuously up forward to make sure that the preparatory work was carried out to the last detail, and that there was full co-operation between all arms.

By 26 October all was ready. The 3rd and 4th Divisions would carry out this phase, a limited attack designed to carry the front 1,200 yards forward. Five days before the attack Currie visited every brigade of the attacking formations, still behind the lines. "The big, smooth-faced, clear-spoken general gave one at every meeting a feeling of confidence."[74]

The men formed a hollow square around him. A table was brought out and the general stood on it in full view of all the soldiers. He spoke simply, sincerely, as soldier to soldier. I am accustomed to great orators . . . I have been bewitched by Laurier. I have witnessed Lloyd George sweeping the House of Commons into frenzied enthusiasm. But this man's speech was different. Its very simplicity was its charm. He told the men exactly what they had to do. He pointed out the difficulties. "The Commander-in-Chief has called on us to do a big job. It has got to be done. It is going to be your business to make the final assault and capture the ridge. I promise you that you will not be called upon to advance—as you never will be—until everything has been done that can be done to clear the way for you. After that it is up to you, and I leave it up to you with confidence."[75]

The Corps Commander made one more change. In previous attacks troops had been brought up from rest areas just before the time of assault. Under the appalling conditions of the ground at Passchendaele, this meant that they often arrived more exhausted than the troops they relieved. Currie put the men in four days early to recover from the arduous march forward and to study the ground over which they were to attack. He preferred risking casualties in the forward positions to the certainty of attacking with tired troops. He could do no more. He ordered the attack for 5:40 A.M. and then, like Haig, awaited the reports of progress.

The forward troops, sheltering in wet and slimy shell holes, shivered under groundsheets throughout the night. At zero they shed their heavy greatcoats to cut down weight and moved forward, blanketed by a cold wet mist, through the fetid mud. The barrage edged forward just in front in perfect fashion, as if inviting them up the ridge. Pillboxes were tackled on the way; while some men held the enemy's attention with rifle grenades and Lewis guns, others worked round to the blind side and tossed in hand grenades from close range.

The mist had now turned to rain, which lasted throughout the day. Almost imperceptibly the attackers struggled forward, in places to the crest of the ridge, but heavy counter-attacks and shelling drove them back. After three days the limited objectives had not been gained. Nevertheless, the attackers were on higher and drier ground—a better base for the next attack—though at heavy cost. In this phase there had been nearly 2,500 casualties.

Currie ordered a pause for road construction. He now wanted tracks to each brigade sector over which mules would bring supplies. The work was done and supplies brought forward in time for another blow on 30 October. That day the line, carried forward by the endurance of determined troops, advanced a thousand yards. The cost in casualties, 2,300, was almost as high as in the three days of the previous phase.

The Canadians were now poised for the final spring but Currie would not make it yet. He was not prepared to take chances with battered troops, and insisted on a seven-day pause to give time to bring up and acclimatize the 1st and 2nd Divisions. At dawn on 6 November a tremendously powerful barrage indicated that he was ready to proceed. The fresh troops broke out of the starting position so impetuously that the German retaliatory fire fell well behind them; they hugged the barrage closely and fell upon the Germans before machine-guns could be manned. In less than three hours after zero the objective had been seized. The crumbling ruins of Passchendaele village, which had obsessed Haig ever since his July dreams of a break-through had been rudely dispelled, were now in Canadian hands. And though the Germans poured shell after shell onto the new defenders, the objective remained secure. A further 2,238 Canadian casualties marked the day's operations.

The capture of Passchendaele relieved Haig's anxiety. The whole offensive had by now become associated with Passchendaele in the public mind. With Passchendaele captured, the operations could be painted as a victory and Haig could hold his own against the politicians. That night Kiggell, his Chief of Staff, phoned Currie to make sure the report was true:

. . . after refusing to speak to anyone other than myself he asked if he might announce in the London Press tomorrow morning that Passchendaele had been taken. When I assured him it was in our possession he uttered a fervent "Thank God!"[76]

Two Canadian divisions, recorded a now jubilant Haig, had "knocked out seven German divisions."[77] "Today was a very important success."[78] It certainly had been a great achievement of Canadian arms, solidly based on the fighting spirit of the men and on the adequate preparations before the battle.

Tributes showered down upon the Corps and they were well deserved. Perhaps the finest came from the Australians, who watched the Canadians exploiting north of the village to take high ground. "Almost

as bad as Pozières . . ." their diarist noted. "The night is simply vile—
and the day too . . . If the Canadians can hold on they are wonderful
troops."[79] The night of 10 November brought an end to Third Ypres.
And though the exploitation phase brought a further 1,100 casualties,
the Canadians continued to hold on.

The offensive, as we have seen, served no useful strategic ends, and
to drive a salient into a ridge four miles forward of the old line was of
doubtful tactical value. What then, was the justification for this long-
continued battle? Was it sheer attrition? If so, the casualties must be
examined.

In a War Office publication,[80] it is stated that 1.6 casualties were
incurred by the British during this period for every one on the German
side. The Australian official historian agrees that the balance of loss
ran strongly against the British. Surprisingly enough, the British official
historian, after giving a British loss for the period of the offensive of
244,897, adjusted the official German figure of 217,000 over a longer
period to a probable loss of 400,000 for the offensive itself! A recent and
careful compilation by the Canadian Army Historical Section places
260,000 on the British side against 202,000 German losses. It would
appear from the weight of evidence, and quite in accordance with
conditions of ground and sophisticated defences, that the balance of
loss favoured the Germans, not the British. And if we accept those
figures, then Passchendaele was justified neither on the counts of
strategy, tactics nor attrition. It was a barren victory.

Canada remained aloof from these dissensions. She had been given
a job to do and had done it well: but at a grim price. In this Ypres
Salient, and especially at Passchendaele, her sons had proved her right
to call herself a nation.

For weeks the dead lay buried amid the mud. In the spring, when
the Newfoundlanders held the ridge, corpses rose out of the softening
ooze and were cleared away. One morning stretcher parties blundered
into a pair of bodies, perhaps symbolic of the whole campaign. One
was Canadian, the other German, grappling still in death. They had
fought desperately and, sucked into the swamp, had died in one
another's arms. All efforts to part them failed and so a large grave was
dug in which to bury the pitiful remains.[81]

ELEVEN.
1918: THE CORPS ADJUSTS TO OPEN WARFARE

In the middle of November, 1917, the Canadian Corps returned to a sector which, ever since Vimy, it regarded almost as its own. On the 20th Sir Arthur Currie took over the line on the Vimy-Lens front with two divisions forward and two in reserve. They had been away from the area for little more than a month, but that month at Passchendaele had contained more misery than a normal lifetime.

The Corps might never have had to endure those horrors of mud and insane frontal assaults if Sir Julian Byng had had his way. Byng's Third Army was on the Cambrai front and it was in this area that a great experiment was tried. It owed its conception to Bullecourt, where a handful of tanks had led Australians through the Hindenburg Line; it had been born out of frustration in the first few days of the Flanders offensive where tanks had bellied down in the broken ground and proved a failure. As early as 3 August, 1917, Colonel J. F. C. Fuller,* then a General Staff Officer at Tank Corps Headquarters, had put forward a proposal for a tank raid of short duration in a sector more favourable to their use. The essence of the raid would be surprise and rapidity of movement: "advance, hit, retire." Byng liked the idea but was disposed to enlarge it from a raid to a full-scale attack on Cambrai and as such he presented it to Haig. He suggested September, and pressed to have his old Canadian Corps as the basic component of a force of tanks, guns, cavalry and infantry. Haig's Chief of Staff, however, argued against another offensive. Every man and gun should be tossed into the Ypres cauldron where he did not recognize the battle as being played out. No firm decision was made then on Byng's proposal; it was neither sanctioned nor turned down. But, inevitably, it was postponed—in the event, until too late for decisive results—and no firm allocation of troops for the proposed attack was made. In the meantime the Canadian Corps had been used to tip the balance at Passchendaele.[1]

As the weeks wore on the failure in Flanders became evident enough, even to Haig, though he would not openly admit it. The Cambrai

*Later Major-General Fuller, the military historian.

proposal promised to redeem it, just as tanks had to some extent redeemed the Somme offensive. A plan was sanctioned in mid-October. By then, Currie's preparations were well in hand to take Passchendaele, and this would put a good face on the termination of the Flanders fighting. The Cambrai assault must not be allowed to degenerate into more attrition; after Passchendaele, an aroused cabinet and public at home would never stand for that. Byng's attack, therefore, could proceed on 20 November, though Haig imposed a two-day time limit.

For the assault, for the first time, there would be a mass of tanks; 381 in all. The sector was quiet, the ground unscarred. In addition Byng had six infantry divisions, the Cavalry Corps (including the Canadian Cavalry Brigade) for exploiting forward, and 1,000 guns. There were no reserves apart from cavalry; every man and tank had to be thrown into the initial break-through effort.

The flaw was that the force was inadequate for Byng's ambitious plan. We have seen that he had changed Fuller's concept of a raid in force to one that envisaged the capture of Cambrai, nine miles beyond the front. He now enlarged on even that and set as the objective the line of the River Sensée, a further five miles beyond Cambrai. And to penetrate in depth at all he had to break three massively defended lines that made up the Hindenburg system. Thus, of Fuller's scheme, only the locality and the employment of large numbers of tanks remained. In that lay the root cause of ultimate disaster.

Nevertheless, the prelude was brilliant. At daybreak on 20 November the long line of tanks rumbled forward on a six-mile front followed by waves of infantry. Simultaneously the artillery crashed out. Because the tanks were able to crush the wire and demolish strongpoints, there had been no preliminary bombardment to alert the enemy. The Germans, surprised and demoralized, streamed back. By nightfall penetrations of up to five miles had been made and the enemy's three main lines of defence overrun; only one half-finished line stood between the British and open country. The infantry and the tank crews, however, had fought all day and were exhausted; and the cavalry, despite the pathetic faith which they still inspired, proved useless for exploitation in the face of modern weapons. Decisive success stared Byng in the face, but he had no reserves with which to reap it. The reserves, which he so desperately needed, had been swallowed up at Passchendaele.

Next day, what few fresh troops Byng himself could scrape together made further gains of up to one and a half miles. The British Commander-in-Chief, impressed with the quick gains which had previously taken months to achieve—and at a tremendously greater cost— decided to extend the time limit. He hoped to capture Bourlon Wood, which threatened the newly gained position. He also hoped to keep German forces occupied and away from Italy. Haig now placed new divisions at Byng's disposal but far too late; worn-out tanks and crews could not maintain momentum.

The battle that developed favoured the rapidly reinforcing Germans more than the British. Finally the enemy produced his own surprise. On 30 November, with no preliminary preparation, the German artillery put down a sudden bombardment, including gas and smoke, followed by storming parties supported by low-flying aircraft through the weak parts of the British line. Successful penetration meant a flood of troops to follow; these reinforced and expanded the "infiltration" until the British gains were largely swept away.

Such was the story of Cambrai. The plain lesson that it taught the British was that the tank, properly used, gave them mastery of the battlefield. Unfortunately, because of German pressure, the lesson could not be applied until the summer and fall of the following year. The final phase of the battle set the pattern for the German method of infiltration, which they used in their great spring offensive of 1918.

While this was taking place, five British and six French divisions, brought by rail from France to bolster up the Italians, helped to establish a firm line on the River Piave, eighty miles behind the former front. Diaz replaced Cadorna as Italian commander. Much as Pétain had done, he first restored the morale of his troops, which had crumbled through their being endlessly hurled at strong defences. By mid-December the crisis had passed. Nevertheless, the Italians strongly opposed any withdrawal of the British and French divisions, thus upsetting still further the balance of opposing forces on the Western Front.

Events in Russia had created an imbalance dangerously in Germany's favour. In November a ruthless Bolshevik minority overthrew the ineffectual Kerensky government that had replaced the Tsar. One of the avowed purposes of the Bolsheviks was to end the war and this they accomplished by a truce signed with the Germans in late December, succeeded in March, 1918, by the Treaty of Brest-Litovsk. Already, in November, 1917, German troops were moving west from Russia to increase the 149 divisions on the Western Front to 161 by December. The Germans then had a slight advantage. The tide swelled to 177 divisions by the end of January with more still to come. Pétain predicted that by 1 March the enemy would have a reserve of 80 divisions, as opposed to 55 reserve divisions on the Allied side. The 1918 campaigning season would open with a German offensive in overwhelming force. Haig agreed. He saw nothing for it but to turn to the defensive and to be braced for a strong hostile attack.

Divisions to redress the balance could not be drawn back from outside theatres. The British, having failed to pierce the Turk's heart at the Dardanelles, were busily engaged in hacking at his limbs in

Mesopotamia and in Palestine; that process would continue. The French were opposed to any curtailment of the Salonika campaign, which had been mounted as an alternative to Gallipoli. The divisions in Italy remained. And for the British Commander-in-Chief there was another disturbing feature. The disastrous squandering of soldiers' lives at Passchendaele had destroyed what little trust Lloyd George had had in Haig. Now unable to oust him, Lloyd George retaliated by withholding reinforcements from France to discourage fresh attrition. On 1 January, 1918, there were 607,403 trained young men in England. Haig demanded 605,000 to make good his losses but did not get them. Instead, he was promised only 100,000.[2] Sir Douglas, therefore, was left with seriously weakened forces with which to oppose the looming German onslaught.[3]

There were two sunlit patches in the whole gloomy panorama. The convoy system had overcome the U-boat menace: in the last half of 1917, monthly sinkings had dwindled from 170 in April to 85 in December. American troops were landing in Europe, four divisions in January had become nine in April, though the balance would not again tip in the right direction until the middle of 1918.

In January, 1918, to meet the serious shortage of reinforcements, the number of battalions in each British infantry brigade was reduced from four to three; troops of the surplus battalion were then used to bring the other battalions up to strength. The result was stronger battalions but fewer of them, and weaker brigades.

The Canadians had generally, in the past, conformed to British changes in organization. Thus it was assumed that the Canadian Corps would follow suit in this case, with a saving of a dozen battalions. With these, and six more battalions then in England, two additional divisions could be formed. The six divisions, reorganized in two corps, would justify a Canadian Army with its own headquarters. This idea appealed to many. In the wake of reorganization, promotions and staff appointments would inevitably flow. But nobody was more delighted than Garnet Hughes, whose father had talked in terms of a Canadian Army even before the Somme. And Garnet a month before had offered Currie any odds he liked that he would take the 5th Division, a strong division employed in England on home defence, to France.[4]

There seemed little doubt that the proposal, formally made by the Chief of the Imperial Staff on 11 January, would be carried out. General Turner lost no time in visiting France to inquire into the availability of staff officers for a second corps. The new Overseas Minister, Sir Edward Kemp, seemed well-disposed to make the change, but before doing so he sought the authority of Borden.[5]

The Prime Minister, though conscription had been forced through the year before, was still grappling with the manpower problem.

Draftees had to be processed, trained and shipped—American troops were now competing for the limited shipping available—and all this took time. He thought it would be difficult, if not impossible, to reinforce six divisions, and would give no firm undertaking to the British to that effect. Recognizing that for the moment, however, "in the presence of a tremendous enemy offensive such as seems imminent," it might be necessary to go along with the British proposal, he gave Kemp the authority to do so if the situation was grave enough. At the same time, after the crisis was past, Borden reserved the right to cut back the Canadian strength to what it had been before. [6]

The marked lack of enthusiasm shown by Sir Robert Borden was matched by Currie's attitude. He saw the proposal as a measure that would break up an efficient fighting machine, and in the meantime had invited the Overseas Minister to come to France and discuss the matter with him. [7] To Kemp, he stressed the team spirit of the Corps, and the damage that would result from a break-up. He then argued cogently against the wastefulness of the scheme: the extra artillery and ancillary services, and the creation of ten additional headquarters from brigade to army level. [8] Kemp remained non-committal, but on his return to London he found Borden's cable waiting. He sent for Arthur Currie.

Kemp's delay in implementing the reorganization prompted a flurry of political manoeuvring in London. The Chief of the Imperial General Staff vainly pressed the Colonial Secretary to intervene. Lord Beaverbrook sought the aid of Lloyd George. The British Prime Minister, however, was too wily a politician to become embroiled in a dispute that was patently a Canadian concern. Beaverbrook, elated as ever by intrigue, reported back to Garnet Hughes in sporting terms: "Our cock won't fight!" [9] The matter was left with Sir Edward Kemp.

Kemp saw Currie on 5 February, 1918. Sir Arthur had had the foresight to arm himself with the opinion of Sir Douglas Haig, who had told him that a change in the Canadian Corps was neither necessary nor desirable; if, however, it was to be done, then Currie must be the Army Commander with the rank of general. Once more Currie outlined his objections: the wasteful overheads and the disastrous effect on the cohesion and morale of the existing Corps. He offered an alternative suggestion. Why not augment the existing battalions by 100 men? Without any increase in staff or services, this would give the four existing divisions more firepower* and 1,200 more men in the line. [10]

This stand by Currie must refute for all time the charge that his actions as leader of the Canadian Corps were motivated by self-interest and "self-glorification." Currie must have known that every army

*There would also be four Heavy Brigades of artillery instead of three and the very-much-wanted Corps Observation and Reconnaissance unit would be formed.

commander in past British wars had been loaded with honours and substantial grants of money. The same held true at the end of the First World War. Haig, as Commander-in-Chief, received an earldom and £100,000; his army commanders baronies and £30,000. And there can be no doubt that Currie would have been an army commander with them if he had not fought against this redundant reorganization as strongly as he did. No Canadian soldier could match him; nor would Haig have accepted any other.

As it was, Currie put the interests of the Corps ahead of his own. His arguments convinced Sir Edward Kemp. Battalions were augmented by a hundred men, and on 8 February the Overseas Minister cabled Borden to let him know that the reduction of battalions on British lines would not be carried out.[11] Later that month, the 5th Division was broken up for reinforcements and Garnet Hughes, having vainly tried to have the capable British commander of the 3rd Division (Lipsett) removed to make room for himself, found employment without pay at the War Office in London.[12]

In their relatively quiet sector, the Canadian Corps, aware that a German offensive was "written in the stars,"[13] strengthened the defences. They also turned to farming. Food shortages in unoccupied France, it was predicted, would become acute if the area under cultivation was not expanded. Land was ploughed and crops sown behind the lines, an occupation that seemed to restore purpose and sanity to the soldiers' lives. The crops were not harvested by the earnest sowers: when that time came, they were reaping a harvest of the enemy in open country far afield.

It was an ominous spring. The British and French were thinly stretched along the Western Front. Haig, in January, 1918, had been forced to take over an extra 25 miles of front to a point five miles south of the Oise. He now held 126 miles of Northern France with 59 divisions. The French had 97 divisions on a front that was 300 miles long. The Belgians had ten divisions, and by the end of the month, the Americans five.[14] For emergencies there was a small reserve of 34 British and French divisions, but these were not centralized. Haig and Pétain agreed that each would assist the other within twelve hours of an attack on either army.

Even the weather contributed to the brooding suspense. March, having opened with snow and bluster, settled down into a period that was sadly quiet like autumn weather; sunny skies, light drifts of wind and mists that shrouded the ground from early morning until the afternoon. The territory behind the enemy lines seethed with secret, stealthy movements. Ludendorff, the *de facto* commander of the German Army, was in fact preparing, with a superiority greater than it had ever been, for an offensive that would end the war. The time factor was all-important. Ground conditions were doubtful until mid-April, but that would be dangerously late in view of the increasing strength of the Americans. He therefore planned the blow for the latter part of March.[15]

It was a desperate gamble but, concluded Ludendorff, it was the only way to win the war. Passchendaele had had its effect on the defending army, too, which thought "with horror of fresh defensive battles and longed for a war of movement."[16] The shortest way home lay through the Allied trenches; thus the enemy moved forward during the final week with a spirit of elation. As with the French a year before, this was to be the knock-out blow. Drawing confidence from the assembled strength in troops and guns which were everywhere in evidence, the German soldiers crept up to their starting positions through blanketing fog during the night of 20 March and with tense nerves awaited the starting signal.

Promptly at 4:40 A.M. on the morning of 21 March, 2,500 guns lashed out on a fifty-mile front at Gough's Fifth Army and at Byng's Third Army further north. There had been no prior preparation by artillery. This was Cambrai on a vaster scale, where guns paralyzed by their very suddenness and mass effect. The pattern, despite its weight, flickered adroitly from nerve-centre to nerve-centre in the British lines, wiping out command posts and signals centres as it passed. It alternated from zone to zone, drenching forward trenches and distant gun lines with gas and high explosive shells. For five hours the bombardment played in rippling waves of dancing fire over the support and reserve lines and then it suddenly concentrated into a steely torrent on the front-line trenches. For five minutes the flood of shells continued before changing, without a pause, into a creeping barrage. Then came the storm troops, the most determined of the German infantry.

The artillery prelude, designed by Colonel Bruchmüller who had arranged the employment of guns in the break-through in East Galicia the previous July,[17] had been a masterpiece. *Durchbruchmüller*—Breakthrough Müller—the Germans called him. The succeeding assault, as tried out on the moribund Russian forces at Riga in 1917 by von Hutier, the apostle of the surprise attack, matched the guns in efficiency. Again, as at Cambrai, storm troops infiltrated through the British lines, ignoring small resisting pockets and pushing deep. Other troops, following closely, widened the breaches and thrust still deeper into the defensive lines.

Although it was long past daylight, the fog still persisted. The surviving British defenders, stunned by the bombardment and blinded by the fog, groped about for targets. But the Germans were elusive in the changing mist. Machine-guns were almost silent. Communications had been destroyed. Confused bodies of troops, muffled in gas masks, waited for orders and quickly succumbed to the German tactics.

Before the sun had reached its zenith and the fog dispersed, the Germans had reached the rearward edge of the Fifth Army defensive zone. Storm troops, in places, were infiltrating through to the Somme. The situation in the Third Army sector, though serious, was not so desperately bad: the defenders still clung to the last of the supporting lines. Under blue afternoon skies the struggle continued until, at nightfall, the Germans had broken clean through the Fifth Army and into open country. The paralysis that had settled over the Western Front at the end of 1914 had thus been shattered in a single day.

So far Ludendorff's bid had been successful. The British defenders of 1918 had not proved so stubborn as those of 1914 and this, in no small part, was due to Passchendaele. It is true that each division, with only nine battalions instead of twelve, had been weaker. It is also true that "never before had the British line been held with so few men and so few guns to the mile"; and that the reserves had been inadequate. But, more significant, nineteen out of twenty-one divisions in the front line of the Fifth and Third armies had been at Passchendaele, and the scars remained. Strong and experienced troops had died there, "a large proportion of their best soldiers," whose places had been filled, "if filled at all, by raw drafts and transfers."[18] And on the German side the tactics had been clever; the troops had been thoroughly trained in methods of infiltration and had advanced rapidly over ground that had not been torn by bombardment of long duration, on the British pattern, "quite unlike the laboured progress of our own troops over the cratered surface and clinging chalk of the Somme, or the liquid mud of the later stages of Passchendaele."[19]

Next day, the German attacks continued, making most progress under Hutier in the sector held by Gough. By nightfall on the 22nd Hutier's troops were on the Somme. Next day he crossed it and occupied Péronne. Haig, fearing the loss of Amiens and, with it, the insertion of a wedge between his forces and the French, appealed to Pétain for twenty French divisions. As it was, the Fifth Army had almost ceased to exist and its collapse opened a dangerous flank on the right of the Third; 23 March was, in fact, the crisis of the battle.

On that day Ludendorff issued fresh orders. Before then, quite rightly, and unlike the Allied generals who had set glorious distant objectives as the target for their troops, Ludendorff had concerned himself with the tactical problem of breaking through. That had now been accomplished on a front of forty miles. His new instructions, astonishingly enough, revealed a lack of strategic grasp that in the long run lost the war. What was required, obvious from the day before, was the employment of Hutier's tactics on a grander scale. His method, as we have seen, was to by-pass resistance and exploit success; infiltration opened a breach, and through the gap all available strength was funnelled, widening it until resistance crumbled.

Of the three armies employed by Ludendorff, only Hutier's was rolling forward without check. Its path might well have been made the axis of advance, with all available force diverted to it. This would have split the French and British forces, driving the former back on Paris and rolling the latter towards the sea. It would have been 1940 fought twenty-two years early.

Instead, Ludendorff set objectives for all three armies, and these diverged both in purpose and direction. On the right the 17th Army battered away at strongly resisting Arras. In the centre, the 2nd Army was held back by the pace of its northern neighbour and when, on the 26th, it did push on, the wilderness of the old Somme battle-ground applied an effective brake. Hutier on the left, though still advancing, was slowed by the pace of the northern armies. Only on the 28th, when an all-out attack by the 17th Army failed to capture "the decisive heights east and north of Arras"—though Ludendorff did not name them, one of these was Vimy—did the German commander at last switch the weight of the attack to Hutier. By then his chance of decisive success had gone.[20] The 18th Army, though stiffened by reserves, now made little progress. British reinforcements, so long withheld from Haig, had quickly become available to him in this dire emergency. British resistance, bolstered by French divisions, had been given time to harden; and though Hutier reached the fringe of Amiens on 30 March, he could not take it. Rather than tie down his forces in another battle of attrition, Ludendorff called off the attempt.

On the 23rd the Allies, unaware of Ludendorff's fatal orders, saw nothing but disaster for themselves. Pétain, though obliged to furnish only six divisions, had placed seven at Haig's disposal. Haig had wanted twenty to knock back the wedge that Hutier was driving towards Amiens. Pétain, who saw his first duty as keeping his army together to cover Paris, refused, and that in turn led Haig to appeal to London for a man of resolution to command the Allied armies. He was willing to subordinate himself to Foch—whose previous interference he had sturdily resisted—if he could be appointed. The Secretary for War acted on Haig's appeal and, on 26 March, Foch was empowered to co-ordinate the French and British Armies. His appointment as Commander-in-Chief of the Allied armies was confirmed three weeks later. Nevertheless, Haig did not get his twenty divisions, only eight in early April, when the crisis had passed. It was due to his own initiative and steady nerves, as well as clear-minded purposefulness, that his forces finally checked the German thrusts. In what appeared to be a hopeless situation, Haig showed a quality of command that had hardly been apparent in the Somme and Passchendaele offensives.

Tactically, Ludendorff scored a huge success; a penetration of forty miles, 80,000 prisoners and 975 guns. Strategically, he had lost the war. The attack had not been decisive; the British and French forces had not been split. The endurance of the German troops, keyed up for what they had thought to be the final battle, would inevitably sag as the fighting still went on. The British, badly mauled, had still not cracked and American troops were arriving in increasing numbers.

On 9 April the Germans turned to Flanders, again a *Durchbruch-müller* masterpiece. The British gains of the 1917 offensive were swept away in a single day, including the blood-soaked Passchendaele feature. Thereafter the defence was well conducted. A ten-mile penetration was stopped just short of Hazebrouck, and Ypres still held out. The Germans had lost 348,300 men since 21 March—slightly more than the British—and by now 179,703 Americans had arrived in France.[21] Of great interest is Ludendorff's own admission: "Certain divisions had obviously failed to show any inclination to attack . . . troops stopped round captured food supplies, while individuals stayed behind to search houses and farms for food. . . This impaired our chances of success and showed poor discipline."[22]

In May, the French reserves having at last been placed at Amiens and on the British front, Ludendorff decided to draw them away by striking at the French in Champagne. He would then turn north to finish off the British. Accordingly, on the 27th, the indispensable Bruchmüller opened a bombardment on the *Chemin des Dames*. Fifteen fresh divisions fell on four French and three unfortunate British divisions that had been put into that sector from Amiens for a rest. The Germans swept over the Aisne. This early success prompted Ludendorff, forgetting his earlier aim, to reinforce in an attempt to seek a decisive victory over the French. The enemy penetrated deeply towards Paris, until Pétain, who refused to throw reserves piecemeal into the battle, established a defensive line on the Marne against which the impetus of the German advance finally died away on 30 May. Two American divisions, around Château-Thierry, fought beside the French. Paris was now within easy reach of the "Big Berthas," enemy guns of surprisingly long range but of short life and little effectiveness; still the Germans could claim—to the consternation of the world and with complete justification—that the French capital was under bombardment.* Nevertheless all that Ludendorff had achieved was a deep salient threatened on both flanks by Reims and Villers-Cotterets, and German strength was fading.

Ludendorff had now carved out two huge bulges, one in Picardy and the other in Champagne, as well as a smaller one in Flanders.

---

*These guns were ungallantly named after Bertha Krupp, the daughter of their manufacturer. The calibre was 8.26-inch; the range about 75 miles. Of three guns which the Germans intended to use on this front, one wore out on the practice range. The breech of the second blew off as it fired its third round. The third gun opened fire as early as 29 March and between then and 8 August hurled approximately 400 shells at Paris.

His next move was an attempt on 9 June to widen the shoulder of the southern bulge in the direction of Compiègne. Though he gained some ground, the offensive failed to reach its objectives, and a month's pause followed.

It was the middle of the year, and despite these substantial gains, the irascible Ludendorff realized that the net was closing. There might be twenty American divisions now in France, he wrote, more than he had believed possible. The superiority that the Germans had enjoyed in March had now been cancelled out. And—though the performance of the new divisions had not impressed him:

The fact that these new American reinforcements could release English and French divisions on quiet sectors weighed heavily in the balance against us. This was of the greatest importance and helps to explain the influence exerted by the American Contingent on the issue of the conflict. It was for this reason that America became the deciding factor in the war.[23]

His own battalion strengths had been reduced, but they were still strong enough to permit him to strike "one more blow that should make the enemy ready for peace." There was, he wrote dolefully, "no other way."[24] Ludendorff had considered going onto the defensive but ruled it out. It would be discouraging to Germany's allies and, apart from that, he was afraid that "the army would find defensive battles an even greater strain than an offensive . . ."[25]

Flanders still obsessed his mind for this last blow, but the British were still too strong there. Again he decided to attract reserves further to the south by an offensive in Champagne, a strong assault by fifty-two divisions attacking on both sides of Reims. On 15 July the last great German surprise bombardment flashed out against the Allied line, and two German armies hurled themselves at the French defenders east and west of Reims. They met with different fortunes, which depended on how closely Pétain's instructions for "elastic defence" had been followed. To the west of Reims two French armies had posted the mass of their defenders too far forward, and they were smashed. The Germans went on to establish a bridgehead four miles deep across the Marne.

On the east of the city, the orders of Pétain, that "cool, unemotional company director of modern war and shrewd economist of human lives,"[26] had been carried out. There the German attack was absorbed by thinly held forward defences, while strongly manned rearward defences awaited the enemy beyond the range of his supporting guns. The French positions in this area, reported a German officer, were "laughing at the withering fire."[27] The German offensive, as a

THE
GERMAN OFFENSIVES
MARCH - JULY 1918

MILES 10 5 0 10 20 MILES

German gains --------- ///////

Compiled and drawn by Historical Section G.S.

result of this repulse, was stalled and halted, cut to shreds by machine-gun fire and counter-artillery bombardment. It was the Nivelle offensive in reverse.

On the other flank, the attenuated enemy thrust, successfully lodged across the Marne, now lay wide-open for a counter-stroke by the French. This was the decisive moment when, in a hush of expectancy, the initiative trembled in Ludendorff's hand and was being reached for by the eager Foch. The Frenchman grasped it firmly.

On 18 July, completely dispensing with a preliminary bombardment, eighteen French divisions stormed forward beind a creeping barrage from the Villers-Cotterets Forest. The attack was led by massed tanks in the Cambrai method. The Germans were hustled back four miles.

Thus began the Second Battle of the Marne, which tied Ludendorff to a grim three-weeks' defensive battle and forced him to abandon any ideas of a Flanders offensive. On 7 August, when the battle ended, the Germans had been forced back bchind the River Vesle. They had lost 29,000 prisoners and casualties estimated at 168,000.[28] By now the Germans' losses since 21 March totalled a million and the lines they had to man were longer than ever before. Three great newly won pockets, insecurely held, offered themselves to Allied attack, and the initiative lay with Foch. Ludendorff's final gamble had failed.

Throughout the period of these giant German blows the Canadian Corps had been virtually inactive; yet, apart from those of Belgium and the United States, its divisions were the strongest in France.

The Canadian divisions would undoubtedly have been drawn into the British defensive battles had it not been for Currie and his insistence on retaining them together under his own control; they were not going to be attached to British formations whenever there was a need to shore up a crumbling front. "He wishes to fight only as a 'Canadian Corps,'" commented Haig bitterly,

and get his Canadian representative in London to write and urge me to arrange it! As a result, the Canadians are together holding a wide front near Arras, *but they have not yet been in the battle!* The Australians on the other hand have been used by Divisions and are now spread out from Albert to Amiens and one is in front of Hazebrouck.[29]

Haig's diary entry is a correct statement of fact. The Australian divisions were dispersed among British formations whilst the crisis lasted and were reunited only when the emergency was over. He intended to do the same with the Canadian divisions. On 23 March the 2nd Division was ordered into the GHQ reserve to be at the disposition of the Commander-in-Chief, and the 1st Division was called into the reserve of Horne's First Army. That left the 3rd and 4th Divisions, still under Currie, to hold an extended line. On the 26th, orders reached Currie that would take his remaining two divisions away from him to stand behind the badly pressed Third Army. (Similarly the Canadian Corps Heavy Artillery found itself a headquarters with no guns to control.) The two adjacent British corps would extend to hold the Canadian line, and Currie's own headquarters would move into reserve.[30]

Currie, left without any of his divisions, protested. He suggested to Horne a readjustment of boundaries that would give him more line to hold, but that would also bring back Canadian divisions under his control. Within twenty-four hours, on 30 March, the 3rd and 4th Divisions returned to his command and on 8 April the 1st Division joined them. Currie now held almost nine miles of front with three divisions, whereas four of his divisions had held only seven miles before.[31]

Arrangements were also made for the 2nd Division, then holding six thousand yards of the Third Army's line, to rejoin the Canadian Corps, but Ludendorff's second offensive caused the move to be cancelled. That division remained with the British until July. British divisions went north to stem the German advance in Flanders, so that by mid-April Currie held sixteen miles of front, which he continued to hold until the crisis had passed. Nor was this task unimportant. Behind Lens and Vimy Ridge lay the only collieries in northern France still working for the French and there were, in addition, the vital communications centres of Arras and Béthune and the important railway lateral running south to Amiens and north to the Channel ports.

Much has been made of Currie's protest against the dispersal of his divisions. Three months later it was still rankling in Haig. He reminded Mewburn, the Minister of Militia, that "the British Army alone and unaided by Canadian troops withstood the first terrific blow made by 80 German Divisions."[32] But Currie's stand was reasonable. As he explained to Haig's Chief of Staff, the formations of the Canadian Corps wished to fight side by side, and that was the wish of the people of Canada. The Corps was used to fighting that way. With one division thrown in here and another there, it had no chance to do its best. He pointed to the close liaison that existed between his headquarters staff and the junior formations. "My staff and myself cannot do as well with a British Corps in this battle as we can with the Canadian Corps, nor can any other Corps Staff do as well with the Canadian Divisions as my own." Under the critical conditions Haig would do what he thought best but, concluded Currie, "for the sake of the victory we must win, get us together as soon as you can."[33]

Currie sent a copy of that letter to the Overseas Minister. Kemp in turn wrote to the British War Minister, pointing out that the efficiency and high morale of the Canadian Corps was due to all its components fighting together under Currie, "in whom the troops have unbounded confidence."[34] The War Minister conveyed this view to Haig, just in time, for Haig had already detached all four of Currie's divisions. As we have seen, three rejoined Currie very soon afterwards.

There was no question of the Corps being permanently broken up by the British, as was hinted in the House by Sir Sam Hughes.[35] That was made quite clear to Kemp by Lord Milner who succeeded Derby as War Minister in mid-April. The past policy of keeping the Corps together, said Milner, had produced tremendous results. Purely on military grounds, quite apart from national sentiment, it would be absolute folly to pursue any other course. If for any military reason the Corps became separated, he pledged that it would be reunited at the first possible moment.[36] The only division not with the Corps, the 2nd, rejoined it on 1 July.

These relatively quiet months were put to good use by Currie. Throughout the summer of 1917 he had encouraged changes in artillery organization and procedures. An effective command and intelligence organization had been built up, as was briefly noted in the account of the Hill 70 battle, and by use of it the guns were kept firing at useful targets long after the prearranged barrages had been completed. The infantry often had the benefit of more than double the rates of ammunition expenditure achieved by British formations. Currie now turned his attention to the other arms.

In March he reorganized the Canadian Machine-Gun Corps. The machine-gun companies with each division were formed into battalions with one extra company, which gave 50 per cent more weapons and machine-gunners per division than previously. A Canadian division now had 96 Vickers guns (as compared to 64 in a British division), while the enlarged infantry battalions gave it 13,200 rifles as opposed to a total of 9,000 in the reduced British units. The most striking departure from existing methods, however, was in the tactical employment of the new machine-gun battalions. From now on they would form a distinctive arm, midway between the infantry and artillery, with tactics of their own. Just as each division had a CRA (Commander, Royal Artillery), who commanded and controlled the divisional guns, so it would have its own Divisional Machine-Gun Commander with whom centralized tactical control of the machine-guns would rest. This gave distinct advantages in command and supply though there was some loss of close touch with the infantry. In November, impressed with the Canadian machine-gun organization, GHQ directed all the British armies to adopt the same system.[37]

During May it was the turn of the engineers. Previously the infantry had provided most of the labour under engineer supervision, but the results had not always been satisfactory; the engineers had been able to exercise little control over infantry working parties, and were themselves subject to dual control. In theory, they were responsible to divisional CRE (Commanding Royal Engineers) for work, but in practice it was the infantry brigadier in whose sector they were working who generally imposed his own ideas as to what was required. Currie solved the problem by pooling all the sappers in each infantry division into an Engineer Brigade made up of a headquarters, three engineer battalions, and a bridging and transport unit. He found the additional engineers who were required from the 5th Divisional Engineers and by disbanding four pioneer and two tunnelling units. In the final days of the war Currie attributed much of the success achieved by the Corps to having enough engineers to do the engineering work and keep the infantry free for fighting.[38]

By the time the German offensive had ended, the Canadians fielded a strong, fresh, well-trained and well-organized corps, ready to play an important part in the fighting that lay ahead. The months spent on the Lens-Arras front had not been wasted, and throughout all those fateful days their line of 1917 had stood firm.

Dominion Day was especially well celebrated that year. The Corps was in reserve. On that day the 2nd Division returned and fifty thousand Canadians assembled for sports at Tincques, fourteen miles west of Arras. A stadium had been knocked together by the engineers, complete with a platform for distinguished guests. Sir Robert Borden, General John J. Pershing (Commander-in-Chief, American Expeditionary Forces) and the Duke of Connaught all attended. There were marquees for refreshments and an open-air theatre where the "Dumbells" gave continuous performances. Planes hovered overhead to protect the Corps from enemy bombing. That night the "Volatiles," the concert party of the 1st Division, presented its revue, _Take a Chance_.[39] Sir Robert Borden inspected units of the Corps next day, and on the 6th, the 3rd Brigade, which had three Scottish battalions, played host to Highland regiments of the British Army. The week was peacetime soldiering, brass and weapons twinkling in the sun, flags, massed bands and stirring music; the Highland Gathering wound it up in proper style with Highland games, skirling pipe bands, and the march of pipes and drums. Morale was extremely high when on 15 July the Corps came out of reserve and relieved XVII British Corps in the line.

Two days later Haig rejected a proposal made by Foch for a British attack in the Festubert sector; he saw no advantage in an advance over that flat and swampy region.* Instead, Haig proposed an operation east and southeast of Amiens and for this, he told Foch, he was

*This was the so-called "Delta" plan. Among other defects, the direction of advance as proposed was at right angles to most main roads.

already secretly preparing an operation north of the Luce. It was
to be a limited blow to give a margin of safety around Amiens and the
railway. The avoidance of marshy ground, secret preparations and
a limited conception: truly, Haig had learned much since Passchendaele!

Foch agreed that the Paris-Amiens line must be cleared and he,
therefore, sanctioned a combined offensive by the British Fourth
Army (Rawlinson) and the First French Army (Debeney). He placed
Debeney under Haig for the operation, which was fixed for 8 August.
Haig directed that Rawlinson would receive as reinforcement the
Canadian Corps, then with the First Army.

In the forthcoming battle, an astonishing departure from the
methods of the Somme and Passchendaele, the British Command
sought to achieve *surprise*. Not only would the Cambrai method be
adopted—no preparatory bombardment and, instead, massed tanks—
but, based on this firm foundation, Haig sought to deceive the enemy
in a variety of subtle ways. Secrecy was, of course, important. To this
end preliminary conferences were never held in the same place twice;
even divisional commanders were kept in the dark about the projected attack until 31 July; and the troops were not informed of it
until thirty-six hours before it was due to start. Movement of the
wildly speculating battalions was made only at night. Were they on
the way to retake Passchendaele Ridge? Were they bound for the
Marne to help the French? But as railway and other transport officials
proved unresponsive to questioning, the riddle became insoluble and
therefore uninteresting. The troops settled down in their boxcars to
games of blackjack, poker, spit-in-the-ocean and seven-toed Pete.[40]
Buses were lined up at the final station to convey the units through
the moonless dark to a nameless crossroads from where they marched
to wooded areas; there, bivouacked on the damp ground, several
other units were lying beneath the cover of the trees.[41]

Carefully camouflaged, . . . innumerable howitzers were emplaced
in clustering groups; tons of shells lay hidden beneath heaps of brushwood; small-arms ammunition, bombs and engineering material of all
kinds were concealed in huge dumps among the trees. Most interesting
of all were the tanks. These monsters were parked in the dark recesses
surrounded at all times by inquisitive infantrymen.[42]

By day planes, as part of their routine missions, patrolled the area
to report on breaches of concealment; the roar of their engines proved
useful later on to drown out the noise of tanks moving to the forward
area. Reconnaissance of the enemy positions by incoming officers
was strictly curtailed so as not to give the game away. Currie, who
considered reconnaissance vital, attached a group of staff officers to
the Australians, who were in the line; there they posed as Australians.

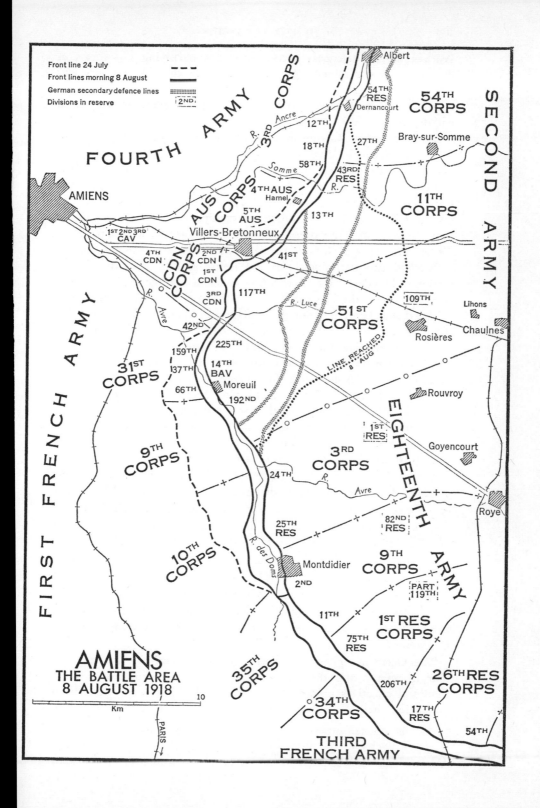

Front line 24 July
Front lines morning 8 August
German secondary defence lines
Divisions in reserve   ⌐2ND¬

FOURTH ARMY

3RD CORPS

AUS CORPS

CDN CORPS

AMIENS

Villers-Bretonneux

R. Ancre

R. Somme

4TH AUS
Hamel

5TH
AUS

1ST 2ND 3RD
CAV

4TH
CDN

2ND
CDN

1ST
CDN

3RD
CDN

12TH

18TH

58TH

13TH

41ST

117TH

43RD
RES

54TH
RES
Dernancourt

27TH

Albert

54TH
CORPS

Bray-sur-Somme

11TH
CORPS

SECOND ARMY

FIRST FRENCH ARMY

R. Avre

42ND

159TH

137TH

66TH

225TH

14TH
BAV

Moreuil

192ND

R. Luce

51ST
CORPS

109TH

LINE REACHED 8 AUG

Lihons

Chaulnes

Rosières

Rouvroy

31ST
CORPS

9TH
CORPS

10TH
CORPS

3RD
CORPS

24TH

25TH
RES

R. Avre

R. des Doms

Montdidier

2ND

11TH

1ST
RES

82ND
RES

9TH
CORPS

PART
119TH

75TH
RES

1ST RES
CORPS

EIGHTEENTH ARMY

Goyencourt

Roye

LINE REACHED 8 AUG

35TH
CORPS

34TH
CORPS

206TH

17TH
RES

26TH RES
CORPS

54TH

THIRD
FRENCH ARMY

AMIENS
THE BATTLE AREA
8 AUGUST 1918

0   10
Km

PARIS
↓

Work on the rear defences still continued, to avoid giving the impression that attack was imminent. And registration by the field artillery was effected by holding some guns silent while slipping newly arrived ones into an unincreased daily rate of fire; the heavy artillery fired without registration.*

By these means Rawlinson's strength grew by 450 tanks, six new divisions, two cavalry divisions and a thousand guns during 1-8 August, and as yet the increase had not been suspected by the Germans. It was considered especially important to conceal the presence of the Canadians. "Regarding them as storm troops, the enemy tended to greet their appearance as an omen of a coming attack."[43] Currie, therefore, directed that the preparations for a projected local attack on Orange Hill, opposite his old Arras sector, should be continued. He also dispatched two battalions, medical units, and the Corps' wireless section to Flanders from where a flow of wireless traffic made it appear that they were the advanced party of the Corps. These measures confused the enemy. He noted the arrival in Flanders, but considered the Scarpe, where the Orange Hill preparations were continuing, as the more likely place for attack. And so that the Canadians should not be recognized up forward, or captured in enemy raids, they did not move into the front line until just before the assault. The Australians relieved the French on the right, thinning out their line to make room for the incoming Corps. Even that was a deceptive measure. For the Germans would not expect attack on a front that had every appearance of being spread out defensively.

The front of the attack was about fourteen miles long, with Debeney's French army holding about half of it south of the Amiens-Roye road. The Fourth Army dispositions consisted of a striking force of two corps—the Canadians and the Australians—which would deliver the main blow south of the Somme. They were the "most formidable troops in Haig's command."[44] The Canadian Corps would operate on the right, adjacent to the French, with the Australians closer to the river. The British III Corps would act as a flank guard north of the Somme on the army's left. A disturbing feature for the Canadians was the River Luce, which cut across the Corps front, and the high ground to the south of it, which completely dominated the Canadian forward area.

The Germans opposite had only seven divisions in the line and four in reserve and these were under strength, estimated at three thousand effectives apiece. Nor, when their whole army had been advancing, had they constructed strong defences. There was little

---

*In the counter-battery groups the pattern on each enemy battery was made up from guns of separate batteries to compensate for any individual errors. The patterns were large but the "mean point of impact" was on the target, and the effect sufficient to prevent the firing of more than a few rounds.

The Great Advance. The Prince of Wales enters Denain after it was
freed by the 4th Canadian Division on 19 October, 1918. He is accompanied by Sir Arthur Currie and (right) the Divisional Commander
Major-General David Watson.

Brigadier-General A. G. L. McNaughton.

digging or wiring done, the main protection consisting of short lengths of trench and machine-gun positions. Currie had made sure that his infantry had been thoroughly trained in the methods of infiltration practised by the Germans in their offensives, and the men were ready for conditions of open warfare.[45]

On 8 August, an hour before dawn, the British tanks lumbered forward through a heavy ground mist. The roar of their engines and the rumble of their tracks sounded strangely hollow in the fog, magnified in the apprehensive ears of the tensely waiting men to a deafening clatter that must certainly arouse the enemy. A bombardment by him would create havoc in the crowded forward areas where tens of thousands of soldiers lay in the open assembly positions. German flares bloomed out over No-Man's-Land. But nothing happened. Suddenly, reassuringly, with a crash that shook the ground, British and Dominion guns flashed out all along the front. The enemy's response was thin and ragged—an incoherent babble, not a firm reply. The infantry attacked simultaneously, counting on the tanks and the barrage to deal with the enemy defences. Unlike the Fourth Army, the French, with few tanks, carried out an artillery bombardment of forty-five minutes; in the interests of surprise, however, this did not begin until Rawlinson's barrage gave the signal. The preparations had been effective. Surprise was complete.

The Canadian and Australian infantry, "matchless attacking troops,"[46] dashed forward wearing for the first time a light "fighting order." This consisted of the bare essentials of ammunition, rations and water bottle, gas mask, entrenching tool, and two Mills bombs. The unhampered men were deployed in an extended order, skirmishers leading, and offered a poor target to the enemy.

The Germans, like the British on 21 March, were, in any case, blinded by the fog. Few machine-guns fired. The front dissolved in panic and confusion as tanks, escorted by grimly determined men, crashed through their positions. Canadian hatred for the enemy had not been so pronounced since the first gas attack at Ypres; the Canadian hospital ship, *Llandovery Castle*, had been torpedoed on 27 June, 1918, carrying to the bottom 234 persons made up of crew, medical staff and nursing sisters, and this battle was looked upon by many as an opportunity for revenge.

Even the Luce proved to be an insignificant obstacle. One bridge was seized intact and at other places attacking troops rushed across on footbridges made from duckboards. The engineers had made adequate preparations for heavier crossings and had two bridges across the stream ready for traffic by 11 A.M. The high ground, which had seemed such a threat in German hands, was of little advantage to them under the prevailing conditions of mist and smoke.

Lipsett, on the right, had the toughest task. It was his job to protect the flank of the Corps until the French, starting forty-five minutes later, should catch up. Consequently his final objective was not so far forward as the objectives of the other divisions. He reached it without incident, and the 4th Division passed through to press the attack forward and keep up the momentum. The general type of opposition up to now had been isolated pockets of German infantry resisting in woods, copses and fields of grain. These, in the main, capitulated when outflanked.

By now the mist had risen and "the spectacle of a lifetime was unveiled."

Topping the long rolling hills, wave upon wave of Canadian infantry were sweeping irresistibly forward, driving before them groups of Germans. Just such a sight, lacking only the actual shelling . . . had been enacted time and again on the . . . manoeuvre area . . . during the summer.[47]

In the forenoon, massed cavalry, accompanied by light "whippet" tanks, came forward. These, taking advantage of the Luce valley and other wooded ravines, cleared villages for the infantry further forward. But in front of General Watson's 4th Division the village of Le Quesnel, heavily defended by machine-guns sweeping the flat fields, proved too much for cavalry; Watson, reluctant to mount a costly frontal attack with infantry and light tanks, ordered his infantry to dig in short of the objective. Elsewhere, by evening, the day's objectives had all been reached and a grip had been obtained on the Amiens outer defence line across the whole of the Corps front.

It had been a magnificent day. The German line had been thrown back eight miles by the strong, fresh, well-organized Canadian Corps, and seven on the Australian front. On the right flank the French had pushed forward five miles, and on the left the British two. Better still, it had been an economical victory. The Fourth Army's casualties were some 9,000. Against that, the Germans lost 27,000 men, 400 guns and large numbers of mortars and machine-guns. Of these, 5,000 prisoners alone and 161 guns fell to the Canadian Corps at a cost of under 4,000 casualties. Much of the credit for the Canadian success was due to the effective contribution of the tanks, especially in the early phases of the attack, and the excellence of the counter-battery programme; the neutralization of the enemy batteries had been very thorough, many being captured without having fired more than a few rounds.

Greater than this material loss was the moral effect that Amiens had on the German Army. This battle was the decisive engagement of the First World War. But though it had been the most brilliant success ever gained on the Allied side during the war, its decisive character did not arise from the extent of the victory or its strategic value. It was not even the turning point of the war; the course of the campaign had already been reversed when the French wrested the initiative out of German hands a month before. What Amiens did was to undermine the morale of the German Supreme Command. It brought home to them with brutal clarity that 18 July had been no temporary reverse. After 18 July, Ludendorff had by no means lost hope; he pressed on with plans for his continued Flanders offensive. After 8 August, he discarded his plans, clearly indicating which battle he thought the more decisive. This he himself admitted:

August 8th was the black day of the German Army in the history of this war. This was the worst experience I had to go through, except for the events that, from September 15th onwards, took place on the Bulgarian Front and sealed the fate of the Quadruple Alliance.[48]

The decline in German fighting power disturbed him most. He had never admitted before, even to himself, that endurance had begun to crack. Strong divisions from the overseas Dominions had now flung the fact in his face. They had attacked with "strong squadrons of tanks, but otherwise in no great superiority," and yet "six or seven divisions, which could certainly be described as battle-worthy, had been completely broken."[49] Now, Ludendorff was forced to acknowledge, the German war machine was "no longer efficient."

The 8th August put the decline of that fighting power beyond all doubt and in such a situation as regards reserves, I had no hope of finding a strategic expedient whereby to turn the situation to our advantage.[50]

Less than a month before Ludendorff had been confident of success. He would make the enemy ready for peace with his next blow. Now the premonition of defeat that swept through Germany and her allies seized him, too. He could see no successful outcome to the four-year-old struggle. "The war," he stated, "must be ended."[51]

TWELVE.
1918: CANADA'S HUNDRED DAYS
FROM AMIENS TO MONS

The Battle of Amiens did not end with the first day's great sweep forward. It continued on 9 August with the object of reaching the line Dernancourt–Bray-sur-Somme–Chaulnes–Roye, and the general offensive was not broken off until 11 August.

The spectacular success of the 8th was not matched on any of the succeeding days; only about half the ground on the way to the objectives was taken. Nevertheless a general advance of about three miles was made. The Germans under Hutier had solved the problems involved in the sudden change from static to mobile conditions of warfare far more efficiently. In the Fourth Army, communications and supplies—and, more seriously, reserves—lagged behind the initial great advance.

On the second day there was no surprise. Tank power, too, had dwindled through mechanical failure and enemy action. Those that were left lumbered forward in clear weather, easy targets for the watchful German gunners, though surviving tanks rendered good service in crushing machine-gun nests and centres of resistance. Rawlinson had only three reserve divisions. The Germans, on the other hand, had by 11 August rushed eighteen divisions forward by train, bus and lorry, committing them piecemeal.

The main reason for the slow-down, however, was the nature of the ground. In the late afternoon of 9 August the attacking troops butted up against the old line of British trenches that had faced the Germans before the Somme offensive of 1916. Badly broken down, it had the appearance of great age with weather-beaten sandbags, crumbling walls, rusty wire and metal fragments. At places in the trenches, bones showed greenish-white in the caved-in sections. The enemy, thankful for its shelter, installed machine-guns and manned it in the reverse direction. Behind it stretched the No-Man's-Land of two years ago, broken by the explosions of forgotten shells, snarled with wire, littered with debris and rank with summer weeds. And across this blasted wasteland lay the mouldering German trenches, grotesque and horrible, with more and still more trenches beyond, carved in the path of struggles long since silent. To the approaching troops, exhilarated by the swift passage through woods and standing grain, the sight was familiar as the sight of death—and as depressing. Morale sagged. From now on, they surely knew, it would be trench warfare once again.

The 10th saw little progress. Haig, remarkably changed since Passchendaele, visited the front and saw the conditions from close quarters.[1] He was amenable to breaking off the battle, but Foch would not relax the pressure. Nevertheless, a passive resistance to the Generalissimo's orders set in on the 11th:

When we came up to the old, but still formidable 1916 line, a cry went up from every throat in the Corps (from the private in the front line all the way back to Corps HQ) to bring down the curtain and to use us elsewhere while we still had a goodly measure of strength left in us. It was a cry no one could fail to hear.[2]

Currie, taking the pulse of this, went at once to Rawlinson. He considered it inadvisable to try to force a way forward by infantry fighting; his recommendation was that the operations should be slackened to give time to prepare a thorough "set-piece" attack on a broad front.[3] Furthermore, Rawlinson advised Currie not to press the attack if that would entail heavy casualties.[4] Later in the day, after conferring with Haig, the Fourth Army commander ordered the offensive to be discontinued.[5]

The outcome was another battle—between Foch and Haig. The Fourth Army, ruled Foch, must maintain the frontal pressure. Haig demurred. Having seen the ground, he considered it a waste of human life; and in a letter dated 14 August he told Foch that he had cancelled any further attack and was preparing one in another sector, north of Albert.[6]

Foch, on the night of the 14th, ordered Haig to maintain the Amiens offensive,[7] which did no more than arouse the other's stubborn streak. Next day Haig visited the Generalissimo at his advanced headquarters. "I spoke to Foch quite straightly," Haig recorded, "and let him understand that *I was responsible to my Government and fellow citizens for the handling of the British Forces.*"[8] Foch gave in; he agreed that the Amiens offensive should not be pressed.[9] There is little doubt that Haig was influenced to take this stand by Arthur Currie, largely at the instance of the Canadian Artillery. On the 13th, Currie, whose Corps would be a major participant in the renewed offensive, had again called on Rawlinson with a letter and air photographs taken that day of the German positions. The letter set forth powerful arguments against renewing an offensive that would be very costly and gain little. If the attack *had* to be resumed, then it should be postponed until there was again some chance of surprise. Far better, however, would be an attack somewhere else. Currie suggested that the Canadian Corps should be taken out of the Amiens sector, rested, and then be moved to Arras for a surprise attack in the direction of Bapaume. Rawlinson saw Haig on the morning of the 14th, taking Currie's letter and the photographs with him.[10]

Haig immediately directed the Third Army, holding a front north of Albert, to push the enemy back towards Bapaume; further north, the First Army would prepare to strike southeastwards from the Arras sector; and the Fourth Army was to be ready to follow up any withdrawal from the Somme. This was better than maintaining frontal pressure at one point: successive attacks at closely related points would keep the enemy off balance, as Pétain had suggested in 1917, and one would be broken off for another as the Germans reinforced.

Moreover, the alternative strategy could well be dovetailed into Foch's own. He had already planned for the French Tenth Army to strike northward from the Aisne; the attack was mounted between Compiègne and Soissons on 20 August and gained five miles in two days. On the 21st, the French Third Army put in a subsidiary attack on the left. That same day Byng's Third Army moved on Bapaume, as directed by Haig; by the 23rd it had advanced two miles and captured 5,000 prisoners. Rawlinson's Fourth, taking advantage of this, pressed hard astride the Somme, where one Australian division smashed two German divisions.

It was now the First Army's move, for which Haig ordered the Canadian Corps northward to Arras.

The territory was familiar and, before the Corps had gone to Amiens, the plan had been matured in detail as a camouflage for that battle. The Canadians moved into their former position east of Arras under General Horne's command. There was no time for rest, for in these last "Hundred Days" one offensive followed another in sharp succession. The Germans were to be forced to a decision by autumn. "If we allow the enemy a period of quiet," Haig declared, "he will recover, and the 'wearing out' process must be recommenced."[11] And on Hutier's pattern, units were to go straight for their objectives, with reserves pushed in wherever progress was made.

In the Bapaume area the attacks of the Third Army were squeezing the enemy out of the Somme salient and back to the Hindenburg Line. Horne's task was to force the defences that screened the flank of the Hindenburg Line facing Arras. He was then to break the hinge of the Hindenburg system and, swinging southwards, to deny those formidable defences to the enemy falling back before the Third Army. The line of Horne's advance would be directly on Cambrai, the hub of the German defensive system on the British front.

The German positions facing the First Army were sited in depth and extremely strong. Immediately in front were the old British trenches in the vicinity of Monchy-le-Preux, lost to the Germans in March, 1918. Behind those was the old German front line. Two miles to the east was a further system, the Fresnes-Rouvroy Line. A mile east of that lay the Drocourt-Quéant Line, a terribly strong and deep system of trenches with concrete shelters and heavy wire designed to block any advance into the Douai plain. Like the Hindenburg Line, of which it was an extension, the D-Q Line had been under construction for almost two years and was counted on as being absolutely impregnable. Between that and Cambrai, the Canal du Nord formed an almost impassable barrier.

The task of breaking these defences was given to Currie with the British XVII Corps co-operating on his right, between the Canadians and Byng's Third Army. It was a tough assignment. The enemy defensive plan was to thin out troops in the Lys and Ypres areas further north,* providing ample reserves to wear out the Allied advance in front of the Hindenburg position. The Germans would then reorganize behind its strong defences. Any voluntary withdrawal to the Hindenburg Line was sternly opposed by Ludendorff; it would have to be approached step by step. No surprise could be hoped for. Successive frontal assaults against the various positions would be necessary against a desperately fighting enemy. The Battle of the Scarpe, 1918, part of Second Arras, began on 26 August.

Currie put the 3rd Division in the centre, between the Scarpe and the road that ran arrow-straight from Arras to Cambrai. On the right was the 2nd Division, and on the left the British 51st (Highland) Division, on loan to the Corps. The 1st Canadian Division, having come from Amiens only the day before, was not employed; and the 4th had yet to arrive.

The objective was a north-south line beyond Monchy-le-Preux, three miles forward. Only three German divisions were as yet on the front, and one of them had evacuated the village of Neuville-Vitasse in the 2nd Division's sector two days before because "the commitment of the Canadians, the best British troops, had been recognized."[12] Currie obtained some surprise by attacking at the early hour of 3 A. M. By nightfall, the German opposition having proved lighter than expected, Monchy and the ground a thousand yards behind it (including both the old British and German trench lines) were in the hands of the Canadian Corps.

Orders for the 27th directed both the Canadian divisions to break through the Fresnes-Rouvroy Line, an advance of five miles. The British division would continue to push forward on the left. The attack

*On 28 September the first two days' fighting by the British Second Army and the Belgian Army in Flanders won back the Messines-Passchendaele Ridge.

began at dawn and though some progress was made, the objective was not reached. The Germans had reinforced with two divisions, and at midday a third came in. All attempts to get forward were met by persistent machine-gun fire.

Next day the fighting was equally bitter. Nevertheless, Lipsett's 3rd Division pierced the Fresnes-Rouvroy Line after calling down heavy concentrations of artillery fire to smother the German machine-gun nests; the position was further improved on the 29th and 30th. But the toll had been heavy. During the first three days, in the teeth of growing German strength, the two Canadian divisions had between them suffered almost 6,000 casualties. One of these was Major Georges Vanier, a future Governor General of Canada, who lost his right leg while commanding the 22nd Battalion; every officer in the unit became a casualty. Three thousand three hundred German prisoners were taken, and a large number of guns. On 30 August the Battle of the Scarpe was brought to an end.

The previous day Haig had received a disturbing letter from Sir Henry Wilson, who had succeeded Robertson as CIGS: "Just a word of caution in regard to incurring heavy losses in attacks on the Hindenburg Line [the Drocourt-Quéant Line was meant[13]] as opposed to losses when driving the enemy back to that line. I do not mean to say that you have incurred such losses, but I know the War Cabinet would become anxious if we received heavy punishment in attacking the Hindenburg Line, without success."[14] Haig's interpretation of this was that Lloyd George was still hunting for his head: "If my attack is successful, I will remain on as C. in C. If we fail, or our losses are excessive, I can hope for no mercy!"[15] Once again, then, as at Passchendaele, Haig's career was in the hands of Arthur Currie, and he was content to let it remain there. He kept the contents of Wilson's discouraging communication to himself, and let his orders stand.

Currie, appreciating the formidable nature of the D-Q Line, which was the next objective, obtained Horne's permission to postpone the attack until 2 September when his preparations would be ready. The 2nd and 3rd Divisions were relieved on the night of the 28th by the 1st Division (right) and the 4th (British) Division (left), and these troops spent the intervening days in wresting from the enemy good jumping-off positions for the main attack. On the night of 31 August the 4th Canadian Division, having arrived from Amiens, entered the line in the centre.

Meanwhile the heavy artillery, the use of which had been made possible by the introduction of the 106 fuse for large-calibre shells, had begun to cut the dense belts of wire. The fighting to obtain satisfactory jumping-off positions continued in places throughout 1 September and German counter-attacks were commonplace; the

12th Brigade, for example, was still fighting at zero hour, and the opening barrage was merely a signal to continue the conflict. A further complication arose when, late on 31 August, the commander of the 4th British Division announced that, because of heavy losses during this preliminary fighting, only one brigade was fit for the assault. Currie made hasty redispositions: his own 4th Division extended to take over half the British frontage. Preliminary preparation, by the standards of 1916 and 1917, was extremely brief, but by now Currie had at his disposal a smoothly functioning machine.

The 1st Division would attack on the right with eighteen tanks, its first objective the support trenches of the D-Q Line. After that its task was to take a connecting system, known as the Buissy Switch, which covered the villages of Buissy and Villers-lez-Cagnicourt. The reserve brigades had the task of exploiting to the Canal du Nord and over; a heavy programme. The 4th Canadian Division in the centre and the British brigade on the left were to pierce the Drocourt-Quéant Line—five rows of trenches—and then would seize the village of Dury beyond and its smooth, bare ridge.

Currie planned to spare the infantry as far as possible and concentrated powerful artillery support: one field gun for every twenty-three yards of front. Behind them were the heavies. So thickly had the defensive wire been installed, however, that it was impossible for the preliminary gunfire to cut it all; the main job for the tanks would, therefore, be to roll paths through the remaining entanglements.

At dawn on the 2nd, behind a barrage heartening in its strength, the infantry went forward. The blundering, swaying tanks clawed through the wire, snapping the strands like cotton. Resistance, unexpectedly, was patchy. These were not the steadily defiant Germans of 1917, though in places isolated pockets held out to the end. Ludendorff's assessment after Amiens matched the Canadian experience of 2 September:

Retiring troops, meeting a fresh division going bravely into action, had shouted out things like "Blackleg," and "You're prolonging the war!" . . . Our fighting power had suffered, even though the great majority of divisions still fought heroically.[16]

The 1st Division at first met little resistance; the enemy surrendered in droves. They came along in battalions, reported the 2nd Battalion, then in reserve, under escort and glad to be done with the fighting. "They could be seen everywhere in column of route . . . it was observed that their march discipline was good, each section of fours was well closed up!"[17] By 7:30 A.M. the left battalion of the right brigade was through the main trenches and had seized its section of the support line, the first objective. A fresh battalion swept through to seize Cagnicourt and "enough Germans to make a full battalion"[18] before going on to take its objective—part of the Buissy Switch in front of Buissy—against stiffer resistance.

The right battalion had a sterner task. Flanking machine-gun and artillery fire from the south hindered the advance. The impasse was broken through the bravery of individual officers and NCOs who guided tanks against the strong points. The first objective—a length of the complete D-Q system—was then captured but, faced by intense fire, the battalion could not reach the Buissy Switch. In the late afternoon it consolidated 3,000 yards short of that objective, and at 6:00 P.M. British troops came forward to close the open flank.

The left brigade, like the right, met with varying fortune. Its part of the line was quickly taken. East of that, the tanks lurched to a stop one by one under bursting enemy shells and the infantry became pinned down by mortars and machine-guns from the Buissy Switch in front of Villers-lez-Cagnicourt. To open the way for the advance of motor machine-guns to seize the Marquion bridge on the Canal du Nord, the artillery fire in a zone 1,000 yards wide from the Arras-Cambrai road had been terminated. This suspension of neutralizing fire had most serious consequences for the attacking troops south of the main road, while armoured cars, fired at by machine-guns and by batteries over open sights, made no progress. Only when the artillery fire had been resumed could the troops go forward; late that night the weary men finally seized the Buissy Switch.

The 4th Division, in the centre, also took its D-Q objectives on schedule, as did the British brigade on the left. The village of Dury fell to the 10th Brigade at 7:30 A.M. but efforts to carry forward down the open slopes of Mont Dury, swept by machine-gun fire directed up the valleys (described as the heaviest ever experienced by the 4th Division), failed. Currie called a halt in mid-afternoon until a further set-piece attack could be laid on; but this proved unnecessary.

Next morning the Corps moved forward for a resumed attack and found—nothing. Only distant artillery fire disturbed the advance as far as the west bank of the Canal du Nord. The east bank was strongly held and the bridges had been destroyed. A pause followed to gather strength for the next great operation. Until the Canal du Nord was crossed, the Hindenburg Line could not be described as having been fully pierced; nor could it be turned.

Though the Corps had not gained its distant objectives on 2 September, it had cleared the much-vaunted D-Q trenches and, beyond it on the right, most of the Buissy Switch, against a numerically superior enemy. This deep penetration of the extension to the Hindenburg Line compelled the hoped-for withdrawal of the enemy along the whole of the Third Army's front further south. On the morning of the 3rd Byng reported that he had occupied both Quéant and Pronville without having to fight for them. This was not all. The wedge that the Canadians had driven in, though still obstructed by the Canal du Nord, threatened to open a flank that would turn the system; thus the Germans felt themselves compelled to withdraw behind the Hindenburg defences, and indeed all along the front as far south as the Aisne, and also in Flanders.

In the words of Hindenburg:

On September 2 a fresh hostile attack overran our lines once and for all on the great Arras-Cambrai road and compelled us to bring the whole front back to the Siegfried [Hindenburg] Line. For the sake of economizing men we simultaneously evacuated the salient north of the Lys which bulged out beyond Mount Kemmel and Merville.[19]

This meant that the whole of the gains of the enemy's March offensive had been relinquished, as had the bulk of those of the April offensive in Flanders. In the south, the German 7th Army was forced to conform by abandoning the Vesle and pulling back behind the Aisne.[20] Nor were these all the consequences of recent developments. Currie's victory of 2 September forced the German High Command to adopt extreme measures. Labour was diverted for the construction of a new defensive line, the Hermann position further back. This was to run, in the northern sector, from the Dutch frontier east of Bruges generally southwards to the Lys, upstream to the east of Courtrai, thence by the Scheldt to Valenciennes, and south on the line Solesmes—le Cateau—Guise. All military material not required for immediate use was to be removed from the region west of that line, railways and roads demolished, and coal mines wrecked. A second line—the Antwerp-Meuse—was reconnoitred. The fortresses in Alsace-Lorraine were put into a state of defence. And to prevent capture, supplies from Germany were ordered to be cut down to the bare essentials. [21]

Well might Currie, though unaware of all this at the time, wonder "whether our victory of yesterday or of August 8th" was the greatest: he was "inclined to think yesterday's was."[22] Though not so decisive as Amiens, by obviating the sustained fighting to the Hindenburg Line that would otherwise have been necessary, it materially shortened the war. This had not been achieved lightly. The fighting between 1-3 September cost 5,500 casualties, mostly inflicted by two of the better German divisions. Although the enemy concealed his total losses, seven divisions are known to have been overcome and 6,000 prisoners taken unwounded.

On 3 September, Haig and his Chief of the General Staff visited Currie to congratulate the Corps on its great victory. Currie learned that there would be a pause to permit the British further south to reach the Hindenburg Line and then to assist in a full-scale attack on the next objective. The Canadian Corps made the most of this lull to reinforce, rest and refit.

That day Marshal Foch outlined his future plans for the Allied campaign on the Western Front. Three British armies, the First, Third and Fourth were either facing the Canal du Nord or approaching the Hindenburg Line for a resumed offensive. To avoid the risk of the enemy massing all his reserves against them, Foch determined on a general offensive all along the front, which would consist of four great blows to be delivered, first, by the three British armies against Cambrai and St. Quentin; second, by the French centre beyond the Aisne; third, by U.S. forces in army strength against the St. Mihiel Salient, later combining with the French in a drive towards Mézières; and finally, by the British and Belgian forces towards Ghent and Bruges.

Next day Currie climbed a ridge overlooking the Canal du Nord. He noted the formidable nature of the barrier. The canal itself was about a hundred feet wide, but the marshes on both sides of it had been extensively flooded to widen the obstacle. Its defences consisted of machine-gun posts close to the canal and, about a mile further back, the Marquion Line. On a lofty hill behind the latter reared Bourlon Wood, and Currie knew from air photographs that between it and Cambrai was yet another line, the Marcoing defence system. Between the Marquion Line and the wood the ground was cut by old excavations that might well house more machine-guns. A frontal attack, he concluded, would be unsound because of the nature of the obstacle: the flooded ground, and the successive defences from which any push to the east would be the more violently enfiladed the deeper it went.[23] To the south, on the other hand, a 4,000-yard stretch of the canal was dry and its excavated bed ran between higher and firmer ground. This was an unfinished section where construction work had been halted by the outbreak of the war. To cover this section the enemy had built further defences, the Canal du Nord Defence Line, and these were densely wired. Nevertheless, the latter appeared to Currie to offer a less costly means of approach than the north, where crossings would have to be confined to hastily constructed and vulnerable bridges.

On 15 September Haig outlined his intentions. The First and Third Armies would operate jointly towards Cambrai, Horne seizing Bourlon Wood and holding the left flank while Byng advanced on the town itself. The Canadian Corps, with the 11th British Division under command, would take the wood and then establish a front along the Sensée Canal. Three days later, Currie submitted his plan to General Horne.

He proposed to take advantage of the dry portion of the canal by having the Corps boundary extended 2,600 yards to the south. Through this one-and-a-half-mile funnel Currie proposed to pass 50,000 men, guns, tanks and transport and, after reaching the further bank, to spread them out fanwise in a 10,000-yard arc to the north and east, enveloping the defences as they went. It was a daring conception calling for skilful leadership and strict discipline. If the enemy artillery should ever become alert to the congestion in the narrow avenue of assault, the attack would break down in a welter of blood that would virtually destroy the Corps. Yet against that risk was the certainty in a frontal assault of extremely heavy casualties, still without assurance of success.

A cautious commander would have accepted the cost of the direct approach. The "brutal expedient of the frontal attack" had become commonplace throughout four years of war. None would have cavilled. And the artillery programme would have been so much simpler: preparation, and then a barrage in front of the long line of attacking men.

For Currie's complicated scheme, only a small portion of the artillery could be positioned forward; there was hardly room enough for the assembly of the infantry. The remaining guns would have to be sited in depth to the rear, where they could help cover the initial assault and must then be brought forward to cover the next stage. The engineers, working to a carefully planned timetable, must by this time have bridges ready to enable the guns detailed for close support to cross the canal and enable them to keep in intimate touch with the later stages of the attack. And not only was the mobility of the guns a problem: the planning of the barrage to cover an assault spreading in different directions on the further bank was extremely intricate. It was the type of battle that would make extreme demands on every arm and service of the Canadian Corps.

The decision demanded great tactical courage on Currie's part. Bourlon Wood being the key to Cambrai, failure would place three armies—the First and Third on Cambrai and the Fourth on St. Quentin further south—in jeopardy. It would tarnish the hitherto un-blemished record of the Canadian Corps—and end Currie's career. Faced with such a decision, perhaps he realized for the first time the terrible loneliness of command. At the same time, it would give the chance of surprise and the possibility of gaining the objectives over better ground at lighter cost. Currie, therefore, accepted the attendant risks and complications. He knew his men and trusted them to sur-mount the difficulties.

Having made up his mind, Currie put in hand the detailed planning. Horne, meanwhile, had serious misgivings and discussed with Byng the advisability of letting the plan proceed. Byng, too, had doubts and saw Currie on the 25th, two days before the assault was due. He went over Currie's plans with him and then said: "Old man, do you think you can do it?" Currie, who had become confident with planning, assured him that he could. Byng was not entirely reassured. He pointed out that it was the most difficult operation that had yet been tried in the war. "If anybody can do it, the Canadians can . . ." he concluded, "but if you fail it means home for you!"[24]

The night before the attack Horne rode over to Currie's headquarters and went over the final plans. Knowing the risks, he was still very anxious, but Currie convinced him that the concept was sound. On his way back, however, a vague uneasiness gripped Horne; he had a strong inclination to turn his horse's head and to cancel the operation. "But the thought came to him that the Canadians had never failed, and so the attack went on next morning at dawn."[25]

The initial crossing of the dry canal was carried out by two divisions. The 4th, on the right, was to push on until it was in possession of Bourlon and Bourlon Wood, by skirting the wood's edges north and south and linking hands at the far end; it would then mop up. The 1st Division would swing left to capture the villages of Sains-lez-Marquion and Marquion (astride the Arras-Cambrai road), both being along the Canal du Nord. This fanlike action, if successful, would expand the front to about 10,000 yards, making room for the 3rd Division to come in on the right of the 4th and for the 11th British Division to come in on the left of the 1st Canadian.

In the second phase, all four divisions were to push outwards. The 3rd, co-operating with the XVII Corps on the right flank, would seize part of the Marcoing Line and push on to the northern outskirts of Cambrai. Right centre, the 4th would seize two villages and the northern part of the Marcoing Line. Left centre, the 1st would move northeast as far as the Douai road; and on the left, the 11th British Division would advance north to seize two villages there.

The advance would then continue, in co-operation with the XXII Corps on the left, to seize important bridges over the Canal de L'Escaut beyond Cambrai. The XVII Corps would perform a similar operation on the right, thus pinching out Cambrai from the north and south.

Of these operations, the 1st Division's were undoubtedly the most complicated. All three infantry brigades and the ancillary services had to cross the canal on a front of no more than 1,100 yards. In the first two hours thousands of men, animals, vehicles and guns were to crowd through this narrow gap. The 1st Brigade had a fairly straightforward job involving only a slight change of direction to carry it through the Canal du Nord and Marquion Lines and thence north of Bourlon. The 3rd was required to swing in a wide arc to the north, in order to get behind the swampy ground in front of Sains-lez-Marquion and then turn towards the canal to attack the village in a direction entirely opposite to the main attack under a reverse barrage. It would then turn west and clean up Marquion and the area back to the canal. The 2nd Brigade would move in the direction of the village of Haynecourt on a line between the 1st and 3rd Brigades. This meant that units of the three brigades would be fighting simultaneously east, northeast, north and west! A special internal barrage would support these intricate manoeuvres. It would first roll forward to the Canal du Nord Line; then, as the 3rd Brigade came along, the barrage would roll back with shells bursting between the troops and their own guns. The clearing of the canal bank was vital. The success of the operation depended on the work of the field gunners and the courage, skill and resourcefulness of the infantry.

In the dusk of the evening of 26 September the assaulting troops tumbled out of dug-outs in the recently seized Drocourt-Quéant Line and fell in by platoons. Platoon commanders called the roll and gave a final briefing. In the gathering darkness of a cold, damp night that threatened rain, the men moved off. The whole area was alive with troops making their way towards the canal. There was no shouting from group to group, and within the platoons men spoke tensely in low voices. By midnight they were assembled opposite the dry section of the canal, huddled together for warmth, and for the most part in the open.

From all around them came the stealthy noises of an immense concentration: the shuffling of men, the jingling of harness chains and the slow rumble of wheels. So far there was no sign that the enemy had singled out the assembly areas for special attention. His shells were scattered along the whole front including back roads and the now deserted rearward areas; some fell amongst huddled men and took their toll. But as yet there was no evidence of enemy counter-preparation.

Apart from light showers, the rain held off and by now the clouds had cleared. The men anxiously watched the brightening eastern sky. Suddenly, with intense, pulsating light, the opening barrage flashed out, shocking the men to action. As they started to their feet a thunderous roar broke behind them, drowning out the sound of the German retaliation. The answering fire, it was heartening to note, had been laid along the length of the Buissy Switch, and it was not before the morning was well advanced that the enemy became alive to his danger and subjected the bed of the canal to a violent bombardment. By that time the initial waves were well over and fanning out from the bridgehead, but the follow-up troops inevitably suffered. Men clambered up the high eastern bank like ants; engineers erected ramps for the artillery and vehicles; guns and limbers, ambulances and wagons, crawled slowly over amid the bursting shells.[26]

The 4th Division, on the right, made good initial progress behind a splendidly maintained barrage, and pierced the Canal du Nord Line. The flanking XVII Corps could not keep up, with the result that the Canadian division was subjected to heavy enfilade fire as it approached Bourlon Wood, and was temporarily checked. In the afternoon machine-gun posts holding up the advance were rushed, and units again moved forward against heavy opposition. After skirting the wood both north and south, a junction was made but the division could do no more that day. The village of Fontaine-Notre Dame, an objective of XVII Corps beyond the wood, remained untaken, and the division dug in facing it for the night, until the British corps could make sufficient progress to attack it; consequently, the 3rd Division did not come forward that day. Nevertheless, good results had been obtained. The division had advanced 6,000 yards, and had captured Bourlon village and the grim eminence crowned by Bourlon Wood.

The 1st Division fulfilled its complicated task on the left. By 9:15 A.M. the Canal du Nord Line had been cleared and Sains-lez-Marquion seized. In conjunction with the 11th Division, Marquion was also captured, and in the afternoon all was in readiness for the second phase. Both the village of Haynecourt and the Douai road were in Canadian hands by nightfall.

On the left, the 11th British Division matched this success. At the end of the day it had gone on to seize both its final objectives, the villages of Epinoy and Oisy-le-Verger, while the XXII Corps mopped up the remainder of the canal bank. The wet portion of the canal had now been bridged, and all the paraphernalia required by a corps in the attack was getting across with ease.

The results of the first day, therefore, had justified Currie's generalship. He had gambled on a difficult manoeuvre to give him the Canal du Nord at light cost. More than that, Bourlon Wood, the essential objective, had also fallen.

Thereafter, the Germans, sensitive to the loss of Cambrai and the railways converging on it, which would threaten their lateral communications both north and south, poured in reinforcements. The enemy strength facing the Corps grew from four divisions on 27 September to ten by 1 October, as well as thirteen Marksmen Machine-Gun Companies that could offer sturdy resistance under conditions of open warfare. The following day saw the capture of the Marcoing Line, but progress afterwards became extremely slow. The 29th was a day of exhausting probing that proved costly and yielded little, and yet the pressure was still maintained until the enemy should crack. Next day a general attack broke down under murderous machine-gun fire and fierce counter-attacks, and the story was the same when the assault was renewed on 1 October. That night, in view of the exhaustion of his troops, Currie broke off the action.

The fighting had continued without respite for five days and the bridges over the Canal de l'Escaut were still defiantly held. Nonetheless, the last organized defences on the Canadian front had been broken through; 205 captured guns and more than 7,000 prisoners were tangible proof of victory. What was not immediately apparent was that the enemy was now fought out. The Canadian thrust, combined with those by the Third and Fourth Armies further south, had so used up the German reserves that the enemy was incapable of any further major resistance.

Foch's offensives had paid good dividends. The German High Command had been forced to shuffle troops from one trouble spot to another. On 12 September the First U.S. Army, fighting its first major battle, St. Mihiel, caught the Germans in a withdrawal and straightened out the salient. Though Pershing had wanted to continue the attack in a divergent direction towards Metz, that had been changed by Foch at Haig's instigation for one converging with the British attack on the Hindenburg Line. On 26 September, in conjunction with the French, the Americans opened the Meuse-Argonne battle on the British right. While this did not succeed in drawing off reserves from in front of Haig's three armies until the Hindenburg Line had been broken, it did gain seven miles and eventually caused the Germans to move troops further south.[27]

The flank protection afforded by the Canadian Corps enabled the Third Army, immediately to the south, to breach the Hindenburg Line southwest of Cambrai on 27 September. The Fourth Army, south of the Third, opened a powerful attack heavily supported by tanks and guns two days later; in an impressive display of strength it bored through the Hindenburg defences north of St. Quentin and burst into the open country three miles beyond. And one day before that, the British Second Army and the Belgians advanced in Flanders, recovered Messines and Passchendaele, and ploughed forward nine miles before being halted by mud and war-torn ground.

Behind the German Army, fighting stubborn rearguard actions, the nation and its allies fell apart. In the middle of September, Allenby's final offensive in Palestine tore the Turks in pieces. The remnants of their forces were driven back towards Damascus in streaming rout. The Allied forces in the much-despised Salonika theatre turned to the offensive against the Bulgarians on 15 September. Bulgaria, standing alone since the recall of German troops to the west, was out of the war by the end of the month.

Ludendorff, with his main defences broken, Turkey and Bulgaria in ruins, and the Allies gathering strength for a renewed onslaught, saw no ray of hope. He had already given orders for the break-up of twenty-two divisions to maintain a reduced battalion strength of 540 men.[28] Prince Max of Baden was brought in as Chancellor to conclude

a peace, and on 4 October the German and Austrian governments despatched notes to President Wilson asking for the opening of armistice
negotiations. "Here," said Foch to Haig, "you have the immediate
result of the British piercing the Hindenburg Line. The enemy has
asked for an armistice."[29]

Unheard-of things were going on in Germany. The army was being
criticized! It was said that the higher staff officers roistered and feasted
while the men who did the fighting starved in the open fields. "This,"
thundered Ludendorff, "was the reward of a grateful people to the
regular officer for his sacrifice and devotion!"[30] On the question of
officers' fare, his conscience pricked him, but the corpulent Ludendorff
knew he was on safe ground. In a letter to Prince Max he declared his
willingness to partake of the food provided by the field kitchens if the
"various Secretaries of State and the whole of Berlin would undertake
to do likewise."[31] The Imperial Chancellor, Prince Max, declined.

The Canadian Corps, refreshed by a week's rest, returned to the
attack on the night 8-9 October. The general plan was to seize the
Escaut bridges leading into Cambrai and then, avoiding house-to-
house fighting, to cut the town off from the north. At the same time the
XVII Corps would carry out similar operations to the south. In the
event the XVII Corps failed to carry a preliminary objective, and the
Canadians attacked alone.[32]

Their assault, in the middle of a pitch-black squally night, caught the
enemy preparing to withdraw. The bridges were reached with almost
ridiculous ease. Before dawn patrols had pushed into Cambrai to find
it deserted except for demolition parties who were busily engaged in
setting the town ablaze. By 8:30 A.M. the whole place was in Canadian
hands and the Corps pushed on to free the district to the north, which
it completed as far as the line of the Sensée by 11 October.

Since 26 August the Corps had fought forward 23 miles through the
backbone of the German defensive system manned in turn by 31
identified divisions. The formidable nature of the task and the severity
of the fighting is revealed by the casualty figures: 30,000 for the six-
week period. German losses, never published, included 19,000 prisoners
as well as 370 guns and 2,000 machine-guns.[33] Currie ascribed the
victories to "iron discipline" and the high standard reached in the
technical knowledge of weapons, as well as the "combined tactical
employment of all your resources."[34] These gains were, as he rightly
said, largely due to all the components of the Corps working smoothly
together in the over-all machine. They were also due in great measure
to careful planning and sound leadership.

That leadership, however, meant nothing to Sam Hughes. Back in
Ottawa, Cambrai became his latest target. Ever since Currie had been

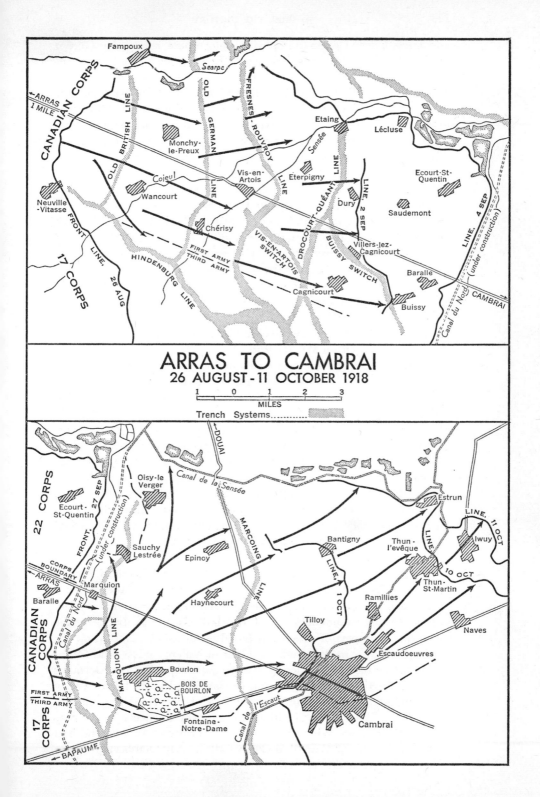

ARRAS TO CAMBRAI
26 AUGUST - 11 OCTOBER 1918

```
1       0       1       2       3
MILES
```

Trench Systems............

appointed Corps Commander, with unfortunate results for Garnet Hughes, Sir Sam had in turn criticized "Lens" (Hill 70) and Passchendaele; without having regard for the true circumstances or bothering to find out—especially the stand taken by Currie over Passchendaele—he painted the Corps Commander as a drover continually prodding men to the slaughter.[35] Currie's opposition to the proposal that two Canadian army corps of three divisions each should be formed also came in for the most unreasoning criticism.[36] And now it was the turn of Cambrai.

In a letter to the Prime Minister dated 1 October, a week before the Canadians even entered the deserted city, Hughes condemned Currie's methods as "bull-head" and sought hard to obtain his removal. The complaint was, as usual, a masterpiece of misinformation. He claimed to know the locality well, "and any General who would undertake to attack Cambrai by suburb or street fighting, should be tried by court-martial."[37] There was, of course, no street fighting in Cambrai; nor could Currie's tactics be described as bull-headed in this battle from the time of the crossing of the Canal du Nord to the actual fall of Cambrai on 9 October. Two major obstacles faced the Canadians— the canal and Bourlon Wood—and, as we have seen, neither was attacked frontally. The method used, and for which Currie assumed responsibility, was the most considerate of human lives.

Yet, though Borden took no action to remove Currie, the abusive sallies of Hughes—a man with "no more conception of a democratic army than a hen of logic"[38]—were bound to take some root. The falsehoods and blatant misrepresentations of the ex-Minister of Militia were allowed to pass to the general public without serious challenge. The Conservatives, reminded of their past praise for Hughes, were reluctant to attack him; the Opposition, on the other hand, treated such an embarrassment to Borden as a political ally. Thus Hughes' dangerous statements, though manifestly untrue, were allowed to grow and fester in the minds of an anxious public.

The Canadian practice on the Sensée Line had been to fire an artillery barrage along its frontage every morning to test the presence of the enemy. On the 17th the usual retaliation failed to materialize. On 16 October Ludendorff had ordered his troops back to the Hermann Line, part of which was based northeast of Cambrai on the Escaut (Scheldt), in the neighbourhood of Valenciennes. The Canadians, having received advice from adjacent troops that the Germans had indeed retired, crossed the Sensée Canal and pushed out cavalry and armoured cars to maintain contact with the retreating enemy. Thus began a pursuit that continued practically unchecked almost as far as Valenciennes. With Currie rode the Prince of Wales, who had been attached to the Canadian Corps staff in early October.

By Ludendorff's order, the countryside had been stripped of every-thing useful, including cattle, pigs and poultry. Bridges had been demolished, railways torn up and roads cratered. It proved extremely difficult to keep up with such an enemy.

This phase of the war seemed almost dreamlike to the marching men. They could hear the loud demolitions ahead but there was a strange absence of gunfire. They moved rapidly, skirting or scrambling over obstacles, and the movement was exhilarating. Bands played as battalions marched through liberated towns and villages to the cheers of French civilians, who proffered wine and coffee and bedecked the men with flowers. For the first time they felt what the newspapers had been calling them for years: "heroes," "liberators" and the "saviours of democracy."

Orders had been given that the enemy was not to be engaged. If he showed signs of fight, the pursuing troops were to go to ground in front of his positions until he pulled back. Casualties were to be avoided.[39] On the 21st, however, the enemy began to show his teeth. Roadblocks were now being covered by fire, and there was some long-range shell-ing. Resistance stiffened during the next two days. The Corps was approaching Valenciennes, and it became more and more obvious that the enemy was prepared to stand and fight. Before further progress could be made the Germans would have to be driven out, and new orders were issued accordingly.

During the evening of 23 October the Canadians reached the Escaut and stretched out eight miles along its length. The Corps lay at the centre of the First Army's front and waited until neighbouring forces— VIII and XXII Corps—should come up into line. The pause stretched into several days while preparations were made for what undoubtedly would be a major operation.

As a key point in the Hermann Line, Valenciennes had been well-chosen. The Canal de l'Escaut barred approach from the west and north. Both banks had been wired, and on the far side trenches had been dug. By opening sluices, low-lying ground west, southwest and north had been extensively flooded. The only dry approaches, there-fore, lay east and south, and these were effectively dominated by the heavily defended Mount Houy. Of five divisions holding Valenciennes, three were concentrated on or near Mount Houy.

Horne planned to attack on the 28th. The 51st Division of XXII Corps, heavily supported by artillery, would take Mount Houy; the Canadian 4th Division would then pass through, carrying the attack to the southern outskirts of Valenciennes and to high ground east of the city. This would effectively outflank Valenciennes, enabling the rest of the Canadian Corps to cross the Escaut from the west and to sweep on towards Mons.

On 27 October, the day on which Italy inflicted a heavy defeat on Austria at the Battle of the Piave, deployment for the Valenciennes battle began. British and Canadian troops were spread along the front, when all at once the sky above the battle area seemed to fill with enemy planes. A lone British fighter dived into the various massed formations. Suddenly German machines began fluttering to the ground trailing plumes of smoke before the eyes of thousands of spellbound troops. The British plane, crippled by now, came down in a low glide and was lost to view behind the trees of Mormal Forest. McNaughton, now the commander of the Canadian Corps Heavy Artillery, described the scene:

The spectacle of this attack was the most magnificent encounter of any sort which I have ever witnessed. The ancient performances of the gladiators in the Roman arenas were far outclassed in the epic character of the successive engagements in which enemy machines, one after the other, were taken on and eliminated. The spectators, in place of being restricted to the stone walls of a Roman arena, had the horizon as their bounds and the sky as their stage. The hoarse shout, or rather the prolonged roar, which greeted the triumph of the British fighter, and which echoed across the battlefront, was never matched in Rome, nor do I think anywhere else or on any other occasion.[40]

The victor, it was afterwards learned, was a Canadian, Major W. G. Barker. He had first shot down an enemy two-seater at the extremely high altitude, for those days, of 21,000 feet—his forty-seventh victim. He himself then came under the fire of a German plane; wounded, Barker fell in a spinning dive into the midst of fifteen Fokkers. He opened fire on these, and accounted for at least one. Wounded for the second time, Barker lost consciousness and spun out of control into a second formation. Rallying, he straightened out and shot down another plane in flames. Under attack by two Fokkers, Barker was again wounded, but managed to shoot down another of his assailants and then crashed behind his own lines. He recovered. For these exploits Barker received the Victoria Cross, joining two other Canadian air VCs, Bishop and McLeod.

At first light on the morning of 28 October the British division, heavily supported by artillery, took Mount Houy against strong opposition but could not hold it. By nightfall the British had been driven off the crest and had to be satisfied with part of the southern slope. The 4th Division could not pass through as had been planned, and Currie asked for and received twenty-four hours' delay in relieving the 51st Division to give time for new planning. This he did at McNaughton's request; the Heavy Artillery Commander wished for a "full and proper opportunity to do our work free from the hysteria of a suddenly improvised attack."[41] The Canadian Corps had by now been ordered to carry out the whole operation, which Currie proposed to do on 1 November.

The fire of the Canadian Divisional and Corps Heavy Artilleries was co-ordinated by Brigadier-General W. B. M. King (4th Divisional Artillery) and Brigadier-General A. G. L. McNaughton (Canadian Corps Heavy Artillery). The work was well done. From noon on 31 October to the same time on 2 November, working to a carefully co-ordinated programme, 2,140 tons of shells were fired, almost as much as had been expended by both sides in the South African War. They smothered the enemy positions, weaving in and out in sophisticated patterns of frontal, oblique, reverse and enfilade barrages, punctuated by solid blocks of fixed bombardment. The result was that one infantry brigade overran Mount Houy. During the morning the canal was crossed, and at noon patrols had pushed well into the city.

It had been a very satisfactory day and the operation, in Currie's words, "one of the most successful the Corps has yet performed."[42] Its essence, the careful co-ordination of tremendous gunfire in close support of a minimum of attacking troops, had brought victory at extremely low cost; 80 Canadians lost their lives, 300 were wounded. Eight hundred German dead alone were buried by the Canadians, and 1,800 prisoners taken.[43] And at Valenciennes Currie's maxim—to pay the price of victory in shells and not in the lives of men—was exemplified.

Currie planned to mount another set-piece attack next morning, but it proved unnecessary. The enemy would not stand up to another ordeal such as that of 1 November. During the night he quitted the Hermann Line entirely and Valenciennes, which had been spared bombardment because of the civilian inhabitants, passed peacefully into Canadian hands. The advance swept on.

The thoroughly defeated Germans reeled back from Verdun to the sea before relentless blue and khaki waves. For a month now armistice negotiations had been in progress. On 9 October Wilson had replied to German and Austrian overtures: his Fourteen Points must be accepted and all occupied territory evacuated before negotiations could proceed. Three days later these terms were agreed, but on the 16th the Allies, realizing the extent of German demoralization, named a stiffer price; the armistice conditions would now be drafted by the Allied commanders. On 24 October a third note from Wilson scrapped the concept of a negotiated armistice for a surrender without conditions. During the first week of November, with the Hermann defences broken, Bulgaria and now Turkey out of the war, and Austria in full retreat from Italy, even this ignominious conclusion to the war could not be avoided by the Germans.

Until the armistice should be finally signed Allied pressure did not relax. The main difficulties now confronting the Corps were not caused by enemy resistance but by the systematic demolitions in the path of the pursuit. But the engineers, working round the clock, kept the advance moving. Bridges were repaired, craters were filled, and unlike the experience of the British,[44] the heavy artillery* managed to get forward to maintain touch with the attacking brigades, whose main task was to dispose of enemy machine-gun posts. There was some German long-range fire, and here the bigger guns proved useful to silence the enemy's still defiant batteries.

By 10 November the leading division of the Corps was on the out-skirts of Mons, poised to take the town. A group of men from one battalion of a reserve division, billeted in a Belgian village, enjoyed a cheerful meal and afterwards sang songs until their repertoire was exhausted.

Unexpectedly a small girl said in French, "I know an English song." The men pressed her to sing it but she was shy. After some persuasion she began to sing in a clear, childish voice:

> Eet's a long way to Teeperaree
> Eet's a long way to go . . .

and she continued, right to the end. The men were astonished to hear that song in territory that had been so long in enemy hands. The girl, who had hidden her face after the song was over, finally recovered from her shyness. The soldiers questioned her and found out that when she was very small, British soldiers had stayed in the house on the way back from Mons. They had not only taught her to sing "Tipperary," but had also told her never to forget it as they would be back some day and would ask her to sing it for them.[45]

The British, represented by the Canadian Corps (with one of the original cavalry units that had served there in 1914), had indeed re-turned to Mons. The town, which had witnessed the first engagement between British and German troops in 1914, changed hands on the night 10-11 November without a struggle.

It was the end of the journey. In their outpost line five miles beyond the town, the troops awaited the cessation of hostilities timed for eleven o'clock. With two minutes to go, one man looked out from behind the corner of a building to see what was happening in the enemy line. He received a bullet in the chest from the Germans who were clearing their weapons in the direction of the enemy. That was the only fatality that day, probably the last casualty of the war.

*The heavy siege batteries had been left out of the line. Their lorries, tractors and men were used to establish depots close up (as the advance pro-ceeded), to support the 60-pounder, 6-inch and some 8-inch batteries, which did most of the shooting during this phase.

The appointed time arrived and firing ceased. There was no cheering to break the quiet, or elated scenes. It would take time to realize that the need for endurance had finally passed; it was too early for the memories that would flood in later. Adjustment would have to wait. Slowly, with difficulty, the men groped for thoughts of home. The transition had been too swift. All they could count on now was that the violent jack-hammer of artillery that had pounded and flayed the ground for four infernal years had at last ceased its monstrous din.

THIRTEEN.
AFTERMATH: THE HOLLOWNESS OF VICTORY AND THE TRANSIENCE OF PRAISE

Currie made his entry into Mons during the afternoon of 11 November. It was a fine day and, as the General rode in with an escort of British 5th Lancers, all of whom had served at Mons in 1914, the narrow streets were thronged with wildly cheering people.

The escorting cavalry must have relished the contrast in the circumstances, so entirely different from those of 1914. At the time of the grim battle during the hot August of four years before, the Belgians had seemed utterly crushed in the shadow of von Kluck's approaching horde. Now, under the weak sun of a winter's day, they were in holiday mood, laughing and shouting and waving the black, yellow and red flags of Belgium.

Bands played in the densely packed Grande Place. Every soldier wore a red carnation stuck into his cap band above his ear. The Canadian Commander and his escort clattered across the rough cobblestones, dismounted, and met the gathered dignitaries of Mons. The Mayor delivered an address of welcome, punctuated at every pause by shouts of *Vive les braves Canadiens!* from citizens almost crazed with joy.

Currie, fresh from Valenciennes where similar scenes had been enacted the day before in the presence of the President of the French Republic, was nevertheless touched by the rapturous welcome. Nor was the historic significance of the occasion lost on him. In reply, the "authoritative voice of the great Canadian General is lifted, clear, vigorous and sincere."[1] Currie echoed the Mayor's words, that the city of Mons had at last been "delivered by the heroism of the British Army, which, at the hour of the Armistice, completes its series of victories in the identical place where, on August 23, 1914, it first engaged the enemy." Then, in a firm yet tactful way to which no one could take offence, he identified Canada with the deliverance. "It was a proud thing—that we, the young whelps of the old lion, were able to

234

take the ground lost in 1914."[2] He then presented to the city the Canadian Corps' flag which, the Mayor assured him, would be forever treasured in the Mons archives.

Selected contingents of the Corps marched past to *La Brabançonne*, the Belgian national anthem, and at the conclusion of the march past Currie was conducted to the City Hall. There he signed the Golden Book of Remembrance immediately under the signature of Albert, King of the Belgians, which had been placed there in 1914, just before his country was invaded.[3]

These were heady days. During the following week the army commanders attended a great military celebration in Mons with Currie, his senior officers and the Prince of Wales. The Place de la Bavarie, where Canadian troops first entered, was renamed the Place du Canada. A gold medal was struck: *La ville de Mons au Lieut.-General Sir Arthur W. Currie en souvenir de la liberation de la cité par le Corps Canadien.* King Albert made a state entry and congratulated Currie on his troops, "unsurpassed by any Corps in Europe." And over the town, from music borrowed from a regimental band, the carillon in the ancient belfry tower pealed out Canada's national airs.[4]

Looking east from the belfry, which rose above a hill surmounted by the citadel of Mons, the Canadian outpost line could be seen. Guns, strangely silent, lay shrouded in tarpaulins; their crews stood boldly on the sky line. Pipes glowed and men moved about no longer fearful of the screaming, whistling death that had dogged them for months and years. Far to the east were hills, rising above the sombre plain, and beyond them, mysterious and somehow fascinating, enemy country.

While at Mons the Canadians learned that they were to march to the Rhineland as part of the British Army of Occupation. Currie received the news with gratification, as an honour that his Corps had well earned. The armistice had provided for the occupation by Allied troops of the left bank of the Rhine together with bridgeheads, each with a radius of thirty kilometres, at the principal crossing places on the other bank. The British would hold one bridgehead in the Cologne area, which would incorporate the bridges at both Cologne and Bonn, and it was planned that the Second and Fourth Armies would comprise the occupation force. In the event, the Second Army alone fulfilled this task, two Canadian divisions forming a sixth of the total force.

On Sunday, 17 November, thanksgiving services were held in Mons and the dead remembered. Next day the 1st and 2nd Divisions crossed the outpost lines and began the long march that would take them through the rugged country of the Ardennes and Eifel districts to the Rhine. The 1st led the march to Cologne, and the 2nd to Bonn. All precautions were taken against surprise and a strict standard of turnout and discipline prevailed. "You must remain what you are," said Currie, "a close-knitted army in grim, deadly earnest":

. . . all external signs of discipline must be insisted upon . . . clothing and equipment must be, if possible, spotless, well kept and well put on . . . in short, you must continue to be and appear to be that powerful hitting force which has won the fear and respect of your foes and the admiration of the world.[5]

The contrast between the steadily marching Canadians and the Germans, whose demoralization was apparent from the litter of army clothing, helmets and even weapons along the roads, must have been very evident to the watching villagers.

On the morning of 4 December the leading units reached the German frontier, but the crossing of the Rhine nine days later was considered more significant. General Plumer would take the salute at the Cologne crossing, the distinction at Bonn being accorded to Arthur Currie.

On the 12th, British cavalry units crossed into Bonn to establish control posts within the town under the protection of batteries of the Canadian Corps Heavy Artillery deployed to cover the bridge and other vital points.* Currie spent the night in the Palais Schaumburg, the home of the German Emperor's youngest sister, where he occupied the Kaiser's suite. The Strathroy farmboy, travelling west on the hard wooden seat of the colonist car to seek his fortune twenty-four years before, had come a long way since then.[6]

Currie made his way to the bridge to take the salute "after a very comfortable night in His Majesty's bed."[7] In the half-light of a wet winter's day, with rain slanting down on the strongly flowing Rhine, the troops crossed the natural frontier of Germany before a handful of apathetic Germans.

"The spectacle was magnificent," said Currie. "The smart, sturdy infantry, with bayonets fixed, marching perfectly with colours flying and bands playing . . . was an impressive sight."[8] The order "Eyes right!" passed successively down the line; steel-helmeted heads jerked precisely over like one man. The figure of the Corps Commander, erect and stern, loomed on the dais by the iron bridge rail—a figure that had proved a strength and an inspiration on many a battlefield. For Currie the task was now almost done.

His final battle concerned demobilization. Plans for this, begun as early as the end of 1916, called for the complete disbandment of the Canadian forces on a "first in, first out" basis, modified by marital status; individuals would be shipped home primarily according to length of service. This would mean the break-up of the Corps, veterans of 1914 going off at once, the later reinforcements leaving by stages.

*A painting of the scene is in the Senate Chamber.

Furthermore, administration would break down. Clerks and cooks, for instance, had been relatively immune from casualties and had thus piled up long-service credits that would ensure their early departure. Currie contended that it was imperative in the interests of morale to send the men back to Canada in the units in which they had fought. They had acquired tradition; far better to return the troops by proud battalions instead of in miscellaneous drafts. This was the wish of the senior officers; it was also the desire of the men who, as one veteran bitterly expressed it, had no wish to be shipped home "like cattle, or a bunch of pre-war draftees."[9] Currie's views had at first been rejected by the Privy Council on the grounds that the existing plans had been arrived at after very careful study!

Currie solicited the support of Sir Robert Borden, who was in England at the time. Borden found his arguments convincing, and in a letter to Sir Thomas White, the acting Prime Minister, asked that the matter be reconsidered.[10] The cabinet at first refused to alter its decision. Borden then cited the example of Australia, which had decided to return its troops by units under their own officers; it would be courting trouble, he warned, if Canadian units "which have fought so magnificently and earned world-wide distinction in keen competition with each other are scrambled into one mass and returned to Canada."[11] With that, the cabinet gave in; it was prepared to defer to General Currie's wishes provided the sanction was limited to combatant units.[12]

Thus the Canadian divisions sailed back to Canada by complete battalions. Currie's stand was justified. Cohesion and discipline were maintained in the fighting units of the Corps until the very end and demobilization proceeded with remarkable smoothness. Other units,* broken up and the men concentrated under strange officers in various camps in England, experienced difficulties. Riots and disturbances broke out. In March at Kinmel Park, for example, 800 soldiers rioted; five men were killed and 23 wounded. In June, at Witley, a large area of the camp was destroyed, including the garrison theatre, following the suppression of gambling. The same month, Canadian soldiers stormed a police station at Epsom; one policeman was killed and seven injured. No such incidents tarnished the record of the divisions of the Corps.

The last of the Canadian occupation troops left the Rhineland in February, 1919. By May every division had returned to Canada.

The Canadian Corps had achieved a reputation unsurpassed in the Allied armies. After the Somme its record was one of unbroken victory. It had emerged successfully from every test, no matter how severe, and its professional ability had proved second to none.

*Nearly 40,000 Canadian troops served in France outside General Currie's command, railway troops, tunnellers, etc.

"Whenever the Germans found the Canadian Corps coming into the line," wrote Lloyd George, "they prepared for the worst."[13] Liddell Hart, the eminent British military historian, said much the same of the Canadians: "Regarding them as storm troops, the enemy tended to greet their appearance as an omen of a coming attack."[14] Another British historian, Corelli Barnett, has described them as the "most formidable troops in Haig's command,"[15] while yet another (C.R.M.F.Cruttwell) speaking of Canadian, Australian and New Zealand troops, said: "These men in physical fitness and strength excelled all the troops of any of the European armies. In their ruthless self-confidence, their individual initiative, their impatience of form, ceremony and tradition, they bore upon themselves the unmistakable mark of the new nations."[16] A German assessment confirms those views. Hindenburg, writing after the war, said: "The English troops were of varying value. The élite consisted of men from the Colonies—a fact which is undoubtedly to be attributed to the circumstances that the colonial population is mainly agrarian."[17]

A comparison of the American performance in the Argonne-Meuse operations with that of the Canadians in the final Hundred Days of the war is not without interest. This is done, in tabular form, not to disparage the efforts of that great republic, but to show what can be accomplished by a country with a small but well-trained force as opposed to another able to furnish larger numbers of troops but not so well prepared. The favourable results obtained were made possible only by the fact that the Canadians had benefited by the experience of training and hard fighting during the previous years.

ARGONNE-MEUSE (American)—"HUNDRED DAYS" (Canadian)

	American	Canadian
Number of troops engaged	650,000	105,000
Duration of operations	47 days	100 days
Maximum advance	34 miles	86 miles
German divisions met and defeated	46	47
Casualties suffered for every German division defeated	2,170	975
Total battle casualties	100,000	45,830
Prisoners captured	16,000	31,537
Guns captured	468	623
Machine-guns captured	2,864	2,842
Trench mortars captured	117	336[18]

Canada, with a small, largely agrarian population in those years, had indeed written her name large over the battlefields of France and Flanders. Great battles—Ypres, Vimy, Hill 70, Passchendaele, Amiens and the Hindenburg Line—will always be associated with the Canadian Corps. Canada began the war with little military experience and with practically nothing in the way of a standing army. She ended it with a superb fighting machine, "the greatest national achievement of the Canadian people since the Dominion came into being."[19]

The reasons for the success of the Canadian Corps must be examined; and any examination must exclude the personality of the dynamic but misguided Minister of Militia and Defence, Sam Hughes. It is, in fact, apparent that the Corps achieved its success despite Sam Hughes. Inflexibility is often taken as the mark of a strong man; some leaders, imbued with that idea, think it a sign of weakness to change their minds, forgetting that what might have been true yesterday need not be so today. Such a man was Hughes. Having decided on the ranges in peacetime that the Ross rifle was a perfect battlefield weapon, he blinded himself to the overwhelming evidence against it in time of war and continued to champion it against all reason. Again, Hughes' advocacy of six Canadian divisions, even before the Somme, continued long after there was any prospect of providing adequate reinforcements for them; in 1918 he came out strongly in favour of breaking up a fully tested and efficient fighting machine to have six divisions, reinforcible or not; and this despite the fact that under his grossly inefficient administration the existing four divisions had been reinforced only with difficulty. Hughes, there is no doubt, was a tragic nuisance whose influence on the Corps was not for good.

The fundamental reason for the effectiveness of the Canadian Corps is that it was an organization in which all the arms and services were balanced in components and integrated in direction, an organization in which the need for the support of the infantry was recognized, at all levels, as the first requirement.[20] This process had already started under Byng at Vimy. It was carried a long way further by Currie, and we have seen something of the reorganization carried out by him in 1918. As a result he created well-balanced and carefully organized components of the Corps and these, imbued with a team spirit that bred co-operation, contributed their own special attributes and were mutually supporting. "The whole was much greater and very, very much more formidable in battle than the sum of its parts."[21]

The capabilities and attitude of staff officers at all levels was considered especially important. They had to know their jobs and be devoted to their tasks; they were encouraged to be helpful towards every problem of the forward troops, no matter how difficult. As a result the staff developed a clearly held purpose: that the fighting troops and those associated with them must have everything it was possible to get to support them and enable them to fulfil their roles. Every available gun supported the infantry; supplies and rations came through on time; the services of road construction and light railway units were provided for communications and supply; pioneer battalions assisted the engineers for fieldworks; and signals, equipped with the best available apparatus, achieved notable efficiency in linking and making coherent every part of the vast machine. The end result was that a remarkable spirit of service and trust pervaded the Corps organization.[22] For this, Currie was largely responsible. As he had done as a brigade commander, he created an atmosphere of friendship and trust at Corps Headquarters. "In it," said a senior British staff officer* serving with the Corps, "friction could not exist. We were like a band of brothers. The very basis of the relationship between Currie's staff and himself was frankness and trust." Yet he never ceased to command. "Nobody ran Currie."[23]

The *Halifax Chronicle* was incisively correct when, immediately after the war, it stated:

The greatest asset of the Canadian Corps is the corps spirit pervading its units. This spirit has given it cohesion, striking power and mutual trust and confidence that has carried it successfully through the severest trials, and often under discouraging conditions to final success . . .[24]

Currie himself recognized "wholeism" as the golden talisman. After breaking the Hindenburg Line he praised his men, pointing to the reason for victory: "In the performance of these mighty achievements all the arms and branches of the Corps have bent their purposeful energy working one for all and all for one."[25] And after the war he spoke strongly to officers of the Corps cautioning them never to forget the lesson. "Men have learned here the value of, and the good that springs from, mutual support, mutual confidence, self-sacrifice, and co-operation; and it will be a good thing not only for ourselves but the country that bred us if these qualities are perpetuated."[26]

The Canadian Corps, a national force, had however been more fortunate than its British equivalents; it enjoyed certain advantages denied to them. A British corps was a formation into and out of which divisions moved as the General Staff saw fit. Its commander and corps staff manipulated divisions which frequently changed. On the divisional level no team spirit could be fostered under such conditions, with the result, as the British official historian points out, that "the co-operation between the divisions of a homogeneous corps, like the Canadian or Australian, was undoubtedly and invariably better than between divisions fortuitously thrown alongside each other in a corps, the name of whose general they did not know and the faces of whose staff officers they did not recognize."[27]

*Lieutenant-Colonel Edmund Ironside, another future British CIGS.

Currie in Mons. On Armistice Day Sir Arthur Currie formally entered Mons, which his troops had occupied the night before. Here he is seen arriving in the Grande Place.

Crossing the Rhine. Currie takes the salute on the Bonn Bridge as Canadian infantrymen march across the Rhine in pouring rain.

The Victory Parade in London. H.M. King George V, Winston Churchill
(Minister for War), Field Marshal Sir Douglas Haig, General Sir Edmund
Allenby and the army commanders await the march past of Canadian
troops. Lieutenant-General Sir Arthur Currie on the dais behind the King.

There were, moreover, other factors. The Canadian wounded or sick were eventually sent back to their own battalions, unlike the British, who "did not take the trouble to sort convalescent reinforcements and, not understanding a soldier's love of his unit as his war home, and the craving for the society of old comrades, despatched these old soldiers to the first unit that required its ranks refilled."[28] And the Canadian Corps had been kept strong. It retained the four-battalion infantry brigade, and even its individual battalions were stronger than the British; by doing so it avoided the dislocation, both tactical and human, which would have attended a break-up of brigades to conform to the British pattern.

The quality of the human material making up the Corps cannot be overstressed. To define the Canadian soldier is no easy task. He was a down-to-earth man, for the most part, realistic but companionable. Eager to be liked, he took you on trust, grinned and gripped your hand and called you Bill or Chuck, and talked in a slow way of the town back home. But if you let him down, you were finished. He liked to fool with things, to improvise, to work out how to do things in a better way. Independent and self-reliant, he chafed under army discipline; but an officer who pitched in, was capable and convinced him that an order was sound, could count on him to the end. He was perhaps the least servile man on earth.

In 1914 he was less urbanized, a harder breed than now. This gave him the stamina to endure. Hindenburg was right when he attributed the hardiness of colonial troops to an agrarian life far removed from the softening influences of the town. General Blumentritt, explaining German failure in Russia during the Second World War, pointed to the sturdiness of the Russians as a major factor. The Western European, he said, was so highly civilized that in many respects he could not stand up to the tougher Easterner who lived closer to nature. The Russian moved freely by night or in fog, through woods or across swamps. He was not afraid of the dark or the cold.[29] In general, the Canadians started off with similar natural advantages over the Germans in 1914, and it became more pronounced with training and front-line experience.

The Canadians, moreover, not only had splendid material to draw on for soldiers; they also recruited officers from a less narrow social background than the British, and these were enterprising and able. Field Marshal Lord Wolseley, when referring to the Red River Expedition in 1903, said of the Canadian Militia:

I was fully aware of the splendid material of which this force was constituted. The men are extremely handy and self-reliant; in fact when well trained they cannot be beaten as fighting soldiers. Their officers, accustomed in civil life to think for themselves, their minds not dwarfed or trammelled by strict rules and regulations, were men after my own

heart and for the work before us they were certainly the best possible material. In parenthesis may I say that if wisdom ruled our councils on military matters—it does so but seldom—we should employ a Canadian division under their own officers in every serious war we undertake. Fortunate indeed will be the Commander-in-Chief who should have such a military force at his disposal in any war into which England may be forced![30]

Haig had not one but four Canadian divisions to count on, and they did not fail. Trained and disciplined, Currie's troops were, in his words, "physically strong, of fine determination, good soldierly qualities, able to endure, carry on, carry through."[31] They did just that.

Above all, the Canadian Corps had a leader of exceptional quality in Currie. His ability was recognized. Lloyd George singled out Currie and Monash as being far more outstanding than the British leaders with whom "Deportment counted for a good deal. Brains came a bad fourth."

The only exceptions were to be found in the Dominion forces. General Currie, the Commander of the Canadian Army, and General Monash, the Commander of the Australian Army, were both in civil life when the War broke out. Both proved themselves to be brilliant military leaders and went right through to the top. It means they had a natural aptitude for soldiering and that the fact of their being officers in unprofessional armies gave full play to their gifts.[32]

In the British forces, on the other hand, "There was no conspicuous officer in the Army who seemed better qualified for the Highest Command than Haig. That is to say, there was no outstanding General fit for so overwhelming a position of the command of a force five times as great as the largest army ever commanded by Napoleon . . ."[33]

Interviewed by Currie's biographer at his home, Bron-y-Churt, in 1934, Lloyd George recalled having been very impressed with Currie. He praised his great ability and strength of purpose.[34] If a change in Commander-in-Chief of the British forces had to be made, Lloyd George said, he had favoured Currie for that appointment. What, then, of Monash?

I had not met Monash at that time and my later idea, after I had got to know Monash, was to make him Chief of Staff and Currie Commander-in-Chief.[35]

It is idle to speculate on a situation that never came about, but the two Dominion leaders would have worked well together. "It was," Monash stated, "Currie's invariable habit to 'deliver the goods,' "[36] and later, when both generals represented their countries at the opening of the parliamentary buildings and Viceroy's palace, New Delhi, in 1931, Monash pointed Currie out to his secretary: "There he stands, McKenna, a giant in stature physically, and he was a giant in mind when he was in France."[37]

As it was, honours were showered on the Canadian leader. As far back as July, 1915, Currie was acclaimed as a hero in England on his first leave following Ypres. The King made him a Commander of the Bath at a Buckingham Palace investiture and he was created a Commander of the Legion of Honour by the French.[38] On 12 July, 1917, following Vimy, he received the accolade of the K.C.M.G. from King George in the ruined square of Albert. Passchendaele brought him further honours. In November, 1917, he went to Paris at the invitation of the French Government who wished to thank him for the "victory." There he was fêted royally, and at a dinner given by the French Minister of War, he received the Croix de Guerre with Palm. The King of the Belgians—for Passchendaele was in Belgium —presented the Belgian Croix de Guerre to Currie and made him a *Grand Officier de l'Ordre de la Couronne*.[39] He received the American Distinguished Service Medal from Pershing. In the New Year's Honours List of 1918 Currie became a Knight Commander of the Bath.

For his part in the final victory the New Year's Honours List conferred the G.C.M.G. on Currie.[40] During February, 1919, Sir Arthur, accompanied by Lady Currie, attended the Peace Conference. In May a contingent of the Corps paraded with the Dominion troops through London. Currie stood by the King while the Canadians marched past; he thought his men looked "simply splendid and' . . . was very proud." That month Currie was the guest of honour at a luncheon given by the Lord Mayor at the Mansion House.[41] On 13 July the Victory March took place in Paris. At a glittering function following the parade, Currie dined at the Palais de l'Elysée with the President and the Allied generals. Six days later similar pageantry took place in London, and once more the Canadians and their commander were acclaimed. Foch, who had come to London to receive the rank of Field-Marshal and the Freedom of the City, sought him out. That month the University of Cambridge conferred an honorary degree on Currie.[42]

On 8 August Sir Arthur and Lady Currie, after a private luncheon with the King and Queen at Buckingham Palace, left for Liverpool and sailed on the midnight tide. The lights faded on the receding coastline and, after almost five years' absence, Canada, looked forward to in high anticipation, lay ahead. At dawn on the 17th the ship docked at Halifax; the Curries stepped ashore that morning.

If Currie had expected a warm welcome on his native soil, he was to be bitterly disappointed. Even on an August morning the almost deserted clearing sheds echoed with chilly emptiness. There were no bands, flags or military display; no crowds or wildly cheering people.

Gloomy customs officials stood around and a few women from voluntary societies handed out coffee and cookies to the disembarking soldiers. But then, as Ibsen pointed out (paraphrasing Scripture), "No one is a prophet in his own country." The General looked around, hurt and bewildered. At length the forlorn figure of the District Officer Commanding came forward to conduct Currie and his wife to the City Hall through silent and empty streets.

He came back to Halifax a world-famous general yet his homecoming compared rather with the burial of Sir John Moore . . . On arrival at the City Hall they were met by a guard of honour, a group of people, chiefly officials, who received Currie in silence, and the garrison band. After inspecting the guard Currie proceeded to the Council Chamber where he was greeted by the Lieutenant Governor of the Province and the Mayor. They presented him with an address of welcome and a piece of silver plate, while flowers were handed to Lady Currie.[43]

The minimum of protocol having been observed, Currie was allowed to depart for Ottawa. He seemed calm and undisturbed. Only once, for a brief moment, did his self-control break down. One of his former officers, who waited for the official welcome to be over, had then come forward:

I managed to salute him and said "Welcome home, sir." Then for a moment he lost control of himself. His eyes got a bit wet, his lips trembled, he put one hand on my shoulder, two fingers of the other in my Sam Browne belt, quietly shook me and never said a word.[44]

Sir Sam Hughes had done his work insidiously and effectively. His indictment of Currie as an incompetent and inhuman leader who had needlessly sacrificed Canadian lives had been given wide publicity. Thousands of persons who had lost sons or brothers or husbands found it impossible to believe that anyone could make such terrible charges without being sure of his ground. And the returning troops had done little to dispel the gathering clouds of suspicion. They knew, for example, that they had suffered heavy casualties at Passchendaele; they did not know of Currie's stand against the resumed offensive and that he had been *ordered* to take the ridge in almost impossible conditions. At the time, inspired by his words, they had been behind him. Now they, too, began to wonder: had it been for self-glorification after all? Honours he had received in plenty; had they been given at the troops' expense?

While the Corps had remained together there had been no moral infection. Disbanded, and its members dispersed to communities across Canada where they were subject to outside influences, there was a natural breakdown in the old cohesion. Currie was powerless to defend himself, and the Canadian Government, uncertain of the temper of the returned soldiers, hesitated to come out in open support of the Corps Commander. The soldiers' doubts, in consequence, intensified. This was no more than a temporary breakdown in morale, symptomatic of what occurred in every country immediately following the war; the spirit of the Canadian Corps, moving deep in human emotions, in time reasserted itself, gathered strength, and swept Currie to victory in the libel trial at Cobourg nine years later.

Ottawa was an even bigger disappointment than Halifax. Broad Street Station was in use at that time as well as the Central Union Station. It was not known at which station Currie would arrive and as a result no crowds lined the streets to Parliament Hill, where he was to be officially welcomed. Now was the time for the government to rally to the support of Currie with a few words of praise that would have been well merited and would have confounded his defamer. But the welcome was frigid. Sir Robert Borden had gone to Saint John to meet the Prince of Wales. Sir George Foster's speech of welcome was cold and non-committal in the extreme. A few thin cheers and then, in a silence that could almost be felt, women were heard to hiss.

As always, Currie remained outwardly calm. Though the proceedings had been a mockery, he thanked Foster in simple and well-chosen words. He was not a stranger to trials and to loneliness but this occasion was the worst of all. Under the eyes of an apathetic, even hostile crowd, he was forced to remain as the centre of a welcome that was not a welcome, unable to be done with it and seek refuge in solitude. He kept his dignity until the whole depressing performance was over.

That evening, invited to the Country Club, he might have expected the ordeal to continue. But, touching as it was unexpected, one person broke through the cold formality with sincerity and warmth. General Mewburn, the Defence Minister, who had visited Currie in France and knew at first hand the esteem in which he had been held, declared flatly that no other living Canadian had done so much as Currie; he was asking him, therefore, to take the senior appointment in the Militia: Inspector General of the Militia Forces of Canada as a full General, the first in the Dominions. Given that lead, the applause was cordial.[45]

Currie accepted the position. He was Inspector General for a year, and then resigned to take up the offer of the appointment of Principal and Vice-Chancellor of McGill University, Montreal. He had not been happy in government employment. The whispering campaign continued and he refused to rebut the criticism that was levelled against him. He made speeches across Canada in which he described the achievements of the Corps but did not champion his own leadership; he let the plain, unvarnished facts speak for themselves.

The bitter experience of Cobourg at last cleared Currie's name and the nation finally knew the lies for what they were. The "great leader who rendered great service to an ungrateful country"[46] was fully restored to his rightful position as a national figure. In 1933, still at McGill, he died.

The course of his last illness had been followed across the country through official bulletins. The King cabled a personal inquiry as to his condition; so did the Mayor of Mons. After his death a memorial service was held in Westminster Abbey. In Canada, the acclamation that had been denied him on his return in 1919 found expression in the full pomp of military ritual when his body, followed by the Governor General, the Prime Minister and all the leaders of the nation, was borne to the grave through the streets of Montreal packed with tens of thousands of his countrymen.[47]

The last written words of Currie concerned Armistice Day:

The recollections that crowd upon some of us, the pictures that so vividly arise from the prints of our remembrance, cannot be classified and cannot be expressed in words. Some of them are too sacred to be clothed in speech ... They cannot be destroyed this side of the grave.[48]

Thus, at the end, he was still preoccupied with the war; he had certain memories about which he could not speak. And it was the same with the veterans of the Corps.

That war had been a foul experience. In the hushed atmosphere of a crowded chamber at Westminster, Lloyd George had described it and described it well. With quiet eloquence, without his usual hurl and sweep of language, he used the imagination of a Celt to conjure up its horrors in telling words:

To this hour I cannot think of the heroism of our soldiers without wonder—without wonder and reverence. There has never been in the history of mankind such a courage as theirs. Never! Think what it was. The least of us is capable of a flash of valour. In a sudden emergency the meanest of us might be brave. Once or twice in his life a coward might do noble things. But think what these men did. It was not for an hour, nor for a day, nor for a week, nor for a month, nor for a year that they did fine things.

Year after year their life was a fine thing. It was not valour they displayed; it was not even heroism; it was something so new and terrible, so undreamed of, that man has created no new word for it. I try to find some word to define it, to suggest it; I can't. The nearest word I can get is Endurance. They were in hell every day of their lives; and they endured. They were in peril of death, and worse than death, day after day, night after night; and they endured. They were exposed to all the nerve-shattering rage of artillery, artillery which rived the soil like an earthquake, which hurled the bodies of the dead into the air, and flung the bodies of the living into a deeper sepulchre; and they endured. They went out into the darkness to storm the trenches of the enemy, to destroy machine-gun nests, to break a line of fire the very thunders of which deafened the men; and they endured. But something more. That is what haunts me. They endured for all these years a manner of life utterly unnatural—utterly unnatural, and horrible beyond the expression of words.

Our people are among the cleanest in Europe; to keep their bodies clean is one of their joys, a part almost of their religion; and think how they lived! They lived in mud and worse than mud; they lived in unutterable filth, breathing an air that choked the lungs with disgust; their young bodies attacked by vermin, their feet sinking into squalor, their hands touching at every turn things which one dare not speak about. And our people are the most domesticated in Europe; our climate has forced us into making indoor life the very heart of existence; and these young men were exiled from their homes, were forced to live almost entirely without the grace and charm and consolation of women, were obliged to herd together in great companies in a foreign country, and not only a foreign country, but a torn and blasted country from which the sulphurous flames of Satanism had scorched the leaf of the meanest weed.

There they lived, always in the presence of death, always in the midst of horror, always on a rack of torture, a rack which stretched and tortured not the muscles of the body, but every nerve, and the whole mind, and the entire soul, and they endured. Yes, they endured, endured inexpressible agony with patience, even with humour, and at the end flinging themselves upon the enemy, they drove him headlong, they drove him out of the trenches, sent him flying, beat him, beat him to his knees. There has been nothing like this in the history of the world.[49]

An old veteran will never tell you this. He would rather forget— and the pity is, he cannot. He will prefer to talk to you of the good things, the *estaminets* behind the line, and of "alcholidays" in Blighty and in Paris.

But when thunder crashes down the empty corridors of the sky you will see his hands twitch and his eyes grow uneasy. At such moments the spectre of memory returns and grips his mind. He is back once more in the flame and fury that was France. He must take a hold on himself not to call out encouragement to comrades long since dead; and not to voice a bitter complaint that to his hearers would sound like the incoherencies of a mad, distorted dream.

NOTES

CHAPTER ONE

1. Public Archives of Canada (PAC), Currie Papers, Testimony, *Currie v. Wilson & Preston*, pp. 993-1005.
2. *Debates, House of Commons*, 25 February, 1919.
3. *Ibid.*, 4 March, 1919.
4. *Loc. cit.*
5. *Loc. cit.*
6. *Ibid.*, 10 March, 1919.
7. *Loc. cit.*
8. *Loc. cit.*
9. *Ibid.*, 14 March, 1919.
10. *Loc. cit.*
11. *Loc. cit.*
12. *Loc. cit.*
13. *Ibid.*, 7 July, 1919.
14. *Ibid.*, 29 September, 1919.
15. *Loc. cit.*
16. *Loc. cit.*
17. PAC, Currie Papers, Testimony, *Currie v. Wilson & Preston*, pp. 9-10.
18. *The Evening Guide*, Port Hope, 13 June, 1927.
19. *Currie v. Wilson & Preston*, pp. 168-178.
20. *Ibid.*, pp. 44-73, 154, 386, 1245.
21. *Ibid.*, pp. 118-119.
22. *Ottawa Journal*, 21 April, 1928.
23. *Ibid.*, 19 April, 1928; *Currie v. Wilson & Preston*, pp. 210-233.
24. *Currie v. Wilson & Preston*, pp. 1647-1656.
25. *Ibid.*, pp. 415, 1090.
26. *Ibid.*, p. 443.
27. *Ibid.*, pp. 1170-1173.
28. *Ibid.*, pp. 1221-1255.
29. *Ibid.*, pp. 1741, 1747.
30. *Ibid.*, p. 1798.
31. *Ibid.*, pp. 1851-1864.
32. *Ibid.*, pp. 1918-1921.
33. *Ibid.*, p. 260.
34. *Ibid.*, pp. 2087-2088.
35. *Ibid.*, pp. 2118-2121.
36. *Montreal Star*, 3 May, 1928.

CHAPTER TWO

1. Henry Borden (ed.), *Robert Laird Borden: His Memoirs* (Toronto: Macmillan, 1938), I, p. 330.
2. *Ottawa Citizen*, 25 April, 1899.
3. *Ibid.*, 6 October, 1899.
4. Army Historical Section, General Hutton's collection of newspaper articles, 1899-1902. Article (newspaper unknown), 28 September, 1899.
5. *Montreal Star*, 4 October, 1899.
6. *Ibid.*, 31 October, 1899.
7. *Toronto Globe*, 2 February, 1900.
8. *Ibid.*, 20 January, 1900.
9. *Ibid.*, 2 February, 1900.

10. *Galt Daily Reporter*, 11 January, 1900.
11. *Sherbrooke Record*, 1 November, 1899.
12. *Parry Sound Canadian*, 12 February, 1900.
13. *Toronto Daily Star*, 23 March, 1900.
14. *Toronto Evening News*, 26 March, 1900.
15. *Toronto Telegram*, 26 October, 1900.
16. *Kingston Whig*, 21 March, 1900.
17. PAC, Borden Papers, OC 55.
18. *Militia Report*, 1911-1916.
19. Colonel G. W. L. Nicholson, *Canadian Expeditionary Force (CEF), 1914-1919* (Ottawa: The Queen's Printer, 1964), p. 12.
20. *Ibid.*, p. 24.
21. *Ibid.*, pp. 10-11.
22. *Loc. cit.*
23. *Ibid.*, p. 12.
24. C. F. Winter, *The Hon. Sir Sam Hughes* (Toronto: Macmillan, 1931), p. 75.
25. C. P. Stacey, *The Military Problems of Canada* (Toronto: The Ryerson Press, 1940), p. 75.
26. Nicholson, *op. cit.*, p. 12.
27. Borden, *op. cit.*, I, pp. 450-1.
28. PAC, *European War Prints*, No. 1, Item 4.
29. Mason Wade, *The French Canadians, 1760-1945* (London: Macmillan, 1955), p. 643.
30. Colonel A. Fortescue Duguid, *Official History of the Canadian Forces in the Great War 1914-1919* (Ottawa: The King's Printer, 1938), I, p. 4.
31. Winter, *op. cit.*, pp. 133, 135-6.
32. *Debates, House of Commons*, 24 March, 1919.
33. B. H. Liddell Hart, *The Real War* (Boston: Atlantic-Little, Brown, 1930), p. 24.
34. *Ibid.*, p. 37.
35. *Loc. cit.*
36. *Ibid.*, pp. 37-8.
37. *Ibid.*, p. 38.
38. *Ibid.*, p. 54.
39. Nicholson, *op. cit.*, p. 6.
40. George F. G. Stanley, *Canada's Soldiers* (Toronto: Macmillan, 1960), pp. 307-8.
41. Nicholson, *op. cit.*, p. 14.
42. *Debates, House of Commons*, 26 January, 1916.
43. Nicholson, *op. cit.*, pp. 18-19.
44. Lt.-Colonel C. L. Flick, *Just What Happened* (London: Privately printed by the author, 1917), pp. 4-5.
45. Winter, *op. cit.*, pp. 47-8.
46. Stanley, *op. cit.*, p. 311.
47. Flick, *op. cit.*, p. 14.
48. *Ibid.*, p. 15.

49. Colonel J. A. Currie, *The Red Watch* (Toronto: McClelland, 1916), p. 32.
50. Flick, *op. cit.*, p. 16.
51. J. A. Currie, *op. cit.*, p. 39.
52. Flick, *op. cit.*, p. 17.
53. Nicholson, *op. cit.*, p. 20.
54. Hugh M. Urquhart, *Arthur Currie: The Biography of a Great Canadian* (Toronto: J. M. Dent & Sons, 1950), p. xii.
55. PAC, Borden Papers, Vol. 298, Secret Memorandum, 15 June, 1918.
56. Urquhart, *op. cit.*, p. 28.
57. Ralph Allen, *Ordeal by Fire* (Toronto: Doubleday, 1961), p. 54.
58. PAC, Borden Papers, Vol. 268, "Memorandum respecting the late Sir Arthur Currie," 13 August, 1943, p. 6.
59. PAC, Currie Papers, Currie to Forsythe, 25 June, 1917.
60. Urquhart, *op. cit.*, p. 30.
61. *Ibid.*, p. 19.
62. *King's Regulations and Orders for the Militia*, p. 639.
63. Urquhart, *op. cit.*, p. 38.
64. *Ibid.*, pp. 23-4.
65. *Canada* Magazine, No. 598, 23 June, 1917.
66. Urquhart, *op. cit.*, p. 32.
67. *Loc. cit.*
68. *Ibid.*, p. 37.
69. PAC, Currie Diary, September, 1914.
70. Nicholson, *op. cit.*, p. 22.
71. *Ibid.*, p. 29.
72. Sir Andrew Macphail, *History of the Canadian Forces, 1914-1919—Medical Services* (Ottawa: Published by the authority of the Minister of National Defence, under the direction of the General Staff . . . F. A. Acland, Printer, 1925), p. 20; Flick, *op. cit.*, p. 55.
73. Flick, *op. cit.*, p. 31.
74. Nicholson, *op. cit.*, pp. 22-3.
75. *Ibid.*, p. 23.
76. Macphail, *op. cit.*, pp. 20, 22.
77. Nicholson, *op. cit.*, p. 24.
78. Duguid, *op. cit.*, I, p. 88.
79. Flick, *op. cit.*, p. 33.
80. *Ibid.*, pp. 21, 41.
81. Allen, *op. cit.*, p. 65.
82. PAC, Creelman Papers, Diary, 8 December, 1916.
83. Currie Diary, September, 1914.
84. *Debates, House of Commons*, I, 1916, 16 January, 1916.
85. Flick, *op. cit.*, p. 73.
86. *Ibid.*, p. 77.
87. *Ibid.*, p. 6.
88. *Ibid.*, p. 7.
89. Macphail, *op. cit.*, pp. 22-3.
90. Flick, *op. cit.*, p. 73.
91. *Ibid.*, pp. 7, 73.

92. Macphail, *op. cit.*, p. 23.
93. Flick, *op. cit.*, p. 39.
94. Macphail, *op. cit.*, p. 23.
95. Flick, *op. cit.*, p. 7.
96. *Ibid.*, p. 6.
97. Nicholson, *op. cit.*, p. 26.
98. *Ibid.*, p. 109.
99. Macphail, *op. cit.*, p. 22.
100. *Ibid.*, p. 23.

CHAPTER THREE

1. Nicholson, *Canadian Expeditionary Force (CEF) 1914-1919*, p. 29.
2. *Ibid.*, p. 30.
3. *Ibid.*, p. 29.
4. Flick, *Just What Happened*, p. 49; *Unknown Soldiers* (Anon.) (New York: The Vantage Press, 1959), p. 24.
5. PAC, Borden Papers, OC 165(1), 12535.
6. Flick, *op. cit.*, pp. 49-50.
7. J. A. Currie, *The Red Watch*, p. 50.
8. Nicholson, *op, cit.*, p. 31.
9. Flick, *op. cit.*, p. 54.
10. J. A. Currie, *op. cit.*, p. 62.
11. Nicholson, *op. cit.*, p. 32.
12. J. A. Currie, *op. cit.*, p. 65.
13. Currie Diary, 15 October, 1914.
14. J. A. Currie, *op. cit.*, p. 64.
15. Currie Diary, 21 October, 1914.
16. Flick, *op. cit.*, p. 63.
17. *Ibid.*, p. 91.
18. PAC, Creelman Papers, Diary, 19 December, 1914.
19. Flick, *op. cit.*, p. 8.
20. Macphail, *History of the Canadian Forces, 1914-1919—Medical Services*, p. 56.
21. PAC, Borden Papers, OC 165(1), 12539, Borden to Perley, 8 October, 1914.
22. Macphail, *op. cit.*, p. 24.
23. PAC, Borden Papers, OC 165(1), 12539, Borden to Perley, 8 October, 1914.
24. Duguid, *Official History of the Canadian Forces in the Great War, 1914-1919*, I, p. 127.
25. Duguid, *Appendices*, No. 118, Hughes to Kitchener, 25 August, 1914.
26. *Ibid.*, No. 119, Kitchener to Hughes, 26 August, 1914.
27. Borden Papers, OC 165(1), 12597.
28. PAC, Kemp Papers, MG 27, Vol. 29.
29. *Loc. cit.*
30. Borden Papers, OC 165(1), 12597.
31. Kemp Papers, MG 27, Vol. 29.
32. *Loc. cit.*
33. Borden Papers, OC 165(1), 12597.
34. *Ibid.*, 12541, N. F. Davidson to Borden, 16 October, 1914.
35. *Ibid.*, 12544.
36. *Ibid.*, Perley to Borden, 23 October, 1914.
37. Cited by Allen, *Ordeal by Fire*, p. 67.

38. Duguid, *op. cit.*, I, p. 127.
39. Borden Papers, OC 183(1), 14788.
40. Duguid, *op. cit.*, p. 127.
41. *Ibid.*, p. 135.
42. Macphail, *op. cit.*, p. 27.
43. W. W. Murray, *The History of the 2nd Canadian Battalion* (Ottawa: The Historical Committee, 2nd Bn., CEF, 1947), p. 16.
44. Currie Diary, 4 December, 1914.
45. Duguid, *op. cit.*, p. 136.
46. *Ibid.*, p. 130.
47. Flick, *op. cit.*, pp. 60, 67-8, 71, 76.
48. *Ibid.*, pp. 81, 93.
49. Duguid, *op. cit.*, pp. 130-1.
50. Murray, *op. cit.*, p. 18.
51. Duguid, *op. cit.*, pp. 132-3.
52. Cited by Urquhart, *Arthur Currie: The Biography of a Great Canadian*, p. 50.
53. Currie Diary, November, 1914-February, 1915.
54. *Loc. cit.*
55. Urquhart, *op. cit.*, pp. 46, 51.
56. *Ibid.*, p. 47.
57. *Ibid.*, pp. 47, 51.
58. Currie Papers, "Confidential Reports on Officers."
59. Urquhart, *op. cit.*, p. 51.
60. Currie Diary, 11 December, 1914.
61. Urquhart, *op. cit.*, p. 47.
62. *Ibid.*, p. 48.
63. *Ibid.*, pp. 48-9.
64. *Loc. cit.*
65. *Loc. cit.*
66. Currie Diary, 28 October-1 November, 1914.
67. Duguid, *op. cit.*, p. 148.
68. Nicholson, *op. cit.*, p. 26.
69. Macphail, *op. cit.*, p. 32.
70. *Ibid.*, p. 33.
71. *Ibid.* pp. 33, 45.
72. *Ibid.*, p. 46.
73. Flick, *op. cit.*, pp. 7, 41.
74. Macphail, *op. cit.*, p. 32.
75. Nicholson, *op. cit.*, p. 27.
76. Macphail, *op. cit.*, p. 46.
77. Nicholson, *op. cit.*, p. 27.
78. Privy Council (PC) 107, 15 January, 1915.
79. Allen, *op. cit.*, p. 97.
80. Duguid, *Appendices*, No. 111.
81. *Loc. cit.*
82. *Loc. cit.*
83. *Loc. cit.*
84. *Loc. cit.*
85. *Loc. cit.*
86. *Loc. cit.*
87. *Loc. cit.*
88. J. A. Currie, *op. cit.*, p. 98.

CHAPTER FOUR

1. Moltke, cited by Correlli Barnett, *The Swordbearers* (London: Eyre & Spottiswoode, 1963), p. 34.
2. Barnett, *op. cit.*, p. 24.
3. Crown Prince Wilhelm, cited by Richard Thoumin, *The First World War* (London: Martin Secker & Warburg, 1963), p. 33.
4. A. Grasset, cited *ibid.*, p. 31.
5. Maurice Paléologue (French Ambassador), *ibid.*, p. 35.
6. Thoumin, *op. cit.*, p. 9.
7. *French Official History*, I, i, p. 54.
8. Barnett, *op. cit.*, pp. 40-1.
9. *Ibid.*, p. 249.
10. Hanson W. Baldwin, *World War I* (New York: Harper & Row, 1962), p. 19.
11. Tappen (Moltke's Chief of Operations) cited Barnett, *op. cit.*, p. 61.
12. Admiral Müller, *ibid.*
13. Cited by Richard M. Watt, *Dare Call It Treason* (London: Chatto & Windus, 1964), p. 63.
14. Barnett, *op. cit.*, p. 83.
15. Winston S. Churchill, *The World Crisis* (London: Odham's Press, 1938), III, p. 946.
16. *Ibid.*, II, pp. 473-4, 486; David Lloyd George, *War Memoirs* (London: Ivor Nicholson & Watson, 1933-1936), I, pp. 356-7, 369-80.
17. Liddell Hart, *The Real War*, p. 150.
18. *Ibid.*, p. 160.
19. British Official History of the Great War (hereinafter referred to as British Official History), *Gallipoli*, I, p. 355.
20. *Ibid.*, II, p. 63.
21. Army Historical Section, J. F. O'Flaherty, "The Royal Newfoundland Regiment."
22. Liddell Hart, *op. cit.*, pp. 123-4.
23. Churchill, *op. cit.*, III, p. 952.
24. *Gallipoli*, I, p. vii.
25. Cyril Falls, *The Great War* (New York: G. P. Putnam's Sons, 1959), p. 136.

CHAPTER FIVE

1. Murray, *The History of the 2nd Canadian Battalion*, p. 30.
2. Currie Diary, 27 February, 1915.
3. *Ibid.*, 10 March, 1915.
4. Baldwin, *World War I*, p. 54.
5. Currie Diary, 14 April, 1915.
6. *Ibid.*, 15 April, 1915.
7. Erich von Falkenhayn, *General Headquarters 1914-1916* (London: Hutchinson, 1919), pp. 65, 84.
8. Liddell Hart, *The Real War*, p. 130.
9. *Loc. cit.*
10. A French army doctor, cited by Thoumin, *First World War*, p. 175.
11. A British officer, *ibid.*, p. 177.
12. Duguid, *Official History of the Canadian Forces in the Great War, 1914-1919*, p. 311.
13. *Ibid.*, p. 307.
14. Nicholson, *Canadian Expeditionary Force (CEF) 1914-1919*, p. 92.

15. Duguid, *Appendices*, No. 111.
16. James E. Edmonds, *Short History of World War I* (London: Oxford University Press, 1951), p. 92.
17. Urquhart, *Arthur Currie: The Biography of a Great Canadian*, p. 66.
18. *Ibid.*, p. 62.
19. *Ibid.*, p. 67.
20. *Ibid.*, p. 68.
21. *Loc. cit.*
22. *Ibid.*, p. 72.
23. *Ibid.*, p. 74.
24. *Ibid.*, p. 75.
25. *Ibid.*, p. 83.
26. *Ibid.*, p. 84.
27. *Ibid.*, p. 85.
28. Nicholson, *op. cit.*, p. 77.
29. Urquhart, *op. cit.*, p. 89.
30. J. A. Currie, *The Red Watch*, pp. 258-9.
31. *Debates, House of Commons*, 16 June, 1920.
32. Urquhart, *op. cit.*, p. 97.
33. Currie Diary, 6 May, 1915.

CHAPTER SIX
1. Duguid, *Official History of the Canadian Forces in the Great War, 1914-1919*, I, p. 426.
2. *Ibid.*, p. 436.
3. Liddell Hart, *The Real War*, p. 187.
4. Watt, *Dare Call It Treason*, p. 70.
5. *Ibid.*, p. 84.
6. Nicholson, *Canadian Expeditionary Force (CEF) 1914-1919*, p. 96.
7. *History of 57th Infantry Regiment*, p. 76, cited Nicholson, *op. cit.*, p. 99.
8. Urquhart, *Arthur Currie: The Biography of a Great Canadian*, p. 106.
9. Nicholson, *op. cit.*, p. 100.
10. Urquhart, *op. cit.*, p. 108.
11. Nicholson, *op. cit.*, p. 107.
12. *Ibid.*, p. 108.
13. *Unknown Soldiers*, p. 67.
14. *Loc. cit.*
15. *Ibid.*, p. 68-9.
16. Nicholson, *op. cit.*, p. 112.
17. *Ibid.*, p. 212.
18. *Ibid.*, p. 114.
19. *Ibid.*, p. 114, *fn.*
20. *Loc. cit.*
21. *Ibid.*, p. 114.
22. *Loc. cit.*
23. Currie Diary, 13-14 September, 1915.
24. Nicholson, *op. cit.*, p. 114.
25. Urquhart, *op. cit.*, pp. 117-8.
26. Nicholson, *op. cit.*, p. 120.
27. Liddell Hart, *op. cit.*, p. 192.
28. Alan Clark, *The Donkeys* (London: Hutchinson, 1961), p. 169.
29. *Ibid.*, p. 172.
30. A German battalion commander, cited *ibid.*, p. 173.
31. Nicholson, *op. cit.*, p. 122.
32. *Ibid.*, p. 121.
33. Urquhart, *op. cit.*, p. 121.

34. British Official History, *France and Belgium, 1916*, I, p. 156, *fn.*
35. Urquhart, *op. cit.*, p. 121.
36. Nicholson, *op. cit.*, p. 127.
37. Murray, *The History of the 2nd Canadian Battalion*, p. 83.
38. *Ibid.*, p. 87.
39. *Ibid.*, p. 83.
40. *Loc. cit.*
41. *Loc. cit.*
42. Nicholson, *op. cit.*, p. 142, *fn.*
43. *Ibid.*, p. 145.
44. *Ibid.*, pp. 146-7.
45. *Ibid.*, p. 147.
46. Duguid, *Appendices*, No. 111.
47. *Loc. cit.*
48. *Ibid.*, Public Archives Records Centre (PARC), Carson file 4-5-13B, Turner to Carson, 4 May, 1916; Ketchen to Carson, 5 May, 1916.
49. Duguid, *Appendices*, No. 111.
50. Murray, *op. cit.*, p. 90.
51. *Ibid.*, p. 81.

CHAPTER SEVEN
1. Liddell Hart, *The Real War*, p. 200.
2. Churchill, *The World Crisis*, III, p. 963.
3. Watt, *Dare Call It Treason*, p. 254.
4. Crown Prince William, *My War Experiences* (London: Hurst and Blackett, 1922), p. 256.
5. Murray, *The History of the 2nd Canadian Battalion*, p. 97.
6. Duguid, *Appendices*, No. 111.
7. Barbara W. Tuchman, *The Guns of August* (New York: Macmillan, 1962), p. 189.
8. *Unknown Soldiers*, p. 77.
9. Murray, *op. cit.*, pp. 104-5.
10. Australian Official History, III, p. 872, *fn.*
11. Sir Charles Lucas, *The Empire at War* (Oxford: Humphrey Milford, Oxford University Press, 1923), II, p. 133.
12. Liddell Hart, *op. cit.*, p. 245.
13. Edmonds, *Short History of World War I*, p. 188.
14. Nicholson, *Canadian Expeditionary Force (CEF) 1914-1919*, p. 171.
15. Liddell Hart, *op. cit.*, p. 257.
16. Currie Papers, Currie to Corps, 16 October, 1916, J-6, 3.
17. Brooke, cited Urquhart, *Arthur Currie: The Biography of a Great Canadian*, p. 134.
18. Nicholson, *op. cit.*, p. 193.
19. Edmund Blunden, *Undertones of War* (London: Richard Cobden-Sanderson, 1928), p. 141.
20. Nicholson, *op. cit.*, p. 199.
21. Lloyd George, *War Memoirs*, VI, p. 3426.
22. Australian Official History, III, p. 872.
23. Nicholson, *op. cit.*, p. 238, *fn.*

CHAPTER EIGHT

1. PAC, Borden Papers, OC 225, 22817, Carson to Borden, 11 January, 1915.
2. *Ibid.*, 22824, Carson to Borden, 20 January, 1915.
3. *Ibid.*, 22829, Borden to Perley, 21 January, 1915.
4. PARC, Carson File, 8-5-10, Carson to Altham, 18 February, 1915.
5. *Ibid.*, 8-5-8, Carson to Hughes, 27 February, 1915.
6. *Ibid.*, 8-5-10, Carson to Hughes, 23 February, 1915.
7. *Loc. cit.*
8. *Ibid.*, Hughes to Carson, 19 March, 1915.
9. *Ibid.*, 8-5-8, Carson to Steele, 25 May, 1915.
10. *Ibid.*, 10-8-22, Hughes to Lougheed, 26 July, 1915.
11. *Ibid.*, 8-5-10-B, Carson to Steele, 6 January, 1916.
12. *Ibid.*, 8-5-43, Carson to Steele, 27 August, 1915.
13. *Ibid.*, Carson to Aitken, 12 October, 1915; Carson to Hughes, 4 October, 1915.
14. *Ibid.*, 8-5-43, Carson to Hughes, 15 November, 1915.
15. *Loc. cit.*
16. Nicholson, *Canadian Expeditionary Force (CEF) 1914-1919*, p. 204.
17. *Loc. cit.*
18. *Loc. cit.*
19. *Ibid.*, p. 205.
20. PAC, Borden Papers, OC 337, 39339, Alderson to Second Army, 8 February, 1916.
21. PARC, Carson File, 8-5-10-C, Carson to French, 29 February, 1916.
22. *Ibid.*, 8-5-10-C, Lt.-Colonel Hilliam to GOC, 8th Infantry Brigade.
23. *Ibid.*, Currie to Carson, 21 June, 1916.
24. *Ibid.*, MacDougall to Carson, 1 March, 1916.
25. *Ibid.*, 8-1-2, Steele to Carson, 11 October, 1915.
26. *Ibid.*, 8-1-87, "Memoir for General Carson," 26 October, 1915.
27. *Ibid.*, 8-5-8-D, Alderson to Hughes, 16 February, 1916.
28. *Loc. cit.*
29. *Ibid.*, 8-5-8-B, Carson to Brade, 8 January, 1916.
30. PAC, Borden Papers, OC 183(2), 14863, Gwatkin to Christie, 14 January, 1916.
31. PARC, Carson Files, 6-A-5, Carson to Hughes, 8 November, 1915.
32. *Ibid.*, 8-1-55, Hughes to Carson, 19 November, 1915.
33. *Ibid.*, Carson to Hughes, 15 December, 1915.

34. *Robert Laird Borden: His Memoirs*, II, p. 556.
35. Winter, *The Hon. Sir Sam Hughes*, pp. 93-4.
36. Allen, *Ordeal by Fire*, p. 96.
37. *Robert Laird Borden: His Memoirs*, II, pp. 559-60.
38. Foster, cited Allen, *op cit.*, p. 94.
39. PAC, Borden Papers, OC 318(1), Perley to Borden, 25 April, 1916.
40. *Ibid.*, OC 280, 31737, Memorandum of Privy Council Meeting, 11 March, 1916.
41. PARC, HQ, Overseas Military Forces of Canada (OMFC) (Argyle House) File, 0-153-33, Vol. 1.
42. PAC, Borden Papers, OC 183(3), 15044, Aitken to Hughes, 10 May, 1916.
43. PARC, Carson File, 8-5-10-E, "Notes on Canadian Training Division, Shorncliffe," 6 June, 1916.
44. PAC, Borden Papers, OC 183(3), 15045, Aitken to Hughes, 10 May, 1916.
45. PARC, Carson file, 8-1-122, Carson to Aitken, 11 July, 1916.
46. PAC, Borden Papers, OC 282, 31826, McCurdy to Borden, 31 July, 1916.
47. PARC, Carson file, 8-1-122, Steele to Carson, 17 June, 1916.
48. PAC, Borden Papers, OC 318(1), 35721.
49. *Ibid.*, OC 318(1), 35722, Perley to Borden, 6 September, 1916.
50. Allen, *op. cit.*, p. 96.
51. PAC, Borden Papers, OC 190, 15814, Borden to Hughes, 31 July, 1916.
52. *Ibid.*, OC 318(1), 35689, Hughes to Borden, 2 August, 1916.
53. *Ibid.*, OCA 189, 80895, Hughes to Borden, 15 August, 1916.
54. *Ibid.*, OC 318(1), 35725.
55. *Ottawa Journal*, 6 September, 1916.
56. Borden Papers, OC 318(1), 35725, Borden to Hughes, 7 September, 1916.
57. *Ibid.*, OC 318(2), 35785.
58. *Ibid.*, OC 318(2), 35782, Aitken to Borden, 11 September, 1916.
59. PARC, Overseas File, Folder 348, "Minutes of Sub-Militia Council."
60. Carson File, 8-1-106, Hughes to Carson, 18 September, 1916, and reply, 21 September, 1916.
61. PAC, Perley Papers, Vol. 6, 190C, Perley to Borden, 11 October, 1916.
62. *Ibid.*, Vol. 6, 183, Perley to Borden, 11 October, 1916.
63. Macphail, *History of the Canadian Forces, 1914-1919—Medical Services*, p. 156.
64. *Ibid.*, p. 166.

65. PARC, Drawer C-275, Folder 6, "Synopsis of Findings of the Baptie Board," 25 July, 1917, and "Observations on Latest Memorandum of Colonel H. A. Bruce," by McComb and Allen.
66. Macphail, *op. cit.*, p. 169.
67. PAC, Borden Papers, OC 318(2), 35835-7, Hughes to Borden, 23 October, 1916.
68. *Ibid.*, OC 318(2), 35838, Hughes to Borden, 28 October, 1916.
69. Montreal *Gazette*, 17 November, 1916.
70. Borden Papers, OC 318(2), 35852, 35853-4, Hughes to Borden, 28 and 30 October, 1916.
71. *Ibid.*, OC 318(2), 35858-9, Borden to Hughes, 31 October, 1916.
72. PC 2656, 31 October, 1916.
73. Borden Papers, OC 318(2), 35860, Hughes to Borden, 1 November, 1916.
74. Hughes, cited Macphail, *op. cit.*, p. 196.
75. Borden Papers, OC 318(2), 35884-5, Borden to Hughes, 9 November, 1916.
76. *Ibid.*, 35887-90.
77. *Ibid.*, 35894.
78. *Ibid.*, OC 230, 22894-D.
79. *Ibid.*, OC 318(1), 35648.
80. *Ibid.*, OC 165(1), 12496.
81. *Ibid.*, OC 165(1), 12485.
82. *Ibid.*, 12583.
83. *Ibid.*, 12597.
84. PAC, Kemp Papers, MG 27, Vol. 29, Toronto *Telegram*, 26 November, 1914.
85. *Ibid.*, 18 November, 1914.
86. Borden Papers, OC 165(1), William H. Price to Borden, 19 November, 1914.
87. *Ibid.*, 12629, 8 December, 1914.
88. *Robert Laird Borden: His Memoirs*, I, p. 463.
89. Borden Papers, OC 165(1), 12553, 18 November, 1914.
90. *Ibid.*, OCA 36, 70829, 23 March, 1911.
91. *Ibid.*, OC 165/3, 12840, Colonel G. H. Bradbury to Borden, 24 October, 1916.
92. PAC, Perley Papers, Vol. 7, 198, Perley to Borden, 27 November, 1916.
93. Borden Papers, OC 176, 13636, Clark to Borden, 9 January, 1917.
94. PARC, Overseas File, 10-8-7, Gow to Perley, 29 June, 1917.
95. PAC, Borden Papers, OC 176, 13685, Currie to Perley, 15 December, 1917.
96. PARC, Overseas File, 10-8-22, Steele to Perley, 6 November, 1916.
97. *Ibid.*, 10-8-7, Folder 348, Perley to Borden, 28 June, 1917.
98. Nicholson, *op. cit.*, p. 208.
99. PAC, Borden Papers, OC 434, 45434, Perley to Borden, 4 December, 1916; 45436, Borden to Perley, 7 December, 1916; PARC, Overseas File, 10-C-12, HQ 4556-2, Vol. 2; *London Gazette*, 30476, 14 January, 1918.

CHAPTER NINE

1. F. A. McKenzie, *Canada's Day of Glory* (Toronto: William Briggs, 1918), p. 9.
2. Murray, *The History of the 2nd Canadian Battalion*, p. 146.
3. Robert Graves, *Goodbye to All That* (London: Jonathan Cape, 1929), p. 297.
4. Clifford Wells, *From Montreal to Vimy Ridge and Beyond*, ed. O.C.S. Wallace (Toronto: McClelland, 1917), p. 252.
5. PAC, Perley Papers, Vol. 7, 205, Perley to Borden, 22 November, 1916.
6. PAC, Turner Papers, 11-78-7186, Turner to Perley, 30 November, 1916.
7. Perley Papers, Vol. 7, 218, Borden to Perley, 2 December, 1916.
8. Urquhart, *Arthur Currie: The Biography of a Great Canadian*, p. 141.
9. *Loc. cit.*
10. *Ibid.*, p. 142.
11. *Ibid.*
12. PAC, Currie Papers, "Notes on French Attacks . . . ."
13. Currie, cited Urquhart, *op. cit.*, p. 142.
14. "Notes on French Attacks . . . ."
15. *Loc. cit.*
16. *Loc. cit.*
17. *Loc. cit.*
18. Nivelle to Haig, 21 December, 1916, British Official History: *France and Belgium, 1917, Appendices*, No. 2.
19. Haig to Nivelle, 6 January, 1917, *ibid.*, No. 7.
20. Barnett, *The Swordbearers*, p. 200.
21. Erich Maria Remarque, *All Quiet on the Western Front* (London: G. P. Putnam's Sons, 1929), pp. 179, 183-7.
22. Robert Graves, *op. cit.*, p. 284.
23. *Ibid.*, pp. 284-5.
24. Barnett, *op. cit.*, p. 276.
25. Macphail, *History of the Canadian Forces, 1914-1919—Medical Services*, p. 57.
26. Byng, cited Murray, *op. cit.*, p. 157.
27. Nicholson, *Canadian Expeditionary Force (CEF) 1914-1919*, p. 250.
28. *Ibid.*, pp. 249-50.

29. *Ibid.*, p. 248.
30. Liddell Hart, *The Real War*, pp. 324-5.
31. Nicholson, *op. cit.*, p. 249.
32. Lucas, *The Empire at War*, II, p. 168.
33. *Ibid.*, p. 169.
34. Nicholson, *op. cit.*, pp. 250-2.
35. *Ibid.*, p. 252.
36. *Ibid.*, p. 253.
37. Wells, *op. cit.*, p. 303.
38. Murray, *op. cit.*, p. 164.
39. *Loc. cit.*
40. Duguid, "Canada on Vimy Ridge," *Canada Year Book*, 1936, p. 57.
41. Wells, *op. cit.*, pp. 304-5.
42. British Official History, *1917*, I, p. 333.
43. Lucas, *op. cit.*, pp. 172-4.
44. Murray, *op. cit.*, p. 167.
45. Nicholson, *op. cit.*, p. 265.
46. PARC, War Diary, G. S., Canadian Corps, April, 1917, Appx. VII.
47. Nicholson, *op. cit.*, p. 265.
48. Paul von Hindenburg, *Out of My Life* (London: Cassell, 1920), p. 265.
49. Erich Ludendorff, *My War Memories*, II (London: Hutchinson, n.d.), p. 421.
50. German Official History, XII, p. 230.
51. Liddell Hart, *op. cit.*, pp. 326-8.
52. Robert Blake (ed.), *The Private Papers of Douglas Haig* (London: Eyre & Spottiswoode, 1952), p. 218.
53. Nicholson, *op. cit.*, p. 243.

CHAPTER TEN

1. Barnett, *The Swordbearers*, p. 209.
2. *Loc. cit.*
3. Watt, *Dare Call It Treason*, pp. 154-5.
4. *Ibid.*, p. 158.
5. Paul Painlevé, *La Vérité sur l'Offensive du 16 Avril 1917* (Paris, 1919), p. 67, cited Thoumin, *The First World War*, pp. 396-7.
6. Watt, *op. cit.*, p. 168.
7. Painlevé, cited Barnett, *op. cit.*, p. 227.
8. Watt, *op. cit.*, p. 175.
9. Blake, *The Private Papers of Douglas Haig*, p. 234.
10. *Ibid.*, pp. 234-5.
11. Edmonds, *Short History of World War I*, p. 242.
12. Pétain, quoted Barnett, *op. cit.*, p. 222.
13. Nicholson, *Canadian Expeditionary Force (CEF) 1914-1919*, pp. 269-70.
14. British Official History, *France and Belgium, 1917*, I. p. 423.
15. *Ibid.*, p. 450.
16. Edmonds, *op. cit.*, p. 238.
17. Lloyd George, *War Memoirs*, VI, p. 3424.

18. Urquhart, *Arthur Currie: The Biography of a Great Canadian*, pp. 157-8.
19. Currie Diary, 3 May, 1917.
20. Nicholson, *op. cit.*, pp. 283-4.
21. *Ibid.*, p. 284.
22. PAC, Perley Papers, Vol. 9, 258, Borden to Perley, 13 June, 1917.
23. Nicholson, *op. cit.*, p. 284.
24. PARC, Overseas File, Folder 348, Perley to Borden, 16 June, 1917.
25. Currie, cited Urquhart, *op. cit.*, p. 165.
26. Urquhart, *op. cit.*, p. 162.
27. Overseas File, 10-8-7, Gow to Perley, 29 June, 1917.
28. PAC, Urquhart Papers, Currie to Forsyth, 25 June, 1917.
29. Perley Papers, Vol. 264, Perley to Borden, 21 July, 1917.
30. Urquhart, *op. cit.*, p. 166.
31. *Loc. cit.*
32. War Diary, G. S., Cdn. Corps, 4 June, 1917.
33. Nicholson, *op. cit.*, p. 281.
34. War Diary, G. S., Cdn. Corps, June, 1917, Appx. 1/3.
35. First Army Message No. G. S. 658/1 (Z), 7 July, 1917, Appx. 1/1 to War Diary, G. S., Cdn. Corps, July, 1917.
36. PAC, Currie Papers, Currie to Ralston, 9 February, 1928, Drawer 1811.
37. *Loc. cit.*
38. *Loc. cit.*
39. Nicholson, *op. cit.*, p. 285.
40. *Ibid.*, p. 287.
41. Currie Diary, 26 March, 1917, to 8 May, 1918.
42. Lucas, *The Empire at War*, II, p. 189.
43. Currie Diary, 15-18 August, 1917.
44. Priestley, cited *History of the Royal Canadian Corps of Signals, 1903-1961*, (ed.), John S. Moir (Ottawa: Published by authority of the Corps Committee, 1962), p. 37.
45. Murray, *The History of the 2nd Canadian Battalion*, p. 202.
46. Currie Diary, 15-18 August, 1917.
47. *Loc. cit.*
48. Nicholson, *op. cit.*, p. 297.
49. *Ibid.*, pp. 292, 297.
50. Blake, *op. cit.*, (Haig's Diary, 12 June, 1917), p. 238.
51. Nicholson, *op. cit.*, p. 303.
52. Blake, *op. cit.*, (Haig's Diary, 19 June, 1917), p. 240.
53. *Loc. cit.*
54. *Ibid.* (Haig's Diary, 21 July, 1917), p. 246.
55. *Ibid.*, Lloyd George, *op. cit.*, IV, p. 2185.
56. Blake, *op. cit.*, p. 252.
57. *Ibid.* (Haig's Diary, 11 October, 1917), p. 260.

58. Liddell Hart, *The Real War*, p. 339.
59. *Ibid.*, pp. 339-40.
60. Edmonds, *op. cit.*, pp. 247-8.
61. Ludendorff, *My War Memories*, II, p. 492.
62. Brig.-General John Charteris, *At GHQ*, (London: Cassell, 1931), p. 250.
63. *Ibid.*, p. 259.
64. Blake, *op. cit.* (Haig's Diary, 5 October, 1917), p. 257.
65. British Official History, *1917*, II, p. 347.
66. Currie Diary, 18 October, 1917.
67. Currie Papers, J-5, 5, Currie to R. J. Patterson, 8 March, 1920.
68. Nicholson, *op. cit.*, p. 327.
69. Currie Papers, J-2, 2, Currie to Beattie, 8 February, 1928.
70. Currie, cited Urquhart, *op. cit.*, p. 264.
71. Lucas, *op. cit.*, II, p. 194.
72. Urquhart, *op. cit.*, p. 178.
73. Charteris, *op. cit.*, p. 264.
74. McKenzie, *Canada's Day of Glory*, p. 116.
75. *Ibid.*, p. 114.
76. Currie, cited Urquhart, *op. cit.*, p. 181.
77. Haig, *ibid.*, p. 181.
78. Blake, *op. cit.*, (Haig's Diary, 6 November, 1917), p. 264.
79. Australian Official History, IV, 1917, p. 935.
80. *Statistics of the Military Effort of the British Empire during the Great War*, (London: His Majesty's Stationery Office, 1922), pp. 326-7.
81. McKenzie, *op. cit.*, p. 181.

CHAPTER ELEVEN

1. Liddell Hart, *The Real War*, pp. 345-7.
2. British Official History, *France and Belgium, 1918*, I, p. 52.
3. Liddell Hart, *op. cit.*, pp. 366-7.
4. Urquhart, *Arthur Currie: The Biography of a Great Canadian*, p. 198.
5. PAC, Kemp Papers, Vol. 169, File 12, Kemp to Borden, 25 January, 1918.
6. Borden Papers, OCA 98, 73868, Borden to Kemp, 31 January, 1918.
7. Kemp Papers, Vol. 182, File 62, Currie to Kemp, 11 January, 1918.
8. Urquhart, *op. cit.*, pp. 199-200.
9. *Ibid.*, p. 202.
10. Borden Papers, OC 494, 52798, Currie to Kemp, 7 February, 1918.
11. Kemp Papers, Vol. 182, File 62, Kemp to Borden, 8 February, 1918.
12. Borden Papers, OCA 98, 73936, Kemp to Borden, 26 February, 1918.
13. Murray, *The History of the 2nd Canadian Battalion*, p. 229.

14. Edmonds, *Short History of World War I*, pp. 279-80.
15. Ludendorff, *My War Memories*, II, pp. 583, 590.
16. *Ibid.*, p. 542.
17. *Ibid.*, p. 606.
18. British Official History, *France and Belgium, 1918*, I, p. 254.
19. *Ibid.*, p. 256.
20. Ludendorff, *op. cit.*, II, p. 604.
21. Barnett, *The Swordbearers*, p. 331.
22. Ludendorff, *op. cit.*, II, p. 611.
23. *Ibid.*, pp. 630, 637.
24. *Ibid.*, p. 638.
25. *Ibid.*, p. 640.
26. Liddell Hart, *op. cit.*, pp. 420-1.
27. General von Einem, cited Barnett, *op. cit.*, p. 337.
28. British Official History, *1918*, III, p. 305.
29. Blake, *The Private Papers of Douglas Haig* (Haig's Diary, 18 April, 1918), pp. 303-4.
30. Nicholson, *Canadian Expeditionary Force (CEF) 1914-1919*, p. 399.
31. *Ibid.*, pp. 378-80.
32. Blake, *op. cit.* (Haig's Diary, 19 July, 1918), p. 319.
33. Kemp Papers, Canadian Corps, File C, 25.
34. *Ibid.*, Kemp to Derby, 30 March, 1918.
35. *Debates, House of Commons*, 1 May, 1918.
36. Kemp Papers, Milner to Kemp, 6 March, 1918.
37. Nicholson, *op. cit.*, p. 383.
38. PAC, Currie Papers, Currie to McGillicuddy, n.d., J-1, "The War —A.W.C.'s Comments."
39. Murray, *op. cit.*, pp. 250-1; Nicholson, *op. cit.*, pp. 384-5.
40. Murray, *op. cit.*, p. 255.
41. *Ibid.*, p. 256.
42. *Ibid.*, p. 258.
43. Liddell Hart, *op. cit.*, p. 434.
44. Barnett, *op. cit.*, p. 348.
45. Lucas, *The Empire at War*, II, p. 219.
46. Liddell Hart, *op. cit.*, p. 435.
47. Murray, *op. cit.*, p. 263.
48. Ludendorff, *op. cit.*, II, p. 679.
49. *Ibid.*, p. 680.
50. *Ibid.*, p. 684.
51. *Loc. cit.*

CHAPTER TWELVE

1. Liddell Hart, *The Real War*, p. 437.
2. General M. Pope to Historical Section, 17 July, 1961.
3. *Report of the Ministry, OMFC, 1918* (London: Printed by authority of the Ministry, Overseas Forces of Canada, n.d.), p. 140.
4. Nicholson, *Canadian Expeditionary Force (CEF) 1914-1919*, p. 417.

5. *Ibid.*, p. 418.
6. Liddell Hart, *op. cit.*, p. 437.
7. French Official History, VII, i, Annex 657.
8. Blake, *The Private Papers of Douglas Haig*, pp. 323-4.
9. *Memoirs of Marshal Foch* (London: Heinemann, 1931), pp. 446-7.
10. PAC, Currie Papers, "Military," G153/2524-4, HQ Cdn. Corps to Fourth Army, 13 August, 1918.
11. Blake, *op. cit.*, p. 324.
12. *History of the 132nd Regiment*, cited Nicholson, *op. cit.*, p. 428.
13. Falls, *The Great War*, p. 380, *fn.*
14. Blake, *op. cit.* (Haig's Diary, 29 August, 1918), p. 325.
15. *Ibid.*, p. 326.
16. Ludendorff, *My War Memories*, II, pp. 683-4.
17. Murray, *The History of the 2nd Canadian Battalion*, p. 286.
18. Nicholson, *op. cit.*, p. 436.
19. Hindenburg, *Out of My Life*, p. 398.
20. Ludendorff, *op. cit.*, II, p. 696.
21. *Ibid.*, pp. 698-9.
22. Currie Diary, 3 September, 1918.
23. Urquhart, *Arthur Currie: The Biography of a Great Canadian*, p. 249.
24. Currie Papers, *Currie v. Wilson and Preston*, pp. 1809-1810.
25. *Ibid.*
26. Murray, *op. cit.*, pp. 300-301.
27. Liddell Hart, *op. cit.*, p. 462.
28. Ludendorff, *op. cit.*, II, p. 725.
29. Blake, *op. cit.*, (Haig's Diary, 6 October, 1918), p. 330.
30. Ludendorff, *op. cit.*, II, p. 648.
31. *Ibid.*, p. 647.
32. Lucas, *The Empire at War*, II, pp. 272-3.
33. *Report of the Ministry, OMFC, 1918*, p. 168.
34. Currie Papers, "Special Order of the Day," 3 October, 1918.
35. *Debates, House of Commons*, 4 March 1919.
36. *Loc. cit.*
37. *Loc. cit.*
38. *Ibid.*, 6 May, 1918.
39. Murray, *op. cit.*, p. 316.
40. General McNaughton to Army Historical Section, 20 February, 1962.
41. Maj.-General A. G. L. McNaughton, "The Capture of Valenciennes," *Canadian Defence Quarterly*, April, 1933, p. 281.
42. Currie Diary, 2 November, 1918.
43. Nicholson, *op. cit.*, p. 474.
44. British Official History, *1918*, V, p. 519.
45. H. R. N. Clyne, *Vancouver's 29th* (Vancouver: Tobin's Tigers Association, 1964), pp. 93-4.

CHAPTER THIRTEEN

1. *Le Petit Parisien*, cited by J. F. B. Livesay, *Canada's Hundred Days* (Toronto: Thomas Allen, 1919), p. 376.
2. Currie, cited *ibid.*, p. 397.
3. Urquhart, *Arthur Currie: The Biography of a Great Canadian*, pp. 258-9.
4. Livesay, *op. cit.*, pp. 398-9.
5. PARC, GAQ File 4-15, "Special Order of the Day," 25 November, 1918.
6. PAC, Currie Diary, 12 December, 1918.
7. *Loc. cit.*
8. *Report of the Ministry, OMFC, 1918*, p. 192.
9. R. C. Fetherstonhaugh, *The 24th Battalion* (Montreal: Gazette Printing Co., Regimental Association, 1930), p. 276.
10. PAC, M.G. 27, Series 11, D9, Borden to White, 18 November, 1918.
11. *Ibid.*, 25 November, 1918.
12. *Ibid.*, Mewburn to Borden, 29 November, 1918.
13. Lloyd George, *War Memoirs*, VI, p. 3367.
14. Liddell Hart, *The Real War*, p. 434.
15. Barnett, *The Swordbearers*, p. 348.
16. C. R. M. F. Cruttwell, *A History of the Great War 1914-1918* (Oxford: Clarendon Press, 1940), p. 138.
17. Hindenburg, *Out of My Life*, p. 330.
18. For U.S. figures, see Colonel Leonard P. Ayres (Chief of the Statistics Branch of the General Staff), *The War with Germany* (Washington: United States Government Printing Office, 1919), p. 113; the Canadian figures were compiled by the Army Historical Section, and are cited by Brig.-General J. A. Clarke, *Debates, House of Commons*, Session 1922, II, 2 May, 1922.
19. Lucas, *The Empire at War*, II, p. 286.
20. General McNaughton to Historical Section, 25 April 1961.
21. *Loc. cit.*
22. *Loc. cit.*
23. Ironside, cited Urquhart, *op. cit.*, pp. 269-70.
24. *Halifax Chronicle*, 2 December, 1918.
25. Currie Papers, "Special Order of the Day," 3 October, 1918.
26. Currie, quoted Urquhart, *op. cit.*, p. 265.
27. British Official History, *France and Belgium, 1918*, V, p. 179.
28. *Ibid.*
29. General Gunther Blumentritt, *The Fatal Decisions* (London: Michael Joseph, 1956), pp. 37-8.

30. Army Historical Section, "History of the Canadian Militia."
31. Currie Papers, *Currie* v. *Wilson and Preston*, pp. 1809-1810.
32. Lloyd George, *War Memoirs*, VI, pp. 3423-4.
33. *Ibid.*, p. 3424.
34. Urquhart, *op. cit.*, p. 226.
35. Lloyd George, cited *ibid.*, pp. 226-7.
36. Monash, cited *ibid.*, p. 227.
37. *Loc. cit.*
38. Urquhart, *op. cit.*, p. 109.
39. *Ibid.*, p. 192.

40. *Ibid.*, p. 263.
41. *Ibid.*, pp. 272-3.
42. *Ibid.*, pp. 273-4.
43. *Halifax Chronicle*, 18 August, 1919.
44. Cited Urquhart, *op. cit.*, p. 280.
45. *Canadian Annual Review*, 1919, p. 42.
46. Brigadier-General W. A. Griesbach, cited Urquhart, *op. cit.*, p. 269.
47. Urquhart, *op. cit.*, p. 356.
48. Cited *ibid.*, p. 357.
49. Lloyd George, cited H. C. Hocken, *Debates, House of Commons*, 3 March, 1919.

INDEX

PUBLISHER'S ACKNOWLEDGMENTS

Grateful acknowledgment is made to the following for permission to quote from copyrighted material:

The Real War 1914-1918 by Captain B. H. Liddell Hart, copyright 1930 by B. H. Liddell Hart, reprinted by permission of ATLANTIC-LITTLE, BROWN & COMPANY.

THE BEAVERBROOK FOUNDATIONS, LONDON, *War Memoirs* by David Lloyd George.

MR. HENRY BORDEN, *Robert Laird Borden: His Memoirs* edited by Henry Borden.

CHATTO & WINDUS, AND SIMON & SCHUSTER INC., *Dare Call it Treason* by Richard M. Watt.

J. M. DENT & SONS (CANADA) LIMITED, *Arthur Currie: The Biography of a Great Canadian* by Hugh M. Urquhart.

DOUBLEDAY & COMPANY, CANADA, *Ordeal by Fire* by Ralph Allen.

EYRE & SPOTTISWOODE, *The Swordbearers* by Correlli Barnett.

HARPER & ROW, *World War I* by Hansen Baldwin.

HUTCHINSON & CO. LIMITED, AND WILLIAM MORROW & CO., INC., *The Donkeys* by Alan Clark.

MACMILLAN & CO. LIMITED, *The French Canadians* by Mason Wade.

THE MACMILLAN COMPANY OF CANADA, *The Hon. Sir Sam Hughes* by C. F. Winter.

ODHAMS PRESS LIMITED, AND CHARLES SCRIBNER'S SONS, *The World Crisis* by Sir Winston Churchill.

G. P. PUTNAM'S SONS, *The Great War* by Cyril Falls.

THE VANTAGE PRESS, INC., *Unknown Soldiers* by "One of Them."

The publisher also wishes to acknowledge his gratitude to MAJOR G. O. CURRIE for permission to reproduce the illustration facing page 144. All other photographs are reproduced by kind permission of THE PUBLIC ARCHIVES OF CANADA.

The maps on pages 66, 72, 102, 150, 169, 183, 201 and 207 first appeared in *Canadian Expeditionary Force, 1914-1919,* by Colonel G. W. L. Nicholson (Ottawa: The Queen's Printer, 1962) and have been reproduced here with the permission of the CANADIAN ARMY HISTORICAL SECTION.

THE TEXT OF THIS BOOK WAS SET IN TEN POINT BASKERVILLE TYPE AND THE DISPLAY MATERIAL IN TWENTY-FOUR POINT NEWS GOTHIC CONDENSED

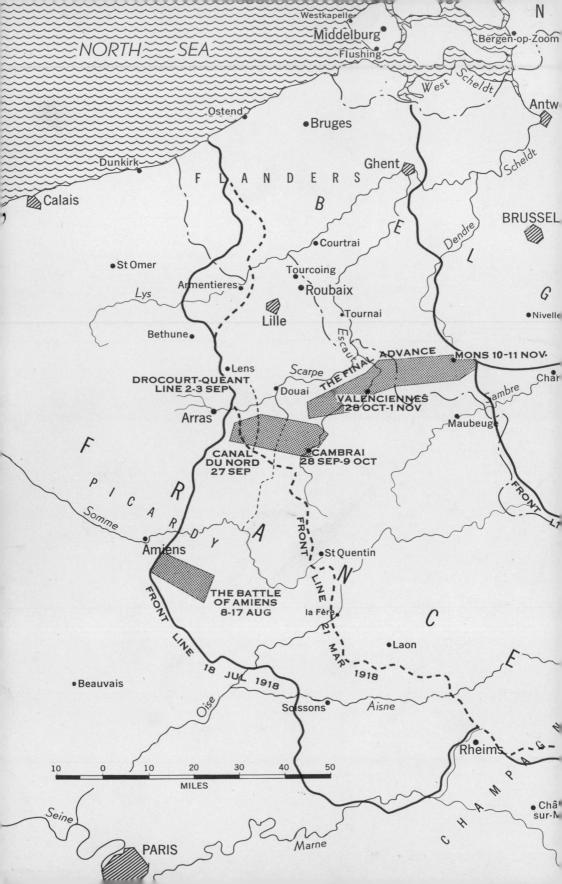

N

NORTH SEA

Westkapelle
Middelburg
Flushing
Bergen-op-Zoom

Ostend
Bruges
Antw

West Scheldt

Scheldt

Calais

F L A N D E R S
B
Ghent
E
BRUSSEL
L

Dunkirk

St Omer
Armentieres
Lys
Courtrai
Tourcoing
Roubaix
Tournai
Escaut
Dendre
G
Nivelle

Bethune
Lille

Lens
Scarpe
Douai
THE FINAL ADVANCE
MONS 10-11 NOV.
Char
DROCOURT-QUÉANT
LINE 2-3 SEP
VALENCIENNES
28 OCT-1 NOV
Sambre

Arras
Maubeuge

F
CANAL
DU NORD
27 SEP
CAMBRAI
28 SEP-9 OCT

P I C A R D Y
A
FRONT
FRONT LI

Somme
Amiens
St Quentin

THE BATTLE
OF AMIENS
8-17 AUG
N
la Fère
C

FRONT
LINE
18 JUL 1918
LINE 21 MAR
1918
Laon
E

Beauvais
Oise
Soissons
Aisne

Rheims

10 0 10 20 30 40 50
MILES

Seine
Marne
Châ
sur-M

PARIS
C H A M P A G N